Directionality
of
Humankind's
Development.
History

Victor Torvich

Publisher's Cataloging-in-Publication data

Names: Torvich, Victor, author.
Title: Directionality of humankind's development. History / Victor Torvich.
Description: Includes bibliographical references and index. | Yury Tomashevich, 2024.
Identifiers: LCCN: 2024904342 | ISBN: ISBN 979-8-218-31334-0 (paperback) | 979-8-218-31335-7 (ebook)
Subjects: LCSH Civilization--History. | World history. | BISAC HISTORY / Ancient / General | HISTORY / Civilization | REFERENCE / Encyclopedias | HISTORY / General
Classification: LCC D20 .T67 2024 | DDC 909--dc23

ISBNs: 9798218313340 (paperback); 9798218313357 (eBook)

Yury Tomashevich, 2024

Table 1. History of Humankind. 42000 BC – 2023 AD.
High-Level Timeline. Classes of Resources. 23 Data Points

Class of Resources, Created by Humankind for Itself	Emergence Date, Year
Novel Mental Images; Art and Music	42000 BC
Man-Made Materials, Substances, and Organisms	34000 BC
People and Societies as Objects of Study	29000 BC
Usage of Domesticated Plants and Animals	32100-16800 BC
Trade with a Use of an Intermediary	11000-8000 BC
Tools, Devices, Machines from Man-Made Materials	8040-7510 BC
Mass Transportation	6500 BC
External Information Storage and Processing	3200–3100 BC
War and Means of Warfare	2700 BC
Transnational Entities	2550 BC
Usage of People as Resource on a Massive Scale	2160-2140 BC
Use of Forces of Nature, Relativity, and Quantum Physics	1346-1334 BC
Mass Education	1292-1190 BC
Independent Communication Channels	550 BC
Mass Production	1320
Mass Media	1455
Technology beyond the Limitations of Human Senses	1590
Usage of the Scientific Method and Information Technology	1642
Usage of Natural Resources on a Massive Scale	1750

Life Expectancy Growth	1770
Massive Involvement of Women in Humankind's Activities	1893
Digital Technology	1924
Artificial Intelligence (AI)	1956

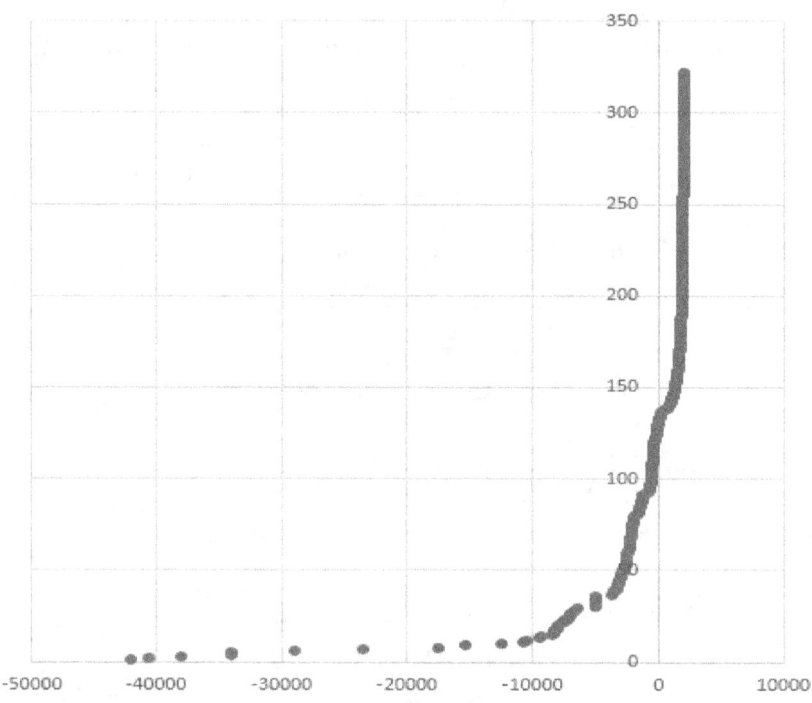

Figure 1. History of Humankind. 42000 BC - 2023 AD.
Vertical - Accumulated number of resources.
Horizontal - Time, years;
Data - from Part 2 and Table B.
Low-Level model of humankind. 318 data points.

Contents

Introduction   5

Part 1. How to Uncover Direction of History   8
Introduction to Part 1   9

History - Linear, Cyclical, or What?   10
   Chapter 1.1. In a Search for the Meaning of Humankind's
     History   11
   Chapter 1.2. Duration of Humankind's History   28

High- and Low-Level Models of Humankind's History   39
   Chapter 1.3. Humankind as a Complex System   40
   Chapter 1.4. Multi-Layer History   43
   Chapter 1.5. Criteria for Resources and Classes of
     Resources   51

Part 2. History of Humankind. 300 Stories   75
Introduction to Part 2   76

First Eight Classes of Resources   77
   Chapter 2.1. Art and Music   78
   Chapter 2.2. Man-Made Materials, Substances, and
     Organisms   89
   Chapter 2.3. People and Societies as Objects of Study   98
   Chapter 2.4. Usage of Domesticated Plants and Animals 107
   Chapter 2.5. Trade with a Use of an Intermediary   114
   Chapter 2.6. Tools, Devices, and Machines from
     Man-Made Materials   117
   Chapter 2.7. Mass Transportation   124
   Chapter 2.8. External Information Storage and
     Processing   128

Next Eight Classes of Resources   132
   Chapter 2.9. War and Means of Warfare   133
   Chapter 2.10. Transnational Entities   139

Chapter 2.11. Usage of People as Resource on a Massive
Scale 143
Chapter 2.12. Use of Forces of Nature, Relativity, and
Quantum Physics 147
Chapter 2.13. Mass Education 150
Chapter 2.14. Independent Communication Channels 153
Chapter 2.15. Mass Production 157
Chapter 2.16. Mass Media 160

Last Seven Classes of Resources **162**
Chapter 2.17. Technology beyond the Limitations of
Human Senses 163
Chapter 2.18. Usage of the Scientific Method and
Information Technology 165
Chapter 2.19. Usage of Natural Resources on Massive
Scale 168
Chapter 2.20. Life Expectancy Growth 171
Chapter 2.21. Massive Involvement of Women in Humankind's
Activities 173
Chapter 2.22. Digital Technology 176
Chapter 2.23. Artificial Intelligence (AI) 179

Part 3. Direction of History. What and Why? **181**
Introduction to Part 3 **182**

Graphs. Turning points. Driving Force. **183**
Chapter 3.1. Humankind's History in Graphs 184
Chapter 3.2. Ways to Use the Subsurface History of
Humankind 198
Chapter 3.3. Turning Points in History 201
Chapter 3.4. Driving Force of Humankind's
Development 212
Chapter 3.5. Various Fields of Humankind's Activity 222
Chapter 3.6. Objectivity and Stability of the Proposed
Models 234

Subsurface History and Conventional History **242**
Chapter 3.7. Ups and Downs in History 243
Chapter 3.8. Subsurface History for Strategic Planning 258

Contents and Introduction

Chapter 3.9. Adding Geography   266
Chapter 3.10. Creativity of Humankind   275
Chapter 3.11. "European Miracle?" and More   287
Chapter 3.12. The East to the West Transfer Patterns   296
Chapter 3.13. Incident or Pattern?   303
Chapter 3.14. Big Questions and Answers   307

Part 4. Past. Present. Future.   **312**
Chapter 4.1. Looking Ahead   313
Chapter 4.2. Big Picture   327

Conclusion   **332**
Definitions and Concepts   **333**

Tables   **339**
List of Figures   **352**
List of Tables   **356**
Notes   **357**
Bibliography   **371**
Image Credits   **417**
Index   **417**

Civilizations... which refused to study their own history... would be doomed to dangers proportional to this peculiar one-sidedness.

Stanislaw Lem

Things are not always what they seem.

Phaedrus

Introduction

Introduction

Answers to the question about the meaning of humankind's history vary. However, research has often been limited to a relatively short period of history or geographic location. We are interested in the world history of humankind, which "adopts the world as its ultimate unit of analysis and looks for phenomena that had an impact on humanity as a whole."[1]

This book gives a clear quantitative answer to the question: In which direction has humanity, as a whole, moved over the past 44 thousand years? This answer does not depend on social structures or subjective concepts like progress, happiness, or morality. The data for analysis was taken from independent original works of researchers.

At the beginning of this book, Table 1 presents High-Level Humankind's History for the time period of the last 44 thousand years. Also, at the beginning of this book, Low-Level Humanity's History is presented in Figure 1, and in Table 2 in the Tables section.

This book's main contents consists of four Parts.

Part 1. How to Uncover Direction of History discusses our approach to modeling humankind's history. Part 1 is for people interested in why the direction of humanity was not discovered sooner and how to find it.

There are 318 short stories in **Part 2. History of Humankind. 300 Stories**. Each entry in Part 2 represents a data point. These data points were chosen based on the approach explained in Part 1. The entire data set from Part 2 is the basis for analyzing the development and direction of humanity in Part 3. Part 2 is intended for people who tend to see the plot side of history or seek encyclopedic knowledge.

Part 3. Direction of History. What and Why? is for people interested in questions, analysis, and answers.

Is there a direction in the development of humanity? Where and how fast is humankind moving? What forces are driving this? Why the last twelve thousand years are different from the previous?

How reliable is the proposed analysis? Why do humans rule the Earth? Part 3 answers all these questions and more.

Part 4. Past – Present - Future provides an overview of the findings of this book and answers the question: is humanity close to a crossroads in its development?

Important Definitions

We will use the following definition of development: The development of something or someone is the process in which that entity changes.

Definitions of resources, families of resources, classes of resources, domains of resources, and some examples are in the Definitions and Concepts section of this book.

About References

It would be better to provide several competing references for each resource. However, in most cases, I use only one reference for each resource to maintain a reasonable balance between this book's text body and bibliography.

We are just in the kindergarten of uncovering things.
Charles Kettering

Part 1.

How to Uncover Direction of History

Introduction to Part 1

Is humanity moving in a certain direction? Is this direction direct, non-linear, cyclical, or what? In the first part of the book, we will look at why the direction in which humankind is moving has not been discovered before. Next we will discuss how to find out such a direction.

We study and describe history in a way that differs from the traditional presentations of historical events. We are looking at a story that is fundamental to conventional history. We call such history the "Subsurface History of Humankind." [1] We will use the terms "subsurface history" and "deep-level history" interchangeably.

This is the history of resources and the history of classes of resources that humanity has created for itself. Definitions of these terms are provided in the Important Definitions and Definitions and Concepts sections of this book.

The main ideas of this book were published in early 2020. [2-6]

The proposed models of humankind's history are dynamic. Over time, humanity will create new resources that can be considered later. Of course, the scientific community might suggest adding or removing some resources from the list.

One can never know enough. The unknown and its call lies even in what we know.

Eduardo Chillida

History - Linear, Cyclical, or What?

History gives answers only to those who know how to ask questions.

Hajo Holborn

Chapter 1.1.

In a Search for the Meaning of Humankind's History

The attempt to extract meaning from the past is as old as culture itself.

Throughout time, many famous thinkers contemplated and analyzed the humankind's history. Philosophers, historians, economists, and so-called visionaries who worked at the intersection of many scientific disciplines, have paid considerable attention to the search for a way to integrate humankind's past with the present.

For many researchers, their statements about historical processes were outside the main themes of their work. However, mentioning the views of some famous thinkers on the search for the sense of humankind's history is worthwhile.

We will soon look at the work of these thinkers from a specific perspective. We are interested to see whether these works will help us better understand the history of such a global entity as humanity. We also look far beyond the "written history" associated with the invention of writing. Understanding history of humankind is closely intertwined with understanding what humanity is and how and why it differs from other animal groups.

Let us look at the works of Karl Marx, Oswald Spengler, Arnold Toynbee, Juli Gutiérrez Deulofeu, Hegel, Pierre Teilhard de Chardin, Vladimir Vernadsky, Nikolai Berdyaev, Karl Popper, and Yuval Harari.

Marx and Engels

These works can be divided into two large groups. One group focused on a local, geographic, or temporal approach. Most of the works of historians and economists belong to this group.

Karl Marx, Oswald Spengler, Arnold Toynbee and Juli Gutiérrez Deulofeu adopted a local approach.

For Karl Marx, analysis of social class, class structures, and changes in these structures was the key to understanding capitalism and other social systems or modes of production. "The history of all hitherto existing society is the history of class struggles."[1] – This is the famous sentence of Marx and Engels from the "Manifesto of the Communist Party." According to Marx and Engels, humanity is moving towards a classless society. According to Marx, the main feature of class society is the struggle between the upper and lower classes.

The Communist Manifesto was first published in 1848. Since then, the Marxist black and white point of view has become obsolete. Marx did not take into account the more prominent role of other classes, such as the middle class.

Per Marx and Engels, the first classes emerged from the massive use of enslaved people. According to scholars, slavery is mentioned as an established institution in the Mesopotamian Code of Hammurabi,[2] which was compiled between 1755 and 1750 BC. Respectfully, class society existed for approximately 3776 years, from 1753 BC to 2023 AD. This means that most of Marx and Engels' views on historical processes cannot be applied to the tens of thousands of years before 1753 BC.

In other words, the views of Marx and Engels are local in comparison with the long history of humankind.

Arnold Toynbee and Juli Gutiérrez Deulofeu

Another prominent group of researchers focused their attention on changes in social structures. Pitirim Sorokin stated that "the cyclical concept of social change is one of the oldest in the history of social thought."[3] Much of the recent work has focused on the rise and fall of civilizations, cultures, and empires.

Arnold Toynbee (1889–1975), in his twelve volumes *A Study of History*, wrote about the rise and fall of civilizations local in geography and time.

Juli Gutiérrez Deulofeu, in his book *The Mathematics of History*, analyzed a small part of the totality of all empires in humankind's history.[4] He derived the exact number for the lifespan of civilizations: 5100 years. He also divided the life of each civilization into three phases, each lasting 1,700 years. Using these figures, Deulofeu was able to make many predictions about future world events. The first edition of his book was published in 1951. Note that the name *Mathematics of History* was invented by Francesc Pujols, a friend of Deulofeu, but not Deulofeu himself. "Despite its name, the theory does not have anything to do with mathematics."[5]

It is generally accepted among scientists that the first civilization arose in Sumer. It flourished between 4100 -1750 BC.[6]

Therefore, both Toynbee's and Deulofeu's views on the cyclical nature of social structures could not be applied to the tens of thousands of years before 4100 BC. Of course, cyclical theories do not apply to a version of the future in which the discussed social structures, such as empires, do not exist. This means that considerations of cyclicity are local in time. And, in most cases, they are local in geography.

Oswald Spengler

Oswald Spengler put forward the idea that "each Culture has its own new possibilities of self-expression which arise, ripen, decay and never return."[7] At the same time, Spengler wrote that history is "the story of specific cultures and their interaction at particular times and places."[8] In other words, the birth and death of local cultures remain local. They add little to the understanding of humankind's history. The first volume of *The Decline of the West* was originally published in 1918, and the second in 1922.

The problem is the lack of specificity of social structures that go through specific cycles - from birth to death. An analogy in biology would be to figure out how different a collection of people and humanity is from a colony of microbes if we only know that people and microbes go through birth and death. We might say that the idea that "every culture" goes through birth and death is too broad to be fruitful for understanding human history.

To summarize the local approach, the fragmentation of the local approach does not allow generalizations to be made at the level of humanity.

Hegel

Some thinkers have been interested in a global approach. This group includes prominent philosophers Hegel and Karl Popper, visionaries Pierre Teilhard de Chardin and Vladimir Vernadsky, and historian Yuval Harari.

Hegel, Pierre Teilhard de Chardin, and Yuval Harari relied on a specific subjective parameter.

According to Hegel, "World history is the progress of the consciousness of freedom - a progress which we have to recognize in its necessity."[9] That is, Hegel saw "progress" in history, understanding that "progress" is "consciousness of freedom." Both "progress" and "freedom" are subjective terms. Moreover, scientists have no consensus on what "consciousness" is. The text of Hegel's book was originally published in 1837.

There is no description of how this progress can be measured by any quantitative method.

Pierre Teilhard de Chardin

Visioners Pierre Teilhard de Chardin and Vladimir Vernadsky subscribed to the noosphere concept. They understand that the noosphere is the newest stage in the evolution of life on Earth. Teilhard de Chardin was a philosopher, scientist, Jesuit priest, paleontologist, and theologian. Vladimir Vernadsky was a philosopher, mineralogist, and geochemist.

Teilhard de Chardin wrote: "Our picture is of Humankind laboring under the impulsion of an obscure instinct, so as to break out through its narrow point of emergence and submerge the Earth; of thought becoming number so as to conquer all habitable space, taking precedence over all other forms of life; of mind, in other words, deploying and convoluting the layers of the noosphere."[10]

There are no proposals to measure the term "conquest of all habitable space" used by Pierre de Chardin. The text of the book by Pierre de Chardin was originally published in 1955.

Vladimir Vernadsky

Vladimir Vernadsky noted: "We can assume that over the course of 5-7 thousand years, at an increasing rate, there is a continuous creation of the noosphere and a steady increase in the cultural biogeochemical energy of humanity, occurring mainly without moving backward , but with stops of decreasing duration."[11] The text of Vladimir Vernadsky's book was initially published in 1977.

This is the qualitative, not quantitative, opinion of Vladimir Vernadsky about the latest, local development of humankind. The term "cultural biogeochemical energy of humankind" is not widely used among scientists.

Nikolai Berdyaev

According to Berdyaev,[12] the character of the religious and historical process presupposes the deepest collision and interaction between the Divinity and man. Note that statements about Divinity are not verifiable by independent researchers. Also, those statements are subject to their author's preferences of one religion over other religions.

Yuval Noah Harari and Karl Popper

Yuval Noah Harari is among the historians who subscribe to the idea that there is a definite direction in humankind's development. "It becomes crystal clear that history is moving relentlessly towards unity."[13] By increasing "unity," Harari understands fewer "isolated human worlds." However, the term "isolated human world" is not defined. Yuval Harari did not specify whether the content of this term is constant or variable throughout humankind's history. Given such uncertainty, it is difficult to assess how subjective the term "isolated human worlds" is and how to properly count "isolated human worlds."

Karl Popper's point of view is different. The text of Karl Popper's book was originally published in 1945. He stated that "history has no meaning."[14]

Conclusion on Well-Known Thinkers

In summary, none of the above-mentioned thinkers, with both local and global approaches, have come close to defining the sense of humankind's history in a way that can be quantified and verified by independent researchers.

Various Takes on the "Meaning of History"

We can also find out which versions of the "meaning of the history of humankind" were explored more often by the authors.

Firstly, there is a special scientific field "Philosophy of History," dedicated to the question of the sense of humankind's history. Daniel Little [15] wrote, "We can usefully think of philosophers' writings about history as domaining around several large questions, involving metaphysics, hermeneutics, epistemology, and ethics: . . . (2) Does history as a whole have meaning, structure, or direction, beyond the individual events and actions that make it up?"

The first group of questions concerns the meaning or sense of history. Those statements are (a) The meaning of human history? [16,17]; (b) Does history make sense?[18]; (c.) History as philosophy: The search for meaning.[19]

The Meaning of Human History by Morris Raphael Cohen [20] was published in 1947. He was famous for his critical mind. It is not surprising that Morris Raphael Cohen in his book criticized the works on the meaning of human history by such great minds as Hume, Bacon, Marx, Freud, and others. D.V. Brogan's work[17] is a short review of "The Meaning of Human History" by Morris Raphael Cohen. This review was published in 1949. Terry Pinkard's book[18] discusses Hegel's philosophy of history in detail. The book was published in 2017.

"Progress"

Another group of questions is centered around the term "progress:" The Idea of Historical Progress [20,21]; Is humanity progressing?[21] History as a process of dialectical change: Hegel and Marx[22]; Human Progress: Not Inevitable, Uneven, and Indisputable.[23]

In his work, Nathan Rotenstreich [19] provided a very broad definition of the term "historical progress" – "The idea of historical progress, despite its many variations, is anchored in a coherent structure of thought which implies a cumulative advance toward an all-encompassing encounter with a universal norm and its realization." He further concludes that "The phenomenological structure of history is, however, inconsistent with the theoretical assumptions on which the idea of progress is based." Nathan Rotenstreich's paper was published in 1971.

Margaret Meek Lange [21] noted in 2011 that "many 20th-century thinkers rejected the notion of progress after horrendous events such as the two World Wars, the Holocaust, and the use of nuclear weaponry."

Marian L. Tupy [22] was interested in "an intelligent debate on the drivers of human progress." Marian L. Tupy cited many indicators of humankind's progress in his article. This once again confirms the subjectivity of the term "progress."

During the 2019 debate, Pinker and Krugman[23] failed to propose a single, agreed-upon measure of human progress. Instead, they prefer to point to numerous measures. For example, Pinker mentioned life expectancy and time spent on housework. These two different measures of progress highlight the subjectivity of the term "progress." Krugman sees a locality, in time, of historical progress. "We're talking about a couple of centuries of progress."

In 2022, Patrick Lancaster Gardiner [24] noted that "Hegel had tended to exhibit "history" as representing the unfolding in time of an inner spiritual principle." So far, there is no tool yet to measure the degree of spirituality.

Replacement of "Meaning" with "Goal"

In several works by philosophers, the search for meaning in humankind's history is replaced with a search for the purpose or mission of humankind's existence in nature. Such works include, for example, Zabelin's essay "Humanity - what is it for?"[25]

Order or Patterns in Humankind's History

Some people have asked a more general question about order or patterns in humankind's history: Contingency, Pattern and the S-curve in Human History[26]; Are there patterns in history?[27]

David Christian [26] examined the patterns of more than ten thousand years of humankind's history. He states, "The feature that distinguishes human history most powerfully from the histories of all other species is our capacity for ... finding new ways of extracting resources and energy from an environment." He did not explicitly define what he meant by "resources." However, starting with Christ's birth date, he uses the per capita gross domestic product (GDP) value.

David Christian pointed to three turning points in humankind's history - the development of symbolic language and the agricultural and industrial revolutions. He identifies "collective learning" as the main feature "unique to our species." However, in his article, "collective learning" remains purely qualitative.

In his book, Ian Morris [27] argues that the only way to answer ..."is by measuring social development to produce a graph that – literally shows the shape of history." "The past ... has strong patterns, and with the right tools, historians can see and even explain what they are." He uses three tools: biology, sociology, and geography.

There is at least one problem with this approach. To use sociology, you need to apply it to social structures. However, it is impossible to find a social structure that has existed for tens of thousands of years of humankind's history, with the possible exception of the family as a social unit. But then we need to know more about family structure, say, thirty thousand years ago. Thus Ian Morris's approach is local in time.

Directionality of Humankind's Development

Various people have raised the question of the direction of humankind's development: Directionality toward Western liberal democracy[28]; Is history cyclical?[29]; Faith forum: Is humanity going in the right direction?[30]; The evolutionary road: The common goal of human as a species.[31]

In his article "The End of History?"[28] Francis Fukuyama wrote, "What we may be witnessing ... is the end point of humankind ideological evolution and the universalization of Western liberal democracy as the final form of human government." Fukuyama is talking about the timeframe in humankind's history, specifically when governments existed, which is local in time. He supports the idea of humankind's history directionality toward Western liberal democracy.

In her article, Megan Erickson [29] wrote, "a British philosopher John Gray told ... that history is cyclical rather than progressive." The idea that history moves in circles is popular in Eastern cultures.

The question before the "group of religious leaders"[30] was: From a religious point of view, is humanity moving in the right direction or does its direction need to be changed? Some of the nine religious leaders believe that humanity is moving in the right direction and some in the wrong direction; however, there was no consensus on what was right and wrong. One religious leader said that "we cannot judge one era over another as "better" — not as people of faith. We "should trust God's presence in every era." All these disagreements confirm that "right direction" and "wrong direction" are subjective concepts.

In his work, Du, D. D.[31] tried to find the "right direction" for humankind.

Ghirath Vermeil defined humanity's directionality as part of directionality, which he saw as a property of broader systems such as living systems. "The particulars of history – participants, dates, events, and places – cannot be predicted and remain profoundly contingent, but production and its regulation by consumers conspire to give history a predictable direction of increased power and reach of dominant members of living systems."[32] However, no quantitative measures were provided.

Biological Evolution

Another group of authors discusses the possible use of the theory of biological evolution as an answer to questions about humankind's development:
-   Where are we heading? The evolution of humans and things[33]
-   Are humans still evolving?[34,35]

Ian Hodder [33] stated that not only do people become dependent on things, but things also become dependent on people. "It is this mutual dependency that creates the dominant trend in both cultural and genetic evolution." It is unclear how the "dependency on things and things' dependency on humans" might affect human genes.

The team of YourGenome.org website[34] gave some examples: "genetic studies have demonstrated that humans are still evolving." However, the number of such examples is minimal.

Debates continue among scientists about the real pace of human biological evolution over the past ten thousand years. David Railton[35] noted that some scientists believe that "no biological change in humans over the past 50,000 years," while others believe that "human evolution has accelerated in the past 10,000 years." Human biological evolution is still ongoing over the past 10,000 years. However, the number of changes observed is small. Four examples of evidence that natural selection alters genes responsible for known human traits are described.

What Makes Humans Different?

A group of thinkers are interested in what distinguishes humans from other species and why humans rule the world: How humanity became the dominant form of life?[36] What makes humans different than any other species?[37] Why humans run the world?[38] What made humans so exceptional among all the species on Earth?[39] The human league: what separates us from other animals?[40]

Frans de Waal [36] wrote, "One oft-mentioned difference between humans and other primates is that we are the only species to cooperate with outsiders and strangers."

Gary Stix[37] wrote about the work done by scientists comparing of human and chimp psychology. Michael Tomasello proposed the hypothesis that "An ability to devise and perceive shared goals" distinguishes humans from other species. However, no tools have been provided to measure the extent of such abilities.

Yuval Noah Harari[38] stated that "humans control the world because we are the only animal that can cooperate flexibly in large numbers." Agustín Fuentes [39] argues, "Our distinctively human capacity for shared intentionality coupled with our imagination is how we became who we are today. "

In his book, Adam Rutherford [40] argues that "Where we stand apart most significantly is in cultural accumulation and transmission. Many animals learn. Only humans teach."

What is a Driving Force of Humankind's Development

Another group of authors is trying to figure out what drives history: What drives human evolution?[41]; War as a driving force of history;[42] What does govern history?[43]

In his extensive review, Joseph Henrich[41] concludes that "cultural evolution was likely a dominant force driving our species' genetic evolution over the last few hundred thousand years." The review was carried out at a qualitative level.

Miguel Alonso [42] argues that war was a driving force of history in the 19th and 20th Centuries. Stephen Nichols [43] discusses from a religious point of view whether "history is subject to the arbitrary governance of fate," or something else. He agrees with Archibald Alexander that providence "governs history." However, different people and societies believed in different Gods at different times. Moreover, there were no proposals for tools to measure the extent of God's providence.

Graeme Donald Snooks states, "The long-run driving force arises from the universal motivation of all living organisms–to survive and prosper at any cost."[44] That, however, does not explain why humans, and not some other "living organisms," rule the Earth. Also, it is not clear how "universal motivation" could be measured.

Complex Systems Theory Perspective

Humankind's history can be viewed from the perspective of complex systems theory, for example, "Complexity rising: From human beings to human civilization, a complexity profile."[45]

Yaneer Bar-Yam stated, "The history of civilization can be characterized through the progressive (though non-monotonic) appearance of collective behaviors of larger groups of human beings of greater complexity." However, in this work, the increase in complexity was discussed at a qualitative rather than a quantitative level.

Tainter's theory of diminishing returns to complexity[46] was applied to a local period of humankind's history, from about 2000 BC to local civilizations. It "was not directly based on quantitative data or models."[47]

The History of Humankind as the Object of Study

At the end of the 20th century, the history of humankind as a whole became the object of study by four different historical disciplines: long history, global history, world history, and deep history.

"Big history is a new disciplinary field of scholarship that studies the past at all possible scales. Its approach is historical, but it links disciplines from cosmology to geology to evolutionary biology and human history."[48] Big history as a historical discipline emerged in the 1990's.[49]

World history is a "branch of history concerned with the study of historical phenomena that transcend national, regional, or cultural boundaries."[50] "World history encompasses a history that is not necessarily completely interconnected through globalization, while global history examines this specific history of interconnectivity."[51] World history as a historical discipline emerged in the 1980s.[52] Global history as a historical discipline emerged in the 1990s.[53] "Deep history [54] is dedicated to studying "the entire duration of human existence on Earth." [55]

Works on Quantifiable Complexity Associated with Milestones in Humankind's History

There are works that are explicitly or implicitly based on the assumption that multiple evolutions move towards increasing complexity. The list of evolutions includes the evolutions of the Universe, geological, biological, and human societies.

Theodore Modis proposed a method for measuring changes in the complexity of a particular evolutionary process. His work quantifies complexity relative to the distance between equally important evolutionary turning points (milestones). "Complexity increases both when the rate of change increases and when the amount of things that are changing around us increase. . . To quantify the complexity associated with an evolutionary milestone we must look at the milestone's importance. Importance can be defined as equal to the change in complexity multiplied by the time duration to the next milestone. The complexity change associated with a certain milestone will then be inversely proportional to the time period to the next milestone."[56]

In his work, Theodore Modis used up to 11 data points from the last 40 thousand years of humankind's history. This data was collected from various sources. Other authors used a similar technique. Alexander Panov[57] considered biological evolution and the evolution of humanity. In his work, Panov used eight milestones from the last 40 thousand years of humankind's history.

The most extensive array of data on milestones over the last 40 thousand years of humankind's history was used in the works of L. Grinin and A. Korotayev.[58] The data set in their work consists of 19 data points from 38000 BC to 1995 AD. The analysis of the curves in the works of Modis, Panov and Korotayev was performed by A. Korotaev.[59] The critique of Panov-Kuzweil's views was done by Modis[60] and Snooks.[44]

Conclusion on 200 Years of the Search for the Sense of Humankind's History

Here is the conclusion of the above review of relevant literature.

There are many works by famous and not so famous authors devoted to a topic that can be roughly defined as the meaning of humankind's history. This debate has been going on for many centuries.

The question of the sense of humankind's history has been posed differently by many thinkers. Accordingly, there are various types of discussions and responses on this topic.

In many cases, aspects have only been studied locally in time and/or geography.

Several articles present quantitative approaches to the last 38–40 thousand years of human history. These articles calculate the rate of change of significant events. However, the data sets were small.

Meaning of History as a Historical Trend in History

Khotsey[61] discusses various meanings of the terms "meaning" and "history," as well as the expression "meaning of history." One such option, per Khotsey opinion, is to consider meaning as a pattern. In this regard, Khotsey quotes from the work of Baranets: "Here it is more important to identify consistency and pattern in history, since for a supporter of this method of research in the field of philosophical understanding of history, the meaning is actually identified with the historical trends. If the historical trend is revealed, then the meaning is revealed."[62]

Understanding the meaning of history as a historical trends in history is closest to what is discussed in our book.

The Need for a Precise Science

The question arises why no one has proven that there is some sense to humankind's history that can be measured and verified.

As Aristotle said: " The right question is half the answer. " The fact is that the term "meaning" or "sense" itself is subjective. Can we reduce this subjectivity? Yes, we can.

We formulated the question like this. Is there a direction in which humanity is developing? In other words, is there a direction in which humankind's history is moving? There is much less uncertainty in "direction" than in "meaning" or "sense."

A satisfactory answer to the question "Is there a direction for the development of Directionality of Humankind's Development. History 24 humanity?" has not yet been provided. We can understand why this has happened. The problem arises from attempts to give and use too broad an understanding of the term "direction."

The original definition of direction is "the path that someone or something moves along when going toward a place."[63] This involves using mathematical calculations to calculate the course from one location point to another location point.

However, it has become common among some researchers to use the term "direction" differently. For example, no one would be surprised by a question like "What is the direction of your future research?" In this sentence, the word "direction" is completely unrelated to the estimated course from one location point to another location point. Instead, this may mean, for example, moving to take a more theoretical rather than experimental approach to the research topic.

The term "direction" has sometimes become unrelated to the original meaning of the term "direction" and can mean almost anything. This is the main reason why there have been no satisfactory answers, even to the correct question.

To get the correct answer to the question, "Is there a direction in which humanity develops?" we need to understand the term "direction" as it is defined in mathematics.

It is known that to determine the direction of movement of an object it is necessary to apply mathematics. The researcher must describe, in a unified form, the coordinates of the points through which the observed object moves. The researcher must then algebraically or geometrically calculate the direction of motion. An example is the well-known movement of a car.

First, we must describe the original data and then apply mathematical methods to this data. In other words, we must apply methods of precise science to the global multi-thousand-year history of mankind.

Direction of History. What is it?

The term history has several different meanings. History "may be used to refer to the past or the historical process, to the study (in particular the scientific study) of history, or to written history or the practice of writing history." [64] One well-known definition of history is that history "is primarily recorded facts of the happenings of the past."[65]

Even this definition still needs to be refined. Something needs to be added here. Here: History of what?

Most definitions of history are not concerned with the history of any particular subject. A history that is not concerned with any specific topic can be about any combination of any objects in this Universe, and therefore such a history is too amorphous to have any direction. In this book, we look at history that "relates to a particular subject, place, organization, etc."[66] We can say that the history of a certain subject is the totality of past changes of that subject over time.

To describe these changes in a measurable way, we need to use at least two dimensions.

"Dimension is a measurable extent of some kind, such as length, breadth, depth, or height."[67] In the case of history, one of the dimensions is time; which we can measure in days, years, thousands of years, and so on. We also need to point out the changes of a particular parameter we want to measure over time to get the history of that parameter.

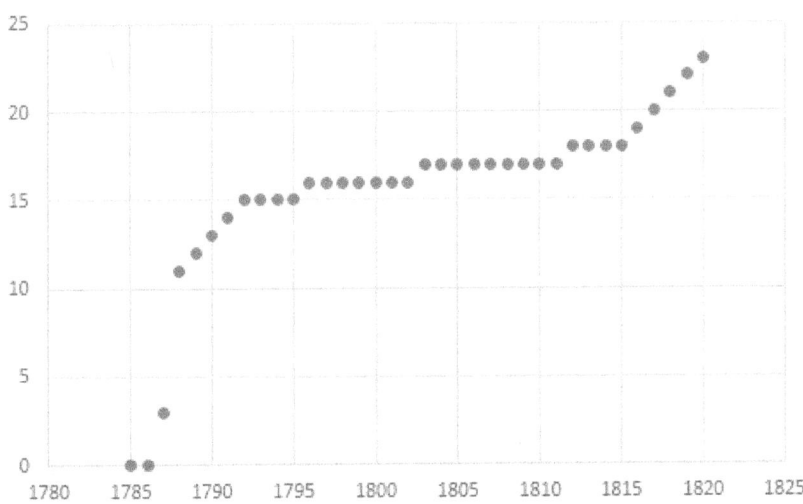

Figure 1.1.1. Total number of states in the USA. 1780 - 1820. Vertical axes – Total number of states. Data from [68]**.**
Horizontal axis - Time, in years.

For example, we want to get US history from 1795 to 1820. We need to focus on a specific parameter that characterizes the United States during this period. Let us use the total number of states as a parameter. This means we use two dimensions: time and the total number of states in the US from 1795 to 1820.

We could then represent changes over time using coordinates. "Coordinates are a pair of numbers that describe the position of a point on a coordinate plane by using the horizontal and vertical distances from the two reference axes."[69] "A coordinate plane is a two-dimensional plane formed by the intersection of a vertical line called the Y-axis and a horizontal line called the X-axis. . . It acts as a map and yields precise directions from one point to another."[70]

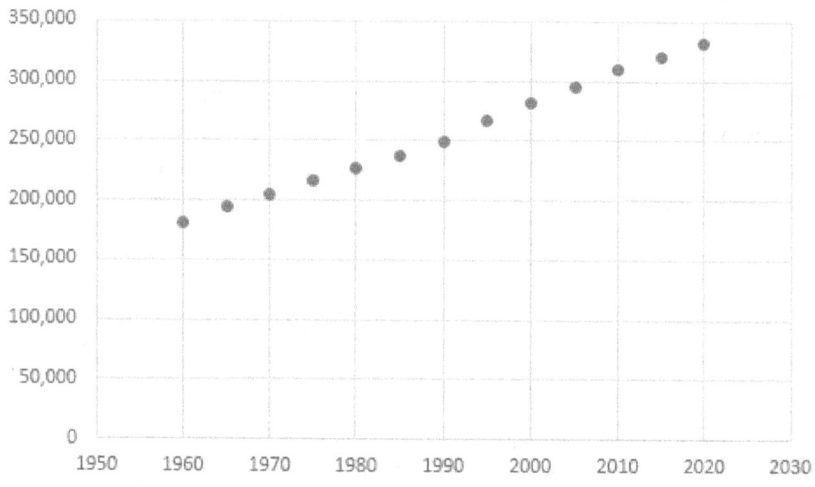

Figure 1.1.2. Population in the USA. 1780 - 1820.
Horizontal axis - Time, in years.
Vertical axes – Population, in Millions. Data from [71].

Figure 1.1.1 shows the history of the United States, specifically the total number of states, from 1795 to 1820. The subject of that history is the total number of states in the United States.

This graph shows the year-over-year change in the total number of states - increasing or not increasing. Over the broader time span, from 1780 to 1820, the general trend was for the total number of states to increase.

In other words, between 1780 and 1820, the United States was on a path to increase the total number of states.

Or we could state that U.S. history from 1780 to 1820, as measured by the total number of states, was directional. The US was moving toward more states.

Nothing in Figure 1.1.1 says anything about the purpose, progress, or reasons behind this directional history. Based on known facts, we have just documented the actual direction of US history in terms of the total number of US states from 1780 to 1820.

For US history, we could choose a different setting and time frame. For example, we could use the total US population for 1960 - 2020.

Figure 1.1.2 shows the history of the United States, namely the total population, from 1960 to 2020.

Both graphs show the direction of the US during a specific period in US history. The graphs also show specific curves, rates of development, etc. In both graphs we see an increase in one or another parameter.

These two examples are presented here to highlight several important points.

First, to get a measurable direction for something in history, you need to have a parameter that can be measured, and then obtain values for that parameter at several points in time. Once you have this data, you can perform data analysis and create graphs. Data can be discussed, verified, and refined by the scientific community.

If you do not have this data, then the history description will not be quantifiable. This description of the history may contain reasoning. This can be an interesting and valuable discussion.

However, suppose you want verifiable data about the direction, form, and pace. In that case, you should start from scratch to get the data first.

Additional Requirements

Both figures 1.1.1 and 1.1.2 characterize the development of the United States. However, we could not compare them because they use different parameters. We need to use the same parameter throughout history if we want to get a coherent picture of history.

We are shaping the world faster than we can change ourselves.

Winston Churchill

Chapter 1.2.
The Duration of
Humankind's History

BC / AD Story

We need to understand the meaning of the time frame of humankind's history. First, let us look at how we count years.

This book was written in 2023. In other words, this book uses the Gregorian calendar with a BC/AD dating system. This calendar uses the term "BC," which means "before the birth of Christ". Two thousand years before the birth of Jesus, the year was 2000 BC. AD in Medieval Latin means "anno Domini," meaning "in the year of the Lord". We could write 2023 AD or 2023 for the current year.

This dating system was not used until 525 AD. In 525 AD, the monk Dionysius Exigus created a new time schema for the Easter table.[1] The most accepted calendar in the world honors the birth of Jesus Christ. However, this calendar has not been used for many centuries since the birth of Jesus Christ.

But that is not all. Another interesting fact is that there is no year 0 in the Gregorian calendar. There is neither a year 0 AD nor a year 0 BC. The year 1 AD follows 1 BC. The origin year, that is, the year of Christ's birth, does not exist in this calendar! Most people do not know this. Historians know, but they don't care.

Imagine arithmetic in which the number 0 is missing. Then not only arithmetic, but all mathematics will crash. But when you have a calendar at hand, it is the exact opposite of mathematics. This calendar system did not collapse at all. Instead, historians agreed to use it in scientific publications on humankind's history.

What does this story about the Gregorian calendar tell us? It tells us that the generally accepted time schema is a product of agreements between people. The importance of the generally accepted time schema in history should not be overrated.

Timeframe of Humankind's History

When did humankind's history begin? Well, time flows without interruption. If we look back at the past years, we will see that some events happened to people while they existed. And we do not want to go back too far, a hundred thousand years ago. We need to draw a line.

Scientists have drawn this line a long time ago. Prehistory is "human history in the period before recorded events."[2]. This is how prehistory is defined. This means that humankind's history began around 3200 - 3100 BC.[3,4]

Of course, written records make the study of ancient events much easier. But such convenience comes at a price. Many important events were relegated to prehistory. The purpose of this book is to provide a general picture of humankind's history. It may be better not to rely on staying in a comfort zone. It is better to abandon the traditional definition of the time frame of humankind's history. Let's think about what to do here.

History is Conditional

No one can claim to know where the first letter came from. We were all born much later. We were not immediately invited to celebrate this event. We must rely on some evidence rather than our personal experience. The history of humankind is a chronicle of events about which we have information in one form or another.

Many of these discoveries happen to us by pure chance. Our ancestors did not want to freeze or burn themselves for our pleasure. They lived their private lives. They did not dream about our archaeologists. Could anyone believe that our ancestors cared so much about us? Why would they think about people who will live several thousand years in the future?

Let us take another look at the first writing in humankind's history as it is known to historians. We could be almost sure that this was not the first writing. Over many thousands of years of history, something may have destroyed the actual first written records. Or these records exist, but are in a place on Earth unknown to us. And remember that archaeologists have not yet excavated all the earth.

Have you been to the Holy Land - Israel? At archaeological sites in Israel, work took place at a level of approximately several meters from the surface. Why is this so? The answer came from a local guide. Jerusalem is the center of the world's major religions. This is why the importance of past events here cannot be overstated.

Thus, the historical layers in the Holy Land are very dense. Scientists in Israel must be very selective. They threw away layers younger than the last 300 years. Imagine if you did this in the US and threw out all the evidence from the previous 300 years!

This adds to the list of missing evidence of past events. No one can guarantee the completeness of existing evidence about the "first" events. We have to live with this.

First "Something"

Humankind's history is not carved in stone. From time-to-time new scientific discoveries occur. Or scientific research technology improves and we may see old artifacts in a new light. Or someone disrupts some commonly held views or assumptions about historical trends.

Our views on history could only be partially correct. There is some variability in history as we know it. Some uncertainty in historical dates is a fact of historical science.

When did humanity first begin to use writing? The answer seems obvious - at the time when the first writing appeared. Well, that answer was too quick. What do we mean by "use"? Are we talking about using writing in a small local place? This may be a very narrow understanding. When someone discusses the "French Revolution," she first mentions France and then goes into detail. Thus, we could be referring to the first use of writing in a particular country.

I want to throw even more firewood into this fire of questions. Shouldn't we also consider how the "first use of writing" spread from its original location? And of course, what we mean by the word "writing" is not as simple as it seems.

Many scientific works are devoted to similar questions. Sometimes you can even find good stories with interesting details. These works are dedicated to a conventional history.

Events in the subsurface version of humankind's history are events of the first use of something important. We need a clear definition of what is "first."

This is how it will be done in the proposed models of the humankind's system. We want to describe the first use of the word "school" in humankind's history. Someone did this somewhere, sometime. We will mark this as the first use of school by humankind. At first it was used by a minimal group of people. But these people are part of humanity. This school was very different from our schools. Details about the specifics of the school are for something other than deep-level history of humankind. We would only record the date when humankind first used the school.

We will always use this approach consistently throughout events on every continent and throughout humankind's history. This consistent approach will give us uniformity in the dates of these events. Then we could have a system with measurable characteristics. We will be able to use the methods of precise science.

Extinct Humans

One idea is to identify a period in history when no-Sapiens humans did not exist. Our last major intelligent competitors were the Neanderthals. We could mark the day of their disappearance as the beginning of humankind's history.

Neanderthals went extinct about 40 thousand years ago.[5] Did Sapiens drive our *Homo* brothers to the extinction? Is there much blood on our hands? That is a pressing and emotional question. We will be back to it later.

We arrived at a solid date when Sapiens became the only humans on Earth. We could mark the beginning of humankind's history at 38 000 BC. It is the easiest way. But is it the best way?

Our task is to find the direction in which humanity is moving. First, we need to define the time frame on which we want to focus. We see that these time frames depend on what we understand by the term "humankind."

Is the history of humankind a history of humans? Or is this the history of *Homo sapiens*? Or is it the same?

The name of our species is *Homo sapiens* or simply Sapiens. *Homo* in Greek means "same." *Homo* is short for "genus *Homo*." The word "man", short for human species, comes from Latin.[6]

The genus *Homo* contains more than ten species of humans. There was a time when several species of people coexisted on this planet. As strange as it may sound, there was a time when our species, Sapiens, was only a tiny part of humanity. There were even times when humanity existed without Sapiens. What should we do with these facts? We cannot ignore them, whether we like it or not.

When people say "humankind's history," they usually mean the history of *Homo sapiens*. In this book we also want to adhere to this understanding. How could we guarantee this? This is where our flexibility in defining the time frame of humankind's history comes in handy.

Compare Sapiens to Cats and Lions

So far, we have looked at Sapiens from the perspective of "what Sapiens is not."

Sapiens are neither Neanderthals nor Denisovans, who are very closely related to each other and to Sapiens. And we all belong to the genus Homo. Sapiens, Neanderthals and Denisovans met and mated with each other; this mating led to the hybridization of their DNA.

The date when Sapiens became the only surviving humans on Earth is very important. Since then, Sapiens have not been able to sleep with Neanderthals and Denisovans. This is exactly what we need to know. From that moment on, Sapiens could not communicate with other people who were not Sapiens. Therefore, Sapiens could not have acquired more Neanderthal or Denisovan DNA to become less Sapiens.

Do we have another option that would define Sapiens through "who we are" rather than "who we are not?" It's like comparing Sapiens to other animals. We could say that Sapiens are not cats, not dogs, not lions or elephants, and the list goes on until, in this case, we run out of mammals.

Or, we could say that Sapiens are animals with some characteristics that no other animal on Earth has. And that would be it! If we knew such a feature and the date when Sapiens acquired it, then such a date would be a better marker of the beginning of humankind's history.

Our Guidance is to Look at Results of Humans' Actions

Let us look at this from a slightly different angle. There were times in the past when even Sapiens could not do what we can do now. And then, at some point, Sapiens acquired the ability to be behaviorally the same as we are now.

We can study and discuss how this happens and when it happens. We can explore how this change was determined by something inside our body and our brain. However, we need confirmation of this change. We need evidence. We cannot know what ancient people thought or felt. But we can see the results of their actions. This is something we could rely on. But first we need to understand what we are looking for.

Behavioral Modernity

Fortunately, scientists discovered this feature a long time ago. Its name is "behavioral modernity." This is how humanity pats itself on the back. "Modern behavior" is determined by a certain set of traits.

However, scientists disagree on which of these traits are most important. First, we need to select a set of these qualities from scientific articles. We will then try to match the archaeological data with this set of features.

Most scientists prefer to include abstract thinking and symbolic behavior in the trait set. What about the date when humans became behaviorally modern? Is there an agreement on this?

When Sapiens Became Behaviorally Modern

There is debate about the timing of the transition to modern behavior. Some scientists believe that this happened about 80 thousand years ago or earlier.[7] Another date 30 – 40 thousand years later. The last viewpoint is that only then did Sapiens get the full package.[8]

Art that depicts figures unseen on Earth is symbolic art. The latest discovery of such art occurred in an Indonesian cave.[9]

Maybe you saw those paintings in some journals. They depict part-human and part-animal figures. The earliest date of this art creation is approximately 44 thousand years ago.

Sapiens carved zigzag patterns much earlier. What art scores highest on the behavioral modernity test? The prevailing view is that hybrids have won over zigzags.

We will choose an Indonesian rock art as more definite evidence. Therefore, in this book we will use 42000 BC as the beginning of humankind's history.

Were Only Sapiens Behaviorally Modern?

There is a small problem with this date. Since then, Neanderthals coexisted with Sapiens for thousands of years. The same goes for Denisovans. Should we consider them part of humankind's history? It depends. Probably yes, if they were "behaviorally modern." Some scientists argue that Sapiens have a cognitive advantage over Neanderthals,[10] while others disagree.[11]

Do we have clear evidence of modern Neanderthal behavior as seen in the Indonesian cave for Sapiens? Probably not yet. For this reason, we will not consider Neanderthals part of humankind's history.

Note that almost no one discussed Denisovans in this regard. It's time to delve deeper into the discussion. Let us hear from neuroscience experts. What development of the human brain might be responsible for behavioral modernity?

Synthesis of *Novel Mental Images*

The hypothesis was put forward by neurologist Andrei Vyshedsky. [12] It involves the process of creating mental images that are new. The process of creating images or thoughts in our heads is fascinating. Of course, this is also a difficult question. It is about the ability to mentally synthesize images that have never been seen before. The process name is PFS. This means prefrontal synthesis.

What items from the archaeological record can be used as evidence of PFS? Help is on the way. In his article, Andrei Vyshedsky compiled a shortlist of such materials. These include composite figurative art and bone needles with an eye.

As for Sapiens, we have a match with the famous Indonesian cave paintings of hybrids. This is it? Well, not yet.

Smart Denisovans

We are talking about an amazing discovery about Denisovans. The name "Denisovan" comes from the name of this place: Denisova Cave in Siberia. There is a photograph of an artifact that belonged to the Denisovans: a bone needle with an eye.[13,14] The possible date for the appearance of the needle is 50 thousand years ago. This needle indicates PFS. Unfortunately, Denisovans were only found at one excavation site. Despite this, some modern human groups have Denisovan DNA of about 3 percent.

What is most important is the quality of the Denisovan bone needle. It speaks for itself. It is on par with the quality of Sapiens' paintings of hybrids.

Sapiens Superiority Complex

The current dominant theory is that Sapiens are exceptional creatures. Somehow, we were chosen. Some supernatural beings have taken us to the top of the food chain on Earth. Or biological evolution favors us for some unknown reason. Either way, we are exceptional and deserve it.

Well, it is up for discussion now. This debate has not yet begun. It is difficult to predict the outcome of this.

In any case, this result will not affect the proposed models of humanity. The reason is simple. Yes, we could include the Denisovans' contribution to humankind's history. However, we know that Denisovans are extinct. We were only able to get one data point from them. Precise science requires more than one data point. Thus, in humankind's history, we will not use data related to Denisovans.

Despite this, the cognitive advantage of Sapiens over other humans is questionable to say the least.

Humankind's History Timeframe

Let us put it all together. In this book, humankind's history began around 42000 BC. Then, Sapiens' status as modern humans was confirmed by images of hybrids in an Indonesian cave.

From 38000 BC to this day, the history of humankind is the history of Sapiens. At that time, Sapiens were the only surviving human species on Earth. Between 42000 and 38000 BC, other people lived on this planet. However, the contribution of Neanderthals to humankind history was absent at that time. Denisovan's contribution is just one data point. It makes no sense to include only one available data point in a model of humankind's history.

Now we can say with a clear conscience that in the proposed models, the history of humanity is the history of Sapiens. Whatever happened to Sapiens before 42000 BC will be called the prehistory of humanity.

What's Next?

We have expanded the time frame of humankind's history from the usual 5150 years to 44 thousand years. This would help us notice important events and trends in humankind's history. At the same time, the search for the direction of humankind's development has become much more complex.

It seems like we need to look beneath the surface of humankind's events. Is it even possible to do this? How to do it?

We could turn to inspiration in our leisure lives. Have you ever enjoyed a beautiful beach? If yes, then you remember this vacation. You love the sun and the beach and want to swim nearby. However, you will probably need some help to see anything interesting underwater near your beach. It would help if you asked locals where the best places to look for colorful fish are. Locals know all the right places. There you will see rich underwater life. Well, even the right site is not a guarantee. Did you forget to take your underwater mask with you? You need to have the right tools to get what you want.

Our situation is very similar. It is very important to know where and how to look.

What Are We Trying to Achieve?

The question is, does humankind's development have any direction at all? The question "What is a right or wrong direction?" does not have a clear answer. We all know that "one man's trash is another man's treasure."

The right direction for one person may be the wrong direction for another. Moreover, we are still determining whether humanity is moving in any direction. First, we need to solve this puzzle. Only after this will everyone be able to decide whether this direction is right or wrong from her point of view.

An answer to the question about direction should exist. The main thing is to find the path along which humanity is moving. We need to measure the position of humanity on this path at different times. Then we will be able to calculate the speed of humanity's movement in this direction. Various mathematical tools are just waiting for us to use them. The desired direction would appear before our eyes.

In a Church

Imagine that you would like to visit a Catholic church. However, you know nothing about Jesus Christ. You are not familiar with Christianity or any religion and do not speak the local language. You walk into some beautiful church and freeze in admiration. Wow! The architecture of the building is magnificent. The lighting is excellent. Paintings and sculptures are everywhere. You are wandering around. You think you are about to get main theme of these paintings and sculptures. Then you go to another church and another.

You realize that there is something intriguing in the architecture of these churches. What it is? Each church building is very different from the others. But you see that there is some commonality in their architecture. You want to solve a puzzle. You have decided to abandon all interior details. You will try to see the "big picture" of the exterior. You rent a helicopter to fly over several churches. Here you are. You wonder why you did not notice this before. The pattern is obvious - the buildings are built in the shape of a cross.

You discover something that has been in front of your eyes all along. But it was hidden until you looked at it from a certain angle. You found the cross in the architecture of these churches.

Your knowledge of the exterior has increased significantly. But how does this relate to the interior? You return to the church to find out.

The big question is whether you can solve the puzzle just by being inside the church. Answer: yes. How? Well, the interior and exterior together form one system that embraces both. You need to imagine this system and understand how it works. However, in real life it takes work to get a clear understanding of what the system is. The solution is to build a model of the real system.

A system is a set of connected things or devices that operate together. [16]

Welcome back from the church to our story. Is humanity a system? Is the history of humankind a system? Of course, both are. We must look at humanity as a system if we want to discover something that we cannot see on the surface. We all probably think that humanity is a complex system. It seems to be complex. However, the term "complex system" should not be taken lightly. "Complex" is not just a word. There is a whole branch of science called "complex systems theory."

Remember, always, that everything you know, and everything everyone knows, is only a model.

Donella H. Meadows

High- and Low-Level Models of Humankind's Development

The only simple truth is that there is nothing simple in this complex universe.

Johnny Rich

Chapter 1.3.

Humankind as a Complex System

The scientific study of complex systems is relatively new and has already proven itself well. It is diverse: many institutes, journals, books, and researchers are devoted to complex systems.

What is a complex system? Are you familiar with the fact that, when we need it most, there is sometimes no clear definition? Well, this will not be the last time you read about complex systems. There is no single agreed-upon definition of the term. We will start with the quote: "the whole is something beside the parts," which is attributed to Aristotle. An individual person is a complex system. There is no doubt about this among scientists. But is it the same for humanity as a whole? Yes. There is recognition in the scientific community that the humankind's system is complex.[1]

One of the advantages of complex systems theory is that it is a hard science and we can obtain quantitative results from it. This is what we are looking for. That is why in this book we will study humanity and its history from the point of view of a complex system.

This view is different from many other positions. In the meantime, we could say what our book is not about. Paleontology or anthropology is not the subject of this book. We also do not investigate archeology or neuroscience. And we will not study evolution or biology. This list goes on and on.

Data from many of these fields of science can and will be used in the proposed models. But the essence of our approach is different from all these areas. The models in this book are models of humankind as a complex system.

Complex Systems around Us

Models are created by researchers and scientists. In short, a written or mathematical description of a system is a model of such a system.

One complex system is right under our feet. Ants. Lots of ants. Together the ants formed a complex system, an ant colony, which is a favorite object of study for scientists.

Researchers decide how many and what elements and interactions to include in a particular model. Sometimes authors use the term "components" instead of the term "elements".

Let us return from ants to humans. And from a colony of ants to humanity. Which collective system looks more complex: an ant colony or humankind? Perhaps it is the size of this complexity gap that matters. This might explain why we still do not have a quantitative model of humanity.

In the proposed models we will use the term element.

Micro and Macro

For some complex systems, so-called macro- and micromodels can be used. The other used terms are the levels to which the models belong. The lowest level is usually called the micro level.

Here is a close analogy. You have storage space with lower and upper shelves. On each shelf you put some of your things. The bottom level will contain your favorite shoes. The top-level shelf is where you place your favorite hats and caps. The contents of your shelves give some insight into who you are. However, each of your shelves holds things that differ individually from each other. Models at the micro and macro levels also differ.

A person can be used as an element of a micromodel of humanity. The level above may be the level with cities as macro elements. Higher up there may be a macro level in which countries act as macro elements.

It makes sense not to mix micro- and macro elements in one model. Just look how different people and cities are.

Traditional Approaches

There are two traditional approaches to modeling humankind. The first way is to use a person as an element of the system. Is it possible to understand all of humanity based only on individual human behavior?

Hardly. Billions of elements would be too much to handle.

A second traditional approach might be based on a macro-level model with social structures as elements. This approach may work for a short period of humankind's history. However, we want to look at 44 thousand years. Do you know of any social structures that have existed all this time?

It seems that both traditional approaches to modeling the humankind's system are not yet suitable for the task at hand.

How and What?

Our "how to look" tool uses a complex systems approach. However, we now know that it has not yet worked when applied to humankind.

We probably need to tweak the second element: "What to look at." Beginning with Herodotus, the typical history of humankind is the history of events that happened to people during a historical period. We need to reconsider our approach to these events.

Elements and Interactions

Typically, the most important part of a complex system is the interactions between the elements of the complex system. However, first we need to define the elements of a complex system. The models of humankind proposed in this book are new. The elements of such systems were not previously known.

Therefore, this book is dedicated to defining these elements. The interactions between these elements can be discussed in future works.

Words can be twisted into any shape. Promises can be made to lull the heart and seduce the soul... Examine his actions. Judge him by them.

Karen Marie Moning

Chapter 1.4.
Multi-Layer History

Let us imagine a diagram with a multi-layered representation of the history of events. At the top we see the layer where people's actions take place. On this top layer we also see the results of people's actions - events.

We'll call this top layer *The Events Layer*.

Two Top Layers

We will follow a top-to-bottom approach. For every two adjacent layers, the lower one determines what happens on the upper one. People's actions are at *The Events Layer*. These actions are based on people's wants and needs. In most cases, people also must consider cooperation and competition. Wants, needs, cooperation, and competition together motivate people to act.

We will call the next layer *The Motivation Layer*. We have two top layers - *The Events Layer* and *The Motivation Layer*.

Going Deeper

We have two layers. Are these two layers enough? No. Wherever people act or want to act, they should think about something else. There are restrictions on what they can and cannot do. What people may want or need is also limited. This is not a generally known fact. These restrictions vary greatly during various periods of humankind's history. Let us dig it up.

If you want to have fun and go to the cinema and watch your favorite movie, can you do it? Sure, you can. If this movie is not on the cinema menu, you can stream the movie online and watch it on your TV, or computer. Your wishes can be satisfied very easily and quickly. Or is it true?

Imagine that you live not now, but a thousand years ago, in 1000 AD. Could you satisfy your desire to go to the cinema and watch your favorite movie? Never! Cinema, film, and television did not yet exist at that time in humankind's history. Your specific desire will hit a stone wall. Your wish at that time could not become a reality in any place on Earth, under any circumstances.

There is a lot to think about here. You would not have the opportunity to even have such a desire. Such wishes did not exist at that time.

In 1000 AD, an opportunity going to the cinema and watching films did not exist. It has not existed throughout humankind's history since the beginning, at least until 1000 AD. We know this now. But no one knew this either in 1000 AD or before. The absence of such an opportunity seriously limits people's desires. The ability to perform certain actions was also limited at that time.

Later in humankind's history, humanity created a new opportunity, i.e., films, cinemas, and televisions. With these capabilities, humankind greatly expands people's ability to act.

The existence or absence of such capabilities is of critical importance to humanity. This effect can be both liberating and limiting. We will call the third layer from the top *The Opportunities Layer*. It affects not only people's abilities to act, but also their desires and needs.

What do we have now? We have built a three-level diagram of events in humankind's history. Each lower layer in this schema controls what happens at the layer above.

Where do new opportunities for humankind come from? In all cases except one, they were created by people, that is, by humanity itself. We will talk about this in detail later. For now, it is enough for us to state that new opportunities have been created by humankind.

The big question is what force pushes humanity to create new opportunities for itself. If such a driving force exists, we will put it in the bottom layer and call it *The Driving Force Layer*."

Of course, this three- or four-level schema of events in humankind's history is just an invented construct. However, it helps to see our history in a new light.

On Which Layer are Hard Facts?

Any representation of a certain set of objects by words or math is called modeling.

Imagine that you see a person crossing a city square and you want to know in which direction he is moving, and also the speed of his walking. You should note several places that this person has passed on his way to get to the indicated direction. You need to know the exact location of these places, and when the stranger stepped on them. You must measure the locations and times, and write the measurements down in mathematical terms. Using only verbal descriptions will not help much. You can use words at first, but then you must convert that verbal description into precise mathematical facts.

The same applies to the model of humankind. If we want to figure out the direction in which humanity is heading, we must use hard facts for every data point we will use in our model. This understanding helps us. Now we need to figure out at which levels of the four-level scheme of events in the history of humankind we can obtain hard facts, and at which we cannot.

Sorting It Out

We will divide information about events into "soft facts" and "hard facts." By "hard" facts we mean just two pieces of information. One of them is the fact that a specific event occurred.

The second is the date when it happened. In other words, we will only get the "what," "when," and nothing else. Taken together, the "what" and "when" represent the quantitative information required by the proposed models. All other information will fall into the group of "soft fact," which are not necessary for the original quantitative models. For example, the location where the event occurred will be a bonus. We won't use this information for models of humankind initially, but we may use it later.

At the top level, we have both soft and hard facts. Let us look, for example, at a recent event - World War II. There is a lot of research available to us. Which countries participated in World War II? What was the political and economic situation in these countries before the war? What were the alliances between some of these countries? What event started the war? The answers to all these and many other questions are in available publications.

Someone can spend a lifetime studying these facts and still see only part of them.

We are not alone in restricting the information on the event. This is not an unusual tactic. Whenever someone writes about an event, that person will always try to choose information wisely.

We just limited the information we wanted to use to the minimum.

Can we extract "hard facts" from the descriptions of people's actions and events that we see in *The Event Layer*? Certainly. However, we already know that too many events were recorded on this layer over 44 thousand years of humankind's history.

Can the second layer, *The Motivation Layer*, help us? Soundly, no. Unfortunately, there are no reliable facts at all on this layer. Each of us can be subjectively confident in our own motives. And that is it. We could not know for sure what was going on in other people's heads. We could guess and assume, but we could not know. This is true even for people living at the same time as us. And this is true for people in history.

What about the bottom, *The Driving Force Layer*, where the driving force behind human development is? Well, events from humankind's history are not listed on this layer.

Since the first, second and fourth layers are not suitable for hard facts, we need to take a closer look at the third layer - *The Opportunities Layer*.

What is the Foundation for Our Actions?

We have said this before, but it is worth repeating. What drives you in your life? Your needs and wants. And, of course, cooperation and competition - because you are not alone. These are the four main things that inspire us to do something. What is the foundation of our actions? What makes these actions possible? The answer is resources at the *The Opportunities Layer*. Let us take a closer look at them.

Resources are behind-the-scenes enablers for actions for all humans. This is also true for all people's communities and humankind.

Resources and Opportunities

Humankind's resources determine what we can do. We call them just resources. Definitions of resources and related terms are in the Definitions and Concepts section of this book.

A wider range of possible actions makes us better prepared for life. This range is determined by the available resources. Resources are opportunities for action.

We obtained data on the first use of resources from scientific publications mentioned in this book. The naming of resources and classes of resources was done by us. Twenty-three classes of resources were found. The range of created by humankind resources is much larger. There are over 300 resources.

With each new resource created, humanity expands its capabilities of action. Creating a new resource is difficult. It requires hard work and creativity. Above all, it requires creativity. There is no single generally accepted definition of creativity. The creativity of humankind has been explored even less.

We focus on *The Opportunities Layer*. History of the last 44 thousand years is the history of the resources created by humankind. Traditional history looks at the top, *The Events Layer*, and often the second, *The Motivation Layer*. The history we are looking at is on the deep, third layer from the surface, *The Opportunities Layer*. That is why we call this history *The Subsurface History of Humanity* or *Deep-Level History*. We could not use the term *Deep History* because it is already reserved for studying "the entire duration of human existence on Earth."[1]

Sapiens used their individual abilities, such as an ability to use and control fire, long before 42000 BC. Whatever abilities humanity had before the beginning of humankind's history; we will call them prehistoric resources. Discussion of prehistoric resources is beyond the scope of this book.

Our story is about resources that appeared at the beginning of humankind's history or after it.

What is Humankind?

Should "model of humankind," "model of humankind development," and "model of humankind history" be considered the same model or not?

It depends on what elements are used in the model. And we need to think about what humanity is, what history is and what development is.

What is humankind? A typical definition is that humankind is "all of the living human inhabitants of the Earth."[2]

We consider this definition too narrow, since it only covers the biological part of humanity. There is so much more to consider: cities, states, cars, cultures, school opportunities, etc. Moreover, [conventional] "history is more than just a set of facts; it also includes the interpretation of facts."[3]

It is difficult to define what humanity is. It makes sense to think about what humankind is by looking at it for one day, such as today.

Humankind and Conventional History

A model is a simplified description of something. Elements of the model of humanity can be individuals, cities, countries, etc.

Conventional humankind's history differs from humankind itself in that conventional humankind's history contains past events, which can be elements of the model. On the other hand, events are not elements of humankind's system.

Therefore, the model of humanity, in which people are the elements of the model, cannot merge with the model of traditional humankind's history, the elements of which are events of the past.

In other words, in general, the models of humanity and the generally accepted history of humankind are different.

Humankind and Development

What about the development of humankind? Development is "the act or process of creating something over a period of time."[4] Development is a process. If we have a model of humanity with elements that have been around for a long time, such as cities, then we could apply that model of humanity to different points in history. We will need to obtain data showing the development of cities over time.

In other words, a model of humankind could be used to describe humankind's development if elements of the model existed in humankind's history during the period of interest.

The simplest model would be one in which each element either exists or does not exist at certain points in the past, but the elements themselves do not change.

Humankind and Subsurface History

The elements of the models of humanity proposed in the book are the resources created by humankind for itself. Simply put, these resources are opportunities that people can use.

Let us visualize the deep-level history of humankind for the first four classes of resources.

The *Arts and Music* class of resources is marked in blue in Table 1.4.1 and in Figure 1.4.1. It can be said that humankind had the opportunity to do something in this area with the advent of the first hybrid rock paintings in Indonesia.

Table 1.4.1. History of Humankind.
First Four Classes of Resources. 4 Data Points

Class of resources		Emergence date
Art and Music		42000 BC
Man-made materials, substances, organisms		34000 BC
People and societies as objects of study		29000 BC
Usage of domesticated plants and animals		32100-16800 BC

Since then, the opportunity to engage in painting, sculpture, playing wind musical instruments, etc. has not disappeared anywhere. This possibility will exist as long as humanity exists. In a high-level model of humankind we consider the class of resources to be invariable. Once introduced, the *Art and Music* class of resources will remain the same class of resources.

In Figure 1.4.1 we can see four classes of resources from Table 1.4.1. These classes of resources are marked with different colors. Each of these classes of resources continues to exist from its inception. The opposite happened with events that occurred at the beginning of these resource classes and only existed at one point in time.

We could now compare the number of classes of resources existing at any given time. For example, from Figure 1.4.1 we see that in 35000 BC there was one class of resources, and in 25000 BC there were three classes of resources.

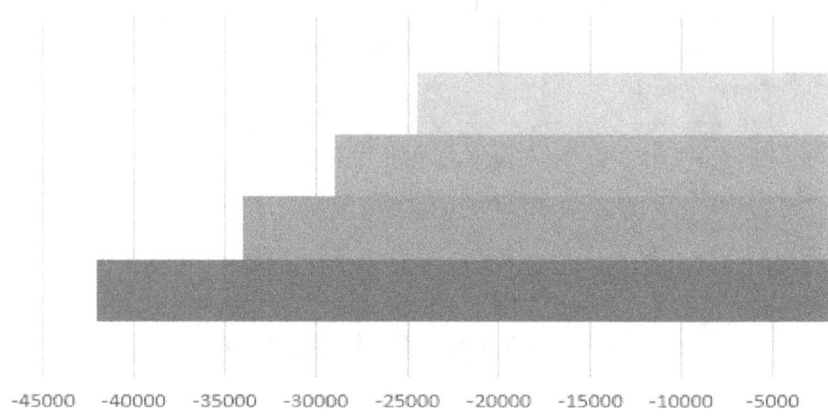

-45000   -40000   -35000   -30000   -25000   -20000   -15000   -10000   -5000

Figure 1.4.1. History of Humankind.
First Four Classes of Resources. 4 Data Points
Vertical – Classes of resources. Horizontal – Time, years.

Using this quantitative approach, we could analyze the subsurface history of humanity.

In other words, models of humankind in deep-level history of humanity can be used to study humankind's development.

Remember that the deep-level history of humankind, unlike the traditional history of mankind, does not include past events. At the same time, resources, or classes of resources, which are very important characteristics of humanity, are part of the deep-level history of humankind.

Humankind, Development and Subsurface History

Let us summarize. In the specific case of the deep-level history of humankind, models of humankind with elements such as resources or classes of resources can be used to describe **humankind's** history and humankind's development.

Measure what is measurable, and make measurable what is not so.

Galileo Galilei

As is known, any new science begins with classifying the research subject.

Genrikh Altshuller

Chapter 1.5.

Criteria for Resources and Classes of Resources

Hierarchical Classification System

When searching for elements of humankind's system, we need to ensure that these elements are not random, or part of data manipulation. We also need to ensure that the model represents an internally consistent system.

One way to do this is to use hierarchical classification system ranks.

For example, in biology, the taxonomy of biological objects is a separate field of practice and research. Zoologists and botanists are using a modified version of Carl Linnaeus's classification. There is even such a profession as taxonomist. "Taxonomy is a particular system of classifying things."[1] Typically, "A common feature of taxonomies is the hierarchical relationship between terms. Terms are linked to each other in a relationship that indicates that one is the broader term (BT) of the other, and in the other direction, one is the narrower term (NT) of the other."[2]

Note that the name taxonomy is reserved for biological hierarchical classification system.

The modern biological taxonomic system has eight levels of hierarchy. "Taxonomic ranks ... are relative levels of grouping organisms in a taxonomic hierarchy."[3] Hierarchical classification system can and is used not only in the field of biology.

Let us look at how we might use hierarchical classification system to study humankind's history at the third level, *The opportunities Layer*. Firstly, we need to determine which resources should have which classification rank.

Also, we must assign some names to the resources that will be placed in the classification levels. For example, in biological taxonomy, some taxonomy ranks have a name class and a kingdom, and the lowest rank has a species name.

As proposed in this book, the hierarchical classification system of resources created by humanity is new. In this hierarchical classification system there are no already established names for the ranks of the classification.

We will use a hierarchical classification system schema for resources like the taxonomy. Specifically, we will divide the classification of resources into 4 levels of classification , which are, from top to bottom, a domain of resources, class of resources, family of resources, and resources. Those names would be used throughout this book. Later, they can be replaced if someone from the scientific community offers better names.

Definitions

Definitions of resources, families of resources, classes of resources, domains of resources, and some examples are in the Definitions and Concepts section.

Filters

Using separate models of humankind for four different hierarchical classification system levels has the additional

Examples of Classes of Resources and Resources
Mass Transportation
/   \
Watercraft   Ground Vehicle

Figure 1.5.1. Partial diagram of

the *Mass Transportation* class of resources
People and Societies as Objects of Study
/ \
Sociology   Dentistry

Figure 1.5.2 Partial diagram of
The *People and Societies as Objects of Study*
class of resources

advantage of serving as a filter against random or manipulated data usage. Including only classes of resources in the high-level model and only resources in the low-level model will ensure internal consistency of the models.   A search for elements of the system of humankind's history could be better understood with several more-or-less apparent examples.

The *Mass Transportation* and the *People and Societies as Objects of Study* are classes of resources. They represent areas of humankind's activity created by humankind since the beginning of its history.

For each class of resources in Figures 1.5.1 and 1.5.2, we see two resources with specific terms. Note that how we differentiate between each other varies greatly for each class of resources.

For the *Mass Transportation* class of resources, we differentiate resources *Watercraft* and *Ground Vehicle* by the media in which *Watercraft* and *Ground Vehicle* operate, i.e., water or surface of the Earth. For the *People and Societies as Objects of Study* class of resources we differentiate resources *Sociology* and *Dentistry* by their relevance to the broader entity to which a particular resource relates. *Sociology* is society-related. *Dentistry* is health-related.

At first glance, those classes of resources and resources appear to be randomly selected. However, they are not. Both classes of resources and resources were carefully selected according to the hierarchy in the proposed classification system, the criteria for resources and classes of resources, and the relationships between these classification ranks.

Of course, in some cases, using more than one type of differentiator is possible. An actual situation is more complex; because a class of resources can contain over 40 resources. With so many resources available, there are many differentiator's designs to consider. This implies some subjectivity in the allocation of resources within families of resources.

This subjectivity differs from the typical subjectivity in humankind's conventional history, where there is dependence on local social structures, geographical, economic, political considerations, or moral and other subjective factors.

Hierarchical Classification System Errors

The subjectivity in the arrangement of classes of resources or resources may affect the total number of data points used in the proposed models. Given this type of subjectivity, it is important to assess the level of misclassification errors.

There is no error-free hierarchical classification system. The hierarchical classification system of resources created by humanity is different from taxonomy. And, of course, we need more scientific discussion about this the hierarchical classification system of resources. Methods for assessing the rate of the classification errors in this new hierarchical classification system have yet to be developed. Respectfully, we will evaluate the rate of classification errors in this new hierarchical classification system of resources by using an analogy with the most developed and researched classification system – biological taxonomy.

Biological taxonomy has been around for centuries, includes a huge amount of data, and is widely studied by scientists. Estimated biological classification error rates vary substantially for different specimen. According to one article, an "overall parataxonomist error rate was 11.1%."[4] Another paper assessed three types of taxonomic errors: straight errors, hierarchical errors, and missing errors. The total percent of errors was 6.9% - 34.4% for a particular specimen.[5]

For now, we will assume that the possible level of classification errors in the proposed classification of resources created by humankind throughout its history may be 7–35 percent.

Domains of Resources

It is intuitively clear that both classes of resources and resources should be important to humankind, with classes of resources having higher importance. However, "importance" is subjective, and a numerical scale has never been proposed for the term. Still, the "importance" of resources must somehow be reflected in the selection criteria for

Table 1.5.1. History of Humankind. 42000 BC – 2023 AD. Domains of Resources. Comparison with Prehistoric Activities.
6 Domains of Resources. 24 Classes of Resources.

Class of resources created by humankind during its history, 42000BC - 2023 AD	Essense of the classes of resources
Domain of resources: New quality	
Novel mental images	Novel mental images
Domain of resources: Personal development and social impact	
Art and Music	Entities for soul and fun
People and societies as objects of study	Study of ourselves and usage of it
Domain of resources: Man-made entities	
Man-made materials, substances, and organisms	Man-made materials, substances, and organisms
Usage of domesticated plants and animals	Domesticated plants and animals
Mass transportation	Man-made transportation
Tools, devices, machines from man-made materials	Man-made Tools, devices, machines
Mass production	Man-made production
Mass media	Man-made media
Domain of resources: Overcoming limits	
Trade with a use of intermediary	Overcoming locality in trade
Transnational entities	Overcoming national boundaries
Independent communication channels	Overcoming locality in communication
Involvement of women in humankind's activities	Overcoming inequality
Life expectancy growth	Overcoming human deceases

Domain of resources: Beyond our body and mind	
External information storage and processing	Outsourcing information storage and processing
Use of forces of nature, relativity, and quantum physics	Consciousness use of laws of physics
Technology beyond limitations of human senses	Going beyond limitations of human senses
Usage of the scientific method and information technology	Usage of verifiable worldview
Digital technology	Highly scalable and expandable technology
Artificial intelligence (AI)	Going beyond limits of human intelligence
Domain of resources: Scale-up to new quality	
War and Means of warfare	Mass human fighting and killing
Usage of people as a resource on a massive scale	Massive human exploitation
Mass education	Mass education
Usage of natural resources on a massive scale	Massive usage of natural resources

domains, classes, families of resources, and resources.

We will follow the approach used by Guy Kahane in his article "Importance, Value, and Causal Impact."[6] He wrote, "genuine importance is, I suggest, difference to value." In his view, "The degree to which something is important, relative to a domain, is a function of how much difference it makes to overall intrinsic value in the domain, compared to other things in the domain; and the more difference to value something makes, in this way, the more attention and concern it merits."

"Domain is a specified sphere of activity or knowledge."[7] With this approach, we need to define the domains to which class of resources could belong. The resources humankind created in history can and should be compared with each other, and with what was available to humans in prehistory.

In this book, we consider that humankind's history began when humans became capable of making Novel Mental Images, which, in turn, was revealed by archeological evidence of art with hybrid figures. As of 2023, that moment is approximately 42000 BC, but it could be moved slightly with possible new discoveries.

We will consider six domains of resources.

The comparison with prehistoric activities is in Table 1.5.1. The right column includes what was created by humankind during its history - classes of resources. The left column shows the base entities to which

Table 1.5.2. History of Humankind. 42000 BC – 2023 AD.
Domains of Resources. The Essence of Classes of Resources.
6 Domains of Resources. 24 Classes of Resources.

Class of resources created by humankind during its history, 42000BC - 2023 AD	Essense of the classes of resources
Domain of resources: New quality	
Novel mental images	Novel mental images
Domain of resources: Personal development and social impact	
Art and Music	Entities for soul and fun
People and societies as objects of study	Study of ourselves and usage of it
Domain of resources: Man-made entities	
Man-made materials, substances, and organisms	Man-made materials, substances, and organisms
Usage of domesticated plants and animals	Domesticated plants and animals
Mass transportation	Man-made transportation

Tools, devices, machines from man-made materials	Man-made Tools, devices, machines
Mass production	Man-made production
Mass media	Man-made media
Domain of resources: Overcoming limits	
Trade with a use of intermediary	Overcoming locality in trade
Transnational entities	Overcoming national boundaries
Independent communication channels	Overcoming locality in communication
Involvement of women in humankind's activities	Overcoming inequality
Life expectancy growth	Overcoming human deceases
Domain of resources: Beyond our body and mind	
External information storage and processing	Outsourcing information storage and processing
Use of forces of nature, relativity, and quantum physics	Consciousness use of laws of physics
Technology beyond limitations of human senses	Going beyond limitations of human senses
Usage of the scientific method and information technology	Usage of verifiable worldview
Digital technology	Highly scalable and expandable technology
Artificial intelligence (AI)	Going beyond limits of human intelligence
Domain of resources: Scale-up to new quality	
War and Means of warfare	Mass human fighting and killing

Usage of people as a resource on a massive scale	Massive human exploitation
Mass education	Mass education
Usage of natural resources on a massive scale	Massive usage of natural resources

classes of resources should be compared. This is either prehistoric activities or locality or limitations. Locality or limitations are not necessarily prehistoric. Table 1.5.1 can be used to estimate the value of a class of resources relative to its prehistoric basis. There is no numerical scale to determine this added value. However, the observer is able to see the significance of a specific class of resources.

To better understand what domains of resources and classes of resources are, we might also look into Table 1.5.2. The list of classes of resources, along with their dates of emergence, was provided in Table 1 at the beginning of this book. The essence of each class of resources is presented in the right column in Table 1.5.2. It shows how classes of resources differ from each other.

Criteria for Resources

How to find out what resources have been developed by humankind? How can we be sure that a new opportunity is not just a minor modification to an old resource? How do you see the event that marked a first use of a new resource?

We identified the following main criteria that we used to search for new resources.

Importance: A difference in the quality of a new resource compared to an old resource in the same class of resources should be very significant.

Durability: A new resource, from the moment it emerges, must be unlimited in time.

Mass Use: The use of resources by humankind should be massive, preferably global, over time.

Are Resources Wide Used?

History is "all the events that happened in the past."[8] The importance of past events to humanity is assessed over time. In other words, in traditional history, the history of events, our assessment of past events is retrospective.

The same is true for deep-level history. Our decision to include a potential resource in the resource list is retrospective. The date of this inclusion is determined by the date of the first publication of the new resource.

Some resources and classes of resources were published in my works in 2020 – 2021[9-13]. The complete list of 318 resources was published in this book in 2024. This date itself is interesting for historiographers. "Historiography is the study of the history and methodology of history as a discipline. Briefly, it is the history of history."[14]

It should be noted, however, that a potential resource should be verified to meet all resource definition requirements before the new resource is first published. In particular, the publication's author must ensure that the potential resource has widespread, preferably global, use as of the publication date.

For example, we know that *Alcohol* was widely used in 2023 and, accordingly, in 2024, *Alcohol* satisfies the requirement for massive use. All the details of how exactly and what types of *alcohol* are used in different countries, when and where the mass use of alcohol began, etc., remain outside the scope of deep-level history. The author verifies that the potential resource at least meets the resource definition. Then, the author publishes data about the new resource, i.e., the name of the resource and the date of first use of the resource.

And, of course, "massive use" is defined differently for various resources. For example, we must have different assessments of what constitutes "massive use" of resources such as *Alcohol* and *Submarine*.

Resource should Give the Most Generalized Idea of the Subject

Per the resource definition, "Resource should give the most generalized idea of the subject."

For example, during the search for a resource, it looks obvious that the "car" is a good candidate for the resource in the *Mass Transportation* class of resources. However, "car" is not the most generalized idea of the subject. We know that there are also trucks, SUVs, buses, etc.

We need to generalize. Will "Ground vehicle on wheels with the engine" be a good enough generalization? Not really. We know that they are also crawler-mounted ground vehicles with engines.

We need to generalize again. The final name for the resource is *Ground Vehicle with Engine*.

Competition Between Resources

"There is no rule without exception". Sometimes resource usage may decrease over time. With the luxury of hindsight, we may see it coming. Consider the usage of *Ground Transportation with a Use of Animal* resource.

Could you imagine a history of humankind without romantic horseback rides and brutal cavalry battles? For thousands of years, horses have made humankind's history very interesting.

Yet, we all know that the use of horses has decreased over time. That decline was caused by a sharp increase in the use of *Ground Transportation with an Engine* resource. "Tractors accounted for about 64 percent of national farm horsepower capacity in 1940."[15]

War – Tool or Event?

Remember, we are under the surface of conventional history. We are on level three from the top. Everything looks different here. You could not see events on the *The Opportunities Layer*. You will recognize tools, things, qualities, and methods as resources or classes of resources for people to act.

Let us look at the *War and Means of Warfare* class of resources. What we see in Table 1 is an emergence date, 2700 BC, of the *War and Means of Warfare* class of resources. It is an opportunity to act for some people.

This book does not link personal morals or other views to objective facts. This means that we are not going to rate this resource on any moral scale. The *War and Means of Warfare* class of resources is a tool. It is an ample opportunity for some people, and many people and societies are taking advantage of it. You will be pressed to find a year in humankind's history without ongoing armed conflict or war.

The specific war between Sumer and Elan is here only as evidence of the first use of the *War and Means of Warfare* class of resources.

No Entry for Revolutions

Does history without revolutions seem strange to you? Many historians view revolutions as the driving force of humankind's history. We can assure you that we have not decided to abandon all revolutions. Their absence from the proposed models of humankind's history is not intentional. This is just a by-product of the proposed approach. However, the absence of revolutions, wars, and dynasties is symbolic.

In the subsurface history of humankind, how we perceive the significance of a particular historical event does not matter much. Did this event create an opportunity that could be used repeatedly? That is what is important. Of course, we have to judge how large or small this opportunity is.

Class of Resources

Many resources could be grouped together. For example, *Mass transportation with Watercraft* and *Mass Transportation with Aircraft* resources could be put together into the class of resources *Mass Transportation*. Of course, such a class of resources did not just pop up altogether.

Every class of resources has its own history. That is a history of emergence dates for resources belonging to this class of resources. Where did the first *Mass Transportation* emerge - in water or on land? When did it happen? What was next?

Classification

The creation of every resource by humankind is a creative act.

We do not know what the creators of such resources thought about their creations. We often have no idea even who these inventive people were. These talented people hardly named those resources the way we did. Sometimes we do not know what language they spoke.

We have the luxury of looking back to categorize resources the way we want. We will name a resource from a particular class of resources that emerged first in this class of resources as a primary one. All non-primary resources are secondary.

Criteria for Classes of Resources

The main criteria we used when searching for a new class of resources are the same as for resources, with the addition of one more criterion. Below is a list of criteria you can use when searching for a class of resources.

Importance: A difference in quality of a new class of resources compared to a cluster of prehistoric resources in the same field of humankind's activity must be very significant.

- *Durability*: A class of resources, from the date of creation of the class of resources, should not be limited in time.

- *Mass Use*: The use of class of resources by humankind should be massive, preferably global, over time.

- *Expand-ability*: Expanding a class of resources by adding new resources should be carried out over time.

Mass Transportation Class of Resources

For a long time, people had an "Individual Mobility" prehistoric resource. If humans wanted to move from one place to another, they had to use their physical abilities. There were no ships, buses, or airplanes for people to ride. Then, tens of thousands of years passed. Humankind developed a new *Mass Transportation* class of resources. Could it satisfy the above criteria? Here is a short analysis.

1. Importance: A difference in the quality of a new class of resources compared to a cluster of prehistoric resources in the same area of humankind's activity should be very significant. - Yes. Current ocean ships could move thousands of people simultaneously.

2. Durability: A class of resources, starting from the creation date of the class of resources, should not be limited in time. - Yes. The *Mass Transportation* class of resources has always been used by humankind since its inception. Its usage only increases over time.

3. Mass use: The use of class of resources by humankind should be massive, preferably global, over time. - Yes. The usage is in every region of the world. Global transportation is integral to the world of humans.

4. Expand-ability: Expanding a class of resources by adding new resources should be carried out over time. - Yes. Over time the *Mass Transportation* class of resources started to include resources, which were not available for mass transportation.

The creation of the *Mass Transportation* class of resources was a dramatic change in the overall resource-ability of humankind.

We will use several different models of humankind. In this book, we will explore mainly two models. The first model is a high-level model consisting of classes of resources. The second model is a low-level model, which includes resources instead of classes of resources.

How the Proposed Approach is Different?

Let us compare the conventional and deep-level descriptions of a complex system of humankind.

A conventional approach is like this. An element of the system could be just a single human being. The other alternative is to use cities, social structures, or alike as system elements. Such elements include big or small gatherings of human beings.

It is reasonable to read a big picture of humankind through people. In the end, without people, humanity does not exist at all. That approach may work for a short period in history and for a much smaller community than humankind.

The problem is that, so far, this standard approach did not deliver to us the direction of humankind's development.

Decoupling from Human Beings

Subsurface models of humankind do not use people or people gatherings as elements of the models.

What does a decoupling of the contents of system elements from human beings allow us to do?

First, it provides independence from social structures, politics, economics, etc.

It also dramatically reduces our dependency on observers' subjective judgments, including this book's author. You could check it out by yourself. You could perform a mental experiment while reading this book. Just imagine some judgment based on morality, progress, or social justice terms. Or it could be an opinion related to happiness, environmental impact, or people's intentions. It could be a viewpoint on the   role of individuals, society, random chance in history, etc.

Then, try to apply this judgment to a high-level model of humankind.

And look for results presented in this book. Results are in Figure 1 for the low-level model and Figure 3.1.4 for the high-level model. Will the form of the curves change? It will not.

You cannot underestimate the importance of this. That independence, in turn, allows us to apply a new approach broadly. The proposed models could be used for any time in humankind's history. The Neolithic time, with a small number of bands of hunter-gatherers, is suited for the model; the current globalized population of billions of people is suited as well.

Granularity

Granularity is the relative size, scale, or level of detail in system elements. Highly aggregated data is low granularity, while highly detailed data is high granularity. In other words, a high granularity level refers to a high level of detail, and a low granularity level refers to a low level of detail. The easy way to visualize granularity is to remember that data used for detailed analysis requires a high level of granularity.

In our case, a low-level model of humankind, with resources as elements, is the model with high-level granularity. We included 318 resources in the low-level model of humanity. The low-level model is much more detailed than the high-level model. The high-level model of humankind has classes of resources that are aggregates of resources. The high-level model has low-level granularity. We included 23 classes of resources in the high-level model of humankind.

System elements with some granularity levels are sometimes called "granules" or "grains."

In our case, the size of "granules" in the high-level model of humankind is approximately 14 (= 318 / 23) times greater than the size of "granules" in the low-level model of humankind.

In many fields, the concept of granularity was applied implicitly. For example, in biological taxonomy, there are eight levels of hierarchy. Objects in higher levels of hierarchy have lower levels of granularity. Respectively, higher levels of hierarchy include multiple objects from lower levels of granularity. The lowest taxonomy level of biological entities is species, next to the bottom - genera. In 2021, there were around "2.13 million species on the planet."[16] "In 2018, the Catalogue of Life quoted 173,363 accepted genus names for both extant and extinct species."[17] That means there were, on average, 12-13 species in one genus. In other words, the granular size at the genera level is 12-13 times greater than the granular size at the species level.

A discussion on granularity is ongoing [18].

In this book, we propose a hierarchical classification system for humankind. That system includes several classification levels. Let us look at them from top to bottom.

The top level is the level of domains of resources. The domains have a maximum size of granules.

Each domain of resources could include several classes of resources, which have granules of a smaller size than those at the domain of resources level.

If the class of resources contains several families of resources, then those families of resources have granules smaller than those at the class of resources level.

Each family of resources includes several resources and has the smallest size of granules.

At each level of hierarchy, we could consider objects on this level as elements of a model of the complex system of humankind. In other words, we could use four different models of humankind.

In this book, we will primarily look at two models. The first model consists of classes of resources. We call it a high-level model of humankind.

The second model consists of resources. We call it a low-level model of humankind.

Manageability of Models

Resources could be used repeatedly. At the same time, those resources appeared only once in the proposed models.

We do not track any use of resources or classes of resources except the first one. For example, we note the first use of the *School* resource and do not track any other uses of the *School* resource. That approach dramatically reduces the number of elements or interactions in the proposed models. Instead of billions of people, we have 318 elements in a low-level model. In a high-level model, there are only 23 elements. That is what makes the proposed models of humankind manageable.

Limiting and Liberating Effects

We could think of resources as something that could be born. The date of a resource emergence is its birthday. For every element in the proposed models, there are only two periods. Those periods are disjoint from each other.

In the first period, before the emergence date, that resource did not exist. The absence of this specific resource had a limiting effect on a range of possible people's actions. You can only go to the cinema if the cinema is invented.

In the second period, after the birth, the resource is alive. It could be used by people. The liberating impact of the presence of this resource is in place. You could go to the cinema if they are around. Moreover, the repertoire of films would increase over time. Every new resource gives people more choices to choose from. It provides a great addition to the arsenal of available resources.

Elements Diversity and Similarity

Did you ever think about something that could be unique and ordinary simultaneously? Maybe you did not, but you know such things very well.

Just look at your carry-on bag when you are at the airport. The contents of the bags are unique. There are tens of other passengers' bags on shelves in the cabin. At first glance, they look different, even on the outside. Some are slightly smaller than others, their forms are various, some are bright-colored, and others look dull.

Yet, for the in-flight airplane system, all those bags are very similar elements of the system. They all satisfied two criteria, which are limits on size and weight. And within those limits, bags can differ from each other tens of times in size and weight.

Elements in the proposed models are like our carry-on bags. You could pick up several items from Table 1 and compare those classes of resources to each other to see it yourself. The contents of every single class of resources in the high-level model are unique. At the same time, they were chosen using the same criteria and are on the same granularity level.

Likewise, the contents of every single resource in the low-level model are unique. *Empire, School,* and *Electronic Logical Gate* are as far from each other as possible. Yet, they all were chosen using the same criteria and are on the same granularity level.

Later, we could assess the difference in granularity size between our four models of humankind.

Ready to Go Under Surface

We defined the beginning date of humankind's history. That history is *Homo sapiens* history.

Are we ready to look at humankind's history as a complex system? We know what we want to investigate. Criteria that must be used while searching for elements of those models are already established. We will validate desired hard facts by scientific publications. Finally, we know how to separate elements of the high-level model from elements of the low-level model by using the difference in proper criteria.

History is like a forest. Some people like to see it from afar. Others prefer to come much closer first and enjoy every tree. Imagine that you have a magic wand, and it could get you to any place you want. Would you prefer to get in front of the forest, observe it for some time, and then move closer to see what types of trees are there?

If you are a big-picture person, you could jump to Part 3. Otherwise, please continue.

How Can Humankind's History Fit into One Chart?

The list of milestones in the deep-level history of humankind looks very short. For a 44-thousand-year period, we counted just 23 data points in the high-level model of humanity and just 318 in the low-level model of humankind.

Let us compare it with the traditional history of events. We may not be fond of everything that happened in humankind's history. But at least we are proud that humankind's history is very rich, correct? How rich is it? How many historic "important" events are contained in the conventional history of the last 44 thousand years? The answer is well over a thousand events.[19-22] The richness of the history of events is a challenge, if you want to discover the direction of humankind's development.

In the proposed models, we are looking below the surface of the history of events. Our history of humankind is very selective. The event cleanup was huge. Because a deep-level history of humankind is not a history of events; all political, economic, geographic, moral, and similar considerations, social structures, and information about great historical personalities or elites, revolutions, wars, and natural disasters was excluded. Please note that the entire cleanup happened automatically.

The subsurface history of humanity is a history of the emergence of new resources created by humankind for itself.

Emergent Behavior

Emergence is a hallmark of complex systems. In the theory of such systems, it is called an emergence behavior.

What does it mean? Let us suppose that we know all parts of the system. An emergence behavior indicates that some features or states cannot be predicted based on that knowledge alone. It does not matter how perfect the knowledge regarding parts of the complex system is.

There is no single agreed-upon definition of what the emergence behavior is. We could quote this definition: "Emergent behavior is a distinctive aspect of systems in which the exhibited behavior of the system is more complex than the behavior of the individual components that shape the system."[23]

There are different types of emergent behavior. Jeffrey Goldstein classified "properties that identify [a system] as emergent."[24] As proposed in this book, models of complex systems of humankind exhibit a dynamical type of emergent behavior. "Dynamical: emergent phenomena … arise as a complex system evolves over time."[24]

To assess whether the proposed model exhibits emergent behavior, we must understand whether it is possible to predict any, some, or all states of the model in the future; assuming we know all the elements that make up the model at any given moment.

Nobody at any moment in humankind's history has been able to predict which resources would emerge next, when they would emerge, and in exactly which form. Our knowledge of all current parts of humankind's system model still does not allow us to predict the whole system's next state. You do not know when a new resource will be added to the model of humankind's system. And nobody envisioned which resource it will be and in which exactly form it will first appear.

For example, at the time when humans invented the use of a horse-drawn carriage as a means of mass transportation, it was impossible to predict that in the future, humans would also use airplanes for mass transportation. This is just one example. However, the same logic can be applied to any state of any of proposed models.

That means low-level, medium-level, high-level, and super-high-level models of humankind are complex systems. Every separate class of resources is also a model of a separate complex system.

Variables and Invariables

Models of systems are always simplified versions of systems with multiple built-in limitations. Models of complex systems of humankind are not exceptions.

The proposed models in this book, like the high-level or low-level models, are systems that change over time by adding new elements. In other words, each proposed model is a variable entity.

At the same time, we already mentioned that for every resource in the model, we use only the date of the first appearance of the resource and do not track any development that could happen with the resource over time. That means that resources are invariables.

As a result, high-level and low-level models cannot be combined and should be treated as separate entities.

Here is an example. Let us consider multiple resources of just one class: Mass *Transportation*, with multiple elements of this class. The elements of this class, such as an *Elevator* or *Ground Vehicle with an Engine*, are invariables. The *Mass Transportation* class of resources itself is a variable. The *Mass Transportation* class of resources is a separate complex system.

On the other hand, if we use a system with classes of resources as elements, those classes of resources are invariables, and a system of classes of resources, i.e., a domain of resources, is variable.

Timeline of a Search for a New Resource

It is helpful to understand the difference between "opportunity to exploit" and "exploitation of opportunity." In our context, "opportunity to exploit" is a resource, and "exploitation of opportunity" is using a resource.

In the tables and graphs of the subsurface history of humankind, the date of the first "use of opportunity" is taken into account. In other words, the date of the first occurrence of the resource, i.e., the date of emergence of the "opportunity to exploit," is considered.

At the same time, the second and all subsequent uses of the resource, i.e., all "opportunity exploits," except the first one, are not considered.

During a search for a new resource, we look at how a potential new resource was used over time to understand if its usage became massive, preferably global, over time. Suppose all items in the resource definition, all items in the search criterion, and other proper details are satisfied, and we move a potential resource into an actual resource status. From that moment, the new-found resource will be characterized only by the date of its emergence, and its uses, except the first one, are not considered.

Typical Resource

We may look at one of the resources created by humankind. A good example would be *Ground Transportation with an Engine* resource, which belongs to the *Mass Transportation* class of resources.

We marked the emergence of the named resource as the date when Bertha Benz, wife of inventor Karl Benz, drove 65 miles from Mannheim to Pforzheim with her sons Richard and Eugen in 1888. As with the emergence of any new resource, only a specific version was introduced at first. In this case, a motorized car was first used as a mass transportation vehicle on a long-distance trip in 1888. However, many more motorized vehicles appeared later in *Ground Transportation with an Engine* resource. In addition to cars, we could name trucks, buses, sport utility vehicles, motorcycles, minivans, scooters, and three-wheeled motorized vehicles.

Is there anybody who doubts that the invention of *Ground Vehicle with an Engine* opened a resource for humankind? There were probably about one billion cars in 2020.[25]

If most of those cars stopped moving, what would happen to the world we live in? The 2020 coronavirus pandemic allowed us to see, with our own eyes, what would happen. That pandemic gave us an impression of how a world without the *Ground Vehicle with an Engine* resource might look.

Timeline of Humankind's History

Let us look at the proposed version of humankind's history chronology, as it is presented in Table 1 at the beginning of this book. What does it tell us?

This list is not a work of fiction. It is a short chronology of deep humankind's history based on hard facts about actual events. Those events' details were retrieved from scientific publications. Details are in Part 2 of this book.

This short deep-level history of humankind deals only with the most significant and impactful breakthroughs.

Subjectivity in Traditional History and in Subsurface History

Subjectivity and objectivity are subjects of lengthy discussions among philosophers, scientists, and alike. We will use a simplified approach and follow this statement: "The term 'subjective' typically indicates the possibility of error."[26] In particular cases, the next question is if this error is measurable or unmeasurable.

Suppose the error related to a particular subject is unmeasurable. In that case, we consider this subject as highly subjective. There is also a specific case when we discuss the subjectivity of some subjects in the past. If the error related to a particular subject is measurable by experts' questionaries now but not in the past, then we consider the use of this subject highly subjective.

Therefore, progress, morale, divine providence, happiness, or alike are highly subjective. Comparative assessment of traditional humankind's history typically involves the mentioned or similar terms and, therefore, is highly subjective.

Suppose the error related to a particular subject is measurable. In that case, we consider this subject as lightly subjective. Typical hierarchical classification schemas have some misclassification errors, which could be discussed by the scientific community, reviewed, measured, and even corrected over time.

Respectfully, we consider hierarchical classification schemas as lightly subjective tools. The subsurface history of humankind is based on a hierarchical classification schema and, therefore, is lightly subjective.

The Spectrum of Humankind's Activities

Please look at Table 1 more closely. The information in it covers a tremendous range of classes of resources created by humankind for itself. You are looking at the deep-level history. It appears that humankind's creativity is in more than just technology and the arts. The proposed high-level model is a witness to that. We capture those classes of resources at the moment of their emergence. Yet, we do not track the usage of emerged resources. That is how we got a high information density in the proposed version of humankind's history.

In the 20th and 21st centuries, we are accustomed to a much narrower view. You have heard this viewpoint often. It says that advances in technology are what define humanity.

Well, the deep-level history of humankind tells us a different story. It is a story about humankind's creativity in any class of resources that it touches; a tale about a humanity who is unsatisfied with what has been achieved. That journey started 44-thousand years ago. The creativity accelerated over time.

Let us look more closely at the creative genius of humankind. Humankind went from the invention of art and music to the creation of text. We moved from the use of people as a resource on a massive scale to external information storage and processing. Those classes of resources look totally unrelated to each other, correct?

Humankind also mastered the creation of man-made materials, substances, and organisms. That, by itself, is a broadly defined class of resources. People gladly embraced mass media. Later, digital technology was born. That humanity baby grew up very quickly, and we all love it. We could not imagine our food without the use of domesticated plants and animals. And mass production conquered the world.

What do transnational entities and the growth of life expectancy have in common? Those were other classes of resources created by humankind. Look also into scaling battles into a war and the emergence of arms of mass damage. There are always some people and countries ready to use them. On the other hand, humankind managed to rise to the creation of mass education.

Various countries are deeply involved in trade with the use of intermediaries. Many independent communication channels are all around us. As you recall, we talked a lot about mass transportation. The latter could not exist without the use of natural resources on a massive scale, at least for now.

Please look again at the areas of humankind's activities. You see the picture. Names of many classes of resources suggest that most of them cover diverse activities. Look, for example, at creating tools, devices, and machines from man-made materials. Some of the mentioned resources look related to each other. Still, most look totally opposite.

We live longer. Thanks, in part, to technology beyond the limitations of human senses. Could we live now without studying a history of people and societies? No way.

Every class of resources counts. Lately, there has been a stream of new resources. What would our world be without using the forces of nature and quantum physics? Never mind that the latter term may be unknown to some people. The names matter much less than the resources and classes of resources they represent. The work of chips in computers and mobile phones is based on quantum physics. Humankind also started catching up on resources that were missed for many thousands of years. We are talking about the massive involvement of women in humankind's activities, which has increased recently.

Two shining examples of technology resources are information technology and artificial intelligence. And, of course, one of the great creative acts of humankind was the birth of the scientific method. When you look at the high-level model of humanity, you will see humankind's creativity everywhere.

If opportunity doesn't knock, build a door.

Milton Berle

Part 2. History of Humankind. 300 Stories

Introduction to Part 2

The emergence of every mentioned resource was triggered by some event created by people. Examples of such events are the creation of the first school, the first cement, the first alcoholic drink, and the first writing – to name a few. There are 318 examples of such events in Part 2.

All stories in Part 2 are about such "first" events. Those events are markers, pointing to a moment in history from which a new resource became available for humankind. This book focuses on resources, but not on the "first" events as themselves.

The proposed models of humankind' history are dynamic. The resources mentioned in this book are the ones I have counted during the writing of this book in 2022-2023. Over time, humankind will create new resources.

Each resource mentioned in this book deserves its own entertaining story. I hope such stories will be written.

At each classification level, we tried to limit classification to the minimal amount of main relevant items. In descriptions, because of a lack of space, we must confine ourselves to just a few phrases with references to the original data sources. For the same reason, in most cases, we refer to just one data source publication in resource descriptions.

In Part 2, we have 23 classes of resources, presented in chronological order of their emergence. Inside each class of resources, we have families of resources listed in the chronological order of their emergence. Inside each family of resources, separate resources are listed in chronological order of their emergence.

Those resources are listed in Table 2, in the Tables section, in chronological order of their emergence. All resources identified in Part 2, are also listed in alphabetical order in the Index at the end of the book.

Domains of resources and classes of resources are presented in Table 1.5.2, in Chapter 1.5. Classes of resources and families of resources are listed in Table 3, in Tables section.

First Eight
Classes of Resources

Art is the stored honey of the human soul.

Theodore Dreiser

Music is the shorthand of emotion.

Leo Tolstoy

Chapter 2.1.
Art and Music

The history of the *Art and Music* class of resources began with the emergence of the resource *Painting* at around 44000 BC. More than thirty resources were created by humankind in the *Art and Music* class of resources during the last 44 thousand years.

We could divide the *Art and Music* class of resources into six families of resources.

Here are those families of resources in the order of their chronological appearance in humankind's history: *Types of Non-Musical Art, Types of Musical Instruments, Types of Art with a Use of Many People, Types of Music, Musical Notation, Types of Technology-Based Art.*

Types of Non-Musical Art

In the family of resources *Types of Non-Musical Art* humankind created the following resources: *Painting, Sculpture, Graphics, Dance, Architecture, Storytelling, and Animation.*

First *Painting* - Locals on the island of Sulawesi in Indonesia knew about nearby cave paintings for years. People thought that these paintings were not very old. Several years ago, archaeologists started dating those cave paintings by using uranium-series isotope analysis to determine the paintings' age. They found that some paintings were around 40 thousand years old. Inspired by that discovery, a team led by Adam Brumm, an archaeologist at Australia's Griffith University, began a search for more art in these caves. In 2017, they found a big painting over 13 feet wide in a limestone cave. On top of the painting, there was a calcite deposit. As determined by the team, the deposit's age was at least

43,900 years old.   The painting tells a fascinating, probably hunting, story. Small buffaloes and wild pigs were chased by people with spears and ropes. Scientists' findings were published in the journal Nature.[1] You can see a short overview of this artwork in the YouTube video "Earliest hunting scene in prehistoric art."[2]

The interesting fact is that the hunters appear to be humans. Yet one human figure has a birdlike head, while another human hunter has a tail. The human-animal figures are hybrids. In mythology, hybrids are known as therianthropes. Anyway, the findings in the Indonesian cave suggest that at around 42000 BC, people could imagine things that did not exist in the world. In this book, this human feature was named *Novel Mental Images*. The found painting marks the beginning, at 42000 BC, of two classes of resources. The first one is named *Novel Mental Images*. The second class of resources is *Art and Music*. In the last class of resources, the painting marks the beginning of the resource *Painting*. We mark 42000 BC as the emergence date of the *Painting* resource.

We also mark 42000 BC as the emergence date of the <u>Art and Music</u> class of resources.

First *Sculpture* - We know that the first sculpture came in the form of the famous "Lion-man." The figurine with a human body and the head of a cave lion was created around 38000 BC in Europe. "Lion-man" was found in the Hohlenstein-Stadel cave in Germany.[3] Scientists tell us that the global climate was cold at that time. Woolly mammoths were still roaming around. People hunters were able to stalk and kill giant mammoths down. From our perspective, an ancient sculptor's choice of mammoth tusk instead of wood was a fortunate one. No wood sculpture would survive 40 thousand years. "Lion-man" is a remarkable sculpture. Archeologists found hundreds of mammoth ivory fragments. As a result of painstaking work, the figure of a lion was assembled from more than 200 pieces. A "lion-man" is regarded by scientists as the oldest known sculpture of a non-existed-on-Earth hybrid. We mark 38000 BC as the emergence date of the *Sculpture* resource.

First *Storytelling* - Storytelling is the art of telling stories. We all know that children can tell us stories through pictures. Stories can be presented orally, pictorially, or in written form. It is not easy to identify which ancient paintings tell us a story. Yet, in 2016, a team of researchers[4] documented "volcanic activity located 35 km northwest of the Chauvet-Pont d'Arc cave, and visible from the hills above the cave entrance" approximately when a particular painting was drawn in the cave. That suggests that "the spray-shape signs found in the cave could be the oldest known depiction of a volcanic eruption." We mark 34000 BC as the emergence date of the *Storytelling* resource.

First *Graphic Art (Drawing)* - Graphic art typically visualizes lines and tones, not color. The primary type of graphic art is drawing. The most well-known oldest cave paintings, from 42000 BC and up, from Indonesia cave, Lascaux cave, etc., are paintings, not drawings. It appears that the oldest known-to-us drawing is the 17,300-year-old drawing of a kangaroo in Australia in the Kimberley province.[5] The drawing was made on the ceiling of a rock shelter.

The age of the drawing was determined by radiocarbon dating using ancient mud wasp nests. That method was pioneered by researcher Damien Finch. Fortunately, archeologists found mud wasp nests on top and underneath a single artwork. That allowed them to establish the artwork's minimum and maximum ages, 15500-15100 BC. A montage of photographs of the kangaroo rock drawing and an illustration of the artwork was presented in the BBC article.[6] We mark 15500-15100 BC as the emergence date of the *Graphics Art (Drawing)* resource.

First *Dance* - Recent advances in the research on ancient human dance have shown that the history of dance can be started much earlier than previously noted. Yosef Garfinkel [7] quoted from Gerhard Bosinski's study that "an unusual assemblage of dancing figures was found at Gönnerdorf, an open-air site on the eastern bank of the Rhine near Koblenz in Germany." Engravings on stone plaques present young female figures. Archaeologists Gerhard Bosinski and Gisela Fischer suggested that these figures are dancing. We will use the 14000-11000 BC date as the mark of the emergence of the *Dance* resource.

First *Architecture* - There is no agreed-upon definition of what art is. Still, architecture has always had a strong association with the art world. Two cities with excavated city architecture remains are considered the oldest in the world - Jericho, in the West Bank, and Göbekli Tepe, in Turkey. However, the amount of architectural art found in Göbekli Tepe is more significant. In 1996, German archeologist Klaus Schmidt and his team dedicated 20 years to excavating the Göbekli Tepe site. Göbekli Tepe is located in the Southeastern Anatolia Region of Turkey.

The site reveals the architecture of one of the oldest cities in the world. A lot of structures and stone pillars are richly decorated. Numerous descriptions and images of architectural art from Göbekli Tepe[8] exist. Several layers of the remains were excavated. Radiocarbon dating shows that the earliest exposed structures at Göbekli Tepe were built between 9500 and 9000 BC.[9] Therefore, we consider that 9500-9000 BC in Göbekli Tepe, in Turkey, marked the emergence of *Architecture* resource.

First *Animation* - In the 1970s, Italian archeologists discovered an ancient Iranian bowl with five images. The images depict a goat leaping to snatch leaves from a tree. Several years later, Iranian archaeologist Mansur Sajjadi recognized those images as sequential, making this image series the world's oldest animation example. You could see a reconstructed animation of a wild goat on that bowl in the article in Animation Magazine.[10] The bowl is approximately 5,200 years old. We mark 3200 BC as the emergence date of the *Animation* resource.

Types of Musical Instruments

In the family of resources *Types of Musical Instruments* the following resources were created: *Aerophone (Flute), Membranophone (Drum), Idiophone (Rattles), Chordophone (Harp)*.

First *Aerophone (Flute)* - Forty thousand years ago, as it is now, people enjoyed both art and music. Archeologists found parts of three flutes at the Geißenklösterle Cave in Germany.[11] One ancient flute was made from mammoth ivory, while the other two - were from swan bones. Thirty-one pieces of highly fragmented carved mammoth ivory have been assembled. The flute had at least three finger holes and a length of 18.7 cm.

People had a deep need for something not required just for survival. They were eager for something for a soul, and, probably, something for fun. People created those opportunities, those tools, which allowed people to express themselves through art and music.

40 thousand years ago was not the best time to create art and music. Just try to picture it out. If you want to make a sculpture or a good flute, then you first need to find a mammoth. Then you must kill that mammoth and not kill or injure yourself in the process. That will give you tusks and bones. Mammoth bones and tusks are very hard material to work with. How would you carve it? It requires a good deal of skill, patience, and time to carve something meaningful from such material. How would you make holes in it? Metallurgy did not exist at the time yet. There was no metal knives or drills. You have to invent the needed instrument from what you had at hand.

An initial estimate was that the ivory flute was about 35 000 years old.

Several years later, the researchers could use advanced dating techniques with improved methods to remove contamination.[12] Per new data, the flute's age was 42,000 to 43,000 years ago. We mark 41000-40000 BC as the emergence date of the *Aerophone (Flute)* resource.

First *Chordophone (Harp)* - In 1922, British archaeologist Leonard Woolley discovered the tomb of Puabi, an important woman in the Sumerian city of Ur. Later, researchers referred to Puabi as a "queen." In Puabi's tomb, a large harp was found. That harp was dated to 3500 BC.[13, 14]. Most excavated artifacts from Woolley's expedition were divided among the British Museum in London, the University of Pennsylvania Museum in Philadelphia, Pennsylvania, and the National Museum in Baghdad. We mark 3500 BC as the emergence date of the *Chordophone (Harp)* resource.

First *Membranophone (Drum)* - The oldest drums were made from clay. According to [15], such drums were already used in China between 4000 and 2000 BC. Clay drums are still popular in some Asian countries. For example, modern Vietnamese use clay drums. Those drums have the drum body made from terracotta and drum faces made from animal skin. We mark 4000-2000 BC as the emergence date of the *Membranophone (Drum)* resource.

First *Idiophone (Rattles)* - The ancient Egyptians used the sistrum (rattle) instrument to provide rhythmical accompaniment to other instruments. "The sistrum and particularly the temple-shaped one, the so-called Naos sistrum, appeared in Egypt for the first time during the Ancient Kingdom period (2700-2200 BC). Even though, in the beginning, it was a simple musical instrument, sistrum turned very quickly into a ceremonial one, held and vibrated by the high priestesses and priests or by the Pharaoh himself when they were offering donations to the goddess Hathor."[16] We mark 2700-2200 BC as the emergence date of the *Idiophone (Rattles)* resource.

Types of Art with a Use of Many People

In the family of resources *Types of Art with a Use of Many People* humankind created the following resources: *Music Ensemble (Band), Theatre, Choral Music, Orchestra, Opera, Circus, Performance Art, Flash Mob.*

First *Music Ensemble (Band)* - Music played an important role in the lives of ancient Egyptians. "Music bands appear on walls as early as the 5th dynasty, some of which were male or female bands or even mixed bands, the number of musicians differed as well."[17] In the majority of the music bands in the Old Kingdom, the most frequent musical instruments are the harps and the flutes. The size of music bands varies, from minimal to seven and, probably, to twelve. At least ten names of musicians are known. The evidence of music bands was provided by the tomb's carvings. Dynasty 5 in the Old Kingdom lasted from 2465 BC to 2319 BC.[18] We mark 2465-2319 BC as the emergence date of the *Music Ensemble (Band)* resource.

First *Circus* - In ancient Rome, the circus was a building featuring trained animals, jugglers, and acrobats, the exhibition of horse races, and more. The first and largest stadium (circus) in Rome was the Circus Maximus, in the valley between the Palatine and Aventine hills. It was built around the 6th century BC by the order of Lucius Tarquinius Priscus.[19] Tarquin, the fifth king of Rome, reigned from 616 to 578.[20] In ancient Rome, the circus was the only public spectacle at which men and women were not separated. The modern concept of a circus as a circular arena appeared in the late 18th century. We mark 616-578 BC as the emergence date of the *Circus* resource.

First *Theatre* - In ancient Greece, there was an annual dramatic festival honoring Dionysus in the City Dionysia. In 534 BC, Thespis became the first to impersonate another person for storytelling.[21] He became the first known actor in written plays. Before Thespis, stories in plays were told in the third person narrative. It is a custom to say that Thespis invented theatre as we know it today. We mark 534 BC as the emergence date of the *Theatre* resource.

First *Choral Music* - Singing in groups and big groups was widely spread in Antiquity. However, there is certainty about the oldest choral repertory, two Delphic Hymns. The Delphic Hymns are two musical compositions from Ancient Greece which survive in substantial fragments. Both were written for performance by Pythaides in 128 BC.[22] Delphic Hymns were addressed to the god Apollo. We mark 128 BC as the emergence date of the *Choral Music* resource.

First *Orchestra* - "An orchestra is an instrumental ensemble consisting of string, brass, woodwind, and percussion sections."[23] In the 1650-1825 book, "The Birth of the Orchestra: History of an Institution, [24] Spitzer John and Zaslaw Neal proposed that "instead of searching for the 'first orchestra,' it is more productive to view the birth of the orchestra as a process stretching over the course of two centuries and culminating around 1800 in a social institution that was distinctive and durable." More precisely, Spitzer and Zaslaw wrote, "The orchestra must have been 'born' at some time between 1600 and 1791." We mark 1650-1791 as the emergence date of the *Orchestra* resource.

First *Opera* - The earliest known opera was composed by Jacopo Peri in 1597, and the libretto was written by Ottavio Rinuccini. Jacopo Peri's "Dafne" was privately performed in the Palazzo Corsi, Florence, in 1597.[25] Most of Peri's music has been lost, but a part of the libretto survived. At the time, the success of "Dafne" was so great that composers Jacopo Peri and Giulio Caccini "were commissioned, in 1600, to write a similar work" [25] for the wedding of Henry IV of France with Maria de Medici. "The result, Euridice, which was performed with Peri himself singing the role of Orpheus, is the earliest surviving complete opera."[26] We mark 1597-1600 as the emergence date of the *Opera* resource.

First *Performance Art* - "Performance [performance art] is a genre in which art is presented "live," usually by the artist but sometimes with collaborators or performers." "20th-century performance art has its roots in early avant-gardes such as Futurism, Dada and Surrealism."[27] For DADA movement it started in 1916. On February 5, 2016, Henri Neuendorf noted that "100 years ago today, on February 5, 1916, the now-legendary Cabaret Voltaire" was opened in Zurich with a DADA performance. "Dada deliberately contravened all known and traditional artistic styles at the time."[28] We mark 1916 as the emergence date of the *Performance Art* resource.

First *Flash Mob* - "The first flash mobbing ... happened in Manhattan, New York, ... on June 17, 2003. ... A crowd of approximately 100 people gathered in the home furnishing section of Macy's department store. The crowd surrounded a rug with a $10,000 price tag. Participants, soon to be known as 'flash mobbers,' were instructed beforehand by 'moberators' to tell the salespeople that they all lived together in a free-love commune and that they wanted to purchase a 'love rug.'"[29] We mark 2003 as the emergence date of the *Flash Mob* resource.

Musical Notation

In the family of resources *Musical Notation* humankind created one resource: *Musical notation*. Resource *Musical Notation* has existed since 450 BC.

First *Musical Composition & Notation* - Dated around 1400 BC, the terra cotta piece transcribed in cuneiform "Hymn to Nikkal" is in National Museum of Damascus. It is "a complete text, with both words and music."[30] This is the oldest known surviving melody. - That is information from this book's "First Song/Folk Song Music" item. A lot of details about Mesopotamian musical notation are in Anne Kilmer's article "The Discovery of an Ancient Mesopotamian Theory of Music."[31] We mark 1400 BC as the emergence date of the *musical notation* resource. However, we will skip this resource in the list of resources because it is already listed under the *Song/Folk Song* resource name.

Types of Music

In the family of resources *Types of Music* humankind created the following resources: *Western Classical music, Song/Folk Song, Blues Music, Jazz Music, Rock Music, Pop Music, and HipHhop/Rap Music.*

First Western Classical Music - The contemporary understanding of *Western Classical Music* remains vague. Here is the often-used musical time period classification. "Western music is music composed/created in Europe, the United States, and societies that were shaped by European immigrants."[32] The eras of Western classical music are as follows: the medieval era (500 - 1450), the Renaissance era (1450 - 1600), the baroque era (1600 - 1750), the classical era (1750 - 1820), the romantic era (1820 - 1900)." We mark 500 as the emergence date of the *Western Classical Music* resource.

First *Song/Folk Song Music* - This is the oldest known surviving melody.[30] The clay tablet was discovered in Ugarit, now part of modern-day Syria. It is dated around 1400 BC. The "Hymn to Nikkal" song is dedicated the Hurrians' goddess Nikkal, the moon god's wife. The hymn is considered the oldest song/folk song. There are several interpretations of music of this hymn. In 2022, Heilung, a group of hardcore folk music musicians, recorded five different versions of "Hymn to Nikkal." You can listen to "Hymn to Nikkal" here.[33] We mark 1400 BC as the emergence date of the *Song/Folk Song* resource.

First *Blues Music* - The exact dates of new types of music are debatable. For blues music, we will go with the date of the first publication of "I Got the Blues." The song was published by Antonio Maggio. He heard some street musician in Louisiana playing three notes for a long time. "I didn't think anything with only three notes could have a title so to satisfy my curiosity I asked him what was the name of the piece. He replied, 'I Got The Blues.' I went home. Having this on my mind, I wrote 'I Got the Blues,' making the three notes dominating most of the time. That same night, our five-piece orchestra played at the Fabaker Restaurant 'I Got the Blues,' which was composed with the purpose of a musical caricature, and to my astonishment became our most popular request number."[34,35] We mark 1908 as the emergence date of the *Blues Music* resource.

First *Jazz Music* - On February 26, 1917, the group Original Dixieland Jass Band (ODJB) recorded music in the New York Studio of the Victor Talking Machine Company. One of the songs on the recorded disk was "Dixie Jass One-Step." Later, the word "jass" was changed to "jazz." That disc was, arguably, the first jazz recording ever.[36] We mark 1917 as the emergence date of the *Jazz Music* resource.

First *Rock Music* - In 1951, Ike Turner and his band recorded a song, "Rocket 88," in Sam Phillips' studio in Memphis, Tennessee.[37] The song's name was born on the band's car trip to the studio. "In 1950, the new Hydra Matic Drive V-8 Oldsmobile "88" was also called "Futurmatic" and advertised as "the lowest-priced car with 'rocket' engine." Considered one of the fastest cars at the time, the "Rocket 88" became the inspiration for the song." [38] This song record is frequently cited as the first rock & roll record. We mark 1951 as the emergence date of the *Rock Music* resource.

First *Pop Music* - Pop is short for popular. The term "pop music" was first used in 1926.[39] However, the meaning of "appealing to a wide audience" originated in the mid-1950s. Pop music was born as a mixture of different music styles. Pop music charts didn't exist until 1952. The "You belong to me" song became a top one on pop music charts in US and UK in 1952.[40] We mark 1952 as the emergence date of the *Pop Music* resource.

First *Hip-Hop Music* - Hip-hop is both a musical genre and a culture. "DJ Kool Herc invented what he called 'The Merry-Go-Round ' in 1973 while DJ'ing his sister's back-to-school party at 1520 Sedgwick Ave. in the Bronx. The Merry-Go-Round involved Herc switching between dual record players in order to draw out the break on a song (generally the most percussive, heavily danced-to part) then switching to another track from a different artist with a similar beat."[41] On the musical side of hip-hop culture, some Hip-Hop scholars include two elements: DJing — the artistic handling of beats and music, and MCing, aka rapping — putting spoken-word poetry to a beat.[42] We mark 1973 as the emergence date of the *Hip-Hop Music* resource.

Types of Technology-Based Art

In the family of resources *Types of Technology-Based Art* humankind created the following resources: *Electronic Music Instruments, Photography, Video Art, Film, Television, Videogame, Computer/Digital Art.*

First *Electronic Music Instrument* - The Czech theologian Václav Prokop Diviš was interested in music and electricity. He built an electrically enhanced musical instrument called "Denis d'or," or Golden Dionysus, before the middle of the 18th century. Unfortunately, surviving descriptions of the Denis d'or are short, and Denis d'or instrument did not survive.[43] In 1759 Jean-Baptiste Thillaie Delaborde, a French Jesuit priest built the clavecin électrique. That is the earliest surviving electric-powered musical instrument.[44] We mark 1759 as the emergence date of the *Electronic Music* resource.

First *Photography* - The earliest photograph produced with the aid of the camera obscura known to survive today was made by Joseph Nicéphore Niépce in France in 1827. This photograph is in "The Niépce Heliograph" article.[45] However, the first commercially viable photographic process was publicly announced in 1839. "Louis-Jacques-Mandé Daguerre invented the daguerreotype process in France. The invention was announced to the public on August 19, 1839, at a meeting of the French Academy of Sciences in Paris."[46] We mark 1839 as the emergence date of the *Photography* resource.

First *Video Art* - Technically, 'videos' and 'films' are the same thing because they are both shot on 'video.' This means that anything described as a 'video,' apart from being shorter and less artistic, is simply not a film. The film has its own category because it is significantly larger in scale.[47] "Most historians have agreed that Louis Le Prince's single-lens camera made in 1888 created the first and oldest motion video in existence. The video is a piece called 'Roundhay Garden Scene' which was a two second silent film of people walking in a garden."[47] Louis Le Prince made his video in Great Britain. We mark 1888 as the emergence date of the *Video Art* resource.

First *Film* - "Auguste and Louis Lumière were photographers by trade, who were inspired to attempt moving pictures after seeing a demonstration of Edison's Kinetoscope ... At the Grand Café on the

Boulevard des Capucines in Paris, on 28 December 1895, the Lumières revealed their device, and nine of their films, to a paying audience."[48] In the Guardian article, you could see a photograph from the first film screened for the public by the Lumiére brothers. We mark 1895 as the emergence date of the *Film* resource.

First _Television_ - "Electronic television was first successfully demonstrated in San Francisco on Sept. 7, 1927. The system was designed by Philo Taylor Farnsworth, a 21-year-old inventor who had lived in a house without electricity until he was 14."[49] "Philo T. Farnsworth ... was the first to successfully demonstrate the principle, in his lab in San Francisco on September 7, 1927."[50] We mark 1927 as the emergence date of the *Television* resource.

First _Video Game_ - In 1962, computer scientist Steve Russell, in collaboration with Martin Graetz and others, created a space combat video game. The game was named "Spacewar!"[51,52] The game was designed to be played on a PDP-1 mainframe computer at the Massachusetts Institute of Technology (MIT). Over time, "Spacewar!" became the first known video game played at multiple computer installations. We mark 1962 as the emergence date of the *Video Game* resource.

First _Computer/Digital Art_ - "Computergrafik was the first exhibition world-wide of graphic works algorithmically generated by a digital computer at the Siemens company, Erlangen (Germany)." The exhibition was from February 4 to February 19, 1965.[53] The other independent show of computer-generated pictures by Bela Julesz and Michael Noll was on April 8 - 24, 1965, at Howard Wise Gallery in New York City. This show was the first computer art show in the United States. A memoir of that show was published in [54] and later in [55]. Bela Julesz and Michael Noll were employees of Bell Telephone Laboratories in New Jersey. We mark 1965 as the emergence date of the *Computer/Digital Art* resource.

Man-made things, buildings, boats, etc., we see more decidedly than the other things in a landscape.

Charles Webster Hawthorne

Chapter 2.2.
Man-Made Materials,
Substances, and Organisms

The history of the *Man-Made Materials, Substances, and Organisms* class of resources began with the emergence of resource *Textile* at around 34000 BC. More than thirty resources were created by humankind in the *Man-Made Materials, Substances, and Organisms* class of resources during the last 44 thousand years.

We could divide the *Man-Made Materials, Substances, and Organisms* class of resources into five families of resources. Here are those families in the order of their chronological appearance in humankind's history: *Soft Materials, Hard Materials, Substances and Liquid Materials, Organisms, Soft-Hard Materials.*

Soft Materials

In the family of resources *Soft Materials* humankind created the following resources: *Textile, Leather, Papyrus Paper, Felt, Paper, Knitted Materials, Genetically Modified (GM) Food (Tomato).*

First *Textile* - An international team of researchers found evidence that people learned to weave plant fibers into textiles around 36000-32000 BC. Fibers of the flax plant were found in Dzudzuana Cave in the foothills of the Caucasus Mountains in the Republic of Georgia. "A small number of fibers are colored black, gray, turquoise, and pink, and the team concludes that they were dyed."[1,2] In Nahal Hemar Cave, in Israel, there were found products made from "plant fiber, that had been processed, spun and plied into yarn suitable for fabric construction".[3]

The estimated date for this textile is around 6500 BC.[3,4] We mark 36000-32000 BC as the emergence date of the *Textile* resource.

We also mark 36000-32000 BC as the emergence date of the Man-Made Materials, Substances, Organisms class of resources.

First *Leather* - According to Massimo Vidale and Muhammad Zahir,[5] there is evidence that leather was produced at Mehrgarh, Pakistan, during Period III. That period lasted from 4000 BC to 3500 BC. We mark 4000-3500 BC as the emergence date of the *Leather* resource.

First *Papyrus Paper* - The papyrus is a form of aquatic plant that grows by the Nile in Egypt. "Excavators of a tomb at Saqqara discovered the earliest known roll of papyrus, dated to around 2900 B.C."[6] Papyrus paper became the world's first smooth, flexible writing material. We mark 2900 BC as the emergence date of the *Papyrus Paper* resource.

First *Felt* - The burials were found at the site of Pazyryk in the Altai Mountains of Siberia, which took place more than 2300 years ago. The felt items were well preserved. For example, you could see felt shabrak with very lively ornament in the photo in the article from Penn Museum.[7] We mark 300 BC as the emergence date of the *Felt* resource.

First *Paper* - The oldest known paper fragments, found in China, were probably made as early as the 3rd Century BC. However, a significant advancement in papermaking technique was made by Cai (Tshai) Lun in 105 AD.[8] "Cai Lun was a eunuch who entered the service of the imperial palace in 75 CE and was made chief eunuch under the emperor Hedi (reigned 88–105/106) of the Dong (Eastern) Han dynasty in the year 89. About the year 105, Cai conceived the idea of forming sheets of paper from the macerated bark of trees, hemp waste, old rags, and fishnets."[9] Cai Lun is traditionally regarded as a father of papermaking. We mark 105 AD as the emergence date of the *Paper* resource.

First *Knitted Materials* - Knitting is making fabric with yarn on two or more needles. One of the earliest knotted items is in the Victoria and Albert Museum in London. "This is the earliest example of true, or double-needle, knitting in the Museum's collections. It was made in North Africa, about 1100–1300, during Islamic rule. The blue and white abstract design echoes the colour combinations and patterning found in Islamic ceramics."[10] We mark 1100-1300 as the emergence date of the *Knitted Materials* resource.

First *Genetically Modified (GM) Food (Tomato)* - "By 1987,

Calgene researchers identified and cloned a tomato fruit PG gene... On May 21, 1994, the genetically engineered FLAVR SAVR tomato was introduced...More than 1.8 million cans, clearly labeled as derived from genetically engineered tomatoes, were sold from 1996 through early 1999."[11] We mark 1987 as the emergence date of the *Genetically Modified (GM) Food (Tomato)* resource.

Hard Materials

In the family of resources *Hard Materials* humankind created the following resources: *Pottery, Composite Materials (Concrete), Faience, Metal (Copper), Synthesized Nanoparticles, Glass, Composite Materials (Plywood), Composite Materials (Cartonnage), Pills (Medicine), Porcelain, Semiconductor Material, Enriched Uranium 235, A Single Atom Thick Material.*

First *Pottery* - The early pottery dating from Xianrendong Cave in China was described in the "Early pottery at 20,000 years ago in Xianrendong Cave" article. [12] Per this article, those pottery sherds are from 18000-17000 BC. Authors noted that "pottery making introduces a fundamental shift in human dietary history, and Xianrendong demonstrates that hunter-gatherers in East Asia used pottery for some 10,000 years before they became sedentary or began cultivating plants." We mark 18000-17000 BC as the emergence date of the *Pottery* resource.

First *Composite Materials (Concrete)* - In 2011 Amelia Carolina Sparavigna wrote, "Concrete was older even than Alexander the Great. Let me show you how we can deduce this fact from some Latin essays and their English translations and from the reports of Schliemann's excavations of Mycenaean archaeological sites."[13] She discussed the findings of concrete floors at Mycenaean palace in Tiryns, Greece. The conclusion is that cement floors at the site date roughly to 1400–1200 BC. Amelia Carolina Sparavigna quoted a "found therein a floor formed of concrete" sentence from famous archeologist Heinrich Schliemann.[14] Tiryns "has been strongly linked with many ancient Greek legends, especially those of Heracles (Hercules), with some sources claiming that the mythical hero was actually born here."[15] We mark 1400-1200 BC as the emergence date of the *Composite Materials (Concrete)* resource.

First *Faience* - "Excavations by the joint University of Pennsylvania Museum/ Yale University/Institute of Fine Arts, New York University expedition, under the direction of Dr Matthew Adams, have recently unearthed part of settlement on the edge of the class of resources of modern settlement, not far from the Early Dynastic Temple of the god Khentiamentiu. The site dates from at least as early as the middle of the Old Kingdom to the early Middle Kingdom, and faience-working class of resources is not associated with any house or workshop structure."[16] The dating of the Old Kingdom and the Middle Kingdom varies slightly in different sources. We will rely on The Metropolitan Museum of Art to date the Old Kingdom and the Middle Kingdom.[17,18] We mark 2470-1900 BC as the emergence date of the *Faience* resource at Abydos in Egypt.

First *Metal (Copper)* - Copper was not the first metal used by people but the first broadly used metal. In a search for the first use of copper, we will skip the use of metal ore and will look at the first form of extractive metallurgy. That is smelting, the process of applying heat to ore, to extract a base metal. "The archeometallurgical analysis of five small copper slags from Trench 3 at Belovode [in Serbia], together with the radiocarbon dating of the excavated horizon in which they were found, ... provided evidence for copper smelting at c. 5000 BC."[19,20]. We mark 5000 BC as the emergence date of the *Metal (Copper)* resource.

First Synthesized Nanoparticles - We are accustomed to thinking that nanotechnology appeared in the 20th century. Yet, the Ancient Egyptians already used nanomaterials more than 4000 years ago. [21] The research team lead, Dr. Philippe Walter, told editors of PhysOrg.com: "When I found an ancient recipe [a hair-dyeing recipe] dealing with the use of lead ...we reconstituted the recipe and observed the formation of galena nanocrystals in the hair."[22] We mark 2000 BC as the emergence date of the *Synthesized Nanoparticles* resource.

First *Glass* - There are conflicting references about when and where the first intentionally created glass appeared. We will follow the book "Early Glass of the Ancient World 1600 B.C A. D 50."[23] "This book presents 155 glass vessels and objects from the Ernesto Wolf Collection, most of which have never been seen by the general public before. The oldest of these pieces date back to the early phase of the glass-making art in the Tigris-Euphrates region around 1600 BC." We mark 1600 BC as the emergence date of the *Glass* resource.

First *Composite Materials (Plywood)* - The oldest piece of plywood was made in Egypt. It consisted of six layers of wood, four millimeters thick, held together by wooden pegs. It was found in a third-dynasty coffin.[24] The dating of the Third Dynasty varies slightly in different sources. For the dating of the Third Dynasty, we will rely on the "Ancient Egypt Site."[25] We mark 2650-2575 BC as the emergence date of the *Composite Materials (Plywood)* resource.

First *Composite Materials (Cartonnage)* - In ancient Egypt, cartonnage was broadly used for composing Egyptian funerary masks. "While Egyptians of the Old Kingdom had attempted to add lifelike features to the outer wrappings of mummies, masks with idealized images of the deceased, designed to cover the head and shoulders of the mummy, were introduced during the First Intermediate Period. By the early Middle Kingdom, they became a standard part of the Egyptian burial assemblage, and they would continue to be used for two thousand years into the Roman era." [26]

The dating of the First Intermediate Period of Egypt varies slightly in different sources. For the dating of the First Intermediate Period of Egypt, we will rely on the "Ancient Egypt Site."[27] We mark 2150-2040 BC as the emergence date of the *Composite Materials (Cartonnage)* resource.

First *Pills (Medicine)* - The famous Ebers papyrus, one of the oldest known medical works, is dated around 1550 BC.[28] It is an Egyptian compilation of medical texts with about 700 formulas. In Ebers papyrus, four recipes describe how to make pills for prescribed remedies.[29] We mark 1550 BC as the emergence date of the *Pills (Medicine)* resource.

First *Porcelain* - Proto-porcelain lacks the translucence of typical porcelain. From the Chinese point of view, proto-porcelain was the origin and irreplaceable link in the evolution to true porcelain in the History of Chinese porcelain production.[30] Proto-porcelain originated in the Shang dynasty (c. 1600–1046 BC).[31,32] We mark 1600-1046 BC as the emergence date of the *Porcelain* resource.

First *Semiconductor Material* - Silicon point contact diode was the first diode fabricated at a large scale. It was first made in 1941 and was primarily used in the Allies' radar systems during World War II. The diode rapidly became a key building element in the front–end mixer within radar systems, so precious in wartime. [33] We mark 1941 as the emergence date of the *Semiconductor Material* resource.

First *Enriched Uranium 235* - "Field tests performed with uranium-235 prototypes in late 1944 eased doubts about the artillery method employed in the uranium bomb. At the same time, Los Alamos shifted from research to development and production".[34] We mark 1945 as the emergence date of the *Enriched Uranium 235* resource.

First *A Single-Atom-Thick Material* - "Novoselov was a postdoctoral associate working with Geim in 2004 when the researchers discovered that they could make atomically thin slabs of carbon by repeatedly cleaving graphite—essentially pencil lead—with adhesive tape. Their 2004 Science paper describing the material and its electrical properties has already been cited more than 3,000 times, according to the Thomson Reuters Web of Science."[35] We mark 2004 as the emergence date of A *Single-Atom-Thick Material* resource.

Substances and Liquid Materials

In the family of resources *Substances and Liquid Materials* humankind created the following resources: *Beer, Alcohol, Liquid Preparations (Medicine), Liquid Fuel (Kerosene)*.

First *Beer* - The first beer was made around 11700-9700 BC at Raqefet Cave, Israel. The team of researchers did a residue analysis of three stone mortars. Scientists were able to recreate the ancient recipe for brewing wheat/barley-based beer in the lab.[36] 13-thousand-year-old beer was made by Natufian people, the same people who later founded the famous city Jericho, which we know from the Torah or the Bible. We mark 11700-9700 BC as the emergence date of the *Beer* resource.

First *Alcohol* - The earliest alcoholic beverage in the world was made in 7000–6600 BC at Jiahu, a Neolithic village in the Yellow River Valley, China. Researchers recovered the residues of the beverage from early pottery at this site. They confirmed this alcoholic drink was a mixed fermented drink of rice, honey, hawthorn fruit, and/or grape.[37] We mark 7000–6600 BC as the emergence date of the *Alcohol* resource.

First *Liquid Preparations (Medicine)* - "Plants, in particular, have formed the basis of sophisticated traditional medicine systems, with the earliest records, dating from around 2600 BCE, documenting the uses of approximately 1000 plant-derived substances in Mesopotamia. These include oils of Cedrus species (cedar) and Cupressus sempevirens (cypress), . . ., all of which are still used today for the treatment of ailments ranging from coughs and colds to parasitic infections and inflammation." [38] We mark 2600 BC as the emergence date of the *Liquid Preparations (Medicine)* resource.

First *Liquid Fuel (Kerosene)* - "The first Muslim scholar to write about the distillation of petroleum was . . . Muhammad al-Razi [Abū Bakr al-Rāzī] . . . In his Book of Secrets, he mentions the use of . . . kerosene lamps, for heating and lighting . . . He gives two methods for making kerosene."[39]   Abū Bakr al-Rāzī spent most of his adult life as a physician and chemist in Baghdad. We will follow the Stanford Encyclopedia of Philosophy for his dates of birth and death, 865–925 CE.[40] We mark 865-925 as the emergence date of the *Liquid Fuel (Kerosene)* resource.

Organisms

In the family of resources *Organisms* humankind created the following resources: *Hybrid (Mule), Transgenic Mouse, Genetically Modified (GM) Organism, GM Animal, Cloned Mammal, Cloned primate, and Genetically Modified Human.*

First Hybrid (Mule) - Mule, the breeding of a donkey stallion with a female horse, is the oldest known man-made hybrid. Encyclopaedia Britannica mentions that mules existed in Asia Minor at least 3000 years ago, but no evidence was provided.[41] The Greek writer and historian Homer repeatedly reported the use of mules in his epic poem Iliad.[42] The date Homer composed the Iliad is not exactly known but is estimated as 760-710 BC.[43] We mark 760-710 BC as the emergence date of the *Hybrid (Mule)* resource.

First *Genetically Modified (GM) Organism* - A genetically modified organism (GM organism) is any organism whose genetic material has been altered using genetic engineering techniques. Herbert Boyer and Stanley Cohen made the first genetically modified organism in 1973.[44] "The two men first discussed collaboration at a deli near Waikiki Beach [in Honolulu, Hawaii]. Their chat over a late-night snack led to a scientific achievement that later rocked the world of science. Within a year, they had cloned DNA molecules made by splicing together DNA fragments of two different plasmids, thus creating recombinant DNA. The foundations for biotechnology were established."[45]

We mark 1973 as the emergence date of the *Genetically Modified (GM) Organism* resource.

First *Transgenic Mouse* - The transgenic mouse is a mouse that has had DNA from another source put into its DNA. In 1974, Rudolph Jaenisch and Beatrice Mintz infected mouse embryos with SV40 virus. They showed that the viral DNA was integrated into the germ line.[46] "Papers published on the use of transgenic mice . . . have grown from zero in 1980, when transgenic mouse was not yet in common use, to over 700 in 1992.[47] We mark 1974 as the emergence date of the *Transgenic*

Mouse resource.

First *Cloned Mammal* - In 1997, "Dolly, the sheep" was successfully cloned at the Roslin Institute in Scotland.[48] "Dolly was important because she was the first mammal to be cloned from an adult cell. Her birth proved that specialized cells could be used to create an exact copy of the animal they came from. This knowledge changed what scientists' thought was possible and opened a lot of possibilities in biology and medicine.   However, Dolly was not the first ever cloned mammal. That honor belongs to another sheep which was cloned from an embryo cell and born in 1984 in Cambridge, UK. Two other sheep, Megan and Morag, had also been cloned from embryonic cells grown in the lab at The Roslin Institute in 1995 and six other sheep, cloned from embryonic and foetal cells, were born at Roslin at the same time as Dolly. What made Dolly so special was that she had been made from an adult cell, which no-one at the time thought was possible."[49] We mark 1997 as the emergence date of the *Cloned Mammal* resource.

First *Cloned Primate* - The first "cloned" primate, a rhesus macaque named Tetra, was created in 1999. She was created by artificial twinning by a team led by Professor Gerald Schatten of the Oregon National Primate Research Center.[50] We mark 1999 as the emergence date of the *Cloned Primate* resource.

First *Genetically Modified Human* - "The world was shocked in Nov. 25, 2018 by the revelation that He Jiankui had used domained regularly interspaced short palindromic repeats ('CRISPR') to edit embryos—two of which had, sometime in October, become living babies."[51] We mark 2018 as the emergence date of the *Genetically Modified Human* resource.

Soft-Hard Materials

In the family of resources *Soft-Hard Materials* humankind created the following resources: *Plastic (Parkesine), Synthetic Polymer, Synthetic Fiber, Synthetic Rubber*.

First *Plastic (Parkesine)* - Alexander Parkes was a well-known inventor in mid-19th-century Britain. His most famous invention was "Parkesine – the first form of celluloid – an early semi-synthetic plastic based on gun cotton. He took out his first related patent in 1855."[52] We mark 1855 as the emergence date of the *Plastic (Parkesine)* resource.

First *Synthetic Polymer* - "In 1863 John Wesly Hyatt was attracted by a reward of $10,000 offered by a New York billiards company to anyone who could invent a satisfactory substitute for ivory billiard balls." Hyatt and his brother Isaiah developed synthetic polymer, which they "patented in 1870 and dubbed Celluloid in 1872."[53] We mark 1870 as the emergence date of the *Synthetic Polymer* resource.

First *Synthetic Fiber* - Joseph Swan, an English physicist and chemist in 1883, "patented a process for squeezing nitrocellulose through holes to form fibers. In 1885, he exhibited his equipment and some articles made from the artificial fibers."[54] We mark 1885 as the emergence date of the *Synthetic Fiber* resource.

First *Synthetic Rubber* - In 1909, the chemist Fritz Hofmann, in Germany, produced the first synthetic rubber." Three patent applications were filed in September 1909. Fritz Hofmann's team increased in size and in 1911 a small commercial production began. Synthetic rubber tires were made and even "placed on the automobiles of the Kaiser and various German princes."[55] We mark 1909 as the emergence date of the *Synthetic Rubber* resource.

Knowing yourself is the beginning of all wisdom.

Aristotle

Chapter 2.3.
People and Societies
as Objects of Study

The history of the *People and Societies as Objects of Study* class of resources began with the emergence of resource *Amputation* at around 29000 BC. More than forty resources were created by humankind in the *People and Societies as Objects of Study* class of resources during the last 44 thousand years.

We could divide the *People and Societies as Objects of Study* class of resources into six families of resources. Here are those families in the order of their chronological appearance in humankind's history: *Related to Physical Health, Related to Society and World, Related to Place in Society, Related to Mental Health, History Related, Tools for Generic Social Impact.*

Related to Physical Health

In the family of resources *Related to Physical Health* humankind created the following resources: *Amputation, Surgery, Dentistry, Medicine (Physician), Physiology, Biology, Anatomy, Pharmacology, Gerontology, Kinesiology, Gender Studies.*

First *Amputation* - "Researchers have found evidence for the earliest known surgical amputation, tens of thousands of years before the advent of modern surgical tools, antibiotics, or painkillers."[1] The dating of this amputation procedure was at least 31,000 years ago. "The individual survived the procedure and lived for another 6–9 years."[2] We mark 29000 BC as the emergence date of the *Amputation* resource.

We also mark 29000 BC as the emergence date of the People and Societies as Objects of Study *class of resources.*

First _Dentistry_ - "Eleven drilled molar crowns from nine adults discovered in a Neolithic graveyard in Pakistan that dates from 7,500–9,000 years ago."[3] We mark 7000-5500 BC as the emergence date of the _Dentistry_ resource.

First _Surgery_ - "A 7,000-year-old burial at Ensisheim, in the French region of Alsace, has yielded the earliest unequivocal evidence for trepanation, according to Kurt W. Alt of Freiburg University and his colleagues."[4] The dating of the procedure is 5100-4900 BC. We mark 5100-4900 BC as the emergence date of the _Surgery_ resource.

First _Medicine (Physician)_ - After his death, Imhotep, a chief minister to Djoser (reigned 2630–2611 BC), was worshipped as the god of medicine in Egypt and Greece. "No contemporary account has been found that refers to Imhotep as a practicing physician." Nevertheless, "Imhotep's reputation as the reigning genius of the time, his position in the court, his training as a scribe, and his becoming known as a medical demigod only 100 years after his death are strong indications that he must have been a physician of considerable skill."[5] We mark 2630–2611 BC as the emergence date of the _Medicine (Physician)_ resource.

First _Biology_ - In 345 BC, Aristotle and Theophrastus took a trip to the island of Lesbos. "Between the two of them they originated the science of biology, Aristotle carrying out a systematic investigation of animals, Theophrastus doing the same for plants."[6] "They set out to bring order to nature by doing something very unusual for the time: they examined living things and got their hands dirty. They turned away from Plato's idealism and looked at the real world. Both Aristotle and Theophrastus believed that the study of nature was as important as metaphysics, politics, or mathematics.... For many years they worked closely together until Aristotle's death in 322 B.C.E. when Theophrastus became his successor at the Lyceum school in Athens."[7] We mark 345-322 BC as the emergence date of the _Biology_ resource.

First _Anatomy_ - "In Alexandria the practice of human cadaveric dissection was the dominant means of learning anatomy and it was here that Herophilus of Chalcedon and his younger contemporary Erasistratus of Ceos became the first ancient Greek physicians to perform systematic dissections of human cadavers in the first half of 3rd century BC".[8] We mark 300-250 BC as the emergence date of the _Anatomy_ resource.

First _Pharmacology_ - Summary by the Library of Congress stated,

"During the first century, the Greek doctor and apothecary Dioscorides, who is considered the father of pharmacology, wrote a very important document on botany and pharmaceuticals." The book "De Materia Medica"[9] is considered the world's first pharmacopeia. "Between about 50-70 C.E., he wrote his fundamental work, Peri ulhV iatrikhV, known in Latin as De materia medica. This five-book study focused on "the preparation, properties, and testing of drugs." It became the most central pharmacological work in Europe and the Middle East for the next sixteen centuries." [10] We mark 50-70 as the emergence date of the *Pharmacology* resource.

First *Physiology* - Historians sometimes correlate the beginnings of early Greek physiology with the theoretical works of Anaximenes (570 BC), Empedocl, Hippocrates, Aristotle, and Erasistratus (302-250 BC). However, a key figure in the early development of Western physiology was Claudius Galenus (129-216 AD), universally known as Galen of Pergamon.[11] Galen was "a great pioneer of experimental physiology."[12] We mark 129-216 as the emergence date of the *Physiology* resource.

First *Gerontology* - Avicenna, in a chapter entitled "Regimen of Old Age" and other chapters of his work "The Canon of Medicine," wrote on issues related to gerontology.[13] John Urquhart, professor of biopharmaceutical sciences, University of California at San Francisco, noted that Avicenna's Canon of Medicine was written about 1012 AD. [14] We mark 1012 as the emergence date of the *Gerontology* resource.

First *Kinesiology* - Kinesiology studies the mechanics and anatomy of human movement and their roles in promoting health and reducing disease. [15] Applied kinesiology was "founded by Michigan chiropractor George J. Goodheart, Jr." in 1964.[16] We mark 1964 as the emergence date of the *Kinesiology* resource.

First Gender Studies - "The first women's studies courses, at postgraduate level were set up in the early 1980s, initially at Kent and Bradford, then York, followed by many others."[17] "Gender studies have emerged from the activism that has long characterized women's studies and associated feminist politics and gender studies in part grew out of the identity politics of the 1980s and 1990s."[18] We mark 1980-1999 as the emergence date of the *Gender Studies* resource.

Related to Society and World

In the family of resources *Related to Society and World*, humankind created the following resources: *Diplomacy, Judiciary, Olympic Games, Philosophy, Theology, Political Science, Logic, Sociology, Economics.*

First *Diplomacy* - "Records of treaties between Mesopotamian city-states date from about 2850 bce. Thereafter, Akkadian (Babylonian) became the first diplomatic language, serving as the international tongue of the Middle East until it was replaced by Aramaic."[19] We mark 2850 BC as the emergence date of the *Diplomacy* resource.

First *Judiciary* - "The Code of Ur-Nammu (c. 2100-2050 BCE) is the oldest extant law code in the world. It was written by the Sumerian king Ur-Nammu (r. 2047-2030 BCE) or his son Shulgi of Ur (r. 2029-1982 BCE) ... The dating of c. 2100-2050 BCE is based on middle chronology; short chronology places the date at c. 2050-2047 BCE."[20] We mark 2100-2047 BC as the emergence date of the *Judiciary* resource.

First *Olympic Games* - "The ancient Olympic Games began in the year 776 BC, when Koroibos, a cook from the nearby city of Elis, won the stadion race, a foot race 600 feet long.... Contrary evidence, both literary and archaeological, suggests that the games may have existed at Olympia much earlier than this date, perhaps as early as the 10th or 9th century BC."[21] We mark 776 BC as the emergence date of the *Olympic Games* resource.

First *Philosophy* - "The cliché runs that Aristotle said that Thales was the first philosopher because he made water the element and principle of the things that are."[22] Historians follow Aristotle and consider Thales as the first philosopher. He was "born c. 624–620 BCE" and "died c. 548–545 BCE."[23] We mark 624-545 BC as the emergence date of the *Philosophy* resource.

First *Political Science* - "Some have identified Plato (428/427–348/347 BCE), whose ideal of a stable republic still yields insights and metaphors, as the first political scientist, though most consider Aristotle (384–322 BCE), who introduced empirical observation into the study of politics, to be the discipline's true founder."[24] We mark 428-322 BC as the emergence date of the *Political Science* resource.

First *Logic* - "The systematic study of logic seems to have been undertaken first by Aristotle. Although Plato used dialectic as both a method of reasoning and a means of philosophical training, Aristotle established a system of rules and strategies for such reasoning."[25] Aristotle lived from 384 to 322 BC. We mark 384-322 BC as the emergence date of the *Logic* resource.

First _Theology_ - "The tenth book of Plato's _Laws_ has for its matter legislation of a peculiar kind and on an unusual subject, namely religion.... That religious legislation provides the frame for the whole body of theological doctrine set forth in this book." [26] Plato was "born 428/427 BCE" and "died 348/347."[27] "At the time of writing the first book of the Laws he was at least seventy-four years of age, if we suppose him to allude to the victory of the Syracusans under Dionysius the Younger over the Locrians, which occurred in the year 356."[28] We mark 354-348 BC as the emergence date of the _Theology_ resource.

First _Sociology_ - "Ibn-Khaldun was one of the early Islamic scholars who explained historical processes explicitly on the basis of social laws...Many of his ideas, like social solidarity, collective consciousness, social change found reflection in the modern sociology".[29] Ibn Khaldūn lived from 1332 to 1406.[30] We mark 1332-1406 as the emergence date of the _Sociology_ resource.

First _Economics_ - "The effective birth of economics as a separate discipline may be traced to the year 1776, when the Scottish philosopher Adam Smith published _An Inquiry into the Nature and Causes of the Wealth of Nations_.[31] We mark 1776 as the emergence date of the _Economics_ resource.

Related to Place in Society

In the family of resources _Related to Place in Society_ humankind created the following resources: _Authored literature, Mythology, Playwright, Genealogy and Family Tree, Ethics, Linguistics, Genetics, Cognitive Science._

First _Authored Literature_ - "Although Enheduanna lived 4300 hundred years ago (ca. 2285-2250 B.C.E.), her existence as a historical personage is well established... she was the daughter of Sargon of Akkad, the first ruler to unite northern and southern Mesopotamia." "She is the world's oldest known author whose works were written in cuneiform...Two of her known works are hymns to the goddess Inanna."[32] We mark 2285-2250 BC as the emergence date of the _Authored Literature_ resource.

First _Mythology_ - "Myths are the narrative patterns that give significance to our existence".[33] "Most scholars of mythology agree that it is a foundational component of how any society, culture, and individual defines themselves, none can agree absolutely on how to define it."[34]

"From the many definitions of myth in books and on the web, we can see that myths have four basic attributes in common: They are cultural — they reflect the beliefs and values of a group of people. They are sacred — they concern the spiritual or divine aspects of existence that human beings cannot understand. They are didactic — they seek to explain the unexplainable, and they teach humans how to behave, live, and relate to each other and the gods. They are foundational — they provide basic rules, beliefs, and rituals for a culture to establish shared beliefs and practices."[34]

The myth known today as the Epic of Gilgamesh was considered in ancient times to be one of the great masterpieces of cuneiform literature".[35] "The Epic of Gilgamesh started out as a series of Sumerian poems and tales dating back to 2100 B.C., but the most complete version was written around the 12th century B.C. by the Babylonians."[36] We mark 2100 BC as the emergence date of the *Mythology* resource.

First *Linguistics* - "The history of linguistics begins not with Plato or Aristotle, but with the Indian grammarian Panini...The first attempt to systematically describe a language as a whole was made in India by Panini."[37] Dates of Panini's life vary between the 6th and 4th century BC.[38,39] We mark 600-401 BC as the emergence date of the *Linguistics* resource.

First *Genealogy and Family Tree* - "The Chinese philosopher, teacher, and politician Confucius have the longest and oldest class of resources tree in the world. The class of resources of Confucius has kept their genealogy records since about 479 BC or over 2,000 years—the records contain millions of names and many generations."[40] Confucius lived from 551 to 479 BC. We mark 479 BC as the emergence date of the *Genealogy and Family Tree* resource.

First *Playwright* - ""Aeschylus, (born 525/524 BC—died 456/455 BC, Gela, Sicily), the first of classical Athens' great dramatists, who raised the emerging art of tragedy to great heights of poetry and theatrical power... Aeschylus wrote approximately 90 plays, including satyr plays as well as tragedies; of these, about 80 titles are known. Only seven tragedies have survived entire... Aeschylus was a notable participant in Athens' major dramatic competition, the Great Dionysia ... Aeschylus is recorded as having participated in this competition, probably for the first time, in 499 BC."[41] We mark 499-455 BC as the emergence date of the *Playwright* resource.

First *Ethics* - "Ancient moral theory tries to provide a reflective account of an essential human activity so one can grasp what is of fundamental importance in pursuing it. In historical order, the theories to be considered in this article are those of Socrates as presented in certain dialogues."[42] Socrates lived from 470 to 399 BC.[43] We mark 470-399 BC as the emergence date of the *Ethics* resource.

First *Genetics* - All present research in genetics can be traced back to Mendel's discovery of the laws governing the inheritance of traits. [44] Gregor Mendel gave two lectures on his work in 1865. [45] We mark 1865 as the emergence date of the *Genetics* resource.

First *Cognitive Science* - "I date the moment of conception of cognitive science as 11 September, 1956, the second day of a symposium organized by the 'Special Interest Group in Information Theory' at the Massachusetts Institute of Technology."[46] We mark 1956 as the emergence date of the *Cognitive Science* resource.

History Related

In the family of resources *History Related* humankind created the following resources: *Archeology, Museum, History,* and *Anthropology*.

First *Archeology* - "About 550 b.c., Nabonidus [the archeologically-minded last king of Babylon] had visited the then-ancient city of Ur and had carried out temple repairs."[47] We mark 550 BC as the emergence date of the *Archeology* resource.

First *Museum* - Ennigaldi was the daughter of Nabonidus, the last king of the Neo-Babylonian Empire. Ennigaldi created her museum at around 530 BC. The museum was private, but it still was a world-first museum.[48]   We mark 530 BC as the emergence date of the *Museum* resource.

First *History* - "Herodotus has been called the 'father of history'."[49] According to the traditional view, "The Histories was brought before the public between approximately 430 and 425 B.C." Challenges to this view were discussed by David Sansone in 1985.[50] We mark 430-425 BC as the emergence date of the *History* resource.

First *Anthropology* - "Anthropology is the study of the human race, especially of its origins, development, customs, and beliefs."[51] "Like many academic disciplines today, the field of anthropology traces its roots back to ancient Greece. The Greek historian Herodotus, in the 4th century B.C., wrote what we might now call "early anthropology" by documenting and attempting to understand the disparate cultures of Greece and Persia."[52] According to traditional view, "*The Histories* was brought before the public between approximately 430 and 425 B.C." We mark 430-425 BC as the emergence date of the *Anthropology* resource.

Tools for Generic Social Impact

In the family of resources *Tools for Generic Social Impact* humankind created the following resources: *False News, Opinion Poll, Propaganda, Mob Mentality,* and *Disinformation.*

First *Propaganda* - Gard Granerød, professor of MF Norwegian School of Theology, Religion, and Society, "discusses the contents of the Persian propaganda text...The main text that the article focuses on is King Darius I's Bisitun [Bisotun, Behistun] inscription."[53] Behistun inscription was created on the orders of King Darius I in 521 BC.[54] We mark 521 BC as the emergence date of the *Propaganda* resource.

First *False News* - Blood libel, also called blood accusation, is "the superstitious accusation that Jews ritually sacrifice Christian children at Passover to obtain blood for unleavened bread ... In 1144 an English boy, William of Norwich, was found brutally murdered with strange wounds to his head, arms, and torso. His uncle, a priest, blamed local Jews, and a rumour spread that Jews crucified a Christian child every year at Passover."[55] We mark 1144 as the emergence date of the *False News* resource.

First *Mob Mentality* – "Mob mentality, herd mentality, pack mentality, groupthink, or crowd psychology — the concept has many names...people conform or change their behavior to match social norms.... [people] conformed mainly because they wanted to fit in with the rest of the group."[56] "The Salem witch trials occurred in colonial Massachusetts between early 1692 and mid-1693. More than 200 people were accused of practicing witchcraft—the devil's magic—and 20 were executed."[57] We mark 1692 as the emergence date of the *Moob Mentality* resource.

First *Opinion Poll* - "The earliest forerunners of the modern public opinion poll appear to be tallies of voter preferences reported by the *Raleigh Star* and *North Carolina State Gazette* and the *Wilmington American Watchman* and *Delaware Advertiser* prior to the presidential election of 1824."[58] We mark 1824 AD as the emergence date of the *Opinion Poll* resource.

First *Disinformation* - "Disinformation is false information targeted to an individual, group or country, created by government ... Disinformation as a KGB weapon began in 1923 when I. S. Unshlikht, Deputy Chairman of GRU, then the name of KGB, the proposed the establishment of a 'special disinformation office to conduct active intelligence operations.' ".[59] We mark 1923 as the emergence date of the *Disinformation* resource.

Related to Mental Health

In the family of resources *Related to Mental Health* humankind created the following resources: *Psychiatry, Psychology, Lie Detector*.

First *Psychiatry* - Western psychiatry emerged as a medical specialty caring for the mentally ill over the course of the late 18th and early 19th centuries. This emergence was a contingent process, dependent on the co-occurrence of three historical developments that together shaped the young discipline.[60] In 1808, Johann Christian Reil published "a 118-page treatise in which he defined the nascent discipline that he called 'Psychiatrie.' "[61] We mark 1808 as the emergence date of the *Psychiatry* resource.

First *Psychology* - Gustav Theodor Fechner (b. 1801–d. 1887) is well known to psychologists as the founder of psychophysics. In 1860, he published his work "Elements of Psychophysics".[62] We mark 1860 as the emergence date of the *Psychology* resource.

First *Lie Detector* - "The first polygraph was created in 1921 when a California-based policeman and physiologist John A. Larson devised an apparatus to simultaneously measure continuous changes in blood pressure, heart rate, and respiration rate in order to aid in the detection of deception (Larson, Haney, & Keeler, 1932; McCormick, 1927)."[63] We mark 1921 as the emergence date of the *Lie Detector* resource.

*Domesticated animals such as dogs and cats are vulnerable and
entirely dependent on us for all of their needs.*

Gary L. Francione

Chapter 2.4.
Usage of Domesticated Plants and Animals

The history of the *Usage of Domesticated Plants and Animals* class of
resources began with the emergence of resource *Dogs* around 32100-
16800 BC. More than thirty resources were created by humankind in the
class of resources *Usage of Domesticated Plants and Animals* during the last
44 thousand years.

We could divide the *Usage of Domesticated Plants and Animals* class of
resources into six families of resources. Here are those families in the
order   of   their   chronological   appearance   in   humankind's
history: *Domesticated Animals, Domesticated Plants (Fruits), Domesticated
Plants (Vegetables), Domesticated Plants (Seeds and Grains), and Inedible
Domesticated Plants.*

Humankind domesticated a lot of plants and animals. The question is
how to choose a set of domesticated plants and animals for our analysis.
We would use the top 25 most valuable domesticated plants and
animals, per gross volume, in metric tons, produced in 2016.[1] Rapeseed
is excluded as it is primarily used for industrial purposes.

Tea and coffee are added as low-weight but highly used drinks. Cacao
(chocolate) is added as highly used dessert. Dogs and cats are added as
highly used people companions. Horses added as highly used animals
throughout humankind's history.

Domesticated Animals

In the family of resources *Domesticated Animals* humankind created
the following resources: *Dogs, Cows, Chicken, Sheep and Goats, Pigs, Cats,
Horses.*

First *Dogs* - "The geographic and temporal origins of the domestic dog remain controversial...Molecular dating suggests an onset of domestication there 18,800 to 32,100 years ago."[2] We mark 30100-16800 BC as the emergence date of the *Dogs* resource.

We also mark 30100-16800 BC as the emergence date of the Domesticated Plants and Animals class of resources.

First *Cows* - Archeozoological, genetic data and mtDNA sequences from 15 Neolithic to Iron Age Iranian domestic cattle "indicate that taurine cattle were first domesticated from local wild ox (aurochs) in the Near East some 10,500 years ago."[3] We mark 10500 BC as the emergence date of the *Cows* resource.

First *Sheep and Goats* - "Sheep and goats (caprines) were domesticated in Southwest Asia in the early Holocene, but how and in how many places remain open questions. This study investigates the initial conditions and trajectory of caprine domestication at Aşıklı Höyük, which preserves an unusually high-resolution record of the first 1,000 y of Neolithic existence in Central Anatolia. Our comparative analysis of caprine age and sex structures and related evidence reveals a local domestication process that began around 8400 cal BC."[4]. We mark 8400 BC as the emergence date of the *Sheep and Goats* resource.

First *Chicken* - Researchers "report ancient mitochondrial DNA sequences from the earliest archaeological chicken bones from China, dating back to ~ 10,000 B.P."[5] We mark 8000 BC as the emergence date of the *Chicken* resource.

First *Pigs* - "Domestication of the pig took place some 9000 to 10,000 years ago independently at two locations: in East Anatolia and in China."[6] We mark 8000-7000 BC as the emergence date of the *Pigs* resource.

First *Cats* - "Around 9,500 years ago, a human, a cat and a rich variety of offerings were buried together on the Mediterranean island of Cyprus. Scientists have now discovered the remains of this burial, believed to be the oldest known evidence of a special friendship between humans and cats."[7] "The cat skeleton lay just 40 centimeters away"[8] from the human skeleton. We mark 7500 BC as the emergence date of the *Cats* resource.

First *Horses* - "Modern domesticated breeds do not descend from the earliest domestic horse lineage associated with archaeological evidence ... at Botai, Central Asia around 3500 bc.[9] ... modern domestic horses ultimately replaced almost all other local populations as they expanded rapidly across Eurasia from about 2000 bc."[10] We mark 3500 BC as the emergence date of the *Horses* resource.

Domesticated Plants (Fruits)

In the family of resources *Domesticated Plants (Fruits)* humankind created the following resources: *Rice, Wheat, Sugar Cane, Corn (Maize), Cotton, Grape, Bananas, Apple, Mango, Tomato, Cucumber, Eggplant, Orange, Watermelon.*

First *Wheat* - The authors reviewed "the available information on the founder grain crops (einkorn wheat, emmer wheat, barley, lentil, pea, chickpea, and flax) that started agriculture in Southwest Asia during the Pre-Pottery Neolithic period, some 11,000–10,000 years ago.... The earliest definite domesticated einkorn wheat appears in two EPPNB sites, namely ca. 10,600–9900 cal BP ...Southern Turkey."[11] We mark 8600-7900 BC as the emergence date of the *Wheat* resource.

First *Sugar Cane* - "Sugarcane has enhanced its status from an unknown wild grass plant to the world's largest cultivated cash crop with its incredible ability to synthesize and accumulate sucrose in its stem. Sugarcane domestication was started around 8000 BC in the region of New Guinea and later it reached Southeast Asia and India."[12] We mark 8000 BC as the emergence date of the *Sugar Cane* resource.

First *Rice* - "Our phytolith data indicate that rice remains retrieved from early stages of the Shangshan and Hehuashan sites have ages of approximately 9,400 and 9,000 calibrated years before the present, respectively."[13] We mark 7400-7000 BC as the emergence date of the *Rice* resource.

First *Corn (Maize)* - "We report starch grain and phytolith data from the Xihuatoxtla shelter, located in the Central Balsas Valley, that indicate that maize was present by 8,700 calendrical years ago (cal. B.P.)"[14] We mark 6700 BC as the emergence date of the *Corn (Maize)* resource.

First *Grape* - "The archaeological record suggests that cultivation of the domesticated grape, *Vitis vinifera subsp. vinifera*, began 6,000–8,000 y ago in the Near East from its wild progenitor, *Vitis vinifera subsp. sylvestris* ...."[15] We mark 6000-4000 BC as the emergence date of the *Grape* resource.

First *Bananas* - "Previous archaeological and linguistic studies have indicated that cultivated banana was initially domesticated by farmers in Southeast Asia about 7,000 years ago..."[16] We mark 5000 BC as the emergence date of the *Bananas* resource.

First *Apples* - "The cultivated apple was initially domesticated from the wild apple *Malus sieversii* (Ldb.) Roem in the Tian Shan Mountains in Central Asia ... Having originated from *M. sieversii* in Central Asia about 4000 to 10 000 years ago, the cultivated apple then underwent hybridization with its wild relatives during its spread from the Tian Shan Mountains westward along the Silk Route."[17] We mark 8000-2000 BC as the emergence date of the *Apples* resource.

First *Tomato* - The history of tomato domestication is complicated. "Razifard, a postdoctoral researcher in the Caicedo lab, says, 'What's new is that we propose [[18]] that about 7,000 years ago, these weedy tomatoes may have been re-domesticated into the cultivated tomato.'"[19] We mark 5000 BC as the emergence date of the *Tomato* resource.

First *Mango* - Mango "has a domestication history of over 4000 years within a large area in the Indo-Burmese and Southeast Asia regions."[20] We mark 2000 BC as the emergence date of the *Mango* resource.

First *Watermelon* - "The diverse evidence, combined, indicates that northeastern Africa is the centre of origin of the dessert watermelon, that watermelons were domesticated for water and food there over 4000 years ago, and that sweet dessert watermelons emerged in Mediterranean lands by approximately 2000 years ago."[21] We mark 2000 BC as the emergence date of the *Watermelon* resource.

First *Cucumber* - "One of the crops domesticated in the Indo-Gangetic plain is cucumber, Cucumis sativus. Evidence for this consists in the occurrence there of a wild progenitor, C. sativus var. hardwickii... and in comparative linguistic evidence..."[22] "Cucumber is originated from India, particularly southern foot-hills of Himalayan region. It was domesticated in India from its wild relative, Cucumis sativus var. hardwickii 3000 years ago."[23] We mark 1000 BC as the emergence date of the *Cucumber* resource.

First *Eggplant* - Authors stated that "records, although rather brief, revealed that the eggplant was already being specifically cultivated in gardens as a crop, not a wild form collected from the surrounding habitat. They also indicate that the domestication of the eggplant took place not later than 59 bc in China."[24] We mark 59 BC as the emergence date of the *Eggplant* resource.

First *Orange* - The dates of domestication of the sour and sweet orange are different. Both types of oranges are hybrids. The review article by Dafna Langgut integrated recent information concerning the history of citrus. According to various textual evidence, the sour orange was brought from India to Oman after 912 AD. The sweet orange hybrid was introduced to Europe much later. "The first mention of the sweet orange in Europe is sometimes said to be in the archives of the Italian city of Savona, in 1471."[25] We mark 912 as the emergence date of *Orange* resource.

Domesticated Plants (Seeds and Grains)

In the family of resources *Domesticated Plants (Seeds and Grains)* humankind created the following resources: *Barley, Sunflower, Cacao (Chocolate)*, and *Coffee*.

First *Barley* - "Remains of barley (Hordeum vulgare) grains found at archaeological sites in the Fertile Crescent indicate that about 10,000 years ago the crop was domesticated there from its wild relative Hordeum spontaneum".[26] We mark 8000 BC as the emergence date of *Barley* resource.

First Cacao (Chocolate) - "We report cacao use identified by three independent lines of archaeological evidence—cacao starch grains, absorbed theobromine residues and ancient DNA—dating from approximately 5,300 years ago recovered from the Santa Ana-La Florida (SALF) site in southeast Ecuador."[27] We mark 3300 BC as the emergence date of *Cacao (Chocolate)* resource.

First *Sunflower* - "Carbonized seeds of domesticated sunflower (Helianthis annus var. macrocarpus Ckill.) recovered from the Hayes site in middle Tennessee yielded an accelerator rate of 4265 +- 60 B.P."[28] "Evidence for early (ca. 2600 cal B.C.) domesticated sunflower (Helianthus annuus) at the San Andrés site in Tabasco, Mexico (1, 2), has reopened discussions about the class of domesticated plants in Mesoamerica."[29] We mark 2600-2265 BC as the emergence date of *Sunflower* resource.

First *Coffee* - "Wild coffee plants, probably from Kefa (Kaffa), Ethiopia, were taken to southern Arabia and placed under cultivation in the 15th century."[30] We mark 1401-1500 as the emergence date of *Coffee* resource.

Domesticated Plants (Vegetables)

In the family of resources *Domesticated Plants (Vegetables)* humankind created the following resources: *Cassava (Yuka), Potato, Onion, Sweet Potato, Tea, Soybeans,* and *Cabbage.*

First *Potato* - "Plant domestication appears in the Peruvian highlands contemporaneously with its appearance in the Northern South America. Potato, ... and jicama were recovered from Tres Ventanas Cave in strata dated to 8000-6000 BC".[31] We mark 8000-6000 BC as the emergence date of *Potato* resource.

First *Sweet Potato* - "All archaeological, linguistic and historical evidence so far establishes the origin of sweet potato as the New World, in either Central or South American lowlands. The oldest remains so far discovered of dried roots are those from the caves of Chilca Canyon of Peru (Engel 1970), which have been radiocarbon dated at 8000-10000 years old. However, it is not certain whether these had been domesticated, or simply collected from wild plants."[32] We mark 8000-6000 BC as the emergence date of *Sweet Potato* resource.

First *Cassava (Yuka)* - Mabrouk A. El-Sharkaw stated[33] that the proposed dates for cassava domestication vary per different researchers from 6000 BC to 4000 BC. We mark 6000-4000 BC as the emergence date of *Cassava (Yuka)* resource.

First *Onion* - "The history of onion can be traced back to at least 5000 years ... In the oldest recorded history, onions were depicted as food in Egyptian tombs as early as 3200 B.C."[34] We mark 3200 BC as the emergence date of *Onion* resource.

First *Tea* - "We note that tea was domesticated around 3000 B.C. either from non-tea wild relatives ... or intra-specifically from the wild ... trees, and that the genetic origins of the various tea varieties may need further inquiry."[35] We mark 3000 BC as the emergence date of *Tea* resource.

First *Soybeans* - "It is commonly believed that soybean was domesticated in ancient China perhaps 3000 to 5000 yr ago from wild soybean ... This estimate derived in part from references to soybean that appeared in Chinese literature."[36] We mark 3000-1000 BC as the emergence date of *sSybeans* resource.

First *Cabbage* - There are many different types of cabbage, and, respectfully, there could be many different dates of a specific cabbage type' domestication. "The oldest written account that we can safely refer to the cole crops is the use of Greek words ... [in] VI century B.C.E. ... [or] V century B.C.E."[37]   We mark 600-401 BC as the emergence date of *Cabbage* resource.

Inedible Domesticated Plants

In the family of resources *Inedible Domesticated Plants* humankind created the following resources: *Cotton*.

First *Cotton* - There are four different cultivated species of cotton. Each of them has its own domestication history. "Colloquially known as the 'A-genome cottons', *Gossypium arboreum* and *Gossypium herbaceum* were both domesticated during the same approximate timeframe as the polyploid species (4,000–8,000 years ago), albeit in southwestern Asia and Africa."[38] We mark 6000-2000 BC as the emergence date of *Cotton* resource.

When goods do not cross borders, soldiers will.

Frederic Bastiat

Chapter 2.5.
Trade with a Use of an Intermediary

The history of the *Trade with a Use of an Intermediary* class of resources began with the emergence of resource *Trade Network* at around 9500 BC.

More than ten resources were created by humankind in the *Trade with a Use of an Intermediary* class of resources during the last 44 thousand years.

We could divide the *Trade with a Use of an Intermediary* class of resources into four families of resources. Here are those families in the order of their chronological appearance in humankind's history: *Types of Goods Delivery Infrastructure, Medium of Exchange, Carriers of Subject of Trade,* and *Components of International Trade.*

Types of Goods Delivery Infrastructure

In the family of resources *Types of Goods Delivery Infrastructure* humankind created the following resources: *Trade Network, Marketplace, Marketplace for Securities Trade, Online Trade.*

First *Trade Network* - Obsidian was widely traded across ancient Mesopotamia. "Our contribution sheds new light on the Late Pleistocene/Early Holocene exploitation of obsidian sources on the island of Melos in the Cyclades reporting dates c. 13th millennium - end of 10th millennium B.P."[1] We mark 11000-8000 BC as the emergence date of *Trade Network* resource.

We also mark 11000-8000 BC as the emergence date of the Trade with a Use of Intermediary class of resources.

First *Marketplace* - The Stoa of Attalos was a stoa (covered walkway) in the Agora of Athens in Greece. [The building] "served a variety of purposes. The spacious colonnades were used as promenades.

The forty-two closed rooms behind served as shops... The Stoa stood, with minor alterations, from about 150 B.C. until the year 267 A.D."[2] We mark 150 BC as the emergence date of *Marketplace* resource.

First *Marketplace for Securities Trade* - "The trade on VOC [The Dutch East India Company (VOC, Verenigde Oostindische Compagnie in Dutch language)] shares started in 1602." VOC had chambers in different cities in the Dutch Republic, including Amsterdam.[3] We mark 1602 as the emergence date of *Marketplace for Securities Trade* resource.

First *Online Trade* - The Boston Computer Exchange (BoCoEx) was the first e-commerce company. BoCoEx was "founded in 1982."[4]   We mark 1982 as the emergence date of *Online Trade* resource.

Medium of Exchange

In the family of resources *Medium of Exchange* humankind created the following resources: *Commodity Money, Fiat Money, Electronic Money*.

First *Commodity Money* - The Code of Ur-Nammu stated: "[If a man caught a fugitive slave in the plain (and)] crossed over the boundary of his (the slave's) city (and) returned him, the owner of the slave shall pay two shekels to the man who had returned him."[5] The Code of Ur-Nammu (c. 2100-2050 BCE) is the oldest extant law code in the world. It was written by the Sumerian king Ur-Nammu (r. 2047-2030 BCE) or his son Shulgi of Ur (r. 2029-1982 BCE) ...The dating of c. 2100-2050 BCE is based on middle chronology; short chronology places the date at c. 2050-2047 BCE.[6] "Silver was unquestionably money in the Ur III Umma economy, as was barley. First and foremost, like its antecedent Sumerian economies the Ur III state was a commodity money economy with silver, it most valued commodity, as a medium of exchange."[7]   We mark 2100-2050 BC as the emergence date of *Commodity Money* resource.

First *Fiat Money* - "Fiat simply means decree, and fiat money is a currency that is decreed and backed by the government that issues it."[8] The Yuan Empire [1271 to 1361] was the first political regime in history that pegged paper money to precious metal and the first that deployed fiat money as the sole legal tender [9] We mark 1271-1361 as the emergence date of *Fiat Money* resource.

First *Electronic Money* - Electronic money is the currency that exists in banking computer systems that may be used to facilitate electronic transactions. Americans process transactions electronically by receiving paychecks through direct deposits, moving money from one account to another via electronic fund transfers, or spending money with credit and debit cards.[10] David Chaum [11] proposed an electronic cash system in 1982-1983. In 1989, Chaum started the DigiCash company with "ecash" as its trademark. We mark 1983 as the emergence date of *Electronic Money* resource.

Carriers of Subject of Trade

In the family of resources *Carriers of Subject of Trade* humankind created the following resources: *Mass Transportation, Electronic Transfer. Mass Transportation* was described in the Chapter 1.5. Mass Transportation.

First *Electronic Transfer* - "1851 - The New York and Mississippi Valley Printing Telegraph Company was founded which later became Western Union... 1871 - Western Union's famous Money Transfer service first became available."[12] We mark 1871 as the emergence date of *Electronic Transfer* resource.

Components of International Trade

In the family of resources *Components of International Trade* humankind created the following resources: *Export, Import, Trade Barrier. Import* was described in the *Export* section.

First *Export* - "It is reasonable to suppose that Indian ports had direct contact with the Sumerian ports in the Akkadian period [about 2350 BC]"[13] We mark 2350 BC as the emergence date of *Export* resource.

First *Trade Barrier* - "Tariff, also called customs duty, [is] tax levied upon goods as they cross national boundaries, usually by the government of the importing country."[14] "Asakura points out that the custom tariffs of Palmira in AD 136 provided different rates for different commodities, thereby ensuring the birth of customs tariff and the customs tariff nomenclature."[14] We mark 136 as the emergence date of *Trade Barrier* resource.

Man is a tool-using animal. Without tools he is nothing, with tools he is all.

Thomas Carlyle

Chapter 2.6.
Tools, Devices, and Machines from Man-Made Materials

The history of the *Tools, Devices, and Machines from Man-Made Materials* class of resources began with the emergence of resource *Human-Powered Machines* around 8040-7510 BC.

More than thirty resources were created by humankind in the class of resources *Tools, Devices, and Machines from Man-Made Materials* during the last 44 thousand years.

We could divide the *Tools, Devices, and Machines from Man-Made Materials* class of resources into nine families of resources. Here are those families in the order of their chronological appearance in humankind's history: *Simple Machines, Sources of Power, Elements of Mechanical Machines, Machine Types, Tool Types, Categories of Electrical Machines, Energy Storage Devices, Components of Electronic Machines (Devices)*, and *Self-Operation Machines*.

Sources of Power

In the family of resources *Sources of Power* humankind created the following resources: *Human-Powered Machine, Water-Powered Machine, Animal-Powered Machine, Wind-Powered Machine, Steam-Powered Machine, Fuel-Powered Machine, Electricity-Powered Machine,* and *Nuclear Energy-Powered Machine*.

First *Human-Powered Machine* - Human-powered machines include human-powered vehicles, i.e., any form of transport that relies on human muscle power. These vehicles range from bicycles to boats and from skateboards to aircraft.

The Pesse canoe is the oldest-known canoe. According to carbon dating, the boat was made "between 8040 BC and 7510 BC."[1] From ancient times, it is known that people used paddles to propel canoes. "Paddling was also used for small, canoe-like vessels in the Bronze Age."[2] The paddle was not found with the Pesse canoe. Yet we could assume that the ancient canoeist propelled the Pesse canoe with a paddle or paddle-like craft. We mark 8040-7510 BC as the emergence date of *Human-Powered Machine* resource.

We also mark 8040-7510 BC as the emergence date of the Tools, Devices, and Machines from Man-Made Materials class of resources.

First Water-Powered Machine - A water wheel is a machine that converts the energy of flowing or falling water into other forms of power, often in a watermill. The earliest waterwheel working like a lever was described by Zhuangzi in the late Warring States period (476-221 BC). It says that the waterwheel was invented by Zigong, a disciple of Confucius, in the 5th century BC.[3] We mark 476-221 BC as the emergence date of *Water-Powered Machine* resource.

First Wind-Powered Machine - "It would seem, then, that we can take the tenth century as the earliest known date for acceptable documentation of the vertical-axis windmill, and the location as most probably West or Central Asia."[4] We mark 901-1000 as the emergence date of *Wind-Powered Machine* resource.

First Steam-Powered Machine - Thomas Savery was an "English engineer and inventor who built the first steam engine." Savery patented it in 1698.[5] We mark 1698 as the emergence date of *Steam-Powered Machine* resource.

First Fuel-Powered Machine - In 1794, Robert Street patented an internal-combustion engine. It was "English Patent No. 1983."[6] We mark 1794 AD as the emergence date of *Fuel-Powered Machine* resource.

First Electricity-Powered Machine - "In 1828 at the University of Sciences of Budapest, the professor of physics Ányos Jedlik constructed the first direct-current motor with electromagnet and commutator ... The activity of Ányos Jedlik is proved by working model of electronic vehicle (auto or locomotive) in 1855."[7] See also.[8] We mark 1828 as the emergence date of *Electricity-Powered Machine* resource.

First Nuclear Energy-Powered Machine - "The first nuclear reactor to produce electricity (albeit a trivial amount) was the small Experimental Breeder reactor (EBR-1) designed and operated by Argonne National Laboratory and sited in Idaho, USA. The reactor started up in December 1951."[9] We mark 1951 as the emergence date of

Nuclear Energy-Powered Machine resource.

Simple Machines

In the family of resources *Simple Machines* humankind created the following resources: *Wedge (Ax), Wheel and Axle, Lever (Balance Weights), Inclined Plane, Pulley,* and *Screw.*

First *Wheel and Axle* - "In 2002 Slovenian archaeologists uncovered a wooden wheel some 20 kilometers southeast of Ljubljana ... The wheel has a radius of 70 centimeters and is five cm thick. It is made of ash and oak ... It was established that the wheel is between 5.100 and 5.350 years old ... The axle, whose age could not be established as precisely, is about as old as the wheel". [10] We mark 3350-3100 BC as the emergence date of *Wheel and Axle* resource.

First *Wedge (Ax)* - Ötzi, also called the Iceman, lived sometime between 3350 and 3105 BC. His mummified body was in the Ötztal Alps on the border between Austria and Italy. A copper ax was found with the Iceman. "Ötzi, the glacier mummy, is displayed in the South Tyrol Museum of Archaeology in Bolzano, Italy together with his clothing and equipment."[11] "The period in which Ötzi lived was determined with the aid of radiocarbon dating, the measurement revealed that he lived between 3,350 and 3,100 BC."[12] We mark 3350-3100 BC as the emergence date of *Wedge (Ax)* resource.

First *Lever (Balance Weights)* - "Secure dating evidence starts with the first king of 4th Dynasty, ... Senofru [Sneferu] ... From his reign we have inscribed balance weights."[13] According to The Oxford History of Ancient Egypt the reign of Sneferu was from 2613 to 2589 BC.[14] We mark 2613-2589 BC as the emergence date of *Lever (Balance Weights)* resource.

First *Inclined Plane* - "From the many inscriptions found on the walls of Hatnub Quarry P, Shaw (1986: 201) notes that the earliest occupation of the quarry was in the time of Khufu (2550 BC)."[15] We mark 2550 BC as the emergence date of *Inclined Plane* resource.

First *Pulley* - "The oldest true pulley found in Egypt dates to the late Twelfth Dynasty."[16] Dates for the 12th Dynasty vary by different sources. We will use 1991-1783 BC.[17] Respectfully, we mark 1887-1783 BC as the emergence date of *Pulley* resource.

First *Screw* - "There are several texts from Antiquity in which the screw-pump is attributed to Archimedes ... [Some authors] have argued that Archimedes invented the screw-pump after having seen in Egypt the operation of a water-drum."[18]. Archimedes was born in 287 BC and died in 212 BC. Dates when Archimedes first described water screw vary from 234 BC to 250 BC. We mark 287-212 BC as the emergence date of *Screw* resource.

Elements of Mechanical Machines

In the family of resources *Elements of Mechanical Machines* humankind created the following resources: *Gears, Bearings,* and *Couplings.*

First *Gears* - "The first documented south-pointing chariot was created by Ma Jun of Cao Wei during the Three Kingdoms." Depending on the legend, it was created as early as 2634 BC by The Yellow Emperor, the Duke Wen of Zhou, or Ma Jun. "The south-pointing chariot was a mechanical vehicle that indicated the southern cardinal direction ... It is believed that most, if not all, south-pointing chariots worked with differential gears."[19] We mark 2634 BC as the emergence date of *Gears* resource.

First *Bearings* - "The remains of ball bearing from the Roman imperial ships of Nemi lake are investigated to understand their mechanical design and to speculate on the machines they were used in. The imperial ships are dated at first century A.D."[20]

We mark 1-100 as the emergence date of *Bearings* resource.

First *Couplings* - "The Flexible coupling was invented by Jerome Carden in 16th century. It was a simple device consisting of two yokes, a cross and four bearings. This joint is still being used with modern modifications and known as the ancestor of all flexible couplings. In 1650 Robert Hooke developed the application of Hooke or Carden Joint."[21] We mark 1650 as the emergence date of *Couplings* resource.

Self-Operation Machines

In the family of resources *Self-Operation Machines* humankind created the following resources: *Automata,* and *Robot.*

First *Automata* - "Few examples of automatons made prior to the 16th century remain, but numerous documents record their onetime existence. Among the earliest references is to a wooden model of a pigeon constructed by Archytas of Tarentum (flourished 400–350 BCE), a Greek friend of Plato. The bird was apparently suspended from the end of a pivoted bar, and the whole apparatus revolved by means of a jet of steam or compressed air."[22] We mark 400-350 BC as the emergence date of *Automata* resource.

First *Robot* - "In 1954, George Devol filed U.S. Patent No. 2,988,237 describing an autonomous machine that could store commands and move parts."[23] We mark 1954 as the emergence date of *Robot* resource.

Machine Types

In the family of resources *Machine Types* humankind created the following resources: *Mechanical Machines, Electric Machines, Computing Machines,* and *Electronic Machines (Devices)*. *Mechanical Machines* were considered in *Simple Machines* class of resources. *Electric Machines* were considered in *Sources of Power* class of resources.

First *Computing Machine* - "The Antikythera Mechanism is an astronomical calculating machine that predicted phenomena involving the Sun, Moon, stars and probably the planets ... The Antikythera Mechanism was on board a ship otherwise laden with fine bronze and marble sculpture and glassware, which sank within a few years after 70 BC off the island of Antikythera, between Crete and the Greek mainland."[24] We mark 70 BC as the emergence date of *Computing Machine* resource.

First *Electronic Machine (Device)* - "The electromechanical relay, used as a constructive part of some early calculators and computers was invented in 1835 by the brilliant US scientist Joseph Henry."[25] We mark 1835 as the emergence date of *Electronic Machine (Device)* resource.

Tool Types

In the family of resources *Tool Types* humankind created the following resources: *Hand Tools* and *Power Tools*. Hand tools are operated by the physical strength of the user.

First *Power Tools* - "Virtually all of today's electric drills descend from the original portable hand-held drill patented in 1917 by S. Duncan Black and Alonzo Decker, whose invention spurred the growth of the modern power tool industry."[26] We mark 1917 as the emergence date of

Power Tools resource.

Categories of Electrical Machines

In the family of resources *Categories of Electrical Machines* humankind created the following resources: *Electrical Motor, Electrical Transformer,* and *Electrical Generator.*

First *Electrical Generator* - The first ever electric generator, with an alternative name, dynamo, was created by Michael Faraday in October 1831. It "is currently on display in the Lower Ground Floor of the Faraday Museum."[27]   We mark 1831 as the emergence date of *Electrical Generator* resource.

First *Electrical Motor* – "1834 - Thomas Davenport of Vermont developed the first real electric motor ('real' meaning powerful enough to do a task) although Joseph Henry and Michael Faraday created early motion devices using electromagnetic fields."[28] "When Davenport traveled to Washington to obtain a patent, however, his application was rejected: There were no prior patents on electric equipment... At last, the first patent on any electric machine was issued to Thomas Davenport for his electric motor on Feb. 25, 1837."[29] We mark 1834 as the emergence date of *Electric Motor* resource.

First *Electrical Transformer* - "The great triad of Miksa Deri, Otto Titusz Blathy, and Karoly Zipernowsky ... was connected by the invention of the transformer and worked at the famous Ganz factory in Budapest ... In 1889 they developed the transformer and the AC (alternate current) energy distribution system."[30] We mark 1889 as the emergence date of *Electrical Transformer* resource.

Components of Electronic Machines (Devices)

In the family of resources *Components of Electronic Machines (Devices)* humankind created the following resources: *Capacitor, Diode, Transistor,* and *Resistor.*

First *Capacitor* - "The first device for storing charge was discovered in the winter months of 1745-46 by two electricians who worked independently. One was Ewald Georg von Kleist, also known as Jurgen das Opfa, a German scientist (there are a few claims that he is from Poland). The other was Pieter Van Musschenbroek, a professor of math and physics at the University of Leyden in Holland."[31] We mark 1745 as the emergence date of *Capacitor* resource.

First *Diode* - "German physicist Ferdinand Braun, a 24-year-old graduate of the University of Berlin, ... demonstrated this semiconductor device at Leipzig in 1876."[32] We mark 1876 as the emergence date of *Diode* resource.

First *Transistor* - "The transistor was invented Dec. 23, 1947 at AT&T's Bell Laboratories by scientists ... John Bardeen, and Walter Brattain."[33] We mark 1947 as the emergence date of *Transistor* resource.

First *Resistor* - "In 1959, Boykin invented his wire precision resistor and two years later invented an improved version that could withstand extreme changes in temperature and pressure. It was cheaper and more reliable than previous types and was in demand by the U.S. military, IBM, and other high-tech organizations."[34] We mark 1959 as the emergence date of *Resistor* resource.

Energy Storage Devices

In the family of resources *Energy Storage Devices* humankind created the following resource: *Electrical Battery*.

First *Electrical Battery* - In 1800, Alessandro Volta invented the first battery. "In 1801 in Paris Volta gave a demonstration of his battery's generation of electric current before Napoleon, who made Volta a count and a senator of the kingdom of Lombardy." [35] We mark 1800 as the emergence date of *Electrical Battery* resource.

Public transportation is like a magnifying glass that shows you civilization up close.

Chris Gethard

Chapter 2.7.
Mass Transportation

The history of the *Mass Transportation* class of resources began with the emergence of resource *Transportation with a Use of Watercraft* at around 6500 BC. More than ten resources were created by humankind in the *Mass Transportation* class of resources during the last 44 thousand years.

Some resources could be placed into several families of resources. For example, resource *Ground Transportation with a Use of Animals* could be placed into all the above families. However, we should count the same resource only once. Therefore, if we put *Ground Transportation with a Use of Animals* resource into *Media* class of resources, then we should not put it into *Transport Driving Force* or *Direction of Movement* families.

What is important is to count all resources in a particular class of resources and not to count any of those resources twice or more times. The placement of resources into this or that family of resources of development is of secondary importance.

We could divide the *Mass Transportation* class of resources into four families of resources. Here are those families in the order of their chronological appearance in humankind's history: *Media of the Mass Transportation, Transport Driving Force, Direction of Movement* and *Driverless Vehicle.*

Media of the Mass Transportation

In the family of resources *Media of the Mass Transportation* humankind created the following resources: *Transportation with a Use of Watercraft, Ground Transportation with a Use of Animals, Icebreaker, Submarine, Amphibious Vehicle, Airplane, Near-Earth Orbit Spaceship.*

First *Transportation with a Use of Watercraft* - The first known boat for several people was built in Europe in 6500 BC.[1] We mark 6500 BC as the emergence date of *Transportation with a Use of Watercraft* resource.

We also mark 6500 BC as the emergence date of the Mass Transportation class of resources.

First Ground Transportation with a Use of Animals - "The Standard of Ur" is the box "decorated on four sides with inlaid mosaic scenes made from shell, red limestone and lapis lazuli, set in bitumen. One side shows a war scene; a Sumerian army with wheeled waggons and infantry charges the enemy; prisoners are brought before a larger individual, who is accompanied by guards and has his own waggon waiting behind him ... Production date 2500 BC".[2] "Horses had not been yet imported to the area so the wagon is probably driven by four asses or onagers."[3]

We mark 2500 BC as the emergence date of *Ground Transportation with a Use of Animals* resource.

First Icebreaker - The first recorded icebreaker ship was a barge. It was used in Bruges in 1383 to help clear the waterways.[4] We mark 1383 as the emergence date of *Icebreaker* resource.

First Submarine - "Sub Marine Explorer was an innovative vessel that was conceived and launched in 1865-1866 with the twin demands of the American Civil War and the Panamanian pearl fishery in mind. The product of the German immigrant ironworker Julius H. Kroehl ... Sub Marine Explorer was one of the most important and successful developments in the early days of the submarine boat".[5] We mark 1865 as the emergence date of *Submarine* resource.

First Amphibious Vehicle - "By the late 19th century, Ontario's lumber industry had harvested much of the timber from along its waterways ... The Alligator or Steam Warping Tug was invented by Joe Ceburn West ... The amphibious [tug named] Alligator was driven by paddle wheels and used a winch to tow log booms and to pull itself over land from lake to lake. In 1889, West began manufacturing the tug in partnership with James Peachey and their Simcoe foundry quickly became the major producer of Alligators."[6] We mark 1889 as the emergence date of *Amphibious Vehicle* resource.

First Airplane - "On Jan. 1, 1914, the world's first scheduled passenger airline service took off from St. Petersburg, FL and landed at its destination in Tampa, FL, about 17 miles (27 kilometers) away."[7] We mark 1914 as the emergence date of *Airplane* resource.

First _Near-Earth Orbit Spaceship_ - "The U.S.S.R. launched the world's first multi-manned spacecraft, Voskhod I ... on October 13, 1964."[8] We mark 1964 as the emergence date of _Near-Earth Orbit Spaceship_ resource.

Transport Driving Force

In the family of resources _Transport Driving Force_ humankind created the following resources: _Rutway for Cargo and Ships, Train with Engine, Transport from Earth to Moon._

First _Rutway for Cargo and Ships_ - The Greek example of a rutway is "the famous Diolkos or railed way across the Isthmus of Corinth ... Archaic letters or monograms cut on many of the stones, interpreted by Verdelis as instructions to the operators ... They, and associated pottery, date the Diolkos to the sixth century BC, in or after the time of Periander, tyrant of Corinth about 600 BC." The carriage was "propelled by horse or by man power".[9]   We mark 600 BC as the emergence date of _Rutway for Cargo and Ships_ resource.

First _Train with Engine_ - "Richard Trevithick, British mechanical engineer and inventor who successfully harnessed high-pressure steam and constructed the world's first steam railway locomotive (1803)."[10] We mark 1803 AD as the emergence date of _Train with Engine_ resource.

First _Transport from Earth to the Moon_ - "The Apollo 10 mission encompassed all aspects of an actual crewed lunar landing, except the landing. It was the first flight of a complete, crewed Apollo spacecraft to operate around the Moon ... Apollo 10 launched from Cape Kennedy on May 18, 1969."[11]   We mark 1969 as the emergence date of _Transport from Earth to the Moon_ resource.

Direction of Movement

In the family of resources _Direction of Movement_ humankind created the following resources: _Elevator, Ground Vehicle with an Engine,_ and _Transport from Moon Orbit to the Moon._

First _Elevator_ - "According to [Vitruvius writings in 236 BC] ... Archimedes designed a primitive lift driven by lifting ropes wrapped around a drum and rotated by human force applied to a winch."[12]

The Roman Coliseum used lifts to raise gladiators and wild animals up from the lower levels to the arena level. "Investigation revealed that there were somewhere between 24 and 28 lifts specifically designed to transport up to 600 pounds each—the average weight of two lions ... Using Beste's findings and ancient texts (including the works of Vitruvius) as guides, Glassman and the documentary team constructed the lift ... The documentary team even put the lift into practice in the film, releasing a wolf onto the Colosseum's floor."[13] "Construction of the Colosseum was begun sometime between 70 and 72 CE ... The structure was officially dedicated in 80 CE by Titus."[14]   Much more is known about Colosseum lifts than about Archimedes lifts. We mark 80-72 as the emergence date of *Elevator* resource.

First *Ground Vehicle with an Engine* - "On 5 August 1888, Bertha Benz, wife of inventor Karl Benz, drove from Mannheim to Pforzheim with her sons Richard and Eugen, over distance 65 miles."[15,16]   We mark 1888 as the emergence date of *Ground Vehicle with an Engine* resource.

First *Transport from Moon Orbit to the Moon* - The primary objective of Apollo 11 was to ... perform a crewed lunar landing and return to Earth ... Apollo 11 launched from Cape Kennedy on July 16, 1969 ... On July 20 ... Partially piloted manually by Armstrong, the Eagle landed in the Sea of Tranquility ... Armstrong stepped onto the moon. About 20 minutes later, Aldrin followed him ... Apollo 11 [returned to Earth] on July 24, 1969."[17]   We mark 1969 as the emergence date of *Transport from Moon Orbit to the Moon* resource.

Driverless Vehicle

In the family of resources *Driverless Vehicle* humankind created the following resource: *Drive-less Approved Vehicle with an Engine*.

First *Driverless Approved Vehicle with an Engine* - is "the world's first purpose-built autonomous robotaxi without traditional driving controls to traverse open public roads with passengers, according to the company. It has undergone thousands of testing scenarios and in July became the first vehicle of its kind to be self-certified by its company to Federal Motor Vehicle Safety Standards, according to Zoox."[18] We mark 2023 as the emergence date of *Driverless Approved Vehicle with an Engine* resource.

All physical systems can be thought of as registering and processing information.

Seth Lloyd

Chapter 2.8.
External Information Storage and Processing

The history of the *External* [to the human body] *Information Storage and Processing* class of resources began with the emergence of resource *Text (Writing, Writing Medium)* in 3200-3100 BC.

More than ten resources were created by humankind in the *External Information Storage and Processing* class of resources during the last 44 thousand years.

We could divide the *External Information Storage and Processing* class of resources into four families of resources. Here are those families in the order of their chronological appearance in humankind's history: *Information Types, Types of Recording, Transforming, and Retrieving Information, Categories of Storage Devices,* and *Types of Inventories of Recorded Information.*

Information Types

In the family of resources *Information Types* humankind created the following resources: *Art,* and *Text. Art* was described in the Chapter 1.1. *Art and Music.*

First *Text (First Writing, First Writing Medium)* - Cuneiform writing was "first developed around 3200 B.C. by Sumerian scribes in the ancient city-state of Uruk, in present-day Iraq."[1] "The people of Sumer, in the ancient Near East – present-day Iraq -created the first script around 3100 B.C."[2] We mark 3200-3100 BC as the emergence date of *Text (Writing, Writing Medium)* resource.

We also mark 3200-3100 BC as the emergence date of the External Information Storage and Processing class of resources.

Types of Inventories of Recorded Information

In the family of resources *Types of Inventories of Recorded Information* humankind created the following resources: *Library,* and *Database.*

First *Library* - The first world libraries were Ebla Archives and Temple Library of Nippur. Ebla was a large walled city in Syria. The Sumerian city of Nippur was a religious center of Mesopotamia.

"The Ebla tablets cover about 150 years, estimated at 2500 to 2360 b.c.e. by one archaeologist, and 2400 to 2250 b.c.e., by another. We know that Ebla was first destroyed around 2200 b.c.e., so it seems the latter dating of Ebla's tablets is probably correct."[3] " 'The Age of the Older Temple Library of Nippur' is next considered, and proofs are advanced that all the tablets from the said library date from the times of the second dynasty of Ur, and the first of Isin (2700-2400 B. C)."[4] We mark 2700-2400 BC as the emergence date of *Library* resource.

First *Database* - "Charlie Bachman and other others from GE's Corporate Services set out to solve the problem. By 1964 they had created and put into production a generic manufacturing system (MIACS), a transaction-oriented operating system, and the first database management system (IDS), all running an 8K GE 225 computer."[5,6] We mark 1964 as the emergence date of *Database* resource.

Types of Recording, Transforming, and Retrieving Information

In the family of resources *Types of Recording, Transforming, and Retrieving Information* humankind created the following resources: *Writing, Printing, Typing, Machine Translation, Search Engine,* and *Virtual Keyboard Typing. Writing* was described in the *Text* section.

First *Printing (Printing Medium)* - "The oldest existing print done with wood-blocks is the Mugujeonggwang great Dharani sutra."[7] It was found in 1966. "The scroll bears no date, but it includes certain special forms of characters created and used when Empress Wu (r. +680-704) was ruling in China. It is believed that this charm must have been printed no earlier than + 705, when the translation of sutra was finished, and no later than + 751, when the building of the temple and stupa was completed."[8] We mark 751-705 BC as the emergence date of *Printing (Printing Medium)* resource.

First _Typing_ - "The real breakthrough was in 1868 when Americans Christopher Latham Sholes, Frank Haven Hall, Carlos Glidden, and Samuel W. Soule from Milwaukee, Wisconsin, patented the first commercially successful typewriter. They created the Sholes and Glidden Typewriter, produced by E. Remington and Sons. They invented the typewriter version that most resemble the typewriters we have today. Their machines also had a QWERTY keyboard, the first of its kind. With the commercial success of their typewriters, QWERTY ended up being adopted as the standard for the keyboard."[9] We mark 1868 as the emergence date of _Typing_ resource.

First _Machine Translation_ - "New York, January 7... Russian was translated into English by an electronic 'brain' today for the first time... A girl who didn't understand a word of the language of the Soviets punched out the Russian messages on IBM cards. The 'brain' dashed off its English translations on an automatic printer at the breakneck speed of two and a half lines per second." [10] We mark 1954 as the emergence date of _Machine Translation_ resource.

First _Search Engine_ - " In 1989, [Alan] Emtage ... wrote some code that would do the searching for him, and named his FTP search engine "ARCHIE" (after "archive", without the "v".) ... [At the time Alan Emtage] was graduate student at McGill University in Montreal, where he'd moved from his native Barbados."[11] We mark 1989 as the emergence date of _Search Engine_ resource.

First _Virtual Keyboard Typing_ - Unlike traditional hardware keyboards, a virtual keyboard is an on-screen graphical representation of a keyboard. An optical virtual keyboard was invented by Hans E. Korth and patented by IBM in 1992.[12] We mark 1992 as the emergence date of _Virtual Keyboard Typing_ resource.

Categories of Storage Devices

In the family of resources _Categories of Storage Devices_ humankind created the following resources: _Writing Medium, Printing Medium, Magnetic Storage Device, Semiconductor Storage Device, Optical Storage Device, Biological Storage Device, Data storage with projected lifespan of 13.8 billion years. Writing Medium_ was described in the _Text_ section. _Printing Medium_ was described in the _Printing_ section.

First _Magnetic Storage Device_ - " The first functioning magnetic recorder was built in 1898 by Valdemar Poulsen, a Danish engineer... He filed a patent application in Germany on December 9, 1898, eight days after the Danish application."[13] We mark 1898 as the emergence date of *Magnetic Storage Device* resource.

First *Semiconductor Storage Device* - "Semiconductor IC [integrated circuit] memory concepts were patented as early as 1963. Commercial chips appeared in 1965 when Signetics, Sunnyvale, CA produced an 8-bit scratchpad memory."[14] We mark 1965 as the emergence date of *Semiconductor Storage Device* resource.

First *Optical Storage Device* - "[During the work at Battelle Memorial Institute], James Russell "succeeded in inventing the first digital-to-optical recording and playback system (the earliest patent by Russell, US3501586, was filed in 1966, and granted in 1970)."[15] We mark 1966 as the emergence date of *Optical Storage Device* resource.

First *Biological Storage Device* - "The Microvenus data base describes a graphic icon that is identical to an ancient Germanic rune... The Microvenus was created by converting this graphic image into a early understood sequence of DNA base pairs... Microvenus plasmids were cloned into several laboratory strains of E. coli (with molecular geneticist Dana Boyd) at Jon Beckwith's laboratory at Harvard Medical School in the spring of 1988 and again at Alexander Rich's Laboratory of Molecular Structure at MIT."[16] We mark 1988 as the emergence date of *Biological Storage Device* resource.

First *Data Storage with a Projected Lifespan of 13.8 Billion Years* - "The storage allows unprecedented properties including 360 TB/disc data capacity, thermal stability up to 1,000°C and virtually unlimited lifetime at room temperature (13.8 billion years at 190°C) opening a new era of eternal data archiving."[17] "In 2018, The Arch Mission Foundation delivered the first library in space, with SpaceX, when it launched a small quartz crystal containing the three books of the Isaac Asimov Foundation Trilogy, into 30 million year solar orbit, in the glove compartment of Elon Musk's tesla. Quartz silica glass is the same material used to make spacecraft windows and is extremely durable in space. Data written into nanogratings in quartz has a projected lifetime of 14B years."[18] We mark 2018 as the emergence date of *Data Storage with a Projected Lifespan of 13.8 Billion Years* resource.

Next Eight
Classes of Resources

War is the statesman's game, the priest's delight, the lawyer's jest, the hired assassin's trade.

Percy Bysshe Shelley

Chapter 2.9.
War and Means of Warfare

The history of the *War and Means of Warfare* class of resources began with the emergence of resource *Conventional War* at around 2700 BC.

More than ten resources were created by humankind in the *War and Means of Warfare* class of resources during the last 44 thousand years.

We could divide the *War and Means of Warfare* class of resources into two families of resources. Here are those families in the order of their chronological appearance in humankind's history: *Types of War,* and *Categories of Means of Warfare.*

Types of War

In the family of resources *Types of War* humankind created the following resources: *Conventional War, Total War, War over the Sacred (not Material) Thing, World War, Proxy War,* and *Nuclear War.* A *Nuclear War* is described in a *Nuclear Warfare* section.

First *Conventional War* - "Conventional weapons refer to weapons that are not weapons of mass destruction."[1] "A weapon of mass destruction is a nuclear, radiological, chemical, biological, or other device that is intended to harm a large number of people."[2] At around 2700 BC, Sumerian king Mebaragesi began a war against Elamites. Sumerians won this war between Sumer and Elam.[3] We mark 2700 BC as the emergence date of *Conventional War* resource.

We also mark 2700 BC as the emergence date of the <u>War and Means of Warfare</u> *class of resources.*

First *Total War* – "Total war is a military conflict in which nations mobilize all available resources in order to destroy another nation's ability to engage in war. The first documented total war was the Peloponnesian War, as described by the historian, Thucydides. This war was fought between Athens and Sparta between 431 and 404 B.C.E. Previously, Greek Warfare was a limited and ritualized form of conflict. Armies of hoplites would meet on the battlefield and decide the outcome in a single day. During the Peloponnesian War, however, the fighting lasted for years and consumed the economic resources of the participating city-states. Atrocities were committed on a scale never before seen, with entire populations being executed or sold into slavery, as in the case of the city of Melos."[4] We mark 431 BC as the emergence date of *Total War* resource.

First *War over the Sacred (not Material) Thing* - "What happens when there is a clash between different systems of meanings around sacred issues? ... Since in wars over the sacred there is no ultimate price that can be paid - any price is acceptable for the sake of the Sacred - the direst scenario can be expected... It turns out that there is no compromise between them. Communities can discuss interests, but not the sources of their political language. In other words, in a war like the Crusade... one symbolic system must disappear and the population that constituted its material cause be absorbed into another community. Therefore, this is the ultimate war, because it is a war without rules ..., a war in which compromise is impossible. It is a war in which violence has no rational limit, a war to the last subject carrier of identity ... There is no political goal to which violence is proportionate in the war of the Crusade."[5] " The armies of the great princes mobilized [for the First Crusade] between August and December 1096."[6] We mark 1096 as the emergence date of *War over the Sacred (not Material) Thing* resource.

First *World War* - World war is "a war engaged in by all or most of the principal nations of the world."[7] June 28, 1914 - "Archduke Francis Ferdinand is assassinated."[8] We mark 1914 as the emergence date of *World War* resource.

First *Proxy War* - Proxy war is "a war fought between groups or smaller countries that each represent the interests of other larger powers, and may have help and support from these."[9] "The First Indochina War was one of the first proxy wars of the Cold War. "[10] " The French Indochina War broke out in 1946 and went on for eight years, with France's war effort largely funded and supplied by the United States. Finally, with their shattering defeat by the Viet Minh at the Battle of Dien Bien Phu in May 1954, the French came to the end of their rule in Indochina."[11] We mark 1946 as the emergence date of *Proxy War* resource.

Categories of Means of Warfare

In the family of resources *Categories of Means of Warfare* humankind created the following resources: *Asymmetrical Warfare, Non-Kinetic Weapons, Warfare with a Use of Gunpowder, Biological Warfare, Information Warfare, Economic Warfare, Chemical Warfare, Nuclear Warfare, Cyber Warfare, Lethal Autonomous Weapon Systems, Radiological Warfare.*

First *Asymmetric Warfare* - Asymmetrical Warfare is "unconventional strategies and tactics adopted by a force when the military capabilities of belligerent powers are not simply unequal but are so significantly different that they cannot make the same sorts of attacks on each other... In the 6th century BCE Darius I of Persia, at the head of the largest and most powerful army in existence at the time, was checked by the Scythians, who possessed a smaller but far more mobile force. As recounted by Herodotus in Book IV of his History, the Scythians retreated before the main body of the Persian army, drawing it deeper into Scythian territory, only to launch lethal mounted strikes on Persian encampments. Darius was forced to retire."[12] With a reference to Herbst L. "the Scythian attack [was dated] back to 513 [BC]."[13] We mark 513 BC as the emergence date of *Asymmetrical Warfare* resource.

First *Economic Warfare* - Economic Warfare is "the use of, or the threat to use, economic means against a country in order to weaken its economy and thereby reduce its political and military power."[14] "Athens imposed economic sanctions in 432 BC when Pericles issued the Megarian import embargo against the Greek city-states which had refused to join the Athenian-led Delian League during the Peloponnesian War."[15] We mark 432 BC as the emergence date of *Economic Warfare* resource.

First *Non-Kinetic Weapons* - Incendiary weapons were, probably, the first in category of non-kinetic Warfare. Incendiary weapons designed to start a fire. The so-called " Greek Fire" was invented in Greece. It is not known who exactly created it. There are two contradictory stories about the origin of it. One story told us that in 660 AD, a man named Kalinkos invented the Greek Fire. He probably was either a Greek architect or a Syrian alchemist. The other story tells us that the Syrian engineer Callinicus invented it in 673 AD. Callinicus was a refugee. But some researchers believe that the creation of the Greek Fire was done by a group of people. Greek Fire was a naval weapon. Greek Fire could float on water. The water alone could not extinguish Greek

Fire. It would ignite upon contact and adhere to surfaces of boats and ships. It was first used at around 673 AD.[16] We mark 673 as the emergence date of *Non-Kinetic Weapons* resource.

First *Warfare with a Use of Gunpowder* - Gunpowder was invented in China. "In 904, at the end of the Tang dynasty, a famous commander named Yang Xingmi was attacking a city, and one of his officers ordered troops to "shoot off a machine to let fly fire and burn the Longsha Gate." Scholars have suggested that this passage may refer to the use of gunpowder arrows... In 970 - very early in gunpowder history - a certain Feng Jisheng was sent by the head of a weapons manufacturing bureau to demonstrate for the emperor a new type of gunpowder arrow."[17]   We mark 904 - 970 as the emergence date of *Warfare with a Use of Gunpowder* resource.

First *Biological Warfare* - "Biological Warfare is the deliberate use of disease-causing biological agents such as bacteria, virus, rickettsiae, and fungi, or their toxins, to kill or incapacitate humans, animals, or plants as an act of war."[18] "One of the first recorded uses of biological Warfare occurred in 1347, when Mongol forces are reported to have catapulted plague-infested bodies over the walls into the Black Sea port of Caffa (now Feodosiya, Ukraine), at that time a Genoese trade centre in the Crimean Peninsula."[19]   We mark 1347 as the emergence date of *Biological Warfare* resource.

First *Information Warfare* - "Information Warfare is a generally Western, late-20th century military term that encompasses a wide range of non-kinetic forms of human conflict."[20] Ems telegram is "a report of an encounter between King William I of Prussia and the French ambassador; the telegram was sent from Ems (Bad Ems) in the Prussian Rhineland on July 13, 1870, to the Prussian chancellor, Otto von Bismarck. ... A telegram describing the incident was sent to Bismarck. Bismarck's edited version, which he published the next day, omitted the courtesies in the two men's exchange and instead made it seem that each man had insulted the other. This touched off an intensified demand for war in Paris and Berlin, and France declared war on July 19."[21] We mark 1870 as the emergence date of *Information Warfare* resource.

First Chemical Warfare - "Chemical weapon, any of several chemical compounds, usually toxic agents, that are intended to kill, injure, or incapacitate enemy personnel."[22] "[On April 22, 1915] the German military launches the first large-scale use of chemical weapons in war at Ypres, Belgium. Nearly 170 metric tons of chlorine gas in 5,730 cylinders are buried along a four-mile stretch of the front. In the end more than 1,100 people are killed by the attack and 7,000 are injured."[23] We mark 1915 as the emergence date of *Chemical Warfare* resource.

First *Nuclear Warfare* – A nuclear weapon is "a device designed to release energy in an explosive manner as a result of nuclear fission, nuclear fusion, or a combination of the two processes. Fission weapons are commonly referred to as atomic bombs. Fusion weapons are also referred to as thermonuclear bombs or, more commonly, hydrogen bombs."[24] "The first atomic bomb detonated over a populated area occurred on August 6, 1945 at 8:15 AM over the Japanese city of Hiroshima."[25] A nuclear war is a war in which countries fight with nuclear weapons. In 1945, during World War II, nuclear Warfare was used by only one country, the USA. We mark 1945 as the emergence date of *Nuclear Warfare* resource.

First *Cyber Warfare* - "Cyber Warfare involves the actions by a nation-state or international organization to attack and attempt to damage another nation's computers or information networks through, for example, computer viruses or denial-of-service attacks."[26] "Cyber Warfare began in 2010 with Stuxnet, which was the first cyber weapon meant to cause physical damage. Stuxnet is reported to have destroyed 20% of the centrifuges Iran used to create its nuclear arsenal."[27] "Stuxnet is a malicious computer worm that became infamous in its use to attack Iranian nuclear facilities."[28] We mark 2010 as the emergence date of *Cyber Warfare* resource.

First *Lethal Autonomous Weapon Systems* - "Lethal autonomous weapon systems (LAWS) are a special class of weapon systems that use sensor suites and computer algorithms to independently identify a target and employ an onboard weapon system to engage and destroy the target without manual human control of the system."[29] "The first use of an autonomous weapon to kill is thought to have occurred in March of 2020 in Libya, but what actually happened in remains murky. According to a UN report, a Turkish-made Kargu-2 drone is reported to have autonomously 'hunted down' members of the Libyan National Army... Turkey denies using the Kargu-2 in this way, though seems to acknowledge the Kargu-2 can be used autonomously".[30] We mark 2020 as the emergence date of *Lethal Autonomous Weapon Systems* resource.

First *Threat of Radiological Warfare Use* - Radiological Warfare is "radioactivity (excluding nuclear bombs) as a means of Warfare...The use of radiological Warfare is becoming a viable possibility as more countries are gaining the technology and materials needed for radioactive weaponry."[31] "Ever since its seizure by Russian forces in March 2022, the Zaporizhzhia nuclear power plant—Europe's largest, with six reactors—has posed a serious danger of a radioactive disaster. Now, Ukrainian officials have charged that Russia has rigged the plant with explosives."[32] We mark 2022 as the emergence date of *Threat of Radiological Warfare Use* resource.

The limits of my language mean the limits of my world.

Ludwig Wittgenstein

Chapter 2.10.
Transnational Entities

The history of the *Transnational Entities* class of resources began with the emergence of resource *Treaty between City-States* at around 29000 BC.

More than ten resources were created by humankind in the class of resources *Transnational Entities* during the last 44 thousand years.

We could divide the *Transnational Entities* class of resources into six families of resources. Here are those families in the order of their chronological appearance in humankind's history: *Empires, International Treaties, World Religions (Each Over 6% of the World Religious Population), Alliances, International Organizations, Global International Organizations, and Global Networks.*

International Treaties

In the family of resources *International Treaties* humankind created the following resources: *Treaty between City-states, Treaty between Nations,* and *Framework for International Monetary Policy, Commerce, and Finance.*

First *Treaty between City-States* - "Mesilim [or Mesalim, born ca. 2600 B.C.] was the ruler of Kish, a kingdom north of Lagashand Umma.... The Mesilim Treaty, concluded in the 25th century B.C. [2550 B.C.] between the two Mesopotamian states of Lagash and Umma."[1]   We mark 2550 BC as the emergence date of *Treaty between City-States* resource. *We also mark 2550 BC as the emergence date of the* Transnational Entities *class of resources.*

First *Treaty between Nations* - "In 1259 BC, 15 years after the battle of Qadesh, the Hittite king Hattusili III drew up a treaty with the pharaoh Ramesses II.1... Two independent versions were composed, one in the Hittite capital Hattusa, the other in Ramesses' capital Pi-Ramesse."[2] We mark 1259 BC as the emergence date of *Treaty between Nations* resource.

First *Framework for International Monetary Policy, Commerce, and Finance* - "The Bretton Woods Conference, officially known as the United Nations Monetary and Financial Conference, was a gathering of delegates from 44 nations that met from July 1 to 22, 1944 in Bretton Woods, New Hampshire, to agree upon a series of new rules for the post-WWII international monetary system. The two major accomplishments of the conference were the creation of the International Monetary Fund (IMF) and the International Bank for Reconstruction and Development (IBRD)."[3]   We mark 1944 as the emergence date of *Framework for International Monetary Policy, Commerce, and Finance* resource.

Empires

In the family of resources *Empires* humankind created the following resources: *Empire, Colonial Empire.*

First *Empire* - The Akkadian Empire was the first empire in the history of humankind. It was the first empire of Mesopotamia. The central city was Akkad. The empire expanded over neighboring territories. That empire united people who had spoken Akkadian and Sumerian languages under one rule. "The... period (ca. 2350–2150 B.C.) is named after the city of Agade (or Akkad), whose Semitic monarchs united the region, bringing the rival Sumerian cities under their control by conquest."[4] We mark 2350 - 2150 BC as the emergence date of *Empire* resource.

First *Colonial Empire* - "Empire is rule over peoples; colonialism is the acquisition of territory for the purposes of settlement and cultivation."[5] W. Y. Adams argues that the first colonial empire was set up by Egypt in neighboring Nubia in 3200 – 1200 BC.[6] We will follow a more common point of view that the first colonial empire was the Portuguese empire. "The Portuguese Colonial Empire was one of the longest-lived empires in European History. Starting in the beginning of the 'Age of Discovery,' with the conquest of Ceuta in 1415, it lasted until 1999, with the transfer of Macau to China."[7]   We mark 1415 as the emergence date of *Colonial Empire* resource.

World Religions
(Each over 6% of World Religious Population)

In the family of resources *World Religions* humankind created the following resources: *World Religion,* and *World Monotheistic Religion.* "The religious profile of the world is rapidly changing... With the help of data from Pew Research Center, we break down the religious composition of the major religions in countries worldwide... Around 31% of the world's population are Christians, 25% are Muslims, 15.2% are Hindus, 6.6% are Buddhists."[8] We will consider only world religions with over 6% of the world population each.

First *World Religion* - "If the Indus valley civilization (3rd–2nd millennium BCE) was the earliest source of these traditions, as some scholars hold, then Hinduism is the oldest living religion on Earth."[9] "The philological and linguistic evidence indicates that the Rig Veda is one of the oldest existing texts in any Indo-European language and that probably originated from the region of present day Pakistan, between 1500 and 1200 BCE."[10] We mark 1500-1200 BC as the emergence date of *World Religion* resource.

First *World Monotheistic Religion* - Council of Jerusalem is "a conference of the Christian Apostles in Jerusalem about 50 CE that decreed that Gentile Christians did not have to observe the Mosaic Law of the Jews."[11] "The Apostle Peter said that... Christians converted from pagan religions did not have to keep the rituals of the law of Moses... St. James approved the opinion of the Apostle Peter... This proposal of the Apostle James was accepted by the apostles, presbyters, and the whole Council unanimously as a resolution of the Council. It was made known to all Christians in a Council decree."[12] We mark 50 as the emergence date of *World Monotheistic Religion* resource.

Alliances

In the family of resources *Alliances* humankind created the following resources: *Multi-City Economic and Defensive Alliance.*

First *Multi-City Economic and Defensive Alliance* - The Hanseatic League was a commercial and defensive coalition of medieval Central and Northern European merchant guilds and market towns. "In 1241 Hamburg joined Luebeck in an alliance which apart from short pauses had endured until the twentieth century."[13] We mark 1241 as the emergence date of *Multi-City Economic and Defensive Alliance* resource.

International Organizations

In the family of resources *International Organizations* humankind created the following resources: *Multinational Corporation*, and *Intergovernmental Organization*.

First *Multinational Corporation* - "The English East India Company, established on December 31, 1600, by a royal charter from Queen Elizabeth I, became one of the most important and influential mercantile companies."[14] We mark 1600 as the emergence date of *Multinational Corporation* resource.

First *Intergovernmental Organization* - "ITU was founded in Paris in 1865 as the International Telegraph Union. It took its present name in 1932."[15] We mark 1865 as the emergence date of *Intergovernmental Organization* resource.

Global International Organizations

In the family of resources *Global International Organizations* humankind created the following resource: *General International Organization*.

First *General International Organization* - "The League of Nations was an international organization, headquartered in Geneva, Switzerland, created [in 1920] after the First World War to provide a forum for resolving international disputes."[16] We mark 1920 as the emergence date of *General International Organization* resource.

Global Networks

In the family of resources *Global Networks* humankind created the following resource: *Global Network (Internet)*.

First *Global Network (Internet)* - "January 1, 1983 is considered the official birthday of the Internet. Prior to this, the various computer networks did not have a standard way to communicate with each other. A new communications protocol was established called Transfer Control Protocol/Internetwork Protocol (TCP/IP). This allowed different kinds of computers on different networks to "talk" to each other. ARPANET and the Defense Data Network officially changed to the TCP/IP standard on January 1, 1983, hence the birth of the Internet. All networks could now be connected by a universal language."[17] We mark 1983 as the emergence date of *Global Network (Internet)* resource.

Exploitation and domination of one nation over another can have no place in a world striving to put an end to all war.

Mahatma Gandhi

Chapter 2.11.
Usage of People as a Resource
on a Massive Scale

The recorded history of the *Usage of People as a Resource on a Massive Scale* class of resources began with written evidence of resource *Corruption* at around 2100 BC in ancient Egypt.

More than ten resources were created by humankind in the class of resources *Usage of People as a Resource on a Massive Scale* during the last 44 thousand years.

We could divide the *Usage of People as a Resource on a Massive Scale* class of resources into two families of resources. Here are those families of resources in the order of their chronological appearance in humankind's history: *Harm to a Person*, and *Harm to a Group of People*.

Harm to a Person

In the family of resources *Harm to a Person* humankind created the following resources: *Corruption, Sexual Violence (Including Rape),* and *Domestic Violence.*

First *Corruption* - "Corruption is an improper and usually unlawful conduct intended to secure a benefit for oneself or another."[1] "The first obvious allusions to bribery would be reflected in the petitions of the Eloquent Peasant."[2] "Among the few literary compositions which have survived from the Middle Kingdom, the tale of the Eloquent Peasant has the distinction of being one of the longest and the most complete."[3] Based on the style of language —so-called Middle Egyptian— the story [in the Eloquent Peasant] seems to have been drafted not too long after the time in which the action is set ...The action takes place in a region called Henenseten, near the Faiyum oasis southwest of modern Cairo.

Nearby Herakleopolis ... was the capital of the ... IXth and Xth dynasties (2160-2040 BC)."[4] We mark 2160-2040 BC as the emergence date of *Corruption* resource.

We also mark 2160-2040 BC as the emergence date of the <u>People as a Resource on a Massive Scale</u> *class of resources.*

First *Sexual Violence (Including Rape)* - "The first rape law appeared in Babylon, ... in the Code of Hammurabi". "The Code of Hammurabi was an extensive code of civil and criminal laws which were said to have been given to King Hammurabi."[5] "Hammurabi ... - sixth and best-known ruler of the 1st (Amorite) dynasty of Babylon *c.* 1792–1750 BCE."[6]   We mark 1792-1750 BC as the emergence date of *Sexual Violence (Including Rape)* resource.

First *Domestic Violence* - According to Dionysius of Halicarnassus, [7] Romulus law stated that "This law obliged both the married women, as having no other refuge, to conform themselves entirely to the temper of their husbands, and the husbands to rule their wives as necessary and inseparable possessions." Romulus, King of Rome, reigned from 753 to 716 BC.[8] We mark 753-716 BC as the emergence date of *Domestic Violence* resource.

Harm to a Group of People

In the family of resources *Harm to a Group of People* humankind created the following resources: *Slavery, Social Deprivation and Exclusion, Massive Forced Displacement/Deportation, Debt Bondage/Bonded Labor, Genocide, Serfdom, Human Trafficking,* and *Child Labor.*

First *Slavery* - The Laws of Ur-Nammu stated, "If someones's slavewoman, presuming herself to be the equal of her mistress, has sworn at her, she shall scour her mouth with one quart of salt."[9] The common assumption is that Sumerian Ur-Nammu Law Code was written in 2100-2050 BC.[10] We mark 2100-2050 BC as the emergence date of *Slavery* resource.

First *Social Deprivation and Exclusion* - "Social exclusion describes a state in which individuals are unable to participate fully in economic, social, political and cultural life."[11] "It is believed that the caste system began with the arrival of the Aryans in India around 1500 BC."[12] We mark 1500 BC as the emergence date of *Social Deprivation and Exclusion* resource.

First _Massive Forced Displacement/Deportation_ - "Expulsion is an act by a public authority to remove a person or persons against his or her will from the territory of that state. A successful expulsion of a person by a country is called a deportation."[13] "Assyrian imperialism is closely associated with the practice of mass deportation... This paper surveys the evidence of deportation in the Levant in the period 745–620 b.c.e. ...Accordingly, this study restricts itself temporally to the age of Assyrian hegemony (c. 745–620 B.C.E.), when deportation was most intensively practiced and done so in the context of a universal empire."[14] We mark 745-620 BC as the emergence date of _Massive Forced Displacement/Deportation_ resource.

First _Debt Bondage / Bonded Labor_ - "In Ptolematic Egypt, for which we have much information from papyri, there is clear evidence both for outright enslavement for debt and for debt bondage."[15] "The Ptolemaic Kingdom was an Ancient Greek state based in Egypt during the Hellenistic Period. It was founded in 305 BC by Ptolemy I Soter, a companion of Alexander the Great, and lasted until the death of Cleopatra VII in 30 BC."[16] We mark 305-30 BC as the emergence date of _Debt Bondage/Bonded Labor_ resource.

First _Genocide_ - "Rome ... began a three-year siege of the world's wealthiest city. At least 150,000 Carthaginians perished. ... Polybius, who participated in the campaign, confirmed that 'the number of deaths was incredibly large' and the Carthaginians 'utterly exterminated'. " In 146, Roman legions under Scipio Aemilianus, Cato's ally and brother-in-law of his son, razed the city, and dispersed into slavery the 55,000 survivors, including 25,000 women."[17] We mark 146 BC as the emergence date of _Genocide_ resource.

First _Serfdom_ - Massive use of serfs began in medieval times. "Medieval Serfs were unfree labourers who worked the land of a landowner (or tenant) in return for physical and legal protection and the right to work a separate piece of land for their own basic needs. ... Serfs might not have been slaves but they were subject to certain fees and restrictions of movement."[18] Nevertheless, serfdom existed long before the feudal system. "A legal code established by the Roman emperor Constantine in 332 demanded labour services to be paid to the lord by the coloni [the dependent peasant]. Although the coloni were legally free, the conditions of fealty required them to cultivate their lord's untenanted lands as well as their leased plot."[19] We mark 332 as the emergence date of _Serfdom_ resource.

First *Human Trafficking* - "Human Trafficking is the recruitment, transportation, transfer, harbouring or receipt of people through force, fraud or deception, with the aim of exploiting them for profit."[20] Gomes Eannes de Zurara, in his Chronicle ..., described in detail "how the Infant Don Henry made Lançarote a Knight" for a successful delivery of 235 African slaves on ships on August 8, 1444[21]. We mark 1444 as the emergence date of *Human Trafficking* resource.

First *Child Labor* - "Child labour is work carried out to the detriment and endangerment of a child, in violation of international law and national legislation."[23] Child labor was used throughout humankind's history. However, "the classic era of industrialization, 1790-1850, apparently saw an upsurge in child labour."[23] We mark 1790 as the emergence date of *Child Labor* resource.

The desire that guides me in all I do is the desire to harness the forces of nature to the service of Humankind.

Nikola Tesla

Chapter 2.12.

Use of Forces of Nature, Relativity, and Quantum Physics

The history of the *Use of Forces of Nature, Relativity, and Quantum Physics* class of resources began with the emergence of resource *use of gravity* around 1346 - 1334 BC.

Six resources were created by humankind in the *Use of Forces of Nature, Relativity, and Quantum Physics* class of resources during the last 44 thousand years.

We could divide the *Use of Forces of Nature, Relativity, and Quantum Physics* class of resources into two families of resources. Here are those families in the order of their chronological appearance in humankind' history: *Forces of Nature,* and *Main Physics Theories.*

"The four fundamental forces act upon us every day, whether we realize it or not. From playing basketball, to launching a rocket into space, to sticking a magnet on your refrigerator - all the forces that all of us experience every day can be whittled down to a critical quartet: Gravity, the weak force, electromagnetism, and the strong force. These forces govern everything that happens in the universe."[1]

Forces of Nature

In the family of resources *Forces of Nature* humankind created the following resources: *Use of Gravity, Use of Electromagnetism, Use of Strong Nuclear Force,* and *Use of Weak Nuclear Force.*

First Use of Gravity - "Gravity is the attraction between two objects that have mass or energy."[1] You have to overcome gravity to lift something up. Shaduf is a hand-operated device for lifting water. "Only in the Amarna period (ca. 1346-1334 B.C.) ...is the shaduf or pole-and-bucket level, singly capable of raising containers of water well over 1 m, verified by the representational art...."[2] We mark 1346-1334 BC as the emergence date of *Use of Gravity* resource.

We also mark 1346-1334 BC as the emergence date of the Use of Forces of Nature, Relativity, and Quantum Physics class of resources.

First *Use of Electromagnetism* - "The electromagnetic force, ... acts between charged particles... The electromagnetic force consists of two parts: the electric force and the magnetic force. At first, physicists described these forces as separate from one another, but researchers later realized that the two are components of the same force."[1] The first electromagnet was created by William Sturgeon, an English electrical engineer. Sturgeon's paper was published in 1824.[3] We mark 1824 as the emergence date of *Use of Electromagnetism* resource.

First *Use of Strong Nuclear Force* - "The strong nuclear force... is the strongest of the four fundamental forces of nature. That's because it binds the fundamental particles of matter together to form larger particles."[1] "When the strong nuclear force that binds protons and neutrons in an atom is broken, extreme high-energy photons are released in the process."[4] That release of energy is used in nuclear weapons. "On the morning of August 6, 1945, the American B-29 bomber Enola Gay dropped an atomic bomb on the Japanese city of Hiroshima."[5] See also *Nuclear Warfare* in Chapter 1.9. We mark 1945 as the emergence date of *Use of Strong Nuclear Force* resource.

First *Use of Weak Nuclear Force* - The weak force, also called the weak nuclear interaction, is responsible for particle decay. The weak force is critical for the nuclear fusion reactions that power the sun and produce the energy needed for most life forms here on Earth. It's also why archaeologists can use carbon-14 to date ancient bone, wood, and other formerly living artifacts. Carbon-14 has six protons and eight neutrons; one of those neutrons decays into a proton to make nitrogen-14, which has seven protons and seven neutrons. This decay happens at a predictable rate, allowing scientists to determine how old such artifacts are.[1] "In 1946, Willard Libby (1908–1980) developed a method for dating organic materials by measuring their content of carbon-14, a radioactive isotope of carbon... The introduction of radiocarbon dating had an enormous influence on both archaeology and geology—an impact often referred to as the 'radiocarbon revolution.'"[6] We mark 1946 as the emergence date of *Use of Weak Nuclear Force* resource.

Main Physical Theories

In the family of resources *Main Physical Theories* humankind created the following resources: *Use of Quantum Physics,* and *Use of General Relativity.*

First *Use of Quantum Physics* - "Quantum Physics also known as quantum theory or quantum mechanics is a major part of modern physics along with general relativity...Quantum theory is used in many ways in everyday life including lasers, CDs, DVDs, solar cells, fiber-optics etc. ...The phenomenon of band structure, which supports the modern semiconductor- based electronics, is fundamentally a quantum mechanism."[7] The first semiconductor material was made in 1941.[8] See also semiconductor material in Chapter 1.3. We mark 1941 as the emergence date of *Use of Quantum Physics* resource.

First *Use of General Relativity* - A prediction of General Relativity is that clocks closer to a massive object will seem to tick more slowly than those located farther away...As such, when viewed from the surface of the Earth, the clocks on the satellites appear to be ticking faster than identical clocks on the ground...The engineers who designed the GPS system included these relativistic effects when they designed and deployed the system.[9] GPS stands for the Global Positioning System. "The launch of Navstar II-1 on February 14, 1989 was the first GPS Block II satellite placed on orbit."[10] We mark 1989 as the emergence date of *Use of General Relativity* resource.

The root of democracy is in mass education.

Narendra Modi

Chapter 2.13.
Mass Education

The history of the *Mass Education* class of resources began with the emergence of resource *School* at around 1292-1190 BC.

Six resources were created by humankind in the *Mass education* class of resources during the last 44 thousand years.

We could divide the *Mass Education* class of resources into three families of resources. Here are those families in the order of their chronological appearance in humankind's history: *Education Levels, Relation to Society,* and *Distant Education.*

Education Levels

In the family of resources *Education Levels* humankind created the following resources: *School, College (University), and Preschool Education.*

First *School* - First schools emerged in ancient Egypt. People who learned to read and write were called scribes. Scribe schools were organized, and discipline was enforced[1,,2]. In the famous "Satire of Trades" the author, Khety, brought his son to the school for scribes. The date of the composition of the text varies depending on the researchers. We will follow the "Satire on Trades" papyrus in the British Museum, dated by the 19th Dynasty[3]. The Nineteenth Dynasty of Ancient Egypt dates are 1292-1190 BC.[4] We mark 1292 – 1190 BC as the emergence date of *School* resource.

We also mark 1292-1190 BC as the emergence date of the <u>*Mass Education*</u> *class of resources.*

First *College (University)* - "If we use the definition of a university as an institution that grants undergraduate and postgraduate degrees The University of Bologna was founded by Italian jurist, Irnerius, in

1088. Located in Bologna, Italy, this institution holds the record for being the world's oldest university in terms of not having experienced even a brief suspension of its operations since its establishment... It might not be the first but it is undisputedly the oldest in terms of uninterrupted operations." [5] We mark 1088 as the emergence date of *College (University)* resource.

First *Preschool Education* - In 1767, Johann F. Oberlin established, at his own expense, the first school for children under the age of six in a rural coal-mining community in the French countryside.[6] We mark 1767 as the emergence date of *Preschool Education* resource.

Relation to Society

In the family of resources *Relation to Society levels* humankind created the following resources: *Mandatory Public Education,* and *Right to Education.*

First *Mandatory Education* - The Aztec empire in America prospered from the 14th to 16th centuries. In education, the Aztecs were well ahead of many other nations. Aztecs made education for all children a mandatory one. Up to a certain age, all children had to be educated at home. From time to time, they were tested at neighboring temples. The age of 15 was a milestone. All children have to leave their homes and go to and stay at school. [7] There were separate schools for boys and girls, as well as separate schools for nobles and commoners. The Aztec Empire flourished in the Valley of Mexico between A.D. 1325 and 1519.[8]   We mark 1325 - 1519 as the emergence date of *Mandatory Education* resource.

First *Right to Education* – The Universal Declaration of Human Rights declared: "Article 26. Everyone has the right to education. Education shall be free, at least in the elementary and fundamental stages. Elementary education shall be compulsory. Technical and professional education shall be made generally available, and higher education shall be equally accessible to all on the basis of merit." The United Nations General Assembly in Paris proclaimed the Declaration on 10 December 1948.[9] We mark 1948 as the emergence date of *Right to Education* resource.

Distant Education

In the family of resources *Distant Education* humankind created the following resource: *Online Learning*.

First *Online Learning* - Online educational programs emerged in 1989, when the University of Phoenix began using CompuServe, one of the first consumer online services.[10] We mark 1989 as the emergence date of *Online Learning* resource.

A good government is one with many information channels, those that give real-time information.

Narendra Modi

Chapter 2.14.
Independent Communication Channels

The history of the *Independent Communication Channels* class of resources began with the emergence of resource *Post* at around 550 BC.

More than ten resources were created by humankind in the *Independent Communication Channels* class of resources during the last 44 thousand years.

We could divide the *Independent Communication Channels* class of resources into two families of resources. Here are those families in the order of their chronological appearance in humankind's history: *Non-Electronic Communication Channels*, and *Electronic Communication Channels*.

Non-Electronic Communication Channels

In the family of resources *Non-Electronic Communication Channels* humankind created the resource *Post*.

First *Post* - Cyrus, the Persian empire's ruler, established a very efficient postal service at around 550 BC.[1] A courier on a horse had to ride from one posting station to another. At those stations, fresh horses were ready for the rider. Now, the written message could travel about 200 miles a day. The media used to transfer messages were horse riders and post stations. Replacing horses, and even horse riders, provided a high speed of message travel. The post was the first long-distance communication channel independent of the message itself. We mark 550 BC as the emergence date of *Post* resource.

We also mark 550 BC as the emergence date of the Independent Communication Channels class of resources.

Electronic Communication Channels

In the family of resources *Electronic Communication Channels* humankind created the following resources *Telegraph, Fax, Telephone, Radio, Television, Video Conferencing, Email, Global Network (Internet), Cell (Mobile) Phone, Text Message,* and *Communication via Hologram.*

First *Telegraph* - "The first two practical electric telegraphs appeared at almost the same time. In 1837 the British inventors Sir William Fothergill Cooke and Sir Charles Wheatstone obtained a patent on a telegraph system...In 1832 Samuel F.B. Morse, a professor of painting and sculpture at the University of the City of New York (later New York University), became interested in the possibility of electric telegraphy and made sketches of ideas for such a system. In 1835 he devised a system of dots and dashes to represent letters and numbers. In 1837 he was granted a patent on an electromagnetic telegraph."[2] We mark 1837 as the emergence date of *Telegraph* resource.

First *Fax* - "The fax, or "facsimile," machine sends text or graphic messages from a scanner through the phone line to a printer, which can print out the message on standard paper for the recipient to read.[3] "The earliest form of the fax machine is attributed to Scottish inventor Alexander Bain (1818-1903). In 1843 Bain created and patented a device that simulated a two-dimensional image, making significant improvements on the telegraph...In 1863 Italian abbot Giovanni Caselli (1851-1891) created the first commercial facsimile system, first used in France between the cities of Paris and Lyon."[4] We mark 1843-1863 as the emergence date of *Fax* resource.

First *Telephone* - "Antonio Meucci, an Italian immigrant, began developing the design of a talking telegraph or telephone in 1849. In 1871, he filed a caveat (an announcement of an invention) for his design of a talking telegraph. Due to hardships, Meucci could not renew his caveat. His role in the invention of the telephone was overlooked until the United States House of Representatives passed a Resolution on June 11, 2002, honoring Meucci's contributions and work. You can read the resolution (107th Congress, H Res 269) on Congress.gov."[5] Alexander Graham Bell was awarded the first U.S. patent for the invention of the telephone in 1876. We mark 1876 as the emergence date of *Telephone* resource.

First *Radio* - "In 1893 the inventor Nikolai Tesla demonstrated a wireless radio in St. Louis, Missouri. Despite this demonstration, it was Guglielmo Marconi who is often credited as the father and inventor of the radio. One of these reasons was that he was given the very first wireless telegraphy patent in England in the year 1896. A year later, however, Tesla filed for patents for his basic radio in the U.S., and they were granted in 1900. On December 12, 1901, Marconi's place in history was forever sealed when he became the first person to transmit signals across the Atlantic Ocean."[6] We mark 1896 as the emergence date of *Radio* resource.

First *Television* - *Television* was described in the *Television* section in Chapter 1.1. We mark 1927 as the emergence date of *Television* resource.

First *Video Conferencing* - "In 1927 Bell Labs connected Secretary of Commerce Herbert Hoover and other officials in Washington, D.C., with AT&T president Walter Gifford in New York City; the two-way audio connection was accompanied by a one-way video connection from Washington. D.C., to New York." [7] We mark 1927 as the emergence date of *Video Conferencing* resource.

First *Email* - "We have Ray Tomlinson to thank for initiating the incredible new era of communication that we now enjoy – he sent the First email in 1971...Email was initially seen as a speedy way for ARPANET programmers and researchers to keep in touch."[8] We mark 1971 as the emergence date of *Email* resource.

First *Global Network (Internet)* - *Global Network (Internet)* was described in the *Global network (Internet)* section in Chapter 1.10. We mark 1983 as the emergence date of *Global Network (Internet)* resource.

First *Cell (Mobile) Phone* - "Motorola developed the first portable cell phone in 1973. The hand-held device was shaped like a brick and weighed around 2.4 pounds. It was called the DynaTAC 8000X... The very first call that was made was by Martin Cooper .... He called Dr. Joel Engel, an engineer at their rival business, Bell Labs."[9] We mark 1973 as the emergence date of *Cell (Mobile) Phone* resource.

First *Text Message* - "In 1992, Neil Papworth, a 22-year-old software programmer from the UK, sent the first ever text message from a computer to his colleague Richard Jarvis. Neil had been working as a developer and test engineer to create a Short Message Service (SMS) for his client, Vodafone. That very first text, sent on the 3rd December 1992, simply said, 'Merry Christmas.'"[10] We mark 1992 as the emergence date of *Text Message* resource.

First *Communication via Hologram* - "Historian Yuval Noah Harari steps into the future — by speaking as a hologram at TED2018: The Age of Amazement, April 11, 2018, in Vancouver. Photo: Bret Hartman / TED".[11] We mark 2018 as the emergence date of *Communication via Hologram* resource.

It never ceases to amaze me what it takes to develop and bring to mass production a product.

Jonathan Ive

Chapter 2.15.
Mass Production

The history of the *Mass Production* class of resources began with the emergence of resource *Standardized Parts* at around 1320.

Nine resources were created by humankind in the *Mass Production* class of resources during the last 44 thousand years.

We could divide the *Mass Production* class of resources into two families of resources. Here are those families in the order of their chronological appearance in humankind's history: *Mass Production Techniques,* and *Manufacturing Engineering.*

Mass Production Techniques

In the family of resources *Mass Production Techniques* humankind created the following resources: *Standardized Parts, Prefabrication, Division and Specialization of Human Labor, Use of Specialized Machinery, Use of Machine Tools, Use of Energy to Run Machines,* and *Precision Interchangeable Parts.*

First *Standardized Parts* - "Standardized parts – The [Venetian] Arsenal introduced the use of standardized parts in ship building".[1] "It was in 1320 that the Arsenal became Venice's premier shipbuilding facility."[2] We mark 1320 as the emergence date of *Standardized Parts* resource.

We also mark 1320 as the emergence date of the Mass Production class of resources.

First *Prefabrication* - "At the Arsenal, shipbuilding parts were standardized, and each major component of this early bill of materials was produced by a specialized team of workers. The necessary parts were then assembled by another team, following which the ship would be moved to another part of the work buildings for furnishing."[3] "It was in 1320 that the Arsenal became Venice's premier shipbuilding facility."[2] We mark 1320 as the emergence date of *Prefabrication* resource.

First *Division and Specialization of Human Labor* - *Division and Specialization of Human Labor* was described in the *Prefabrication* section in this Chapter. We mark 1320 as the emergence date of *Division and Specialization of Human Labor* resource.

First *Use of Specialized Machinery* - " The flying shuttle was invented by John Kay in 1733; this machine represented an important step toward automatic weaving."[4] We mark 1733 as the emergence date of *Use of Specialized Machinery* resource.

First *Use of Machine Tools* - "Invention of machine tools – the first machine tools were invented included the screw-cutting lathe, the cylinder boring machine, and the milling machine. Machine tools made the economical manufacture of precision metal parts possible, although it took several decades to develop effective techniques."[5] "John Wilkinson invents the first machine tool: a boring machine for cylinders and cannons in 1774."[6] We mark 1774 as the emergence date of *Use of Machine Tools* resource.

First *Use of Energy to Run Machines* - James Watt was "Scottish instrument maker and inventor whose steam engine contributed substantially to the Industrial Revolution... In 1782, at the height of his inventive powers, he [James Watt] patented the double-acting engine, in which the piston pushed as well as pulled."[1] Such an engine could be used to directly drive the rotary machinery of a factory or mill.[7] We mark 1782 as the emergence date of *Use of Energy to Run Machines* resource.

First *Precision Interchangeable Parts* - "In 1803, Marc Brunel, famous engineer, along with the help of others was first able to mass-produce interchangeable parts. He streamlined a process of creating pulley blocks for naval shipyards using metal machines and a crew of only 10 men... By 1816, a man by the name of Simeon North had created the world's first metal milling machine. This machine allowed manufacturers to create parts with tight tolerances, which would've been a key aspect needed to create metal interchangeable parts on a large scale."[8] "It appears that all the essential elements of the modern milling machine existed at Simeon North's factory no later than 1831 or 1832."[9] We mark 1803-1832 as the emergence date of *Precision Interchangeable Parts* resource.

Manufacturing Engineering

In the family of resources _Manufacturing Engineering_ humankind created the following resources: _Production Factory,_ and _Modern Production Factory._

First _Production Factory_ - The Venetian Arsenal "had similarities to the modern way of producing goods using both the mass production and lean techniques: standardized parts..., moving assembly line..., continuous improvement..., engineering with production in mind..."[1] We mark 1320 as the emergence date of _Production Factory_ resource.

First _Modern Production Factory_ - Mass production is an "application of the principles of specialization, division of labour, and standardization of parts to the manufacture of goods. Such manufacturing processes attain high rates of output at low unit cost, with lower costs expected as volume rises... Much of the credit for bringing these early concepts together in a coherent form, and creating the modern, integrated, mass production operation, belongs to the U.S. industrialist Henry Ford and his colleagues at the Ford Motor Company, where in 1913 a moving-belt conveyor was used in the assembly of flywheel magnetos."[10] We mark 1913 as the emergence date of _Modern Production Factory_ resource.

There's plenty to criticize about the mass media, but they are the source of regular information about a wide range of topics.

Noam Chomsky

Chapter 2.16.
Mass Media

The history of the *Mass Media* class of resources began with the emergence of resource *Mass Printing* around 1455.

There are different opinions on what constitutes mass media. Tomi Ahonen coined the term "Seventh of the Mass Media" in 2006.[1] That implies the existence of six other types of mass media. [2] First six were prints, recordings, cinema, radio, television, and the Internet. The seventh one is mobile phones.

Seven resources were created by humankind in the *Mass Media* class of resources during the last 44 thousand years.

We will correlate the *Mass Media* class of resources with one family of resources *Mass Media*.

Mass Media

In the family of resources *Mass Media* humankind created the following resources: *Mass Printing, Recording, Film, Radio, Television, Global Network (Internet), Cell (Mobile) Phone.*

First *Mass Printing* - "Johannes Gutenberg is known as the Father of Printing" because he was the first to combine the use of molded movable metal type, a press, and printer's ink."[3] "Metal moveable type was developed in Korea in the 13th century...Gutenberg's invention allowed the mass production of books for the first time and changed the world. Before Gutenberg, every book (outside of Asia where some printed books had been produced much earlier) had to be copied by hand. Now it was possible to speed up the process without sacrificing quality. The Gutenberg Bible was printed in Mainz in 1455 by Johann Gutenberg and his associates, Johann Fust and Peter Schoeffer."[4] We mark 1455 as the emergence date of *Mass Printing* resource.

We also mark 1455 as the emergence date of the <u>Mass Media</u> class of resources.

First *Recording* - "Thomas Edison amazed the world in 1877 when he invented his "talking machine," the first instrument ever to record and play back sound"[5] "Audio historians have found a sound recording that predates Edison's phonograph by nearly 20 years. The "phonautograph" was patented in 1857 by Edouard-Leon Scott de Martinville."[6] We mark 1857-1877 as the emergence date of *Recording* resource.

First *Film* - *Film* was described in the *Film* section in Chapter 1.1. We mark 1895 as the emergence date of *Film* resource.

First *Radio* - *Radio* was described in the *Radio* section in Chapter 1.14. We mark 1896 as the emergence date of *Radio* resource.

First *Television* - *Television* was described in the *Television* section in Chapter 1.1. We mark 1927 as the emergence date of *Television* resource.

First *Cell (Mobile) Phone* - *Cell (Mobile) Phone* was described in the *Cell (mobile) phone* section in Chapter 1.14. We mark 1973 as the emergence date of *Cell (Mobile) Phone* resource.

First *Global Network (Internet)* - *Global network (Internet)* was described in the *Global network (Internet)* section in Chapter 1.10. We mark 1983 as the emergence date of *Global Network (Internet)* resource.

Last Seven
Classes of Resources

Once we accept our limits, we go beyond them.

Albert Einstein

Chapter 2.17.
Technology beyond the
Limitations of Human Senses

The history of the *Technology Beyond the Limitations of Human Senses* class of resources began with the emergence of resource *Equipment to Observe Objects* at around 1590.

"Traditionally, humans have five recognized senses: sight, touch, taste, smell, and sound. In the strictest sense, our reality is defined by anything and everything we experience through those five senses, but today's technology is allowing us to live in a world beyond them. Rapidly improving technology and a deeper understanding of how our senses work are allowing us to fundamentally change our perception of the world".[1] Three resources were created by humankind in the class of resources *Technology Beyond the Limitations of Human Senses* during the last 44 thousand years.

We will correlate the *Technology Beyond the Limitations of Human Senses* class of resources with one family of resources *Technology Beyond the Limitations of Human Senses*.

Technology beyond the
Limitations of Human Senses

In the family of resources *Technology Beyond the Limitations of Human Senses* humankind created the following resources: *Equipment to Observe Objects, Matter Identification Technique*, and *Sonic, Ultrasonic and Infrasonic Devices*.

First *Equipment to Observe Objects* - The Netherlands is the birthplace of the first microscope. It was invented in 1590. An inventor could be Zacharias Janssen or his father, Hans Martens. [2] Or it could be that the microscope was invented by Hans Lippershey.[3] We mark 1590 as the emergence date of *Equipment to Observe Objects* resource.

We also mark 1590 as the emergence date of the <u>Technology beyond the Limitations of Human Senses</u> class of resources.

First *Matter Identification Technique* - "Analytical chemistry

is the science of obtaining, processing, and communicating information about the composition and structure of matter."[4] "A revolution in qualitative analysis was brought about by spectral analysis...Complete success was attained, however, by Bunsen and Kirchhoff only, with their spectroscope. They were both famous scientists in 1859, when they came out with their spectroscope."[5] We mark 1859 as the emergence date of *Matter Identification Technique* resource.

First Sonic, Ultrasonic and Infrasonic Device - Per the

Recording section in Chapter 1.16, the first sound recording was at 1857-1877. "The first observation of naturally occurring infrasound ever recorded with instruments was in the aftermath of the 1883 eruption of the Krakatoa volcano in Indonesia. Infrasonic waves circled the globe at least seven times, shattering windows hundreds of miles away and were recorded worldwide."[6] We mark 1857-1883 as the emergence date of *Sonic, Ultrasonic and Infrasonic Devices* resource.

The real purpose of scientific method is to make sure Nature hasn't mislead you into thinking you know something you don't actually know.

Robert M.Pirsig

Chapter 2.18.
Usage of the Scientific Method and Information Technology

The scientific method was first used in hard sciences. "Hard sciences use math explicitly, they have more control over the variables and conclusions. They include physics, chemistry and astronomy."[1] Nowadays, IT is used mainly in business operations, as opposed to technology used for personal or entertainment purposes. The relevant definition is "According to ND Century Code (Chapter 54.59. 01), Information Technology means the use of hardware, software, services, and supporting infrastructure to manage and deliver information using voice, data, and video."[2] We will consider the usage of the scientific method and information technology together.

The history of the *Usage of the Scientific Method and Information Technology* class of resources began with the emergence of resources *Mechanical Calculator (Pascaline)* at around 1642 and *Use of Scientific Method* at around 1687. Ten resources were created by humankind in the *Usage of the Scientific Method and Information Technology* class of resources during the last 44 thousand years.

We could divide the *Usage of the Scientific Method and Information Technology* class of resources into two families of resources. Here are those families in the order of their chronological appearance in humankind's history: *Information Technology (IT)*, and *Scientific Method*.

Information Technology (IT)

In the family of resources *Information Technology (IT)* humankind created the following resources: *Mechanical Calculator (Pascaline)*, *Computer in Business, Compiler, Database, Global Network (Internet)*, and *Big*

Data Processing.

First *Mechanical Calculator (Pascaline)* - "Pascal's invention of the mechanical calculator in the early 1640s was born out of a desire to help his father in collecting taxes...Production of the machines started in 1642."[3] We mark 1642 as the emergence date of *Mechanical Calculator (Pascaline)* resource.

We also mark 1642 as the emergence date of the Usage of the Scientific Method and Information Technology *class of resources.*

First *Computer in Business* - "In the late 1940s, J. Lyons and Co., the country's largest caterer, made the prescient decision to invest, both financially and by offering staff support, in the computer developments being made at Cambridge University (EDSAC) on condition that they could copy their 'electronic calculator' if it worked. From this collaboration came Lyons' own version, the Lyons Electronic Office (LEO), now acknowledged as the world's first business computer."[4] "LEO, which occupied all the space in a large room, was ready to attempt its first business program in November 1951. It was called Bakery Valuations, and computed the costs of all the ingredients that went into the bread and cakes produced at the Lyons factory at Cadby Hall in west London."[5] We mark 1951 as the emergence date of Computer in Business resource.

First *Compiler* - "In 1952 she [Grace Hopper] developed the first compiler called A-0, which translated mathematical code into machine-readable code—an important step toward creating modern programming languages."[6] Over time, A-0 transformed into FLOW-MATIC, and, later, COBOL compiled programming language. We mark 1952 as the emergence date of *Compiler* resource.

First *Database* - *Database* was described in the *database* section in Chapter 1.8. We mark 1964 as the emergence date of database resource. We mark 1964 as the emergence date of *Database* resource.

First *Global Network (Internet)* - *Global Network (Internet)* was described in the *Global network (Internet)* section in Chapter 1.10. We mark 1983 as the emergence date of *Global Network (Internet)* resource.

First *Big Data Processing* - "In 2009, Hadoop was successfully tested to sort a PB (PetaByte) of data in less than 17 hours for handling billions of searches and indexing millions of web pages."[6] We mark 2009 as the emergence date of *Big Data Processing* resource.

Scientific Method

In the family of resources *Scientific Method* humankind created the following resources: *Use of Scientific Method, Diffusion of Scientific Knowledge, Falsifiability as a Criterion,* and *Scientific Paradigm.*

First *Use of Scientific Method* - Below is a short sequence of steps in the scientific method in a nutshell. Identify the problem or question. Provide a hypothesis for a potential reason for the observed phenomena. Put in place an experiment or test the prediction and hypothesis. Take the data from the experiment and perform analysis to prove the hypothesis or reject it. Many scholars[7] see Isaac Newton's book "Principia Mathematica" as the first major publication with the use of scientific method. "The Principia appeared in three editions during Newton's lifetime: the first in 1687."[7,8] We will mark the date of this publication, i.e., 1647, as an emergence date of *Use of Scientific Method* resource.

First *Diffusion of Scientific Knowledge* - "The first great scientific school of the modern world, the École Polytechnique in Paris, was founded in 1794 to put the results of science in the service of France. The founding of scores more technical schools in the 19th and 20th centuries encouraged the widespread diffusion of scientific knowledge and provided further opportunity for scientific advance."[9] We mark 1794 as the emergence date of *Diffusion of Scientific Knowledge* resource.

First *Falsifiability as a Criterion* - "Another approach that took off from the difficulties with inductive inference was Karl Popper's critical rationalism or falsificationism [in the book 'The Logic of Scientific Discovery']."[10] "The Logic of Scientific Discovery is a translation of Logik der Forschung, published in Vienna in the autumn of 1934 (with the imprint '1935')." [11] "In so far as a scientific statement speaks about reality, it must be falsifiable: and in so far as it is not falsifiable, it does not speak about reality."[11] We mark 1934 as the emergence date of *Falsifiability as a Criterion* resource.

First *Scientific Paradigm* - "Thomas Kuhn [in his book *The Structure of Scientific Revolutions* [11] published in 1962] argued that science does not evolve gradually toward truth. Science has a paradigm that remains constant before going through a paradigm shift when current theories can't explain some phenomenon, and someone proposes a new theory."[12] We mark 1962 as the emergence date of *Scientific Paradigm* resource.

> *We survived on natural resources, so we should take care of the earth.*
>
> Alek Wek

Chapter 2.19.
Usage of Natural Resources on a Massive Scale

The history of the *Usage of Natural Resources on a Massive Scale* class of resources began with the emergence of resource *spike in fossil fuel mining* at 1750.

Over ten resources were created by humankind in the *Usage of Natural Resources on a Massive Scale* class of resources during the last 44 thousand years. *Usage of Natural Resources on a Massive Scale* is an exception in Class of Resources because, without proper management, humankind's natural resources are dwindling.

We will correlate the *Usage of Natural Resources on a Massive Scale* class of resources with one family of resources *Usage of Natural Resources on a Massive Scale*.

Usage of Natural Resources on a Massive Scale

In the family of resources *Usage of Natural Resources on a Massive Scale*, humankind created the following resources: *Spike in Fossil Fuel Mining, Multi-Times Increase in Coal Mining, 50 Times Increase in Fossil Fuel Consumption, Consumption of Gas and Oil Together Overcome Coal, 400 Times Increase in Fossil Fuel Consumption, Consumption of Oil Became Top One, 800 Times Increase in Fossil Fuel Consumption, 1400 Times Increase in Fossil Fuel Consumption,* and *Sizable Increase in Renewable Energy Sources Consumption.*

First *Spike in Fossil Fuel Mining* - The first used on massive scale natural resource was coal, one of fossil fuel resources. During 50 years, from 1700 to 1750, the amount of coal used in the world increased from

2.7 million tons to 4.7 million tons.[1,2] That is a seventy-five percent increase in 50 years. We mark 1750 as the emergence date of *Spike in Fossil Fuel Mining* resource.

We also mark 1750 as the emergence date of the Usage of Natural Resources on Massive Scale class of resources.

First *Multi-Times Increase in Coal Mining* - During 50 years, from 1750 to 1800, the amount of coal used in the world increased from 4.7 million tons to 10 million tons.[1] That is 3.7 times increase in 50 years. We mark 1800 as the emergence date of *Multi-Times Increase in Coal Mining* resource.

First *50 Times Increase in Fossil Fuel Consumption* - From 1800 onward, we can look at global primary energy consumption by fossil fuel sources, measured in terawatt-hours (TWh). In 1800, global primary energy consumption by fossil fuel sources was 97 TWh.[3] Calculations based on available data[[3]] shows that, in 1888, there was a 50 times increase of global primary energy consumption by fossil fuel sources over level of consumption in 1800. We mark 1888 as the emergence date of *50 Times Increase in Fossil Fuel Consumption* resource.

First *Consumption of Gas and Oil Together Overcome Coal* - In 1960, global primary energy consumption by fossil fuel sources was 4,472 TWh for gas, 11,097 TWh for oil, and 15,442 TWh for coal.[4] We mark 1960 as the emergence date of *Consumption of Gas and Oil Together Overcome Coal* resource.

First *400 Times Increase in Fossil Fuel Consumption* - Calculation based on available data[[3]] shows that, in 1963, there was 400 times increase of global primary energy consumption by fossil fuel sources over the level of consumption in 1800. We mark 1963 as the emergence date of *400 Times Increase in Fossil Fuel Consumption* resource.

First Consumption of Oil Became Top One - In 1965, global primary energy consumption by fossil fuel sources was 6,304 TWh for gas, 17,997 TWh for oil, and 16,140 TWh for coal.[4] We mark 1965 as the emergence date of *Consumption of Oil Became Top One* resource.

First 800 Times Increase in Fossil Fuel Consumption - Calculation based on available data[3] shows that, in 1990, there was an 800 times increase of global primary energy consumption by fossil fuel sources over the level of consumption in 1800. We mark 1990 as the emergence date of *800 Times Increase in Fossil Fuel Consumption* resource.

First 1400 Times Increase in Fossil Fuel Consumption -

Calculation based on available data [[3]] shows that in 2020 there was 1400 times increase of global primary energy consumption by fossil fuel sources over level of consumption in 1800. We mark 2020 as the emergence date of *1400 Times Increase in Fossil Fuel Consumption* resource.

First *Sizable Increase in Renewable Energy Sources Consumption* - "Globally we get the largest amount of our energy from oil, followed by coal, gas, then hydroelectric power. As we look at in more detail below – 'How much of global energy comes from low-carbon sources?' – the global energy mix is still dominated by fossil fuels. They account for more than 80% of energy consumption [in 2022]."[5] Renewable energy sources count for over 14% of all energy sources in 2022. Renewable energy sources include hydropower, wind, solar, biofuels and other renewables.[1] We mark 2022 as the emergence date of *Sizable Increase in Renewable Energy Sources Consumption* resource.

Infant mortality and life expectancy are reasonable indicators of general well-being in a society.

P. J. O'Rourke

Chapter 2.20.
Life Expectancy Growth

The history of the *Life Expectancy Growth* class of resources began with the emergence of resource *Life Expectancy at Birth Over 28 Years* at around 1700. Three resources were created by humankind in the *Life Expectancy Growth* class of resources during the last 44 thousand years.

We will correlate the *Life Expectancy Growth* class of resources with one family of resources *Life Expectancy Growth*.

Life Expectancy Growth

In the family of resources *Life Expectancy Growth* humankind created the following resources: *Life Expectancy at Birth Over 28 Years, Ten Times Increase in an Average Annual Growth Rate of Life Expectancy at Birth,* and *Increase in Life Expectancy in Developed Counties (England and Wales) is Primarily Driven by Declining Old-Age (60-Year-Old) Mortality.*

First *Life Expectancy at Birth Over 28 Years* - Transition from hunter-gathering to settlements began with domestication of cows at 10700 BC – see the "*Cows*" section in Chapter 1.4. The other name for this transition is Agricultural / Neolithic Revolution. We will use estimates for life expectancy at birth for period 17000-7000 BC (with average 12000 BC) based on data in Table 11 in.[1] Estimates for life expectancy in that pre-Agricultural Revolution period varied greatly geographically. An average over five available data points is 28 years. We estimate life expectancy at birth to be roughly 28 years at around 12000 BC. After the Neolithic Revolution, for some time, life expectancy declined.[1] There were periods of life expectancy and decline. More robust data about global life expectancy at birth appeared for period from 1770 AD. Global life expectancy at birth in 1770 was 28.5 years,[2] which is roughly equal to pre-Agricultural Revolution life expectancy. We mark 1770 as the emergence date of *Life Expectancy at Birth Over 28 Years* resource.

We also mark 1770 as the emergence date of the Life Expectancy Growth class of resources.

First *Ten Times Increase in an Average Annual Growth Rate of Life Expectancy at Birth* - Life expectancy at birth from 1770 to 2023[2,3] are known. Analysis of those data shows that there were two distinctly different periods – from 1770 to 1900 and from 1913 to 2023. The average annual growth rate 1770 to 1900 was around 0.42 month per year. The average annual growth rate 1913 to 2023 was around 4 month per year. In other words, an average growth rate for life expectancy at birth jumped ten times in 1913. We mark 1913 as the emergence date of *Ten Times Increase in an Average Annual Growth Rate of Life Expectancy at Birth* resource.

First *Increase in Life Expectancy in Developed Counties (English and Wales) is Primarily Driven by Declining Old-Age (60-Year-Old) Mortality* - "During this stage [lasting until the middle of the twentieth century in developed countries], the increase in life expectancy was primarily driven by declines in infant and child mortality... "In the second stage of population ageing, which is the current situation, population ageing is primarily driven by the increase in life expectancy, which is now due to declining old-age mortality."[4]

The above observation is supported by the analysis of the chart "Life Expectancy by Age in England and Wales, 1700-2013" in.[5] Percentage estimates for life expectancy increase from 60 to 70 years. Also, the percentage of life expectancy increases from birth to 10, which allows us to build the proper charts, by using data for the years 1841, 1950, and 2013. Furthermore, linear approximation shows that around 1982, an increase in life expectancy in developed counties (England and Wales) became primarily driven by declining old-age (60-year-old) mortality, instead of infant and child mortality. We mark 1982 as the emergence date of *Increase in Life Expectancy in Developed Counties (English and Wales) is Primarily Driven by Declining Old-Age (60-Year-Old) Mortality* resource.

In the future, there will be no female leaders. There will just be leaders.

Sheryl Sandberg

Chapter 2.21.
Massive Involvement of Women in Humankind's Activities

According to the origin story of the Abrahamic religions, Eva was the first woman, and, of course, she was the first to be involved in humankind's activities, per written sources. Yet, the dates of Eva's life are unknown. In this Chapter, we will not discuss individual women's activities. Instead, we will look at known breakthrough dates of the massive involvement of women in humankind's activities.

The history of the *Massive Involvement of Women in Humankind's Activities* class of resources began with the emergence of resource *Country Where Women Right to Vote Accepted Legally* at 1893.

Until recently, almost any society in history guarded its tradition of viewing women as inferior to men. A few exceptions to this rule in humankind's history were local geographically and short-lived. Finally, a new trend emerged at the end of the 19th and beginning of the 20th Century.

Seven resources were created by humankind in the *Massive Involvement of Women in Humankind's Activities* class of resources during the last 44 thousand years.

We will correlate the *Massive Involvement of Women in Humankind's Activities* class of resources with one family of resources *Massive Involvement of Women in Humankind's Activities*.

Massive Involvement of Women in Humankind's Activities

In the family of resources *Massive Involvement of Women in Humankind's Activities* humankind created the following resources:

Country Where Women Right to Vote Accepted Legally, Over 10% Share of "Self-Made" Women at the Top of the Social Hierarchy, Over 39% Percentage of Employed Women, Over 50% Share of Women in Higher Education in OECD Countries, Less than 20 % Gap with Men in Years of Schooling, Over 3% of Women of Working Age Have Legal Equality to Men, and Less than 21% Gap with Men in Earnings.

First *Country Where Women Right to Vote Accepted Legally* - New Zealand was the first country, which acknowledged women's right to vote.[1] In 1893 the women's suffrage bill was adopted weeks before the general election of that year. At the time, New Zealand still was a self-governing British colony. Saudi Arabia was "the last country to allow women the right to vote, leaving Vatican City to claim that top spot, in 2015."[2] "In some countries or regions, women have the legal right to vote, but are prevented from doing so by societal norms, harassment and violence at the polls, or pressure from their husbands."[3] We mark 1893 as the emergence date of *Country Where Women Right to Vote Accepted Legally* resource.

We also mark 1893 as the emergence date of the *Massive Involvement of Women in Humankind's Activities* class of resources.

First Over 10% Share of "Self-Made" Women at the Top of the Social Hierarchy - "We measure the female share of people at the top of the social hierarchy in each era as a proxy for women's status. ... For most of history, women who became part of the elite were either born into influential families or married into them." Data "shows a rising prevalence of women who were not born into families or married to males with power and fame, a group we call 'self-made.'"[4,5] In 1900, the global women's share of self-made women at the top of social hierarchy exceeded 10%. We mark 1900 as the emergence date of *Over 10% Share of "Self-Made" Women at the Top of the Social Hierarchy* resource.

First *Over 39% Percentage of Employed Women* - The percentage of employed women among all working population was 39.4% in 1990 and 39.5 in 2022. [6] We mark 1990 as the emergence date of *Over 39% Percentage of Employed Women* resource.

First *Over 50% Share of Women in Higher Education in OECD Countries* - "Of the 18 countries for which data were available in 1985 and 2005, women students were in the majority in 5 countries in 1985 compared with 16 in 2005. In 2005, the average share of the student population accounted for by women amounted to 55% in the OECD area

(1.2 women to every man)."[7] The Organization for Economic Co-operation and Development, abbreviated as OECD is an international organization of 38 countries committed to democracy and the market economy.[1] We mark 2005 as the emergence date of *Over 50% Share of Women in Higher Education in OECD Countries* resource.

First *Less than 20% Gap with Men in Years of Schooling* - "Female-to-male ratio of the average number of years people aged 15-64 participated in formal education. Values below 100% mean that fewer women were educated."[8] Over 80% (Less than 20% gap) was achieved in 2010 for all world regions (Advanced Economics, Eastern Europe, Latin America and Caribbean, Sub-Saharan Africa, Middle East and North Africa, Asia and the Pacific). Advanced Economics, Eastern Europe, Latin America and Caribbean achieved rate over 80% in 1935 and 100% in 2010. Advanced Economics, Eastern Europe, Latin America and Caribbean achieved a rate of over 80% in 1935 and 100% in 2010. We mark 2010 as the emergence date of *Less than 20 % Gap with Men in Years of Schooling* resource.

First *Over 3% of Women of Working Age Have Legal Equality to Men* - "93 million women of working age (15–64)" in 2022 had "same legal rights as men in the areas measured." "Nearly 2.4 billion women of working age still do not have the same legal rights as men. Over 90 million women of working age gained legal equality in the last decade."[9] Over 3% of women of working age had same legal rights as men in 2020. The rest, 73% of women have much less legal rights. "In 2022, the global average score on the World Bank's Women, Business and the Law index rose just half a point to 77.1 — indicating women, on average, enjoy barely 77 percent of the legal rights that men do."[10] We mark 2020 as the emergence date of *Over 3% of Women of Working Age Have Legal Equality to Men* resource.

First *Less than 21% Gap with Men in Earnings* - "On average, women globally are paid about 20 per cent less than men, the International Labour (ILO) Organization said on Sunday, International Equal Pay Day."[11] Gap = 20% in 2022. We mark 2022 as the emergence date of and *Less than 21% Gap with Men in Earnings* resource.

Digital transformation represents a break from the past and presents a high level of impact and complexity.

Pearl Zhu

Chapter 2.22.
Digital Technology

The history of the *Digital Technology* class of resources began with the emergence of resource *Electronic Logic Gate* at 1924.
"Digital technology encompasses digital devices, systems, and resources that help to create, store, and manage data."[1]

Eight resources were created by humankind in the class of resources *Digital Technology* during the last 44 thousand years.

We will correlate the *Digital Technology* class of resources with one family of resources *Digital Technology*.

Digital Technology

In the family of resources *Digital Technology* humankind created the following resources: *Electronic Logic Gate, Digital Computer, Mathematical Theory of Communication, Integrated Circuit (Microchip), Cost-Effective Digital Storage, Decisive Usage of Mobile Phones, Decisive Usage of Internet,* and *Digital Transformation Definition.*

First *Electronic Logic Gate* - The first modern electronic logic "AND" gate was invented in 1924 by famous physicist Walther Bothe. In 1954, Bothe shared Nobel Prize in physics for this achievement.[2] We mark 1924 as the emergence date of *Electronic Logic Gate* resource.

We also mark 1924 as the emergence date of the Digital Technology class of resources.

First *Digital Computer* - The first digital computer - "The machine was designed and built by Atanasoff and graduate student Clifford Berry between 1939 and 1942."[3] "Iowa State mathematician and physicist John Atanasoff designed the first electronic digital computer [Atanasoff-Berry Computer (ABC)]. It would use binary numbers (base 2, in which all numbers are expressed with the digits 0 and 1), and its data would be stored in capacitors."[4] ABC computer was not programmable.

The first digital programmable computer - "The ENIAC, or Electronic Numerical Integrator and Computer, was... a huge machine, taking up a 1,500-square-foot room at the Moore School... The machine was completed in February 1946."[5] A 1973 court ruling on patent infringement declared John V. Atanasoff and Clifford E. Berry were the digital computer's inventors and that the ENIAC had been derived from their design."[6] "The original group of ENIAC programmers" consisted of six women.[7] We mark 1944-1946 as the emergence date of *Digital Computer* resource.

First *Mathematical Theory of Communication* - "How did it all [digital transformation] start? The actual basis lies in a mathematical paper ("A Mathematical Theory of Communication") written [in 1948] by Dr. Claude Shannon,[[8]] which is the founding theory behind our current internet."[9] We mark 1948 as the emergence date of *Mathematical Theory of Communication* resource.

First *Integrated Circuit (Microchip)* - "Jack Kilby was an electrical engineer who joined Texas Instruments in the summer of 1958. Because he was a new employee and had not accumulated enough vacation time, he stayed in the office while the rest of his department took its annual two-week vacation in July. While the office was deserted, Kilby studied how to effectively and efficiently reduce the numbers. Reid says, "Every computer of that time had miles and miles of wiring and Jack said, 'Why do we need the wires? If I make the parts all out of the same material, I could just carve them into one block of that material and...no wires.' " By inventing the integrated circuit (IC), now commonly called the microchip, Jack Kilby reduced the "tyranny of numbers" to one. Suddenly, engineers really could design a computer that could do anything. And they could build it small enough to fit in your pocket. Jack Kilby's invention of the integrated circuit was the genesis of almost every electronic product used today."[10] We mark 1958 as the emergence date of *Integrated Circuit (Microchip)* resource.

First *Cost-Effective Digital Storage* - "[In 1996] Digital storage becomes more cost-effective for storing data than paper according to R.J.T. Morris and B.J. Truskowski, in "The Evolution of Storage Systems," IBM Systems Journal, July 1, 2003." [11,12]"] We mark 1996 as the emergence date of *Cost-Effective Digital Storage* resource.

First *Decisive Usage of Mobile Phones* - We will consider usage of some technology being a decisive factor if over 40% of world population uses that technology. Number of mobile phone users worldwide in 2006 were 2,679 million.[13] The world population in 2006 was 6,641 million.[14] That means that 40.3% of world population was using mobile phones in 2006. We mark 2006 as the emergence date of *Decisive Usage of Mobile Phones* resource.

First *Decisive Usage of Internet* - The number of Internet users worldwide in June, 2014 were 3,035 million, which were 42.3% of world population.[15] We mark 2014 as the emergence date of *Decisive Usage of Internet* resource.

First *Digital Transformation Definition* - "Digital success isn't all about technology: The 2015 Digital Business Global Executive Study and Research Project by MIT Sloan Management Review and Deloitte identifies strategy as the key driver in the digital arena...2015 global study of digital business found that maturing digital businesses are focused on integrating digital technologies, such as social, mobile, analytics and cloud, in the service of transforming how their businesses work. Less-mature digital businesses are focused on solving discrete business problems with individual digital technologies."[16] We mark 2015 as the emergence date of *Digital Transformation Definition* resource.

By far, the greatest danger of Artificial Intelligence is that people
conclude too early that they understand it.

Eliezer Yudkowsky

Chapter 2.23.
Artificial Intelligence (AI)

The history of the *Artificial Intelligence (AI)* class of resources began
with the emergence of resource *Artificial Intelligence (AI) Conference* at
around 1956.

Three resources were created by humankind in the *Artificial
Intelligence (AI)* class of resources during the last 44 thousand years. We
will correlate the *Artificial Intelligence (AI)* class of resources with one
family of resources *Artificial Intelligence (AI)*.

Artificial Intelligence (AI)

In the family of resources *Artificial Intelligence (AI)* humankind created
the following resources: *Artificial Intelligence (AI) Conference,* and
Acknowledgment of AI Creativity by People Globally.

First *Artificial Intelligence (AI) conference* - Computer scientist
John McCarthy coined the term "Artificial intelligence (AI)" in 1955 in his
proposal for the first AI conference.[1] "Artificial intelligence (AI) refers to
the simulation of human intelligence in machines that are programmed
to think like humans and mimic their actions."[2]

The first conference on AI was organized in Dartmouth, the USA, in
1956. We mark 1956 as the emergence date of *Artificial Intelligence (AI)
Conference* resource.

We also mark 1956 as the emergence date of the Artificial Intelligence (AI)
class of resources.

First *Acknowledgment of AI Creativity by People Globally* -
Board game Go is a game of strategy. Go is a much more complex game
than chess. The standard board size in Go is 19 by 19. The number of
possible legal positions on such board size in Go is larger than the
number of atoms in the observable Universe.[3] That implies that Go

players could not calculate all possible moves and have to "cut corners." They should play creatively.

In 2016, the computer program AlphaGo beat a 9-dan professional Go player, Lee Sedol, in a five-game match.[4] Lee Sedol was among the top world Go players in the world. A huge worldwide Go players community assessed some AlphaGo moves in that match as creative moves.[5] Of course, not everybody agrees with this opinion. Yet, it was the first time in humankind's history that millions of people acknowledged that computer program's moves in a game were creative ones. We mark 2016 as the emergence date of *Acknowledgment of AI Creativity by People Globally* resource.

How do you know where you're going if you don't know where you've been.

Todd Stocker

Part 3.

Direction of History.

What and Why?

Introduction to Part 3

In Part 2, we presented the data for the subsurface history of humankind, which we gathered from independent publications.

We will analyze the data in Parts 3 and 4 in different ways and with several models of humankind. In a few cases, we will draw a comparison with conventional history.

Several "Big questions" about humankind will be answered.

Roads were made for journeys, not destinations.

Graphs.
Turning Points. Driving Force.

There is a magic in graphs. The profile of a curve reveals in a flash a whole situation... The curve informs the mind, awakens the imagination, convinces.

Henry D. Hubbard

Chapter 3.1.

Humankind 's History in Graphs

Four Models of Humankind's History

Four separate complex systems of humankind correlate with the proposed models: super-high-level, high-level, middle-level, and low-level models.

The elements of the super-high-level model are domains of resources. The elements of the high-level model are classes of resources. The elements of the middle-level model are families of resources. The elements of the low-level model are resources.

Graphs from Four Models of Humankind

This book focuses on resources and classes of resources. However, in this Chapter, we will present graphs for all four models, from top to bottom. Those graphs cover the entire course of humankind's history, 44 thousand years. Elements of Super-High-Level model, Domains of Resources, presented in Table 3.1.1.

Table 3.1.1. History of Humankind. 42000 BC – 2023 AD. Super-High-Level Timeline. Domains of Resources. 5 Data Points

Domain of resources, created by humankind for itself	Emergence Date, year
Personal development and social impact	42000 BC
Man-made entities	34000 BC
Overcoming limits	11000-8000 BC
Beyond our body and mind	3200-3100 BC
Scale-up to a new quality	2700 BC

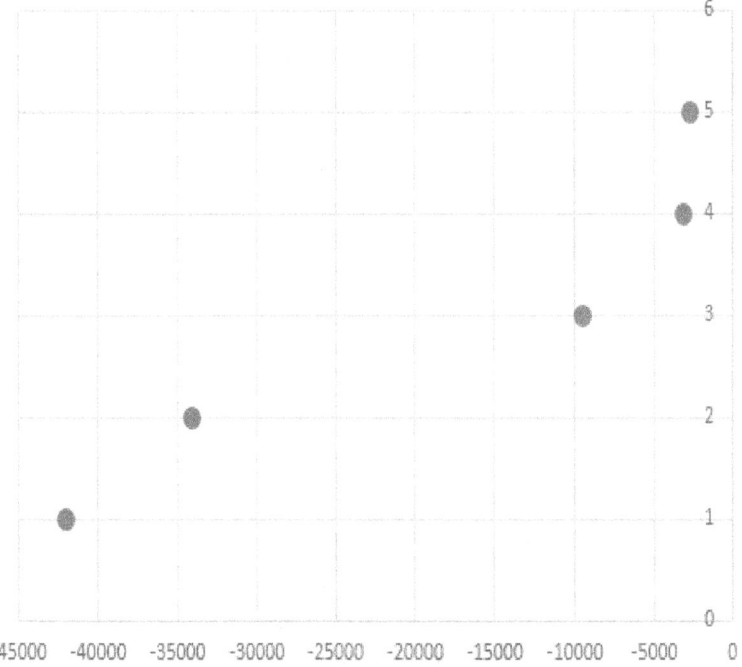

Figure 3.1.1. History of Humankind. 42000 BC - 2023 AD
Vertical - Number of accumulated domains of resources.
Horizontal - Time, years. 5 data points. Data from Table 3.1.1.
Super-high-level model of humankind.

Details on the contents of each domain of resources, i.e., which classes of resources belong to which domain according to the proposed hierarchical classification system, are presented in Table 3 at the end of this book.

The next is the high-level model, a model of classes of resources. The data for this model are presented in Table 1 at the beginning of this book.

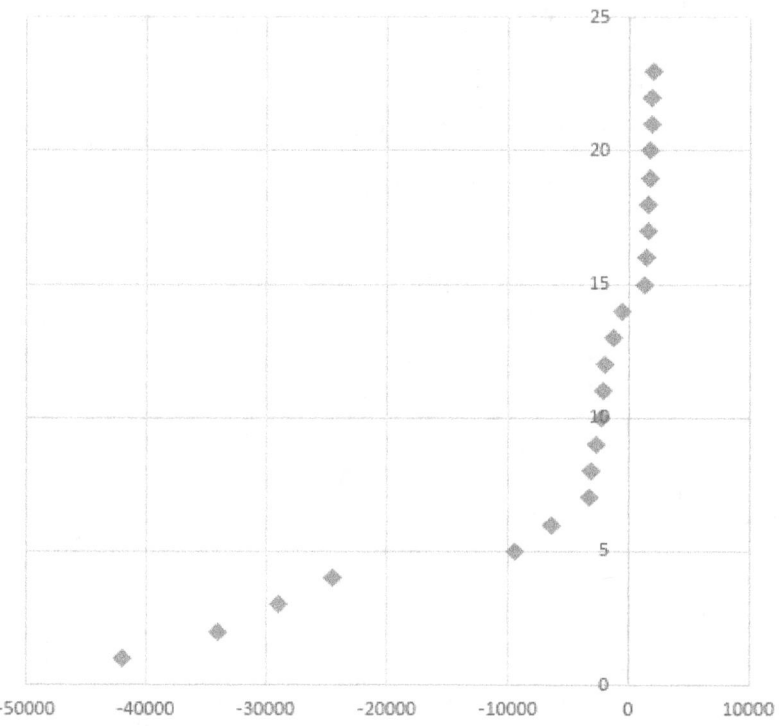

Figure 3.1.2. History of Humankind. 42000 BC - 2023 AD
Vertical - Number of accumulated classes of resources.
Horizontal - Time, years.
23 data points. Data from Table 1.
High-level model of humankind.

The next is the middle-level model, the model of families of resources. The data for this model are presented in Table 3 at the end of this book.

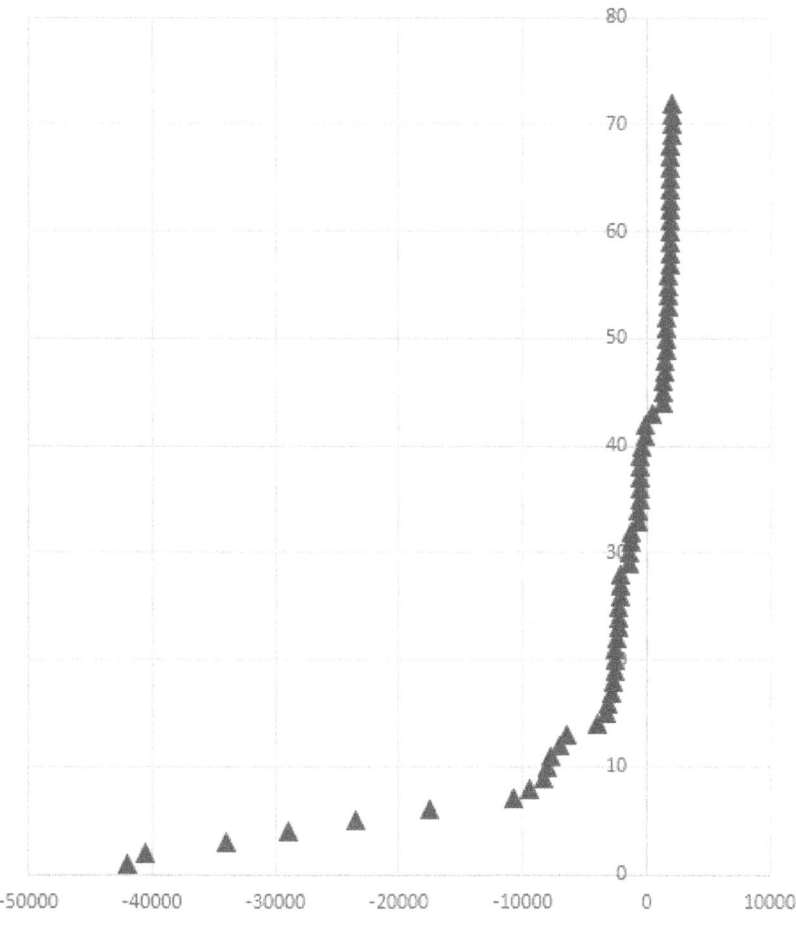

Figure 3.1.3. History of Humankind. 42000 BC - 2023 AD
Vertical – Number of accumulated families of resources.
Horizontal – Time, years.
72 data points. Data from Table 3. Middle-level model of humankind.

The most detailed model is the low-level model, the model of resources. The curve of humankind's development from 42000 BC to 2023 AD in a low-level model is based on 318 data points in Part 2 of this book. This data is also conveniently placed in Table 2 in chronological order of dates of creation of those resources by humankind. The chart for this model is presented in Figure 1 at the beginning of this book. The same curve is presented on Figure 3.1.4 with two added trendlines.

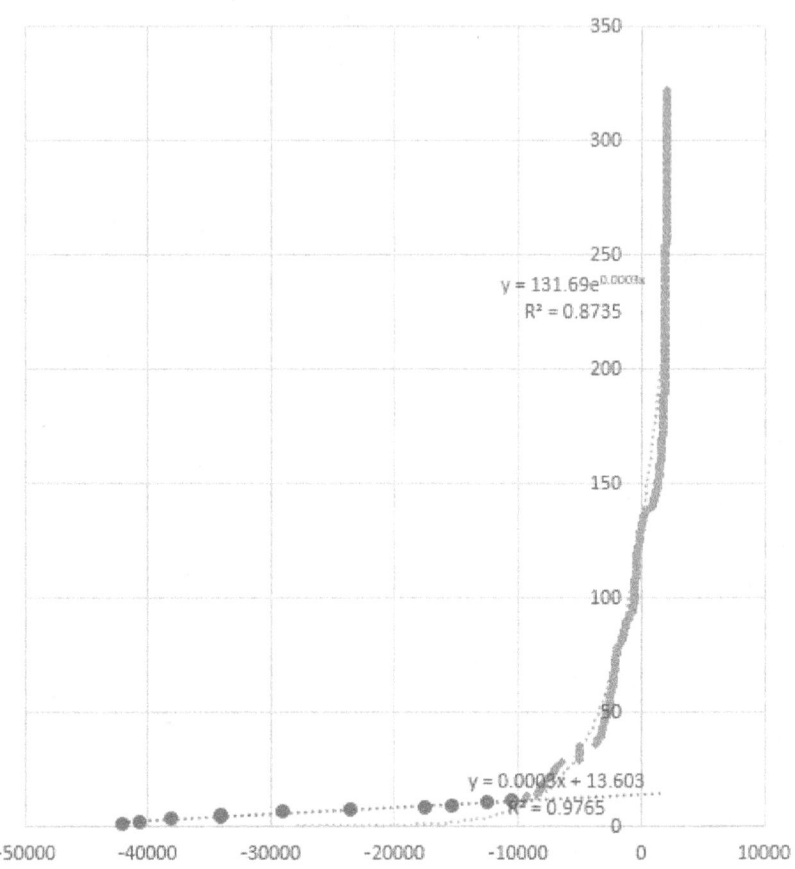

Figure 3.1.4. History of Humankind. 42000 BC - 2023 AD
Vertical – Number of accumulated resources.
Horizontal – Time, years.
318 data points. Low-level model of humankind.
Trendlines added – (a) Linear for 42000-10700 BC,
(b) Exponential for 10500 BC – 2023 AD

The curves in Figures 3.1.1 – 3.1.4 show the total number of resources (families of resources, classes of resources, domains of resources) at any point in humankind's history. You can draw a curve through all the data points on a particular graph.

In Figures 3.1.1 – 3.1.4 you can see four snapshots of humankind's history at different levels of detail.

Granularity Levels of Four Models of Humankind

Table 3.1.2. History of Humankind. 42000 BC – 2023 AD.
Granularity of Models of Humankind

Model Type	Type of elements	Number of elements in the model	Normalized garnularity (= 1 for high-level model)	Granularity level	Difference in granula size, times (compared to high-level model)
Low-level model	Resource	318	0.07	Super-high	13.8
Middle-level model	Family of resources	72	0.32	High	3.1
High-level model	Class of resources	23	1	Middle	1
Super-high level model	Domain of resources	5	4.6	Low	4.6

Data granularity measures the level of detail in the data structure. The summary of information on granularity in the proposed models is in Table 3.1.2.

We took the level of granularity of elements in the high-level model to be 1 compared to other models of humankind. We could then describe the level of granularity for other models and calculate the size of the "granules" using the ratio of the number of elements in the high-level model to the number of elements in the different models.

From Table 3.1.2 it can be seen that the levels of detail of the presented models vary significantly - from approximately five to almost 65 times. This is a significant factor.

First, such a large jump in detail from one model to another helps to significantly reduce the likelihood of incorrectly assigning an element of a system to an inappropriate model type.

Second, having multiple models of humanity at very different levels of detail allows us to compare the consequences that arise from these models. Note that the four proposed models of humanity differ significantly from each other. Table 3.1.2 shows that the difference in the size of "granules" between neighboring models is in the range of 3.1 – 4.6.

The overall direction of humankind's development is evident in all four models. **Humankind is moving in the direction of increasing the arsenal of resources created by humankind for itself. The pace of this movement is increasing over time, more sharply in later times.**

10,000 Years of History in Three Models of Humankind

For any period in humankind's history, we can compare the development of humanity based on data from at least three models of humankind.

Let us take a closer look at one period of humankind's history, from 10000 BC to 1 BC. We could use the corresponding data for high-level, middle-level, and low-level models. Comparison curves are presented in Figure 3.1.5.

The trends are similar. However, each model provides us with some additional information.

The interesting phenomenon is the period between 6500 and 3150 BC.

According to Figure 3.1.5.a, there was no activity of humankind to create classes of resources for 3350 years in this interval.

Figure 3.1.5.b shows that at the edges of this period, in 4000 BC and 3225 BC, humankind created two new families of resources in classes of resources that already existed before 6000. The window of missing creativity of humankind has shrunk to 2,500 years on a level of families of resources.

Even on the level of resources, according to Figure 3.1.5.c, the creative activity of humankind, except for a few new resources created at around 5000 BC, was absent for 2,250 years, between 6250 BC and 4000 BC.

As we move from less detailed models to more detailed ones, from high-level to middle-level to low-level, it is natural to expect additional data to become available at the end of the period of the "frozen creativity" period. Our suspicion about 5000 BC data points in the low-level model is confirmed by 8000 BC – 2000 BC data from a low-level model. The dates of the emergence of several resources were highly uncertain. For example, the date of creation of the domesticated grape is between 6000 BC and 4000 BC, with the midpoint of this range being 5000 BC. The situation is even worse with the available information about the data for the domesticated apple's creation date. The estimated

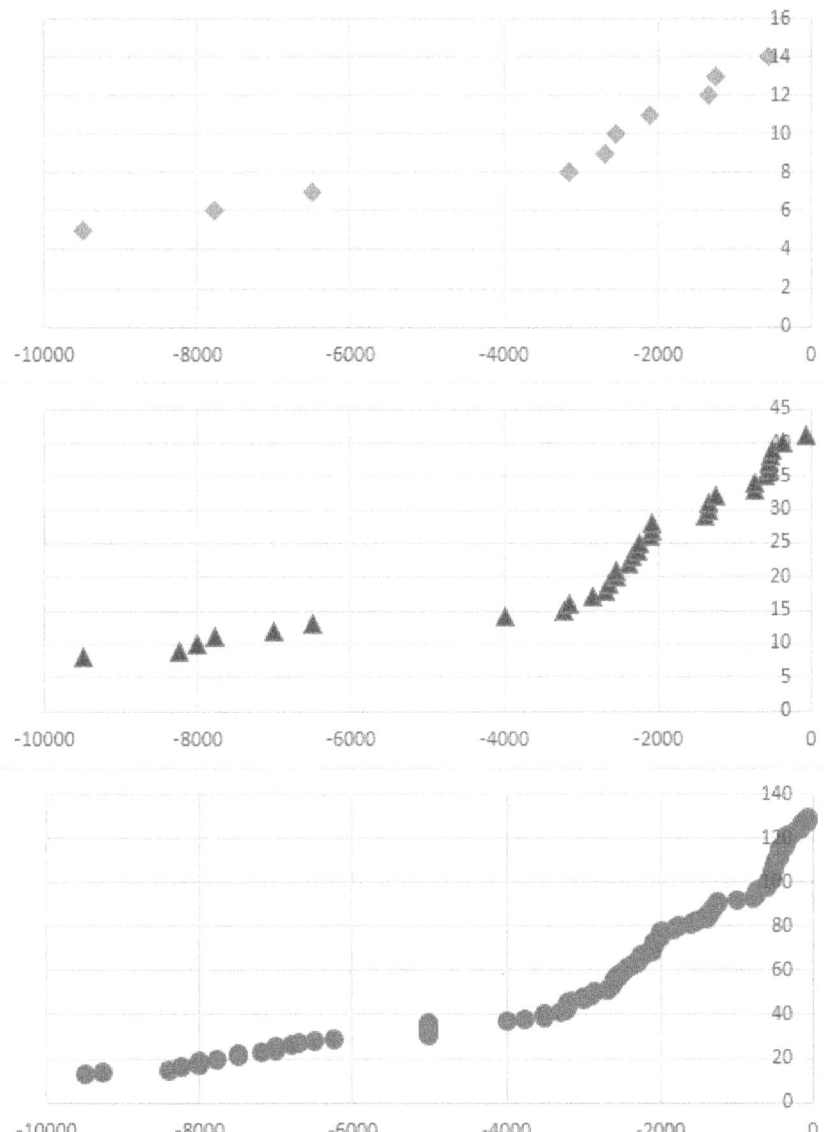

Figure 3.1.5. History of Humankind. 10000 BC – 1 BC
(a) Top chart - high-level model, (b) Middle chart – middle-level
model, (c) Bottom chart – low-level model of humankind.
Vertical axis – Number of accumulated (a) classes of resources, (b)
families of resources, and (c) resources.
Horizontal axis – Time, years. Data – from Part 2.

range of dates is 8000 BC – 2000 BC, with the midpoint of this range of 5000 BC. It may be that actual emergence dates for those resources are within the date ranges mentioned, but closer to their edges. In other words, the outstanding data at 5000 BC may be the result of high uncertainty of dates and do not negate information from two other models about the found period of "frozen creativity" of humankind.

Graphs in Low-Level Model
of Humankind's History

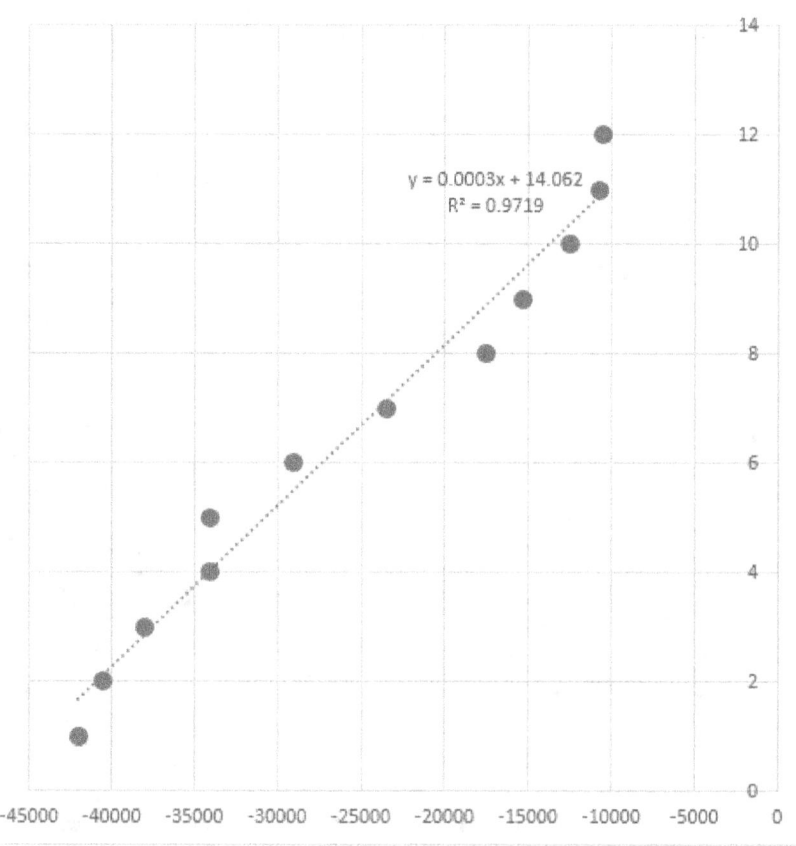

Figure 3.1.6. History of Humankind. 42000 BC - 10500 BC
Vertical – Number of accumulated resources.
Horizontal axis – Time, years.
Low-level model of humankind. Linear trendline added.

The curve of low-level humankind's development is complex. We could divide the history of humanity into two periods with one transition point of the development curve from one period to another. The change point of the development curve is at approximately 10700 BC - 10500 BC.

The first period of humankind's development lasted from 42000 BC to 12700 BC. The approximation curve in Figure 3.1.6 shows that during this period of time, the pace of humankind's development was approximately even. A linear function of time could describe the number of emerged resources.

That pattern changed dramatically around 10700 – 10500 BC.

Below are data points from Figure 3.1.6 in chronological order of dates of creation of those resources by humankind.

Table 3.1.3. Details on Resources Created by Humankind During Period from 42000 BC to 10500 BC

Resources	Emergence date, Year
painting	42000 BC
aerophone (flute)	41000-40000 BC
sculpture	38000 BC
storytelling	34000 BC
textile	36000-32000 BC
amputation	29000 BC
dogs	30100-16800 BC
pottery	18000-17000 BC
graphic art (drawing)	15500-15100 BC
dance	14000-11000 BC
beer	11700-9700 BC
cows	10500 BC

For any period of humankind's history, a similar table can be presented based on the data from Table 2. The first column indicates a resource such as amputation, based on when a particular entity of the mentioned resource was created for the first time in history. For example, as we now know, the first amputation of a human leg was performed on the island of Borneo. A source link for the first known amputation was mentioned in Part 2.

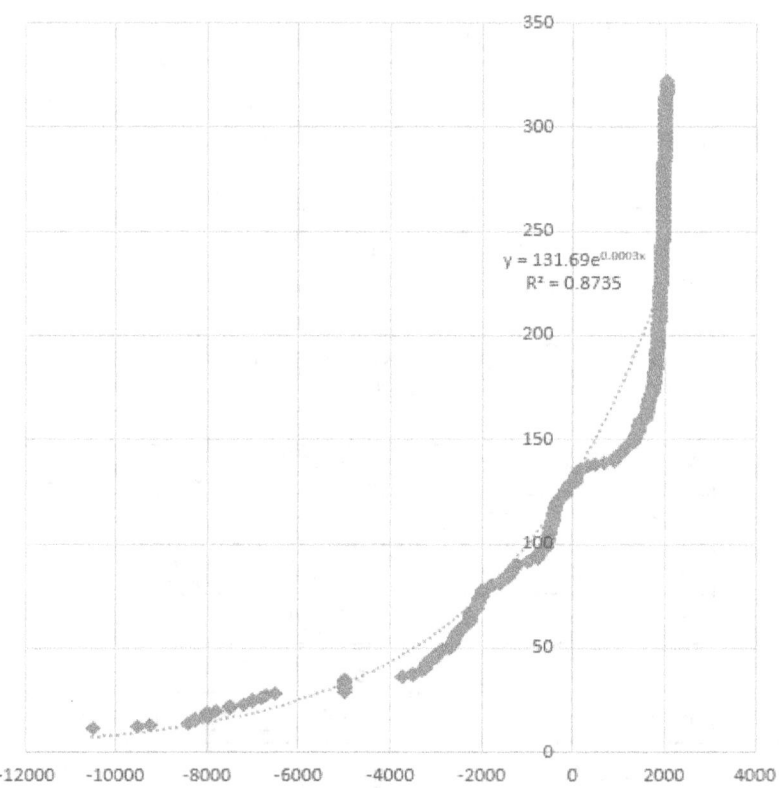

Figure 3.1.7. History of Humankind. 10500 BC - 2023 AD
Vertical – Number of accumulated resources.
Horizontal – Time, years.
Low-level model of humankind. Exponential trendline added.

The second period of humankind's development began around 10500 BC; currently, in 2023 AD, it is still ongoing. The approximation curve in Figure 3.1.2 shows that during this period, the pace of humankind's development has become very uneven. The number of emerged resources could be roughly approximated by an exponential function of time. In addition, recently the actual curve has become even steeper than the exponential curve, perhaps closer to hyperbolic.

At the same time, we see that an actual curve is much more complex than an ideal exponential curve. This is not surprising given the uneven composition of humanity and the many complex interactions between different parts of humanity and its interactions with the environment.

Graphs in Both Models of Humankind's History

We can compare low-level subsurface history, based on the accumulation of resources, with high-level history, based on the accumulation of classes of resources.

Let us look into humankind's high- and low-level history during the same time period: from 12000 BC until 2023 AD. High-level and low-level graphs of humankind's history are both different and similar.

They are different because they include different types of elements and different number of elements. The high-level history of humankind from 12000 BC to 2023 AD consists of 19 classes or resources. The low-level history of humankind during the 12000 BC to 2023 AD interval includes 312 resources. The details of humankind's history in those two models differ by more than tenfold.

Yet both models show that humankind is moving toward increasing the arsenal of opportunities created by humankind for itself, regardless of whether these opportunities are presented on the level of resources or the level of classes of resources. Both models show that the pace of humankind's move in that direction is increasing over time.

Brief Analysis of High-Level Curve of Humankind's Development

What conclusion could we draw from the observed curves of humankind's development over the last 44 thousand years?

The direction of development and the pace of development of humankind are clearly defined in Figures 3.1.3 and 3.1.4 and can be measured quantitatively. Humanity is developing not according to a linear law and not according to some cyclical law. The curve of humankind's development is non-trivial and changes over time.

First, the intervals between subsequent creation dates of classes of

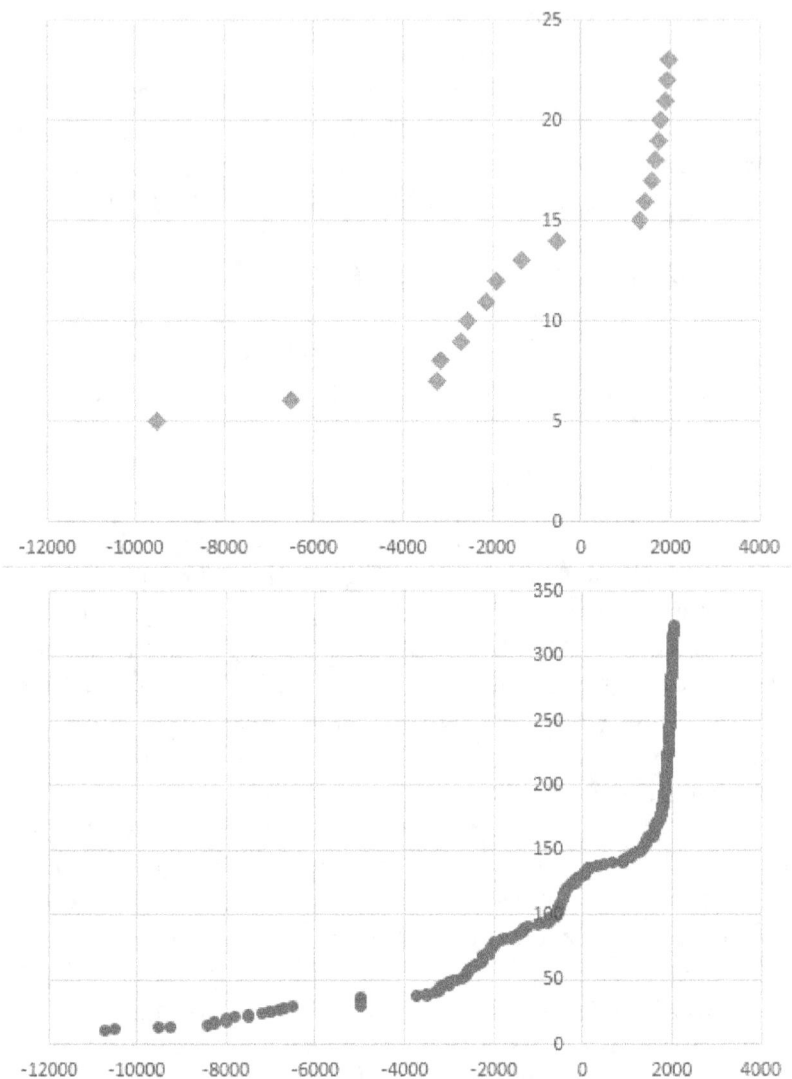

Figure 3.1.8. History of Humankind. 12000 BC - 2023 AD
Top chart – (a) High-level model of humankind,
(b) Bottom chart – Low-level model of humankind.
Vertical – Number of accumulated (a) classes of resources, (b)
resources. Horizontal axis – Time, years. Data – from Part 2.

resources fluctuate. This is understandable; the development of humanity is influenced by many factors.

Second, the overall direction of humankind's development is evident. *Humankind is moving towards increasing the arsenal of resources and classes of resources that humankind creates for itself.*

We could say: *the meaning of humankind's history is that humanity is moving towards increasing the arsenal of resources created by humankind for itself.*

Third, the rate at which new resources are being added is increasing over time.

Fourthly, we can distinguish several periods of enhanced creativity of humankind. These periods are separated by periods of slowdown, or periods that lack creativity. The duration of periods of absence or slowdown of creativity is much greater than the fluctuations within adjacent periods of increased creativity. Therefore, the existence of periods of absence or slowdown in creativity cannot be characterized by fluctuations within periods of increased creativity.

The influence of any single factor cannot explain such a complex curve. The overall shape of the curve may be due to one major influencing factor. The alternation of periods of intensification and slowdown or lack of creativity and the parameters of these periods may depend on secondary factors.

Research is creating new knowledge.

Neil Armstrong

Chapter 3.2.

Ways to Use the Subsurface History of Humankind

The deep-level history of humankind is based on the data presented in the second part of this book. This data can be combined, analyzed, and presented in a variety of ways.

We look at four levels of the hierarchical classification system of resources that humanity has created for itself. At each level, a different model of the complex system of humankind can be considered.   At the low level of this classification system, the level of resources, 318 data points constitute a low-level model of a complex system of humankind. Elements of the low-level model - resources - are presented in Table 2 and Figure 3.1.1.

At the middle level of the hierarchical classification system of resources , the level of families of resources, the 72 data points represent a middle-level model of a complex system of humankind. The elements of the middle-level model - families of resources - are presented in Table 3.

At a high level of the hierarchical classification system of resources, the level of classes of resources, 23 data points comprise a high-level model of a complex system of humankind. The elements of the high-level model - classes of resources - are presented in Table 2, Figure 1, and Figure 3.2.4.

At the super-high level of the hierarchical classification system of resources , the level of domains of resources five data points comprises a super-high-level model of a complex system of humankind. The elements of the super-high-level model - super-high-level - are presented in Table 3.1.1.

Each of those four models considers humankind's creativity in all fields of humankind's activity. We will call those models a general type of model.

Every class of resources is a separate complex system with elements – resources. This means that we have 23 complex systems models of humanity, each dedicated to a specific area of humankind's activity. We will call these models regional-type models.

Table 3.2.1. Complex System Models of Humankind

Model Type	Level of Model	Number of Models	Number of data points in the model
General	Low-level model	1	318
General	Middle-level model	1	72
General	High-level model	1	23
General	Super-high-level model	1	5
Regional	Super-high-level model	23	Art and Music - 33, ... , Mass transportation - 14, etc.

Models of complex systems usually include elements of the models and interactions between these elements.

This book is dedicated to revealing the elements of humankind's complex systems. The interactions between the found elements can be studied later.

How can you use the information presented about the history of humankind, information about a large set of resources created by humanity for itself?

First, it can be used to analyze the long history of humanity. We could explore the direction of humankind's development, its speed, acceleration, or deceleration at different times. Possible correlations or causes of the entire movement of humanity or the irregularities of this movement can be explored.

More broadly, comparisons could be made between the humankind's development curve and other natural phenomena.

Moreover, we can now conduct numerous studies of various localities of humankind's history.

We could explore different periods in detail; for example, from 8000 BC to 7500 BC, or from 150 to 750 AD. We could compare different periods of humankind's history with each other. That is research of localities in the time.

We can now conduct other studies of various localities of humankind's history.

Another type of locality is the locality of the type of humankind's activity. We could study humankind's activity in specific areas, such as *Transnational Entities* or *Mass Education*.

We could also add additional information to the model elements. For example, we could add available information about the place of where a new resource or resource class emerged. Throughout humankind's history, 44 thousand years, we can use the most common geographical units, such as continents. For periods of history that have reasonably good written records, we could add geographic information at the country level.

Methods for analyzing the presented data may also vary. We could examine the raw data. We could also analyze data averaged over a certain number of time intervals between dates of emergence of resources, etc.

We could study history at a more detailed level than the low-level model. In other words, we could treat each resource as a separate family of sub-resources and study their history. For example, for the resource *Mass Transportation with Watercraft*, we could explore the emergence of sub-resources such as boats, rafts, ships with sails, ships with engines, etc.

As we continue to study subsurface humankind's history, we could add information from traditional history and study both histories together.

In the following chapters, we will touch on some of these methods.

History is important. More than any other topic, it is about us. Whether one deems our present society wondrous or awful or both, history reveals how we got to this point.

James W. Loewen

Chapter 3.3.

Turning Points in History

Two Turning Points in of Humankind's History

High-level and low-level timelines of human history lead us to the same essential conclusion: there have only been two major turning points in humankind's development.

The first big turning point was that humans became behaviorally modern and humanity began to create new resources and classes of resources for itself for the first time. We base this date on evidence of the first depiction of hybrids in an Indonesian cave around 42000 BC. Since this date, humanity has continued to create new resources. As a result, humankind began to move towards increasing the arsenal of resources that humanity creates for itself.

For thousands of years after the first turning point, humanity steadily created new resources. This pace can be approximated by a linear function of time. Humankind has created twelve resources in the 31.5 thousand years since the first big turning point in humankind's development.

Then, around 10700–10500 BC in the low level model and in 9500 BC in the high-level model, we observe the second inflection point of the curve. The linear curve has transformed into an exponential or even steeper curve. The pace of humanity's movement towards increasing the arsenal of created resources has become very uneven.

The low-level model shows that over the next 12.5 thousand years, humanity created 312 new resources for itself. That is, the creation of new resources on average every 40.9 years. According to the high-level model, over the past 11.5 thousand years, humanity has created 19 new classes of resources for itself. This means the creation of a new resource class every 606 years on average.

There is nothing in humankind's history over the past 44,000 years that can compare in importance to these two turning points.

First Turning Point in Humankind's History

Let us look at the first turning point more closely. There were times in the past when we, Sapiens, could not do what we can do now. And then, at some point, Sapiens acquired the ability to be behaviorally the same as we are now.

We can study and discuss how this happened and when it happened. We can explore how this change was determined by something inside our body and our brain.

However, we need confirmation of this change. We need evidence. We cannot know what ancient people thought or felt. But we can see the results of their actions. This is something we can rely on. But first, we need to understand our objectives.

Novel Mental Images

The first class of resources, *Novel Mental Images*, differs from all other resources. All other classes of resources were developed by humankind itself. The ability to produce *Novel Mental Images* was granted to humans from Nature.

Novel Mental Images are the mental images shared by people with other people. Otherwise, we would know nothing about any particular novel mental image. The *Novel Mental Images* term does not emphasize this "sharing" only because we wanted to keep the term relatively short.

Novel Mental Images were new when they were first created by some people. Those people then shared their images with other people. If someone's personal *Novel Mental Image* is not transmitted to others in a community, then no one, except that one person, knows about it. If you don't know about *Novel Mental Image*, then you won't be able to use it. Thus, it is of no use to humanity. So it goes without saying that humanity shared generic images.

We will continue to use the term *Novel* both when the mental image first appears and after it has been shared with others.

After humans acquired the ability to produce *Novel Mental Images,* humankind used this ability extensively. That was the first turning point in humankind's history. What are those images, how are they created, how could we identify and differentiate them from anything else, and how could we count them? There are no clear-cut answers to those questions. To answer the first two questions, we refer to neurologist Andrey Vyshedskiy.[1]

What could people do with *Novel Mental Images*? A million things. Look at a small portion of these images expressed in words. Villages, cities, and countries. Love, feelings, compassion. We use these words in all corners of every society. We talk about them to each other. These mental images are everywhere you look.

Hard to Measure

People use thousands and thousands of *Novel Mental Images.* How do we measure the amount of those images?

Every mental image is represented by its name in our languages. That name is a word or combination of words that we attribute to a specific *Novel Mental Image.* The shortest way to describe democracy is to use the word "democracy."

The study of the relationship between words and mental images is a complex problem and the subject of numerous discussions among scientists.[2,3,4] Not every lexicalized word represents a novel mental image. We will focus on the possible upper limit on the number of *Novel Mental Images.* This possible upper limit could be close to the number of words in a dictionary of a language. The actual number of new mental images will, of course, be less than the upper limit. However, the upper limit's curve will indicate a trend in the number of *Novel Mental Images* over time. This would be a simple but very imprecise measure of the number of *Novel Mental Images.*

Words counted in dictionaries are known. However, there are thousands and thousands of languages. We must choose a sequence of them to rely upon. In other words, our count would be a ballpark number. We are fortunate that we are only aiming for a rough estimate and not an exact figure. What language is currently most used internationally? English. We can use English dictionaries and dictionaries of predecessor languages to find out how many words those languages had at a particular time.

Proto-Indo-European language - There are conflicting dating hypotheses about when Proto-Indo-European, or PIE, originated and when it split into separate languages. According to two sources, PIE as a linguistic and cultural phenomenon existed from 4500 BC to 3000 BC [5] or 4000 BC to 2500 BC [6]. PIE is now reconstructed language. Linguists reconstructed a few thousand words in the PIE lexicon.[7,8] We mark 4500-2500 BC as the date when Proto-Indo-European language vocabulary included 3.5 thousand entries.

Table 3.2.2. The Potential Upper Limit of Items
in the *Novel Mental Images* Class of Resources.
Vocabulary in English and Its Predecessors,
In Thousands of Words.

Source	The potential upper limit of items, in Thousands	Time of record
Proto Indo-European language	3.5	4500-2500 BC
Old English	50	1150
Early Modern English	43	1755
Modern English	544	1900
Modern English	600	2023
Modern English	1022	2023

Old English language - "Old English – the earliest form of the English language – was spoken and written in Anglo-Saxon Britain from c. 450 CE until c. 1150"[9] "At the end of the Old English period the size of the lexicon stood at something over 50,000 different words. Many words then fell out of use, but the rate of replacement was such that by the end of the Middle English period we see this total doubled."[10] We mark 1150 AD as the date when Old English language vocabulary included 50 thousand entries.

Early Modern English language – Early Modern English language period is considered to be from 1500 to 1800.[11] "However, the first reliable dictionary is considered to be Samuel Johnson's 'Dictionary of the English Language' (1755) which had 43000 words."[12] We mark 1755 as the date when Early Modern English language vocabulary included 43 thousand entries.

Modern English language – "Using this technique, we estimated the number of words in the English lexicon as 544,000 in 1900, 597,000 in 1950, and 1,022,000 in 2000."[13] "The Oxford English Dictionary provides an unsurpassed guide to the English language, documenting 600,000 words through 3.5 million illustrative quotations from over 1,000 years of history across the English-speaking world."[14] We mark 1900 as the date when Early Modern English language vocabulary included 544 thousand entries, and 2023 as the date when Early Modern English language vocabulary contained 600-1022 thousand entries.

The potential upper limit for items in the *Novel Mental Images* class of resources is shown in Table 3.2.1.

We can visually represent how human vocabulary size has changed over time.

Figure 3.3.1 compares this curve of human vocabulary size with population growth.

That Figure shows that the Sapiens population growth curve and the curve of the imprecise possible upper bound for the number of *Novel Mental Images* are similar.

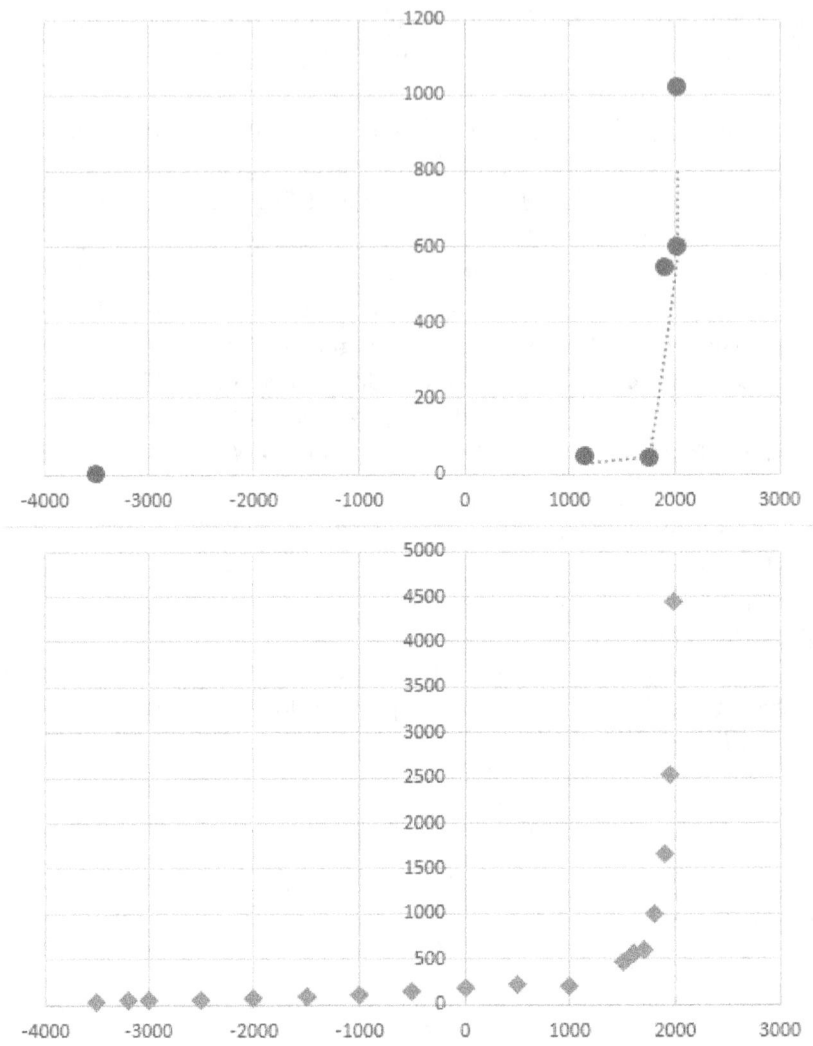

Figure 3.3.1. History of (a) Human Vocabulary Size (top chart), and (b) Humankind's population (bottom chart).
Vertical axis – (a) The number of words in the English Language and Its Predecessors, in thousands, (b) Population, in millions. Horizontal axis – Time, years.
Words data – from Table 3.2.1. Population data – from [15].

Second Turning Point in Humankind's History

We know that humankind's activity and survival are largely dependent on global climate fluctuations. Let us turn to the available scientific data in this area.

A sharp increase in global temperature occurs around 10000 BC. Temperature rise around 10000 BC was a gift from nature. However, for people to have a chance, more was needed. As you can see in Figure 3.3.2, sudden increases in temperature have already happened many times during the Ice Age. But over the past 450 thousand years there have been no examples of long periods with stable and sufficiently warm climatic conditions.

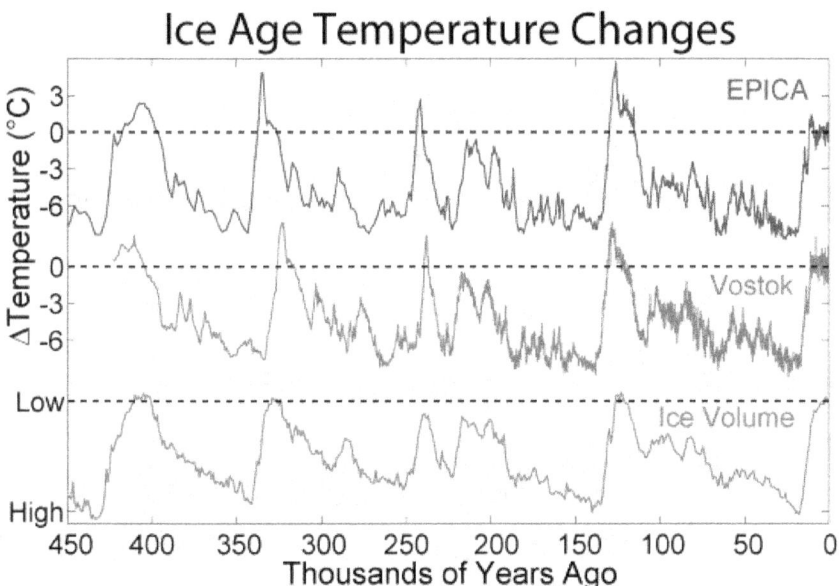

Figure 3.3.2. Ice age temperature and ice volume [16]
(a) Top chart – EPICA site, (b) Middle chart – Vostok site, (c) Bottom chart – Global ice volume.
Vertical axis – (a) and (b) local changes in temperature at two sites in Antarctica, (c) global ice volume. Horizontal axis – Time, thousands of years
The present-day (the year 2000) is at 0 on the right.

Look at the temperature peaks in Figure 3.3.2. Before the *Holocene*, all those peaks were sharp. Surprisingly, per Figure 3.3.3, a unique *Holocene* period has a very stable climate. Such relatively long and stable periods with warm enough temperatures rarely happen. From the available data, it looks like one chance in at least 450 thousand years. And already having a "modern behavior" at that time - probably much less than a one-in-million chance.

It can be argued that "small" fluctuations of 0.5–1 degree Celsius have greatly affected humanity. We have confirmation of this from our history [18].

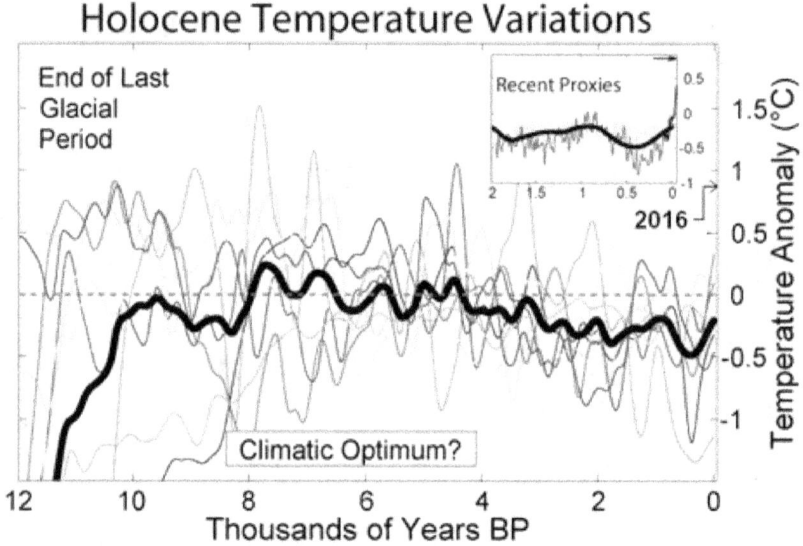

Holocene Temperature Variations

Figure 3.3.3. Holocene Temperature Variations.
10000 BC to 2000 AD [17]
Vertical axis – Global temperature deviation from **the mid-20th-century average temperature.**
Horizontal axis – Time, thousands of years.
The present-day (the year 2000) is at 0 on the right. BP stands for Before Present. The thick black line is an average of eight different reconstructions of Holocene temperature.

The Rhine froze over on New Year's Eve 406 AD. "Many believe that widespread drought in central Eurasia triggered migration to both China and the Roman Empire from around 300 to 500 AD." The ice on the Adriatic Sea near Venice was very thick in 858-860 AD. Then came the so-called "Little Ice Age," which was conveniently defined as the period from 1600 to 1850 AD. In the first half of the 1600s, China experienced floods and droughts. As a result, peasants were unable to pay taxes. The peasants rebelled. These circumstances led to the Manchu conquest of China and then the establishment of the Qing dynasty.

Yes, we could see that even "small" changes in average temperature could lead to dramatic events in some or all human societies.

However, for humankind as a whole, those 12 thousand years of stable *Holocene* climate are a surprisingly good period.

Holocene temperature variations are small compared to other variations during the previous 450 thousand years. And the *Holocene* temperatures were warm enough for humans to start farming.

Scientists have frequently participated in debate about when this or that geological era begins and ends. The last word in this debate belongs to a certain decision-making body to which scientists have delegated such authority. That body is the Executive Committee of the International Union of Geological Sciences (IUGS). In June 2018, IUGS decided that the start of the *Holocene* era was 9700 BC. [18] We will stick to this definition.

From the proposed models of humankind's development, we have established that the point in time when the pace of humankind's development radically changed was approximately 10700 BC – 10500 BC. Two different resources were created by humankind in 10700 BC and 10500 BC. The date assigned by the scientific government body for the beginning of the *Holocene*, 9700 BC, is within 1000 years of 10700 BC and 800 years from 10500 BC.

A detailed discussion of the impact of input data uncertainty on the sensitivity and stability of models will follow.

Here we can note a good coincidence of the declared decision of the IUGS on the date of the beginning of the *Holocene* and the two dates of the creation of resources at the turning point of a radical change in the pace of humankind's development.

Conclusion 1: The beginning of the unique geological period of the *Holocene* created favorable conditions for the rapid creation of new resources by humanity starting from 10500 BC – 10000 BC.

Conclusion 2: The proposed models of humankind's development at important moments in humankind's history correlate with processes on our planet that had or could have a significant impact on humanity.

Conclusion 3: The curve of humankind's development is complex and is not smooth. Unusual data points or periods detected by high- or low-level models of humanity are likely not statistical noise. Instead, these dates or date periods may be caused by important processes.

Changes in Environments Were Not Fast Enough

As we can see from Figure 3.3.3, the global climate has been warm and remarkably stable over the past twelve thousand years.

Imagine that you are watching the ceremony in a stadium. This is the procedure for awarding the winners of the heavyweight competition. The contest category was the "main driving force of humankind's development." Before the *Holocene,* climate change proudly took first place on the podium. Forces of well-known biological evolution got the silver medal. That was the norm.

There were only two competitors and no newcomers. That situation was unshaken for millions of years.

Then, in the *Holocene,* climate stability pushed the force of climate change off its pedestal. We are also unaware of any significant changes in human biology over the past 12,000 years. In other words, both the first and second guys were almost completely passive during these short 12 thousand years. They don't seem to have competed at all during the *Holocene.*

This was not a normal situation. This opened the door for a new player to enter the competition.

At this time, humankind's development was accelerating. A well-known fact is the correlation between a stable climate in the *Holocene* and the rapid development of humankind.[20] However, there has been no serious scientific discussion on this matter. No new driving force has been proposed or identified.

Look again at the data in Table 1. Over the past 12.5 thousand years, starting from 10500 BC, humanity has created 23 new classes of resources for itself. How many classes of resources were created in the previous 12.5 thousand years? Zero. From 23000 BC to 10500 BC humanity did not produce any classes of resources.

What happened at the dawn of the *Holocene*? There was an almost unbelievable leapfrog jump in humankind's capabilities in a super short, by historical count, time. How could that happen?

In 1785, a book, which is famous now, was published. In that book, Baron Munchausen pulls himself out of a mire by his own hair.[21] That was an impossible event. Of course, it was fictional. We should reject the notion that, somehow, humankind pulled itself from being an unremarkable animal in the swamps of time.

There should exist something in the *Holocene* forcing that remarkable transformation of humankind. Yet, we have already found that it was not a force of climate change, and it was not the force of biological evolution. Then, what is this yet-unknown force? Can we even propose a candidate for this force?

Anytime you have population growth, there are business opportunities.

Roland Darson

Chapter 3.4.

Driving Force of Humankind's Development

Which Force is Driving Humankind's Development?

Criteria for a Search of the Driving Force

We know that external forces have been overthrown since the arrival of the *Holocene*, a time of astonishing acceleration in humankind's development. We must investigate humanity itself.

But what should we look for in our search for new driving force? Let us think about this. There are three questions to ask here. A yet undiscovered force must influence all of humanity to do "what?" Do "when?" Do "how often?"

Conventional history will not help us answer the "what" question. We are not interested in why people managed to start a new war. Or how some rulers happily inherited the long tradition of a dynasty ruling over a country.

We should consider the essence of humankind's development. And this is a subsurface history, revealed in the proposed high- or low- level models. If you look at Table 1 or Table 2, you already know the answer.

The driving force must push humanity to increase the totality of resources or classes of resources created by humankind for itself. We have already said earlier that the essence of the deep-level history of humanity is in the creation of new resources for humankind to act. Act on what? New resources should help people solve big problems and find new ways of development.

The answer to the question of "when" is also before our eyes. These new resources must be created frequently with the onset of a stable and warm *Holocene* climate.

"How often?" There is no easy answer to this question. However, we have already seen the exact pattern of how often this happens in the actual history of humankind. Look at the curve in Figure 1 as humanity's response to a driving force. The answer was not clear. It was not even over time. Closer to the present time it has accelerated. Therefore, the driving force does not always have to be the same. The value of this force must change over time.

There must also be an unmistakable correlation between the driving force and humanity's response to it.

Different Uses of the Term Driving Force

The term driving force has three completely different meanings, which is a source of confusion and misunderstanding.

In mechanics and physics, several forces can act on one object. The produced vector quantity when two or more forces act on one object is called net force or resultant force. In mechanics there is a precise definition and formulas for calculating the resultant force.

Suppose the net force pushes the object in the direction in which it is already moving. In this case, it accelerates the object. Sometimes such a net force in mechanics is called a driving force. With this understanding of the driving force, it has a precise definition and can be calculated.

However, the term driving force in mechanics is excessive. Therefore, professional physicists rarely use this term.

Over time, people began to use the term driving force in a similar way to mechanics. Examples are electrochemical driving force,[1] or thermodynamic force.[2] In such cases, the driving force directly affects the object and can still be calculated. This is the first type of use of the term driving force.

However, most meanings of the term driving force now are very different. In these cases, the driving force is essentially a substitute for the term "main force(s)" or "primary force(s)," which are not clearly defined and cannot be calculated. When used in this manner, it is impossible to prove that the driving force is the primary or only force that causes an object to move in a particular direction or manner. In this usage, the term driving force of the object is merely an opinion expressed in unverifiable terms, an undeclared substitute for the term "one of the forces acting on an object." This is the second type of use of the term driving force.

There is also a third type of use of the term driving force. In this case, researchers try to prove a cause-and-effect relationship between the behavior of the driving force and the behavior of the object on which the driving force acts.

The term driving force is now used in biology,[3] psychology,[4] history ,[5] and more. The tendency to use the term driving force in this way often results in the presentation of not one, but many driving forces that still need to be prioritized.

Biological evolution is generally considered to have four driving forces: mutation, gene flow, genetic drift, and natural selection. "Low levels of gene flow are sufficient to counteract opposing mutation, drift, and selection." [5]

Historian Halfdan Kocht, in his book "Driving Forces in History,"[6] listed at least nine driving forces of history: religion, cooperative spirit, economics, class consciousness, state power, rebellion and obedience, science, war and internationalism. None of the proposed driving forces in his book were quantifiable. They were not measured or prioritized among themselves.

To prove a cause-and-effect relationship between phenomena, a researcher usually needs to have a sufficiently large statistical data set, then prove a mathematical correlation, and finally, a cause-and-effect relationship. This is a known problem in science.

Recently, a new scientific direction has emerged - the theory of causal inference. "This theory can be thought of as an algebra or language for reasoning about cause and effect."[7]

There are several examples of the application of the theory of causal inference to the term driving force.[8]

However, in the humankind's history, we were only been able to find articles on driving forces with opinions expressed in unverifiable terms.

The main problem is the lack of statistics on humanity's supposed driving force and expected development of humankind.

One of the results of this work is a large but compact set of more than 300 data points on the dynamics of humankind's development over a very long period. This data set provides the basis for a hypothesis about the driving force of humankind's development with possible, over time, analysis using statistics and causality theory.

Not everyone in the scientific community accepts the concept of driving force. One possible reason is that it is difficult to prove it in specific circumstances.

It may take many years for scientists to recognize this. Here is a famous example. We all like to draw dinosaurs. They have been the kings of the world on our planet for millions of years. For decades, researchers have tried to figure out what caused the extinction of dinosaurs. Over time, the picture became more obvious. There is now a generally accepted theory about how this happens. The so-called Alvarez theory was put forward in 1980.[9]

A giant comet, or perhaps an asteroid 6 to 9 miles wide, collided with Earth about 66 million years ago. This was the trigger for a chain of global events. First, the interaction of the asteroid with the Earth led to a multi-year global winter.

The global winter was a dramatic and sharp climate change. Its influence on life on the planet was colossal. After the meteor impact, more than two-thirds of the animals went extinct within the next tens of thousands of years after the impact. It was an unfortunate dead end for the dinosaurs. Many biological niches were devastated, which, in turn, led to the rise and dominance of mammals. Without the spread of mammals there would be no great apes and people would not walk the Earth.

Sudden climate change caused a sharp change in the direction of biological evolution. Scientists have debated the evidence, pros, and cons of Alvarez's hypothesis for many years. It took more than twenty years for this hypothesis to become generally accepted.

However, it is much more difficult to prove a cause-and-effect relationship with climate change when the events are not so catastrophic.

This is why climate change as a driving force is still considered a hypothesis and not a fact in the scientific community[10].

Naturally, our upcoming conclusion about the driving force of humankind's development in the Holocene will also be a hypothesis.

The Driving Force Hypothesis

We have considered driving forces external to humanity. They do not explain the overall rapid development of humanity in the *Holocene*. This result is an invitation to look at possible driving forces within humankind.

What events occurred at the beginning of the *Holocene*? What major event was valued most by scientists? Well, the answer is simple. We know that researchers of conventional history consider revolutions to be the main events.

From a traditional history of events standpoint, the agricultural revolution is a convenient answer. Could this be the driving force for the last twelve thousand years? Of course not. This revolution did not last twelve thousand years.

Let us look at trends that began at the dawn of the *Holocene*. We also need to understand how long these trends have been viable. Of the significant trends that emerged 12 thousand years ago, two interrelated trends could be candidates for the role of driving force. The first of them is the increase in humankind's population. The second is the increased use of domesticated plants and animals.

Can we determine if either of these two might be the driving force? There was no exchange of views among scientists about humankind's driving forces within *Holocene*. However, there is another discussion. It is still ongoing. This is the discussion about which of the two mentioned trends provoked another one at the beginning of the *Holocene*.

According to some scientific estimates, the world population of people at the time when the domestication of plants and animals began to take shape, in 10000 BC, was about 1–10 million people. At that time, most people lived in small bands located far apart from each other.

Since this time, the growth of humankind's population has been astounding. It rose to 2–20 million in 5000 BC, approximately 27 million in 2000 BC, 150 million in 200 BC, 443 million in 1340 and 2000 million in 1925. According to the latest United Nations estimates, there were 7.7 billion people on Earth. as of October 2019.[11,12,13] That is a million-fold increase since 10000 BC to 2019.

We propose that humankind's population change has been the driving force behind humankind's development since the beginning of the *Holocene*.

First Criterion for a Driving Force

We noted that the role of population growth and domestication during the early *Holocene* is still part of an ongoing debate.[14] This discussion is about which one was a trigger for the other.

We look at it from a completely different point of view. Our question is, which of the two candidates better meets our criteria for being a driving force?

According to the first criterion, a new resource must help people solve big problems and find new ways of development.

Let us look at the *Independent Communication Channels* class of resources. The first use of this class of resources was made possible by the creation of a postal system with changing stations. This happened in the Persian Empire in 550 BC. Creating a new and fast communication channel was a brilliant solution to some problems.

What makes people create such a solution? Was there a problem in controlling a thriving population in an expanding territory? Or was it a response to the growing number of domesticated plants and animals? This is just one example. This example shows that the problems that arose in society had their source in population growth. The problems were not related to the growing number of cows.

Second Criterion for a Driving Force

The second criterion concerns the continuity of the driving force. The system must respond to driving forces throughout the entire period of humankind's activity since the beginning of the *Holocene*. Is this the case with domesticated plants and animals? Well, at the beginning of the *Holocene*, the use of domesticated plants and animals influenced some decisions of some people. Is this the same situation now? No. Now everything is different in both developing and developed countries.

In the former, "children are needed as a labor force and to provide care for their parents in old age."[15] In other words, food availability is currently at least not the only factor influencing people's decisions to have children. In developed countries, concerns about food availability have dropped from the top of the list altogether. The *Usage of domesticated plants and animals* may still be a factor. However, this is not the main factor. We can also look at a simple forecast for the near future.

With approximately 8 billion people living on Earth, agriculture has already placed a heavy burden on our planet. Moreover, in the future, agriculture may not be able to provide enough food for an ever-growing population. Are there any solutions to this problem? Yes, there are. One solution is the production of artificial meat. Its quality is getting better and better. Its price is falling very quickly.[16] We could imagine a future where most of our food comes from artificial food factories. It is doable.

We could summarize the arguments presented this way. We must reject the possibility that changes in food availability are the driving force behind humankind's development. Otherwise, we may soon bring ourselves to declare artificial food production as the driving force of humankind's development.

So far, the domestication of plants and animals has not held scrutiny of our second criterion.

On the other hand, changes in humankind's population numbers hold up throughout the *Holocene*. The population continues to grow, creating new problems and providing new opportunities for humankind's development.

The key test is whether there is an unmistakable correlation between the driving force and humanity's response to it.

We have data on population growth since 10000 BC. This chart is shown in Figure 3.4.1 in this book. Compare this to Figure 1, which shows the totality of classes of resources over time. Both curves are not proportional to each other. However, there is a clear correlation between the development of the curves over time.

We will hypothesize that "a population change is a driving force of humankind's development in the *Holocene*." This hypothesis has yet to be confirmed by independent researchers. We do not believe that such a reminder is necessary in this book going forward. Therefore, in further chapters of this book, the term "hypothesis" associated with the driving force of humankind's development in the *Holocene* will be omitted.

Population Growth Trend

Scientists have been tracking the global population for a long time. It has been established that its growth curve is hyperbolic. This growth is faster than exponential. To show this growth during the *Holocene*, we present two graphs at different scales in Figure 3.4.1. On the top one we could see how quickly the Sapiens population grew from 10000 BC to the beginning of the era AD. However, as you can see, this growth is negligible compared to what we have over the last two thousand years in the bottom graph.

Look at the curve in Figure 3.4.1 as the driving force behind humankind's development. You can compare this force with humanity's response to it, the curve in Figure 1. The correlation between them is obvious. However, the rate of emergence of new classes of resources is slower than population growth. This is expected, since nonlinear relationships are a hallmark of complex systems. The sharp rise in both curves over the past hundred years is beyond doubt.

The Significance of a New Driving Force

With the onset of the *Holocene* geological period, for the first time, the physical or biological environment on Earth was no longer the primary driving force for the development of one species - humans. This is not simply replacing one driving force with another.

According to our hypothesis, one species, Sapiens, under certain conditions acquired the ability to be independent of external driving forces. It does not matter that humanity did not do it consciously. This is still a tectonic shift in the development of life on our planet. Could such a thing be sustainable in the future?

500 million Years of Climate Changes

In other words, can humankind's development still be driven by population change rather than climate change? There are many variables to consider when looking for a likely answer. Here we will look at just one factor to consider when looking for a possible answer. Scientists have yet to figure out the reason for the long-term climate stability in the *Holocene*. This is not an expected climate behavior on this planet.

We could see an analogy in the behavior of the stock market. The market experiences regular intervals of ups and downs to varying degrees. However, sometimes there are outstanding market moves. An example would be an unusually long bull market. The longer we have this situation, the more we should expect a "return to the mean" in market behavior.

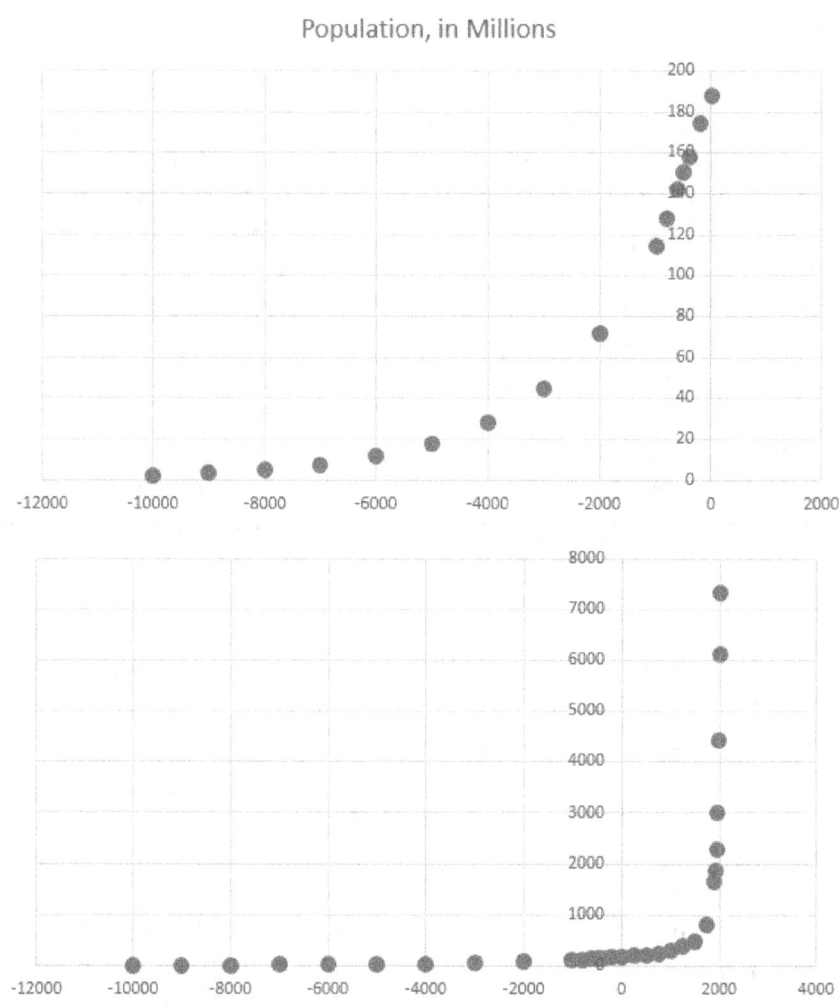

Figure 3.4.1. Humankind's population.
(a) Top chart – 10000 BC - 1AD, (b) Bottom chart – 10000 BC to 2018 AD.
Vertical axis – Population, in Millions.
Horizontal axis – Time, years. Data were provided in US Census
Bureau contributors (2012).[13]

Likewise, we should expect Earth's climate to return to its typical periodic pattern of ups and downs.

The dramatic change in climate away from the *Holocene* temperature plateau is long-awaited. We do not know why this did not happen, say, ten thousand years ago. This makes us wonder what will bring the *Holocene* to an end and when.

This could happen in just a thousand years or even less. It should not be forgotten that at the beginning of the *Holocene*, in just ten years, "the temperature in Greenland rose with an impressive 8 degrees, which corresponds to that North Europe's climate was replaced with a Mediterranean climate."[3]

Our planet has enormous diversity. Humanity conquered the planet. People live in all climate zones of the Earth, even in Antarctica. Humanity has become a technological power. We are on the verge of becoming an interplanetary species.

Sapiens existed on Earth for about 200 - 300 thousand years. According to Figure 2, over the past 150 thousand years, global temperatures have ranged from minus 6 degrees Celsius to plus 4 degrees Celsius compared to current temperature levels. In the *Holocene*, on average, according to Figure 3, we have changes of only 0.5 degrees Celsius. Temperature swings up and down before the *Holocene* were enormous.

What do you think? Will we experience an abrupt transition to a much colder or hotter climate?

The current debate about "climate change" has largely avoided ending the *Holocene* topic. In the recent Intergovernmental Panel on Climate Change (IPCC) report,[15] the word *Holocene* was not even mentioned. The end of the *Holocene* could lead to a much larger change in global temperatures than is assumed in the "current climate change" debate.

Try different activities to see which skill is best suitable for your success. Without variety, you'll never truly know.

Mitta Xinindlu

Chapter 3.5.

Various Fields of Humankind's Activity

The variety and richness of data presented in the subsurface history of humankind allows us to study the history of various areas of humankind's activity. We counted twenty-three classes of resources created by humanity over the past 44 thousand years.

We could construct a graph for each area, showing the pace and direction of development of specific areas of humankind's activity. It makes sense to compare the development trajectories of different classes of resources.

The overall pace of humankind's development is very uneven. Therefore, a comparison of classes of resources will only be representative if the two classes of resources are neighbors in terms of the classes' appearance dates.

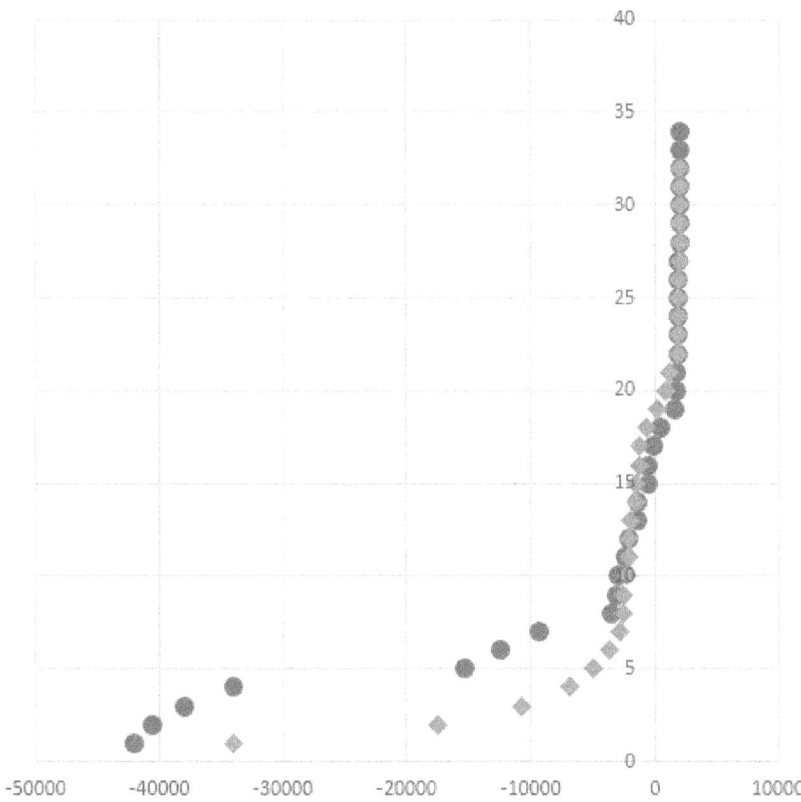

Figure 3.5.1. History of Humankind. 42000 BC - 2023 AD
Vertical – Number of accumulated resources.
Horizontal – Time, years.
1. *Art and Music* **(dots) – 34 data points.**
2. *Man-Made Materials, Substances, and Organisms*
(diamonds) – 32 data points.
Regional low-level models of two classes of resources.

The *Art and Music* class of resources emerged in 42000 BC. The *Man-Made Materials, Substances, and Organisms* class of resources emerged in 34000 BC.

The pace and shape of the development curves of both fields of humankind's activities are similar. In both areas, there are two different periods of growth acceleration.

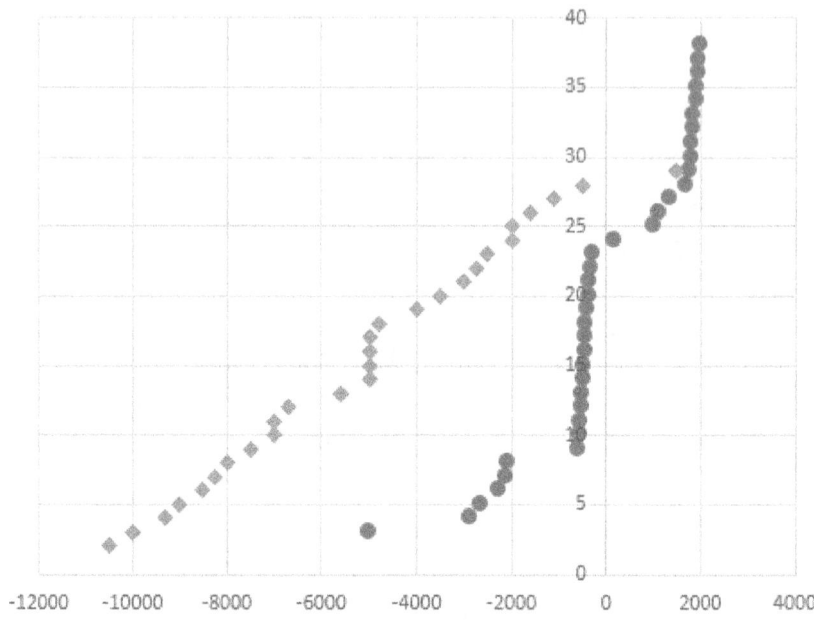

Figure 3.5.2. History of Humankind. 42000 BC - 2023 AD
Vertical – Number of accumulated resources.
Horizontal – Time, years.
1. *People and Societies as Objects of Study*
(dots) – 40 data points (Two first points combined).
2. *Usage of Domesticated Plants and Animals*
(diamonds) – 32 data points (Two first points combined).
Regional low-level models of two classes of resources.

The *People and Societies as Objects of Study* class of resources emerged in 29000 BC. The *Usage of Domesticated Plants and Animals* class of resources emerged in 32100-16800 BC, with an average date of 24450 BC.

Both classes of resources started to grow rapidly from the beginning of the *Holocene*. Unlike most classes of resources, the *Usage of Domesticated Plants and Animals* class of resources grew differently.

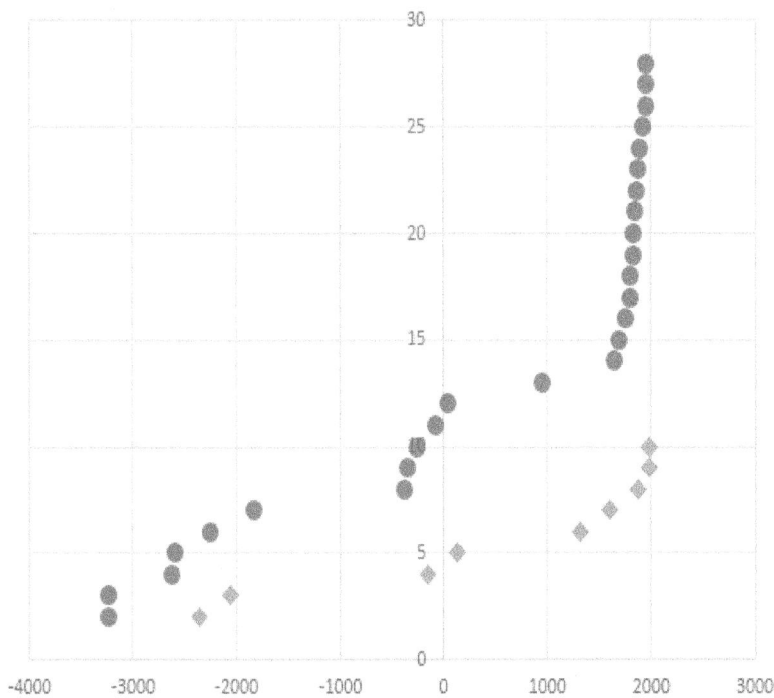

Figure 3.5.3. History of Humankind. 42000 BC - 2023 AD
Vertical – Number of accumulated resources.
Horizontal – Time, years.
1. *Trade with a Use of anIintermediary*
(diamonds) – 10 data points (Two first points combined).
2. *Tools, Devices, and Machines from Man-Made Materials*
(dots) – 28 data points
(Two first points combined).
Regional low-level models of two classes of resources.

The *Trade with a Use of an Intermediary* class of resources emerged in 11000-8000 BC, with an average date of 9500 BC. *Tools, Devices, and Machines from Man-Made Materials* class of resources emerged in 8040-7510 BC, with an average date of 7775 BC.

Both classes of resources have similar curves until about 1800. The number of resources that emerged in the first class of resources were almost three times less than in the second class of resources.

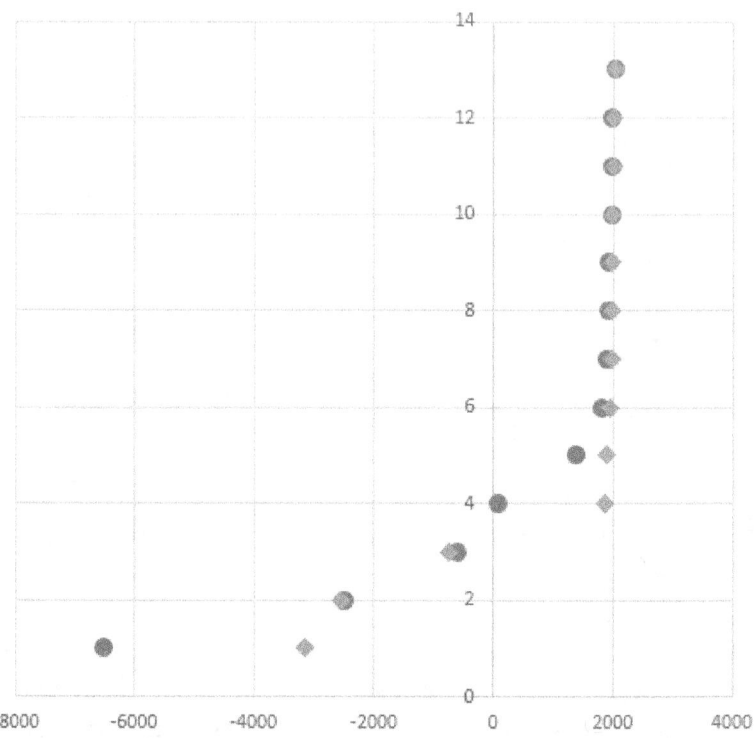

Figure 3.5.4. History of Humankind. 42000 BC - 2023 AD
Vertical – Number of accumulated resources.
Horizontal – Time, years.
1. *Mass Transportation* (dots) – 14 data points.
2. *External Information Storage and Processing*
(diamonds) – 13 data points.
Regional low-level models of two classes of resources.

The *Mass Transportation* class of resources emerged in 6500 BC. The *External Information Storage and Processing* class of resources emerged in 3200-3100 BC, with an average date of 3150 BC.

The curves of both classes of resources have a high degree of similarity.

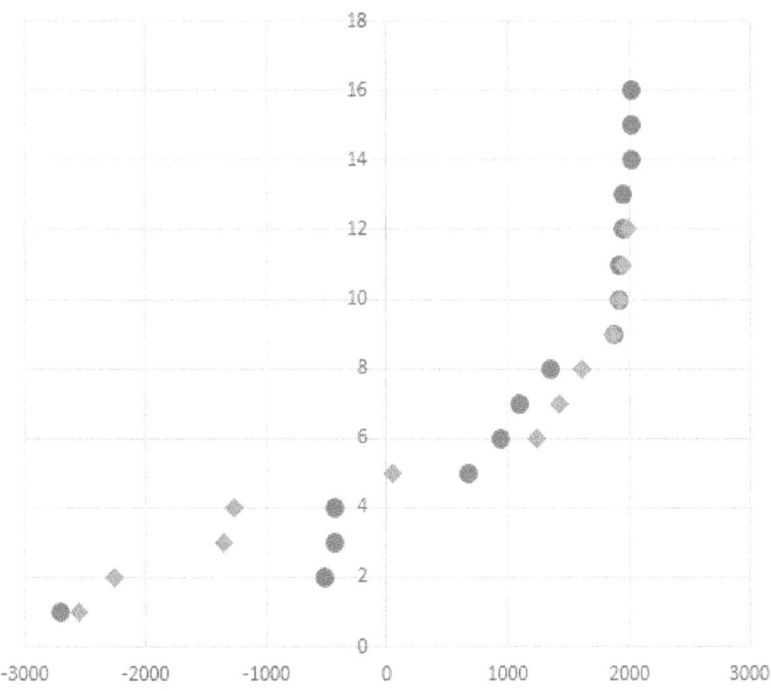

Figure 3.5.5. History of Humankind. 42000 BC - 2023 AD
Vertical – Number of accumulated resources.
Horizontal – Time, years.
1. *War and Means of Warfare* **(dots) – 16 data points.**
2. *Transnational Entities* **(diamonds) – 12 data points.**
Regional low-level models of two classes of resources.

The *War and Means of Warfare* class of resources emerged in 2700 BC. The *Transnational entities* class of resources emerged in 2550 BC.

The War and Means of Warfare class of resources is about fighting with others, while the *Transnational Entities* class of resources is about cooperation with others. However,, these two opposing areas of humankind's activity exhibit similar shapes of development curves.

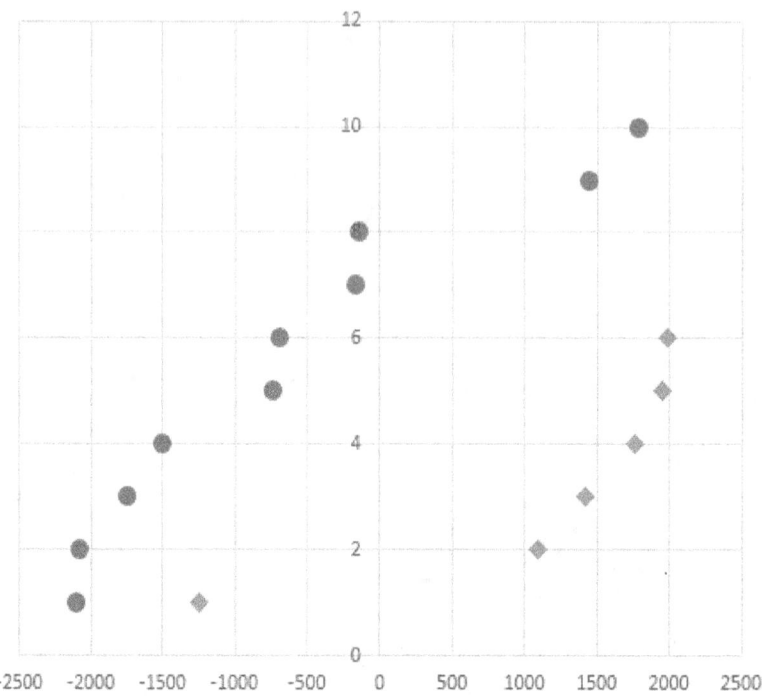

Figure 3.5.6. History of Humankind. 42000 BC - 2023 AD
Vertical – Number of accumulated resources.
Horizontal – Time, years.
1. *People as a Resource on a Massive scale*
(dots) – 10 data points.
2. *Mass Education* **(diamonds) – 6 data points.**
Regional low-level models of two classes of resources.

The *People as a Resource on a Massive Scale* class of resources emerged in 2160-2140 BC, with an average date of 2150 BC. The *Mass Education* class of resources emerged in 1292-1190 BC, with an average date of 1241 BC.

Like most other classes of resources, the *Mass Education* class of resources has a pace that accelerates over time. The *People as a Resource on a Massive Scale* class of resources does not exhibit similar behavior.

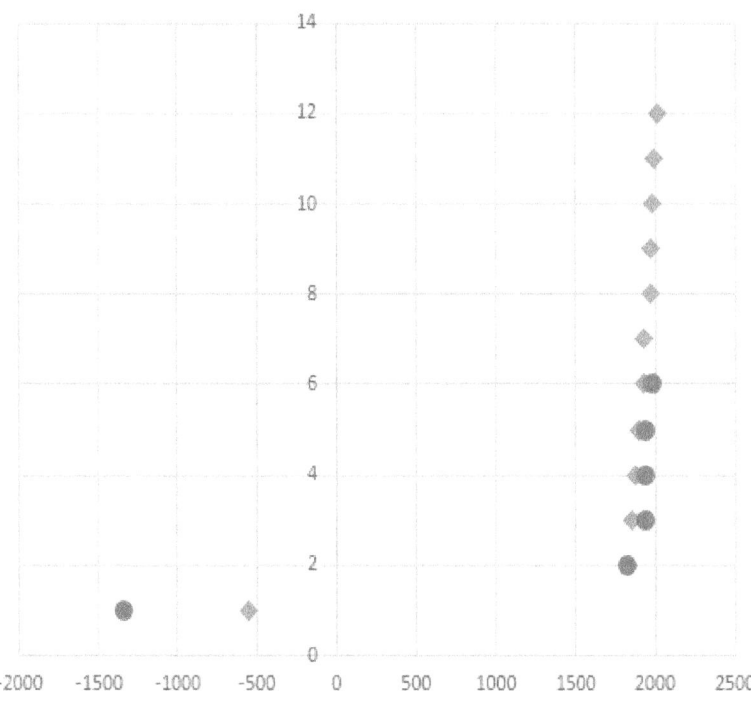

Figure 3.5.7. History of Humankind. 42000 BC - 2023 AD
Vertical – Number of accumulated resources.
Horizontal – Time, years.
1. *Use of Forces of Nature, Relativity, and Quantum Physics*
(dots) – 6 data points.
2. *Independent Communication Channels*
(diamonds) – 12 data points.
Regional low-level models of two classes of resources.

The *Use of Forces of Nature, Relativity, and Quantum Physics* class of resources emerged in 1346-1334 BC, with an average date of 1340 BC. The *Independent Communication Channels* class of resources emerged in 550 BC.

Both classes of resources show a similar shape of development curves.

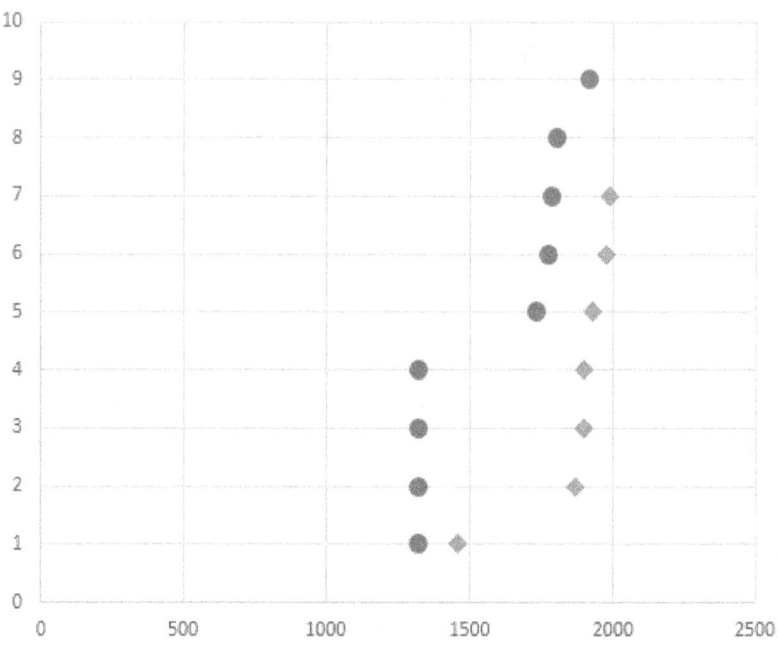

Figure 3.5.8. History of Humankind. 42000 BC - 2023 AD
Vertical – Number of accumulated.
Horizontal – Time, years.
1. *Mass Production* (dots) – 9 data points.
2. *Mass Media* (diamonds) – 7 data points.
Regional low-level models of two classes of resources.

The *Mass Production* class of resources emerged in 1320. The *Mass Media* class of resources emerged in 1455.

The *Mass Production* class of resources is atypical because almost half of the resources in this class of resources were created at around the same time at one factory in Venice.

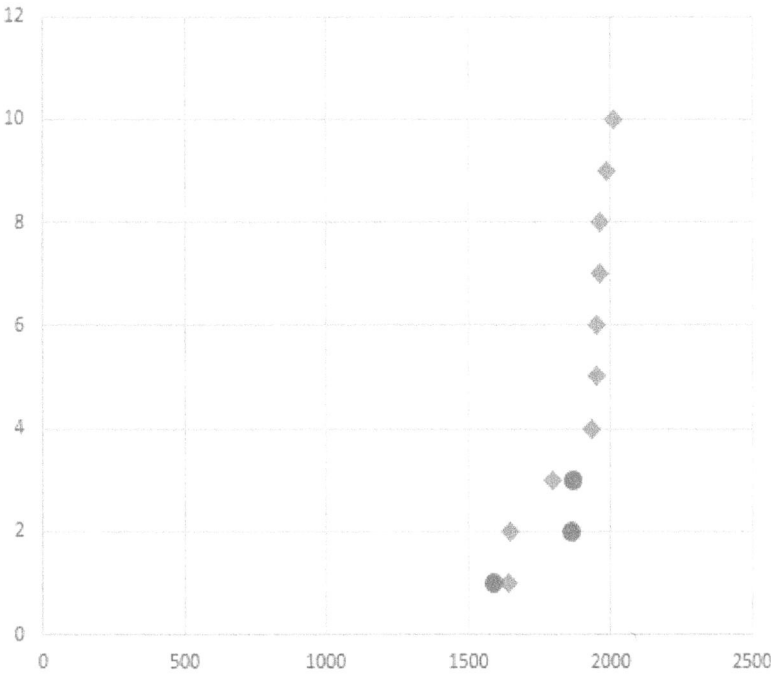

Figure 3.5.9. History of Humankind. 42000 BC - 2023 AD
Vertical – Number of accumulated. Horizontal – Time, years.
1. *Technology beyond the Limitations of Human Senses*
(dots) – 3 data points.
2. *Usage of the Scientific Method and Information Technology*
(diamonds) – 10 data points.
Regional low-level models of two classes of resources.

The *Technology beyond the Limitations of Human Senses* class of resources emerged in 1590. The *Usage of the Scientific Method and Information Technology* class of resources emerged in 1642.

Humans possess only five senses, and consequently, the resources available in this class of resources are limited.

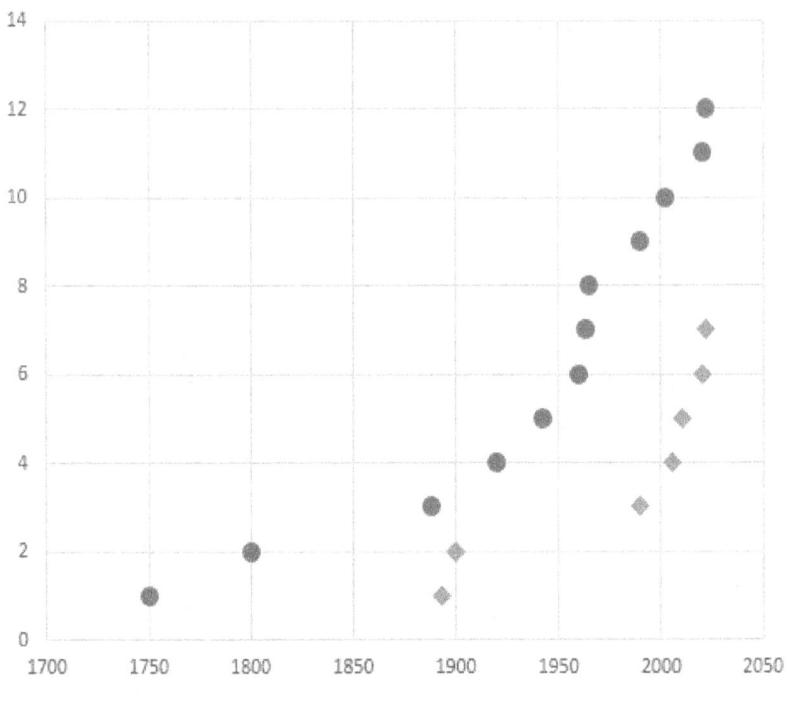

Figure 3.5.10. History of Humankind. 42000 BC - 2023 AD
Vertical – Number of accumulated resources.
Horizontal – Time, years.
1. *Usage of Natural Resources on a Massive Scale*
(dots) – 12 data points.
2. *Massive Involvement of Women in Humankind's Activities*
(diamonds) – 7 data points.
Regional low-level models of two classes of resources.

The *Usage of Natural Resources on a Massive Scale* class of resources emerged in 1750. The *Massive Involvement of Women in Humankind's Activities* class of resources emerged in 1893.

Many dates of emergence of resources in those two classes of resources were defined as some global milestones, instead of local inventions, as in most of the other resources created by humankind. Still, the curves of development of those two classes of resources are very similar to other classes of resources.

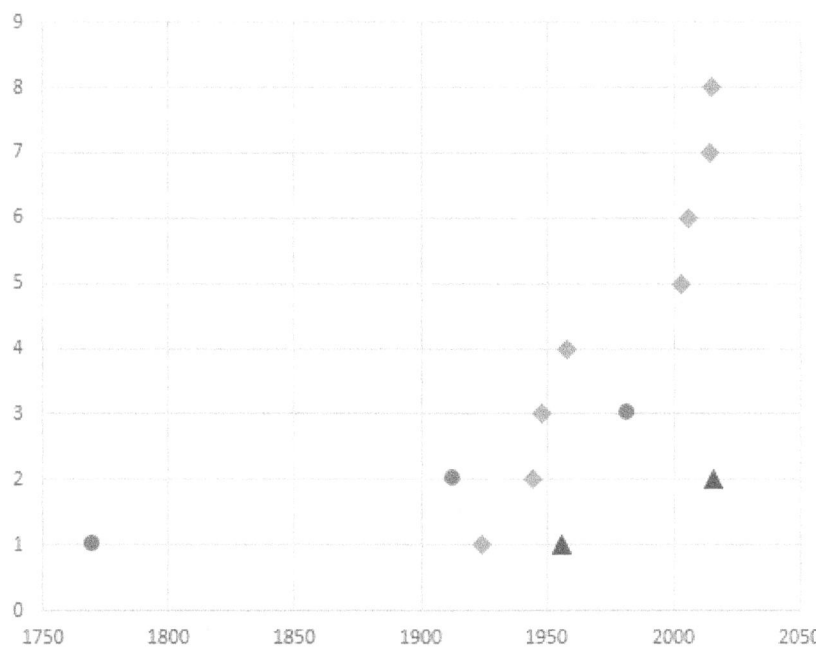

Figure 3.5.11. History of Humankind. 42000 BC - 2023 AD
Vertical – Number of accumulated resources.
Horizontal – Time, years.
1. *Life Expectancy Growth* **(dots) – 3 data points.**
2. *Digital Technology* **(diamonds) – 8 data points.**
3. *Artificial Intelligence (AI)* **(triangles)**
– 2 data points.
Regional low-level models of three classes of resources.

The *Life Expectancy Growth* class of resources emerged in 1770. The *Digital Technology* class of resources emerged in 1924. The *Artificial Intelligence (AI)* class of resources emerged in 1956.

Those three classes of resources are the ones that emerged most recently. Consequently, they have a smaller number of emerged resources in each class compared with the oldest ones.

Objectivity requires taking subjectivity into account.

Lorraine Code

Chapter 3.6.
Objectivity and Stability of the Proposed Models

How Objective are the Proposed Models of Humankind?

We drew the whole history of humankind as a simple graph. The curves in Figure 1 and Figure 2 show us the dynamics of humankind's development over many millennia.

The names of classes of resources or resources were taken from scientific publications or assigned by us. Those names are not set in stone and could be fine-tuned. Instead of the name *Mass Transportation,* we could use *Mass Transportation of People and Cargo* name or something similar. Yes, the names of resources or classes of resources are subjective, but they do not impact what is under those names.

The essence of the resource or class of resources under that subjective name has an objective value. Mass transportation exists independently of our views on it. It does not matter if you see it as beautiful, ugly, dangerous, or comfortable. Specific cars or tanks may become obsolete, not used, or destroyed. Still, mass transportation continues to exist and be used by people.

Choices on Dates

The quantitative model of humankind requires us to use events together with dates, which indicate when those events happened. Researchers try to identify the dates for events as precisely as possible. However, history is not a precise science. Many factors come into play here. We need to find out the possible variations of the dates. There is also some flexibility in choosing an inception date for specific resources.

We should consider that, also. Even all that knowledge is not enough for us. We must check to what extent we can withstand the named imprecision. Most importantly, we want to ensure the reliability of our model results.

When did the *Technology beyond the Limitations of Human Senses* class of resources emerge?

In the 13th century, the first eyeglasses were invented. Time passes. In the 16th century, the first microscope was invented. Which one of those dates is better to mark as the first use of the *Technology beyond the Limitations of Human Senses* class of resources?

Well, in this case, a choice is easy. Eyeglasses are used to help people who do not have typical "normal" vision. Eyeglasses aim to return to the norm and to stay within that. What was the purpose of the invention of the microscope and telescope? The inspiration and ambition of the creators was to create technology that allows you to see much more than what the naked eye can see. They succeeded. We also know that the microscope was created before the telescope. This is why we chose the date when the microscope was first manufactured.

There were times when the choice was not so obvious. Of course, our choice may later be challenged by researchers.

Other Sources of Individual Dates Imprecision

There are other problems. It is hard to find evidence for an emergence date for resources created before writing was invented. Consider, for example, the date when animals or plants were first domesticated. It could be that the same type of animals was domesticated independently in different parts of the world. We must choose the earliest one or a range to include both events.

The other case could be when a domesticated variant did not survive. Or it could be that all current variants of the domesticated animal are descendants from another lineage. Which date should we choose?

For consistency's sake, we always look for the earliest dates. That means we use the earliest dates around the globe and for any variants.

From time to time, an advancement in technology and discoveries forced researchers to revisit previous dates.

The latest such change recently happened right before our eyes. We are talking about the famous lion-man figurine, found in the 20th century in Germany. The date of the lion-man creation was estimated to be around forty thousand years ago. The scientific community almost unanimously considered this figurine the first confirmation of modern-behaved humans.[1,2]

Yet, in 2020, an article was published in the *Nature* journal about Indonesian cave paintings, which were 44 thousand years old[3,4]. Those cave paintings depicted part-human, part-animal figures. Then, what? The scientific community must move the date of the behavioral modernity of humans four thousand years back.

Imagine that this book was written in 2018 instead of 2023. We then had to define the beginning of humankind's history as 38000 BC instead of 42000 BC. Will it impact our high-level model of humanity and conclusions from that model? Yes and no. It is "yes" because specific date will change. It is "no" because the model's results will remain the same. The direction of humankind's development will be the same. The shape of the curves on a scale in Figure 1 or Figure 2 will be pretty much the same.

Figure 3.6.1 compares two curves of humankind's development in a high-level model. The top chart shows humankind's history if we assign the emergence date of the first class of resources, *Art and Music*, as 38000 BC according to the data available in 2018 AD - the data point at 38000 BC marked by a green triangle.   The bottom chart shows humankind's history with the emergence date of the first class of resources, *Art and Music*, as 42000 BC, according to data available in 2023 AD - the data point at 42000 BC marked by a red diamond.

We see that the shape of the curve, the direction of humankind's development, and the pace of humankind move in most periods of humankind's history are the same.

Over time, we will have to adjust the position of some individual points on the humankind's development curve. However, we have just seen that even moving one data point by four thousand years did not change the curve much.

Conclusions from the subsurface history of humankind still hold in the high-level model of humankind's history. Note that in the high-level model, we have 23 data points. In the low-level model, with 318 data points, the mentioned change in the date of the first emergence of the first resource in the *Art and Music* class of resources, from the *Sculpture* resource in 38000 BC to the *Painting* resource at 42000 BC, will be almost invisible on the graph.

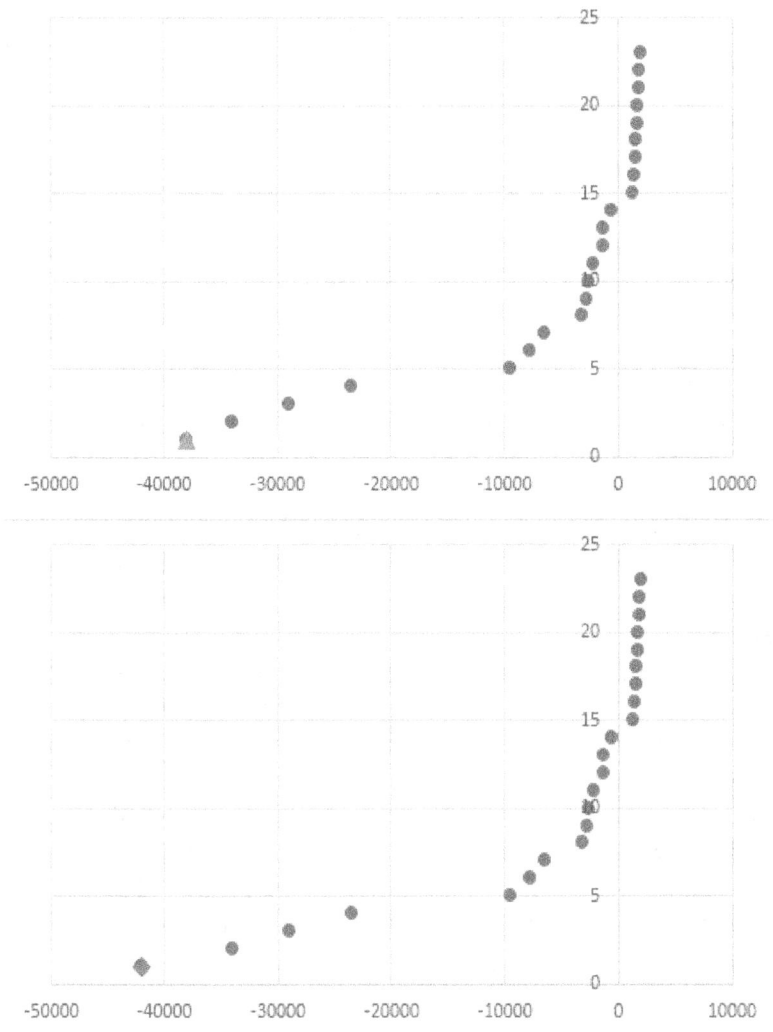

Figure 3.6.1. History of Humankind.
(a) Top chart - 38000 BC - 10500 BC (per data from 2018 AD); (b)
Bottom chart - 42000 BC - 10500 BC
(per data from 2023 AD)
Vertical – Number of accumulated classes of resources.
Horizontal – Time, years.
High-level model of humankind.

The Dominance of Statistical Errors

An average error in high-level model is around 2.3% for BC dates and 0.07% for AD dates.[5] Those values are small.

There is one other significant factor besides an individual margin of error. Let us say it's a sunny day and you're traveling along a beautiful road. On both sides of the road, you see many planted trees. These trees are like our data points. This beautiful path was drawn to have the minimal average distance to the trees. This is our path, the direction of humankind's development.

Individual inaccuracies in potted trees have little effect on the accuracy of road direction. This is the advantage of using many data points to form a curve. The tighter the grouping of these points, the more accurate the curve.

In traditional history we are used to studying individual events, such as the reigns of kings such as Henry IV or Henry V. How long was the king on the throne? This is a big part of the whole story in traditional history.

But the deep-level history of humanity is different. The inaccuracy of the dates of the first writing or the first invention of the microscope has lost its significance. More important is how dense the community of data points on both sides of the road is.

The transition from traditional history to deep-level history led to a transition from the dominance of individual event errors to the dominance of statistical errors. This is the beauty of our ability to use a quantitative model of humanity. This, in turn, increases the reliability of the proposed models.

Misclassification Errors

In the section "Hierarchical classification system errors" we have already indicated that there are no error-free taxonomies. What are the possible types of misclassification errors in proposed models of humanity?

We could have mixed up the models, i.e., mistakenly assigned a resource to a high-level model or assigned a class of resources to a low-level model. We could omit or assign an excessive resource or class of resources to low- or high- level models.

As of 2023 AD, we counted 318 resources in the low-level model and 23 classes of resources in the high-level model. We have already mentioned that the *Novel Mental Images* class of resources is a separate case, and we do not consider it here.

This means that each class of resources contains on average 318/23 = 14 resources. In other words, the granularity size of classes of resources is 14 times the resource granularity. Such a large difference in the size of detail makes it difficult to make mixing-up-models mistakes. This also makes it difficult to exclude or assign an excessive class of resources to a high-level model.

It is still possible to skip or assign excessive resource to a low-level model. A few of these possible errors should only slightly affect the low-level model, since the data set in the low-level humanity model is currently 318 data points, which is a good number for statistical distributions.

With Weight or without Weight?

Should we assign different weights to different objects on the same granularity level? The usual answer is No.

Typically, in hierarchical classification systems, complex system models, etc., on the same granularity level, no weight is assigned to different elements of the system.

For example, in biological taxonomy, we could compare the Southwest African lion, a large cat of the *Panthera* genus, with the bee hummingbird, a small bird of the *Archilochus* genus. Despite a vast difference in appearance, the Southwest African lion and bee hummingbird are merely species that are at the same level of detail in biological taxonomy, with no weight assigned to the lion or the bee hummingbird.

We should note that unlike sets from taxonomies on the same level of granularity, there are multiple lists of "the most important events." Many such lists came from the field of Big History. Items on such lists do not seem to be on the same granularity level. An example is the list of milestones in "Cosmic Calendar" outlined by Carl Sagan.[6] The list consists of 47 items. Zero weights were assigned to items on the list. That includes, for example, events like the "Big Bang," item 1 on the list, and "Zero and decimals invented in Indian arithmetic; Rome falls; Moslem conquests," item 44 on the list. References to similar lists compiled by other authors can be found in Modis' article.[7]

We will not assign any weights to resources in the low-level model or to classes of resources in the high-level model of humankind.

Overview of the Impact of Misclassification Errors

As mentioned, the level of subjectivity in resource classification and its impact on the model's outcome is greatly reduced by combining the following factors.

1. A hierarchical classification schema with a separate model on each hierarchy level corresponds to different granularity sizes of elements in different models.

2. Application of combined factors like resource criteria, resource search criteria, hierarchical classification schema, use of different models, etc.

3. Greatly reduced the importance of individual errors of events because of the transition to mainly statistical errors.

Nevertheless, a total extermination of misclassification errors in classification schemas is impossible. Further reduction of possible misclassification errors could be done in several ways.

The first method uses a broad scientific discussion with multiple participants with an outcome of non-weighted consensus on resources to be included in the models. The other option is to use some known methods of quantifying the weights of decision criteria in the choice of resources, for example, the use of the analytic hierarchy process (AHP).[8]

Both ways require multiple participants, preferably experts in a chosen field. Therefore, the possible use of such methods has to wait for a time when a discussion of proposed models of humankind's history will involve a broad array of specialists.

With publications done by a single author, the proposed methods, their analysis, and outcomes should be considered as a first iteration, a base for future research.

What People Do with Resources

It is important to note that in all cases the resource itself does not and cannot be held responsible for its use. It is people who decide how to use each resource.

What people did and are doing with these opportunities is another story, and is not the topic of this book. For example, people may use school buses to take their children to school. Or they could use tanks to destroy schools. Humankind's history would have been different if people had used resources without harming others. But we must not deceive ourselves. We humans are who we are. It's just a fact.

The history of humankind would also be different if humankind did not develop new resources for itself. People could not use school buses to drive kids to schools or tanks to destroy schools until the *Mass Transportation* class of resources was added to humankind's resources.

From Table 1, we see that in 4000 BC, seven classes of resources were available for humankind to use. In other words, humankind created six classes of resources during its history up to that point in time. The number of classes of resources grew up to eleven in 2000 BC. There are many ways to use the presented data - you could look up history from 42000 BC to 4000 BC, 3500 BC to 1650 BC, or 2000 BC to 2000 AD.

The graph of humankind's history in Figure 1 is very concise. The subsurface history of humankind was cleaned up from any references to social structures and political or economic considerations.

Humankind's history in Figures 1 and 2 is cleared of connections with concepts such as morality, progress, or happiness.

The deep-level history has been compiled using objective facts about the emergence of resources or classes of resources.

The charts with the curves of humankind's development or the development of various fields of humankind's activity do not indicate the names of resources or classes of resources. Therefore, any possible shortcomings in naming are excluded.

In this deep-level history of humankind, you see an underlying foundation for people's actions and events. And you see how humanity has developed this foundation over time.

There is more going on beneath the surface than we think.
Malcolm Gladwell

Subsurface History and Conventional History

Life is not linear; you have ups and downs. It's how you deal with the troughs that defines you.

Michael Lee-Chin

Chapter 3.7.

Ups and Downs in History of Humankind

We have 318 data points in the low-level model of humankind's development. Having that many data points allows us to look more closely into relatively short periods in humankind's history.

We already know that since 42000 BC, humankind has been headed toward increasing the arsenal of resources created by humankind for itself. Overall, the tendency so far is an increase in rate at which humanity moves in that direction. However, on the way, there were multiple periods of speed-up and slowdown.

Because of the highly uneven pace of humankind's development, a comparison of the development's rate makes sense only for neighboring to each other periods.

Below is the history of speed-up and slowdown periods in humankind's development in the last 44 thousand years.

We have 318 data points in the low-level model of humankind's development. Having so much data allows us to take a closer look at relatively short periods of humankind's history.

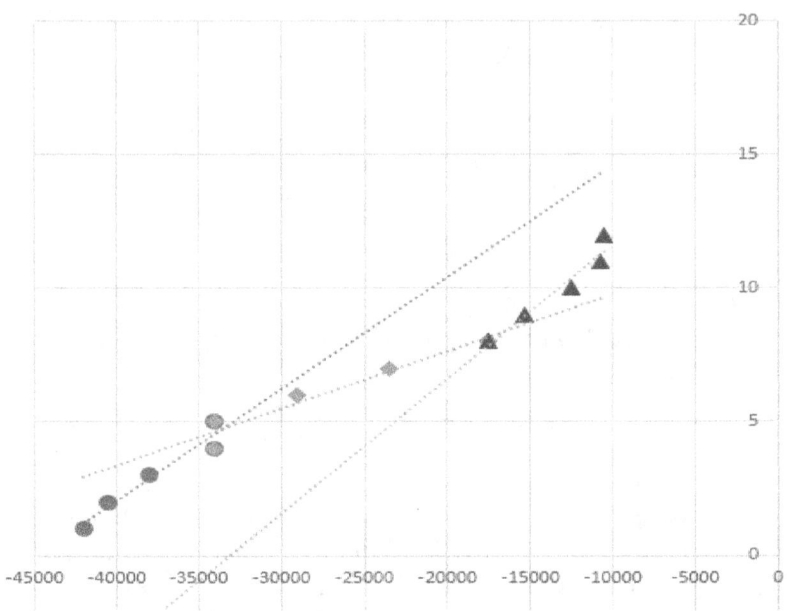

Figure 3.7.1. History of Humankind. 42000 BC - 10500 BC
Vertical – Number of accumulated resources. Horizontal – Time, years.
Low-level model of humankind.
Periods: Initial (left, dots), slowdown (middle, diamonds), speed-up
(right, triangles)

42000 BC to 10500 BC – in this period of time we see three distinctly different periods. 42000 BC to 34000 BC - Initial period of humankind's history. The gap between the emergence of resources adjacent in time amounted to an average of 2000 years.

34000 BC to 17500 BC was the first slowdown period in humankind's history. The gap between the emergence of resources adjacent in time amounted to an average of 4125 years. The slowdown, compared to the previous adjacent period, was 4125/2000 = 2.1 times.

17500 BC to 10500 BC was the first speed-up period in humankind's history. The gap between the emergence of resources adjacent in time amounted to an average of 1250 years. The speed-up, compared to the previous adjacent period, was 4125/1250 = 3.3 times.

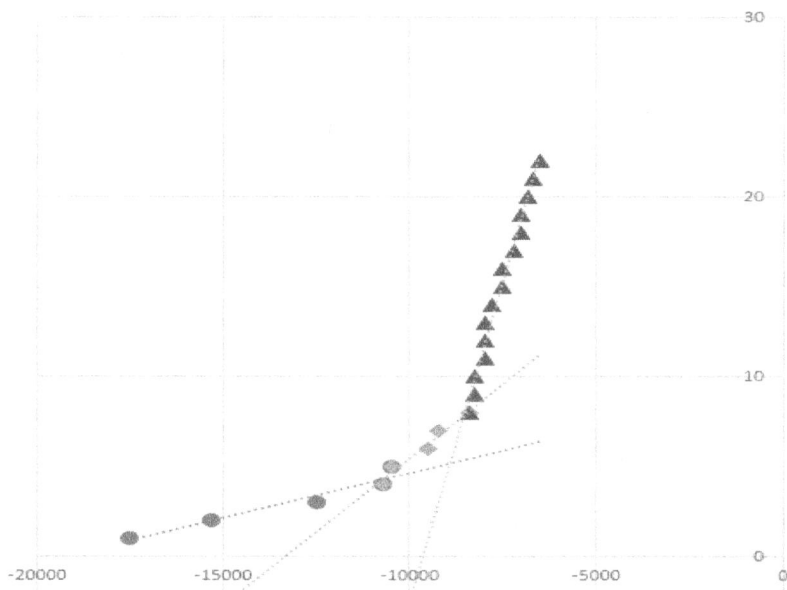

Figure 3.7.2. History of Humankind. 17500 BC - 6500 BC
Vertical – Number of accumulated resources. Horizontal – Time, years.
Low-level model of humankind.
**Periods: speed-up (left, dots), speed-up (middle, diamonds), speed-up
(right, triangles)**

17500 BC to 6500 BC – We could divide this period of time into three
distinctly different periods. 17500 BC to 10500 BC is a period of speed-up
in humankind's history. The gap between the emergence of resources
adjacent in time amounted to an average of 1250 years. The speed-up,
compared to the previous adjacent period, was 4125/1250 = 3.3 times.

10500 BC to 8400 BC is a speed-up period. The gap between the
emergence of resources adjacent in time averaged 525 years. The
slowdown, compared to the previous adjacent period, was 1250/525 = 2.4
times.

8400 BC to 6500 BC is a speed-up period. The gap between the
emergence of resources adjacent in time amounted to an average of 136
years. The speed-up, compared to the previous adjacent period, was 3.9
times.

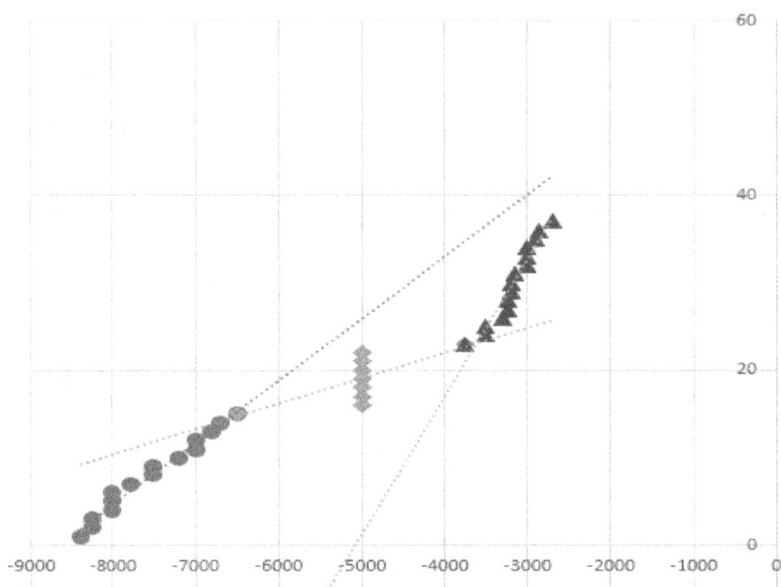

Figure 3.7.3. History of Humankind. 8400 BC - 2700 BC
Vertical – Number of accumulated resources. Horizontal – Time, years.
Low-level model of humankind.
Periods: speed-up (left, dots), slowdown (middle, diamonds), speed-up
(right, triangles)

8400 BC to 2700 BC – During this timeframe, we see three distinctly different periods. 8400 BC to 6500 BC is a speed-up period. The gap between the emergence of resources adjacent in time amounted to an average of 136 years. The speed-up, compared to the previous adjacent period, was 3.9 times.

6500 BC to 3750 BC is a slowdown period. The gap between the emergence of resources adjacent in time amounted to an average of 344 years. The slowdown, compared to the previous adjacent period, was 2.5 times.

3750 BC to 2700 BC is a speed-up period. The gap between the emergence of resources adjacent in time amounted to an average of 75 years. The speed-up, compared to the previous adjacent period, was 4.6 times.

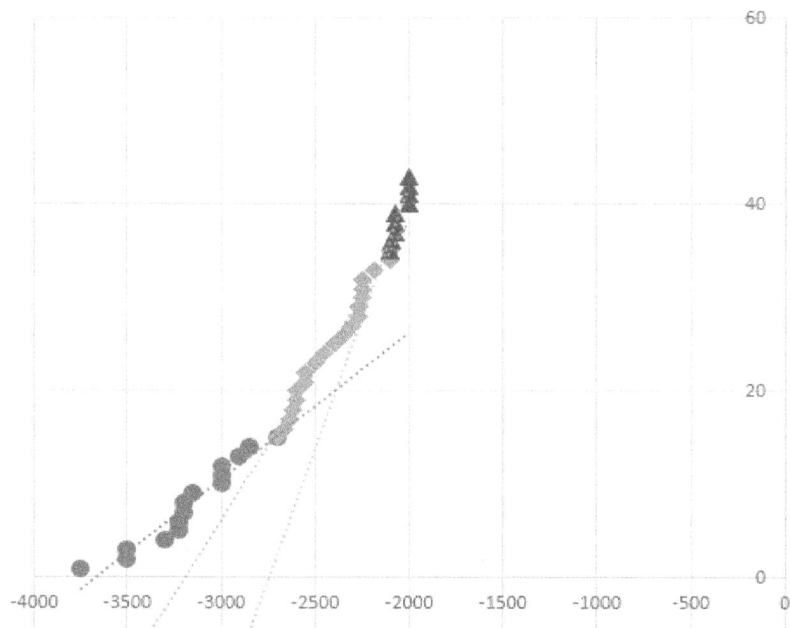

Figure 3.7.4. History of Humankind. 3750 BC - 2000 BC
Vertical – Number of accumulated resources. Horizontal – Time, years.
Low-level model of humankind.
Periods: speed-up (left, dots), speed-up (middle, diamonds), speed-up (right, triangles)

3750 BC to 2000 BC – We could divide this timeframe into three distinctly different periods. 3750 BC to 2700 BC is a speed-up period. The gap between the emergence of adjacent in time resources amounted to an average of 75 years. The speed-up, compared to the previous adjacent period, was 4.6 times.

2700 BC to 2100 BC is a speed-up period. The gap between the emergence of adjacent in time resources amounted to an average of 30 years. The speed-up, compared to the previous adjacent period, was 2.5 times.

2100 BC to 2000 BC is a speed-up period. The gap between the emergence of adjacent in time resources amounted to an average of 11.1 years. The speed-up, compared to the previous adjacent period, was 2.7 times.

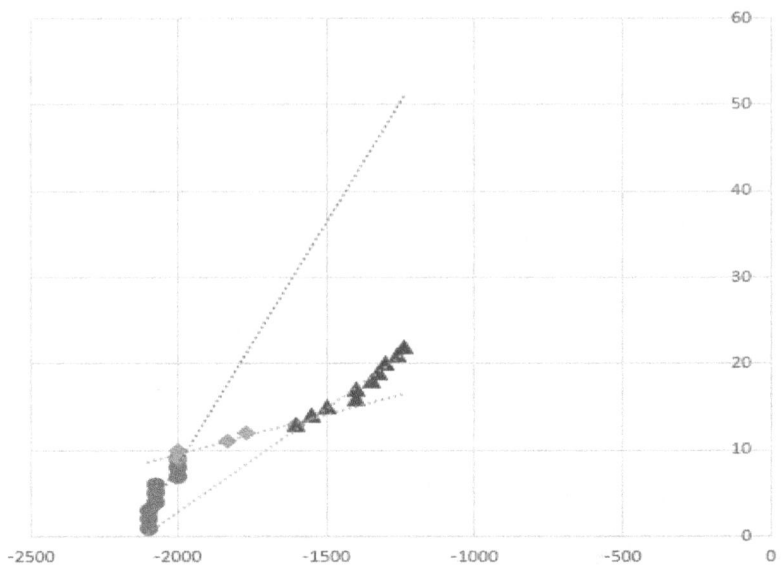

Figure 3.7.5. History of Humankind. 2100 BC - 1241 BC
Vertical – Number of accumulated resources. Horizontal – Time, years.
Low-level model of humankind.
Periods: speed-up (left, dots), slowdown (middle, diamonds), speed-up
(right, triangles)

2100 BC to 1241 BC – During this timeframe, we see three distinctly different periods. 2100 BC to 2000 BC is a speed-up period. The gap between the emergence of adjacent in time resources amounted to an average of 11.1 years. The speed-up, compared to the previous adjacent period, was 2.7 times.

2000 BC to 1600 BC is a slowdown period. The gap between the emergence of adjacent in time resources amounted to an average of 100 years. The slowdown, compared to the previous adjacent period, was 9 times.

1600 BC to 1241 BC is a speed-up period. The gap between the emergence of adjacent in time resources amounted to an average of 39.9 years. The speed-up, compared to the previous adjacent period, was 2.5 times.

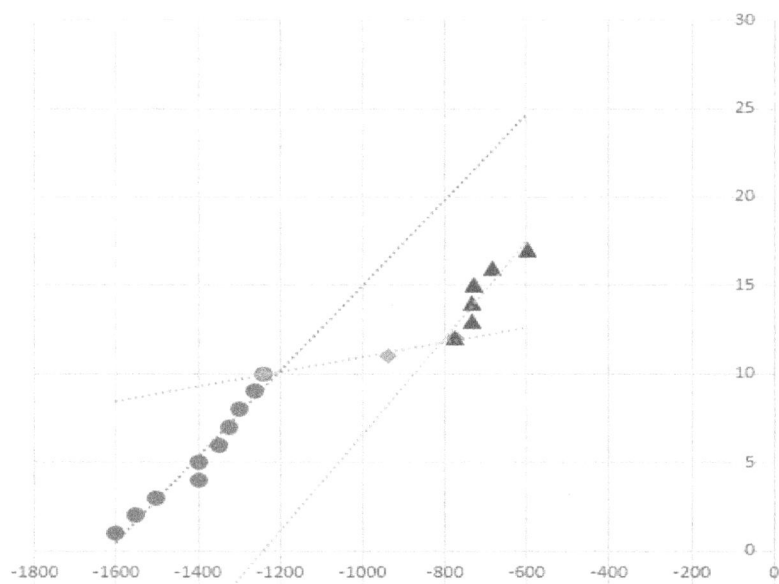

Figure 3.7.6. History of Humankind. 1600 BC - 597 BC
Vertical – Number of accumulated resources. Horizontal – Time, years.
Low-level model of humankind.
Periods: speed-up (left, dots), slowdown (middle, diamonds), speed-up (right, triangles)

1600 BC to 597 BC – We could divide this timeframe into three distinctly different periods. 1600 BC to 1241 BC is a speed-up period. The gap between the emergence of adjacent in time resources amounted to an average of 39.9 years. The speed-up, compared to the previous adjacent period, was 2.5 times.

1241 BC to 776 BC is a slowdown period. The gap between the emergence of adjacent in time resources amounted to an average of 155 years. The slowdown, compared to the previous adjacent period, was 3.9 times.

776 BC to 597 BC is a speed-up period. The gap between the emergence of adjacent in time resources amounted to an average of 29.8 years. The speed-up, compared to the previous adjacent period, was 5.2 times.

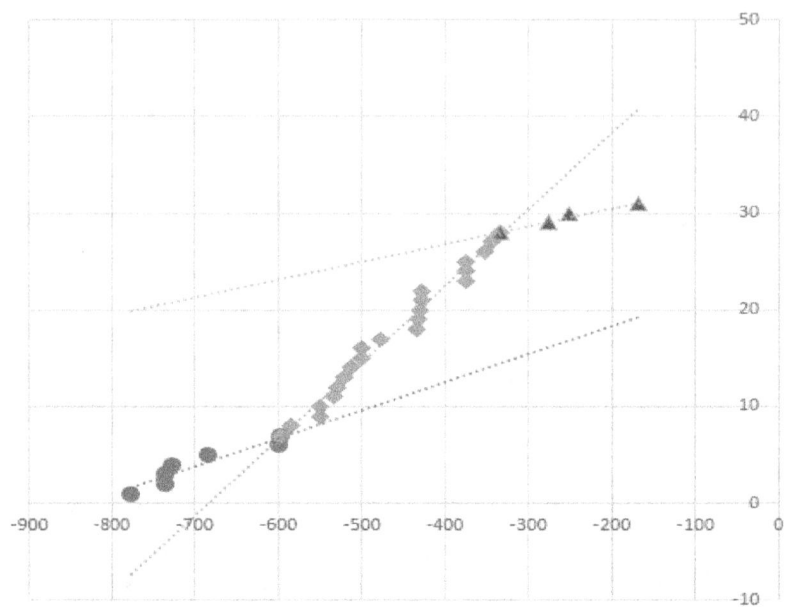

Figure 3.7.7. History of Humankind. 776 BC - 168 BC
Vertical – Number of accumulated resources. Horizontal – Time, years.
Low-level model of humankind.
Periods: speed-up (left, dots), speed-up (middle, diamonds), slowdown (right, triangles)

776 BC to 168 BC – During this timeframe we see three distinctly different periods. 776 BC to 597 BC is a speed-up period. The gap between the emergence of adjacent in time resources was, on average, 29.8 years. The speed-up, compared to the previous adjacent period, was 5.2 times.

597 BC to 334 BC is a speed-up period. The gap between the emergence of adjacent in time resources was, on average, 12.5 years. The speed-up, compared to the previous adjacent period, was 2.4 times.

334 BC to 168 BC is a slowdown period. The gap between the emergence of adjacent in time resources was, on average, 55.3 years. The slowdown, compared to the previous adjacent period, was 4.4 times.

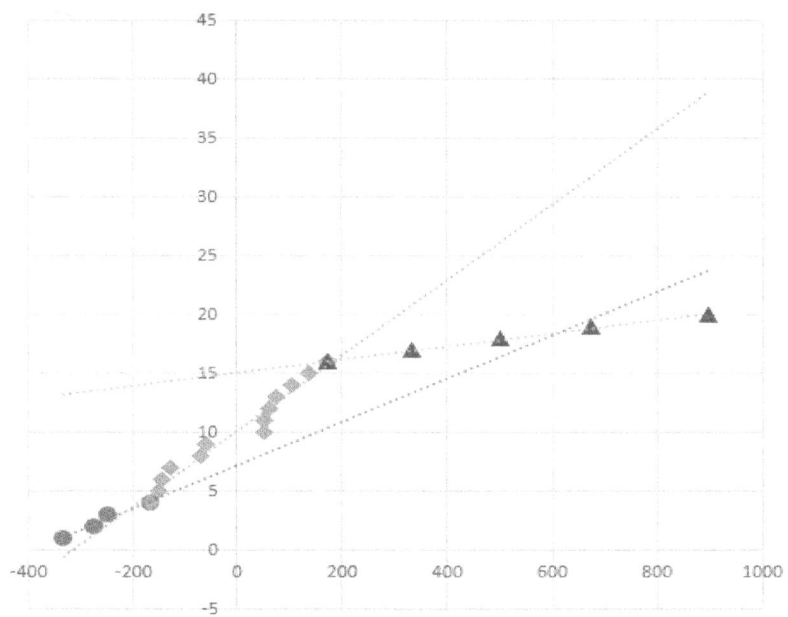

Figure 3.7.8. History of Humankind. 334 BC - 895 AD
Vertical – Number of accumulated resources. Horizontal – Time, years.
Low-level model of humankind.
Periods: slowdown (left, dots), speed-up (middle, diamonds),
slowdown (right, triangles)

334 BC to 895 AD – We could divide this timeframe into three distinctly different periods. 334 BC to 168 BC is a slowdown period. The gap between the emergence of adjacent in time resources was, on average, 55.3 years. The slowdown, compared to the previous adjacent period, was 4.4 times.

168 BC to 173 AD is a speed-up period. The gap between the emergence of adjacent in time resources was, on average, 28.4 years. The speed-up, compared to the previous adjacent period, was 1.9 times.

173 to 895 is a slowdown period. The gap between the emergence of adjacent in time resources was, on average, 180.5 years. The slowdown, compared to the previous adjacent period, was 6.4 times.

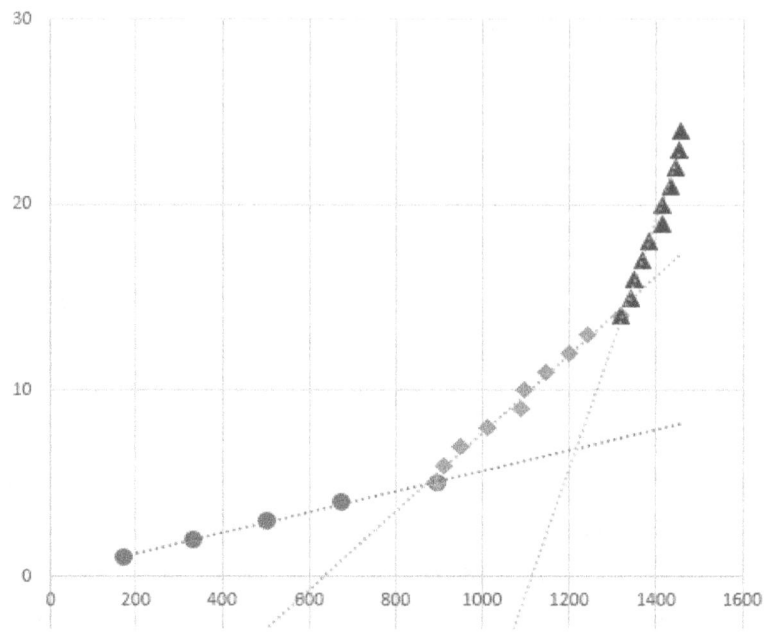

Figure 3.7.9. History of Humankind. 173 - 1455
Vertical – Number of accumulated resources. Horizontal – Time, years.
Low-level model of humankind.
Periods: slowdown (left, dots), speed-up (middle, diamonds), speed-up
(right, triangles)

173 to 1455 – During this timeframe, we see three distinctly different periods. 173 to 895 is a slowdown period. The gap between the emergence of adjacent in time resources was, on average, 180.5 years. The slowdown, compared to the previous adjacent period, was 6.4 times.

895 to 1316 is a speed-up period. The gap between the emergence of adjacent in time resources was, on average, 46.8 years. The speed-up, compared to the previous adjacent period, was 3.9 times.

1316 to 1455 is a speed-up period. The gap between the emergence of adjacent in time resources was, on average, 13.9 years. The speed-up, compared to the previous adjacent period, was 3.4 times.

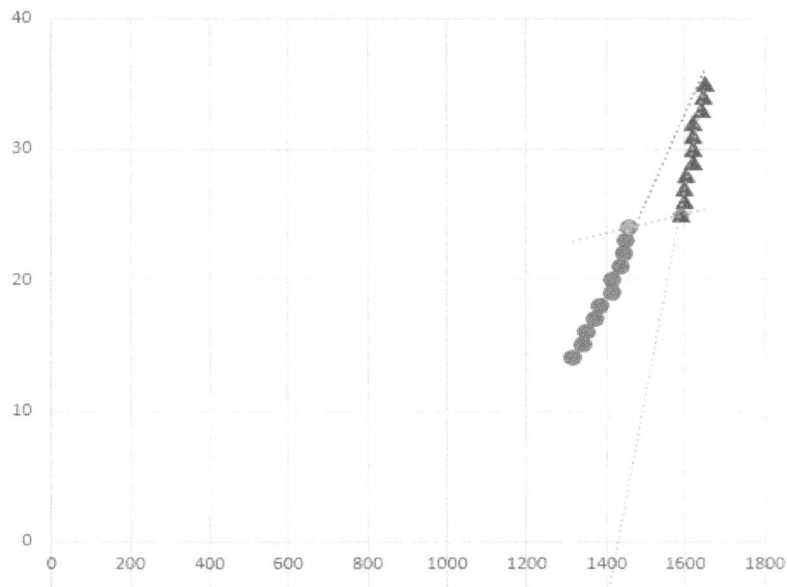

Figure 3.7.10. History of Humankind. 1316 - 1650
Vertical – Number of accumulated resources. Horizontal – Time, years.
Low-level model of humankind.
Periods: speed-up (left, dots), slowdown (middle, diamonds), speed-up (right, triangles)

1316 to 1650 – We could divide this timeframe into three distinctly different periods. 1316 to 1455 is a speed-up period. The gap between the emergence of neighboring in time resources was, on average, 13.9 years. The speed-up, compared to the previous adjacent period, was 3.4 times.

1455 to 1590 is a slowdown period. The gap between the emergence of neighboring in time resources was, on average, 135 years. The slowdown, compared to the previous adjacent period, was 9.7 times.

1590 to 1650 is a speed-up period. The gap between the emergence of neighboring in time resources was, on average, six years. The speed-up, compared to the previous adjacent period, was 22.5 times.

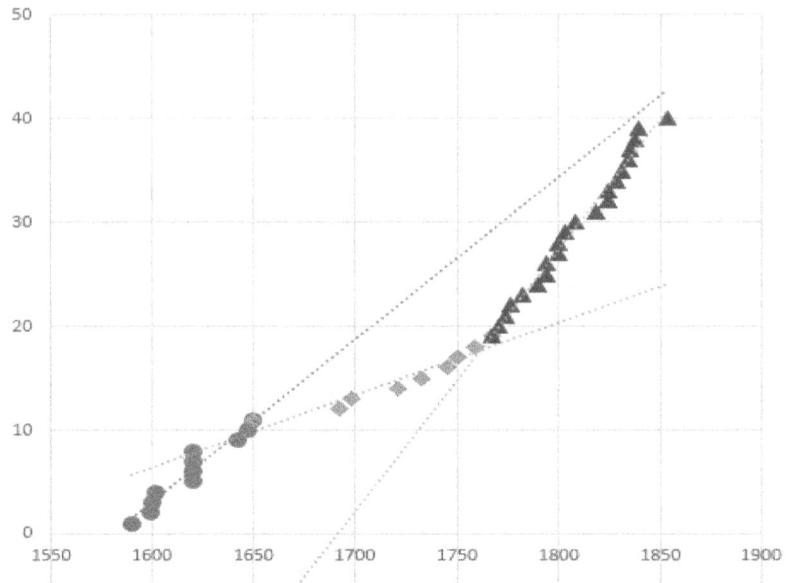

Figure 3.7.11. History of Humankind. 1590 - 1853
Vertical – Number of accumulated resources. Horizontal – Time, years.
Low-level model of humankind.
Periods: speed-up (left, dots), slowdown (middle, diamonds), speed-up
(right, triangles)

1590 to 1853 – During this timeframe, we see three distinctly different periods. 1590 to 1650 is a speed-up period. The gap between the emergence of neighboring in time resources was, on average, six years. The speed-up, compared to the previous adjacent period, was   22.5 times.

1650 to 1767 is a slowdown period. The gap between the emergence of adjacent in time resources was, on average, 14.6 years. The slowdown, compared to the previous adjacent period, was 2.4 times.

1767 to 1853 is a speed-up period. The gap between the emergence of adjacent in time resources was, on average, six years. The speed-up, compared to the previous adjacent period, was 4.1 times.

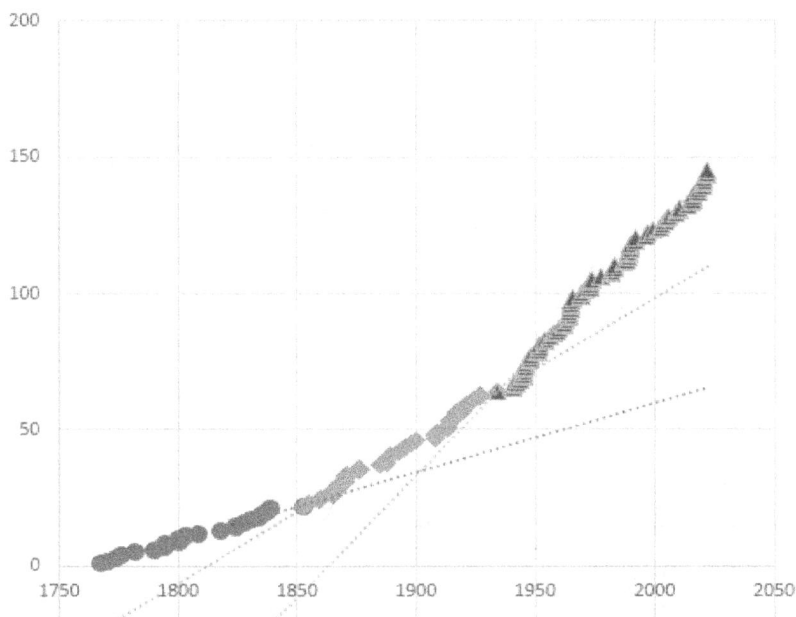

Figure 3.7.12. History of Humankind. 1767 - 2023
Vertical – Number of accumulated resources. Horizontal – Time, years.
Low-level model of humankind.
Periods: speed-up (left, dots), speed-up (middle, diamonds), speed-up (right, triangles)

1767 to 2023 – We could divide this timeframe into three distinctly different periods.

Table 3.7.1. History of Humankind. Low-Level Model.
42000 BC to 2023 AD. Speed-ups and Slowdowns in the Pace of
Humankind to Increased Number of Resources.

Period of humankind's history	Start year	Finish year	Speed-up, times
Initial	42000 BC	34000 BC	
Slowdown	34000 BC	17500 BC	-2.1
Speed-up	17500 BC	10500 BC	3.3
Speed-up	10500 BC	8400 BC	2.4
Speed-up	8400 BC	6500 BC	3.9
Slowdown	6500 BC	3750 BC	-2.5
Speed-up	3750 BC	2700 BC	4.6
Speed-up	2700 BC	2100 BC	2.5
Speed-up	2100 BC	2000 BC	2.7
Slowdown	2000 BC	1600 BC	-9
Speed-up	1600 BC	1241 BC	2.5
Slowdown	1241 BC	776 BC	-3.9
Speed-up	776 BC	597 BC	5.2
Speed-up	597 BC	334 BC	2.4
Slowdown	334 BC	168 BC	-4.4
Speed-up	168 BC	173 AD	1.9
Slowdown	173 AD	895	-6.4
Speed-up	895	1316	3.9
Speed-up	1316	1455	3.4
Slowdown	1455	1590	-9.7
Speed-up	1590	1650	22.5
Slowdown	1650	1767	-2.4
Speed-up	1767	1853	4.1
Speed-up	1853	1934	3.2
Speed-up	1934	2022	1.7

1767 to 1853 is a speed-up period. The gap between the emergence of adjacent in time resources was, on average, six years. The speed-up, compared to the previous adjacent period, was 4.1 times.

1853 to 1934 is a speed-up period. The gap between the emergence of adjacent in time resources was, on average, 1.9 years. The speed-up, compared to the previous adjacent period, was 3.2 times.

1934 to 2023 is a speed-up period. The gap between the emergence of adjacent in time resources was, on average, 1.1 years. The speed-up, compared to the previous adjacent period, was 1.7 times.

In this Chapter, we presented the subsurface history of humankind as a history of speed-up periods and slowdown periods in humankind's development. Of course, those speed-ups and slowdowns are relative to the overall direction toward increased resources and classes of resources.

Throughout humankind's history, from 42000 BC to 2023 AD, there were sixteen periods of speed-up and eight periods of slowdown.

The question is whether the reasons for these relatively small ups and downs can be identified, or whether humankind's development has been influenced by so many factors that there is no point in even studying these accelerations and deceleration periods at a deeper level. There are no studies on this issue yet, because these periods of acceleration and deceleration are published in this book for the first time.

Some of the following chapters will be dedicated, for the first time, to a study of two periods of speed-up and one period of slowdown in the deep-level history of humankind in comparison with conventional history.

Time transforms risk, and the nature of risk is shaped by the time horizon.

Peter L. Bernstein

Chapter 3.8.

Subsurface History for Strategic Planning

From Chapter 3.8, the subsurface history of humankind can be represented as a sequence of periods, each of which can be approximated as linear development.

That understanding can have important implications for strategic analysts and decision-makers.

"Time horizon" is an essential element of strategic thinking by analysts and decision-makers.[1,2,3,4] Thinking from a global perspective is important for decision-makers in international relations.

Typically, the term "time horizon" is applied to some interval from when the forecast was made to some point in the future. "Time horizon may be defined as: that distance into the future to which a decision-maker looks when evaluating the consequences of a proposed action."[5]

However, it is important to include in the analysis not only the current situation but also trends and precedents from the past. We can call the span of history contained in strategic thinking as a "back time horizon."

There is a far-reaching marker of how the back time horizon is used by analysts. One way is to stay within the back time horizon, which is limited to a period of history with a uniform, for example linear, trend of development. A much broader view will be taken if the analysts look into a back time horizon, which includes two or more periods with different rates of humankind's development.

Table 3.8.1. History of Humankind. Low-level model.
10500 BC to 2023 AD. Essential Back Time Horizons.

Possible date of analysis with a use of essential back time horizon	Essential back time horizon per criterion 1
34000 BC	
17500 BC	
10500 BC	23500
8400 BC	25600
6500 BC	27500
3750 BC	4650
2700 BC	3800
2100 BC	1650
2000 BC	4500
1600 BC	2100
1241 BC	759
776 BC	824
597 BC	644
334 BC	442
168 BC	429
173	507
895	1063
1316	1143
1455	560
1590	274
1650	195
1767	177
1853	203
1934	167
2023	353

We know there were multiple periods of slowdown and speed-up in humankind's development. However, periods of deceleration and acceleration did not always alternate. Figures from Chapter 3.8 revealed many historical cases with two or three consecutive speed-up periods. If an analyst uses a back time horizon, which includes only speed-up periods, the analysis could be deficient because of tunnel vision thinking.

Therefore, it makes sense to include in the back time horizon three or four consecutive periods with different rates of humankind's development. For simplicity, let us call a back time horizon per that criterion an "essential back time horizon."

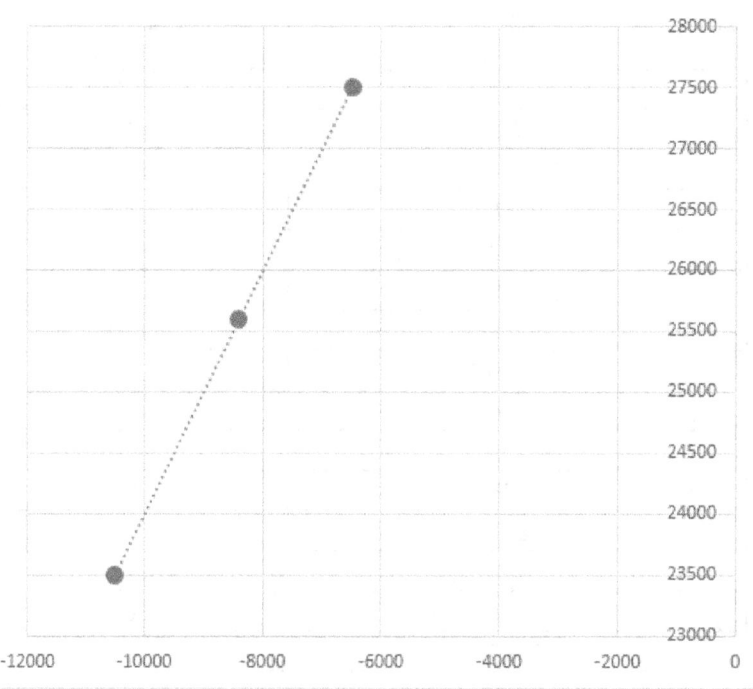

Figure 3.8.1. History of Humankind. 10500 BC - 6500 BC.
Vertical – An essential back time horizon, years.
Horizontal – Time, years. Low-level model of humankind.
The trend with a linear approximation added.

10500 BC to 6500 BC was a period with the most extended essential back time horizons, from 23.5 to 27.5 thousand years. At that time, there was no one in humankind who could use such huge back time horizons.

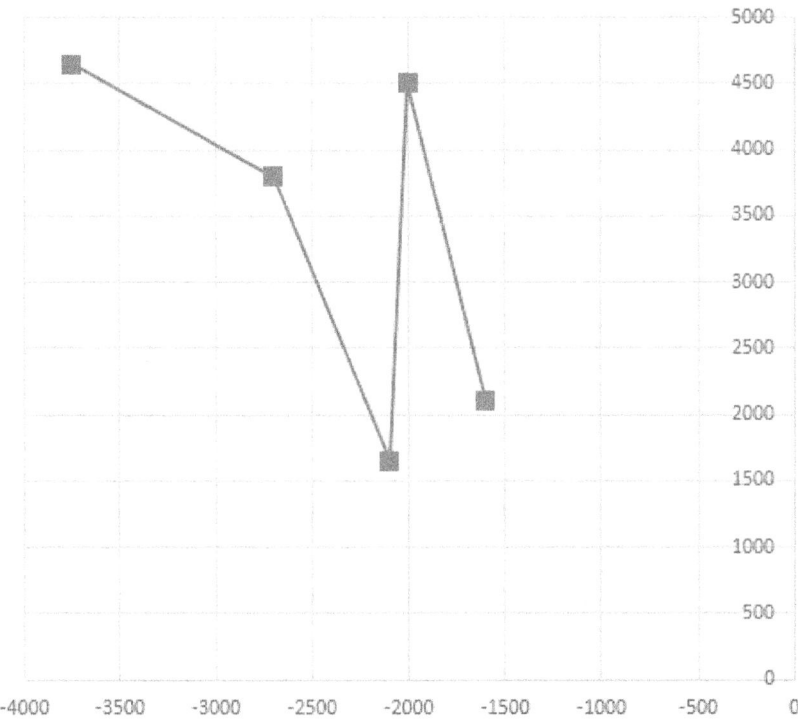

Figure 3.8.2. History of Humankind. 4000 BC - 1500 BC.
Vertical – An essential back time horizon, years.
Horizontal – Time, years. Low-level model of humankind.

During 4000 BC - 1500 BC, an essential back time horizon was approximately the same, in a range of 1650 - 4650 years. During this period, the written history of humankind began.

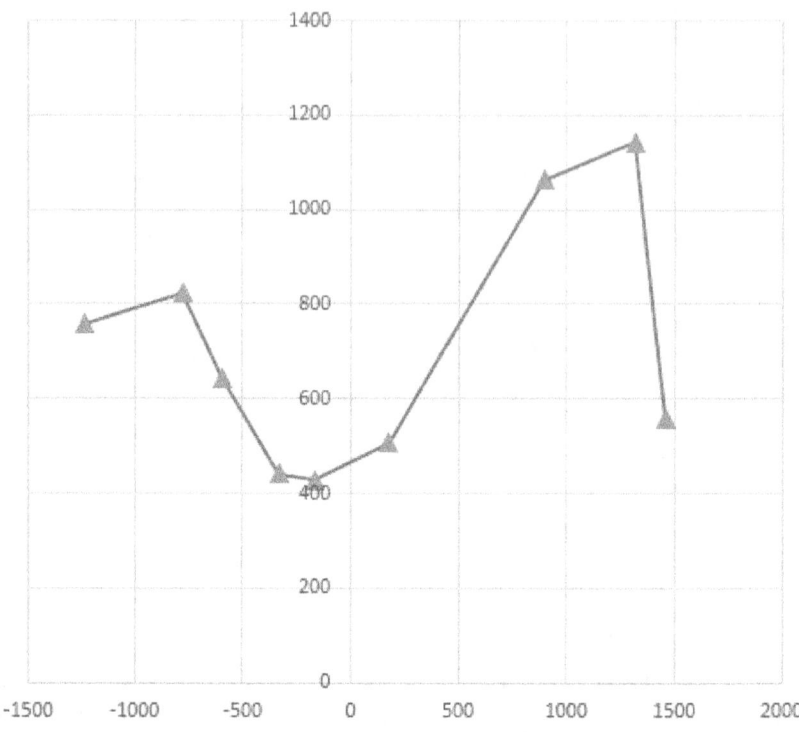

Figure 3.8.3. History of Humankind. 1500 BC – 1500 AD.
Vertical – An essential back time horizon, years.
Horizontal – Time, years. Low-level model of humankind.

From 2700 BC to 2000 BC, the essential back time horizons was in range of 430 – 1140 years.

There were Mesopotamia, Ancient Egypt, and Ancient India civilizations during this period.

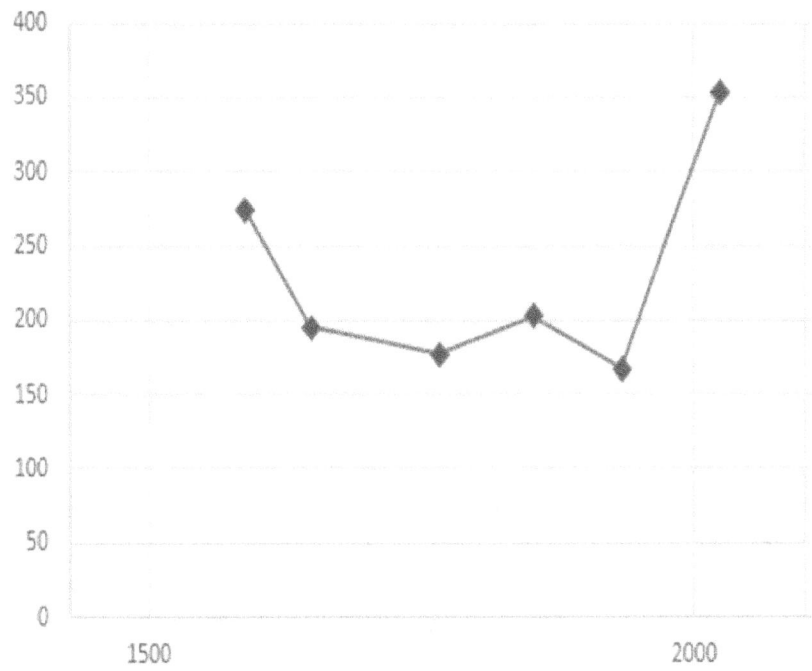

Figure 3.8.4. History of Humankind. 1500 – 2023.
Vertical – An essential back time horizon, years.
Horizontal – Time, years. Low-level model of humankind.

Between 1500 and 2023, there were significant fluctuations in an essential back time horizon. There is no point in drawing a trend line on an essential back time horizon in this timeframe.

The value of an essential back time horizon during this period was always at least 167 years. The essential back time horizons was in range of 167 – 353 years.

We assume that the lifespan of one generation is 25 years. With that, for a horizon of 353 years, it is necessary to know what happened approximately 14-15 generations ago.

Since the beginning of the 16th century, people have known that humanity is global. However, knowledge about the various parts of the world, especially the history of these parts, was scarce. As a result, it was probably impossible to use an essential back time horizon of 200 years.

It can be assumed that at around 1750, it became possible to use scientific method and math to take into account back time horizon with duration around 200 years. Also, that was a period between the establishment of multiple colonial empires and the decolonization era, when strategic analysts had to think globally.

Since then, analysts have been able to use not only a short-term back horizon, but also an essential back time horizon or even a longer back horizon.

How many analysts know that today, in 2023, the essential back time horizon is over 350 years?

How many analysts use such a long back time horizon? I think we will have a hard time finding the proper analysts and decision makers.

The very rapid pace of change in the modern world implicitly suggests that it is likely to be sufficient to limit the back time horizon of strategic planning to a short time frame.

From Table 2 we know that in 50 years before 1750 humankind created 4 resources while in 50 years before 2023 - 44 resources. That means the pace of creation of resources by humankind increased from 0.8 per year in 1750 to 8.8 per year in 2023. That is 11 times increase. However, as we can see from Figure 3.8.4 the essential back time horizon did not decreased from 1767 to 2023. Instead, it increased from 177 years in 1767 to 353 years in 2023. That is a counterintuitive fact, which is probably unknown to strategic analysts and decision-makers.

The "Rise and Fall of Civilizations" is still a hot topic among researchers, and many articles and books have been published in this area. However, the role of the inability of pre-18th century decision makers to use an essential back time horizon in the fall of "civilizations" has not been explored.

Since about 1750, decision-makers have had the technical ability to exploit an essential back time horizon. It is well known that decision-makers in many countries from the 18th century to nowadays made many strategic mistakes. The role of failure to use an essential back time horizon in the strategic mistakes made over the past few centuries has also yet to be examined.

A study can be conducted to reanalyze some known situations. In such cases, it is known what time horizon was used in the analysis and what action options were proposed in the forecast for that time horizon. The situation could be reanalyzed using an essential back time horizon.

The two resulting sets of options can then be compared. Comparing several situations will provide an initial assessment of the impact of using an essential back time horizon in decision-making.

How does an essential back time horizon correlate with decision makers' actual use of a back time horizon?

It is difficult to find in public sources information about the time horizon analysts and decision-makers use. Therefore, the information below is only a rough estimate of how time and back time horizons are used in the 21st century. And, of course, the duration of the time horizon and back time horizons depend on the field in which the analysis is conducted.

In 2018, using a 20-30-year time horizon in military equipment forecasting in the US was considered a long-term forecast. [4] Assuming that in this case, the time horizon and the back time horizon are approximately the same, we got the used back time horizon as less than 20% of an essential back time horizon.

There were two different instances in 2023 where we could make an estimate of the time horizon used.

First, US President Joe Biden gave a speech to the nation. Kempe wrote: "Historians may come to know US President Joe Biden's speech to the nation this week as his 'Inflection Point Address'... I consider Biden's inflection point to be the fourth since the early twentieth century. The previous ones set the stage for the periods after both world wars (1918-1945 and 1945-1990), the period after the Cold War (1990-2022), and now the period beginning with Russia's war in Ukraine. As was the case previously, expect this defining 'moment' in history to open up an era that could stretch for three decades or more, perhaps until 2050."[6]

Second, Ukraine's commander-in-chief, General Valery Zaluzhny, gave an interview to The Economist magazine. "Ukraine's military chief, Gen. Valery Zaluzhny, says in a long essay and interview with the Economist that 'just like in the First World War, we have reached the level of technology that puts us into a stalemate.'"[7]

The back time horizon used in Biden/Kempe and Zaluzhny's analysis was around 109 years. That is close to 60% of an essential back time horizon.

You may not notice a pattern until you pay attention to timing.
Efrat Cybulkiewicz

Chapter 3.9.
Adding Geography

Speed-ups vary from 1.6 to 22.5 times. Let us investigate the period of not very big speed-up. Between 597 BC and 334 BC, there was a speed-up of 2.4 times in the pace of humankind's movement to the increased number of resources.

Which resources were created by humankind during this period?

Table 2 shows that during this timeframe, humanity created 23 new resources. For each of those resources, we could find out from the research articles what was the geographic locality where the resource was created. For example, the *Archeology* resource was created in Sumer around 550 BC.

Wherever we have a range of dates for the emergence of some resource, then in graphs and tables, we use the midpoint of the range. We already mentioned this unified approach as accepted throughout this book.

Every resource created during humankind's history is characterized by two parameters – the name of the resource and the date of its emergence. Please note that the graphs use only one parameter - the emergence date of the resource.

Information about the geographic area where a particular resource was created is not necessary to analyze the direction of humankind's history, since we consider the history of humankind as a single global whole.

However, we could use this optional geographic locality information for additional research.

Table 3.9.1. History of Humankind.
Low-Level Model. Resources, Emerged During Period from 597 to 334 BC. Data from Table 2 with Added Country of Origin

Resources	Emergence date, Year	Average date	Country of origin
circus	616-578 BC	-597	Rome
philosophy	624-545 BC	-585	Greece
archeology	550 BC	-550	Sumer
post	550 BC	-550	Percia
theatre	534 BC	-534	Greece
museum	530 BC	-530	Sumer
propaganda	521 BC	-521	Percia
asymmetric warfare	513 BC	-513	Iran (Scythians)
cabbage	600-401 BC	-501	Greece
lingiustics	600-401 BC	-500	Greece
cucumber	5000 BC	-500	India
genealogy and family tree	479 BC	-479	China
playwright	499-455 BC	-477	Greece
ethics	470-399 BC	-435	Greece
economic warfare	432 BC	-432	Greece
total war	431 BC	-431	Greece
history	425-430 BC	-428	Greece
anthropology	425-430 BC	-428	Greece
political science	428-322 BC	-375	Greece
automata	400-350 BC	-375	Greece
logic	384-322 BC	-353	Greece
theology	354-348 BC	-351	Greece
water-powered machine	476-221 BC	-344	China
biology	345-322 BC	-334	Greece

In the conventional history of Ancient Greece, the period from 700 BC to 480 BC is called Archaic Greece.[1] The period from 480 BC to 323 BC is called Classic Greece.[2]

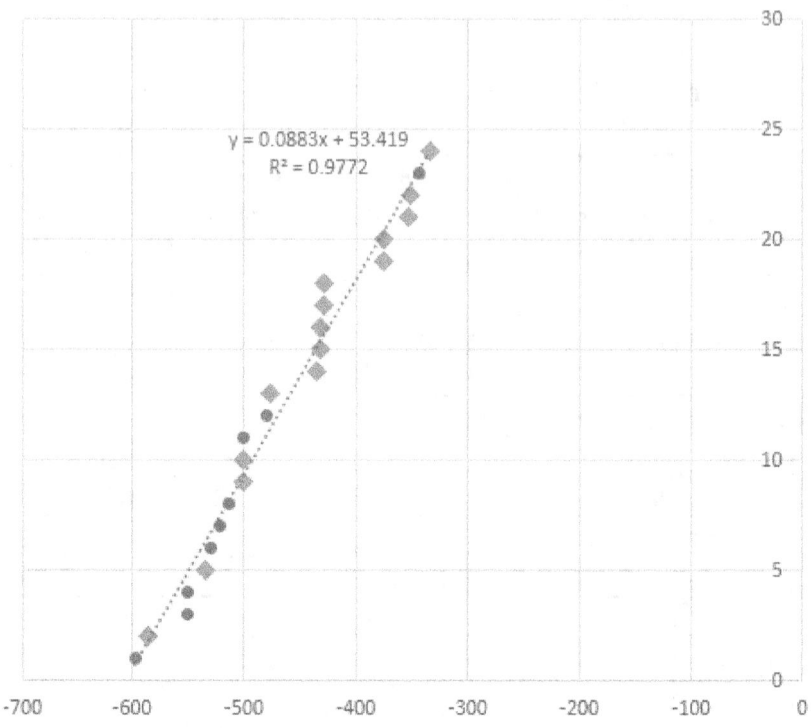

Figure 3.9.1. History of Humankind. 597 BC - 334 BC
Vertical – Number of accumulated resources.
Horizontal – Time, years.
Low-level model of humankind. Resources created in Greece, marked as diamonds. Resources, created at any other place on Earth, marked as dots.

The importance of Ancient Greece is well known. Ancient Greek civilization was "the period following Mycenaean civilization, which ended about 1200 BCE, to the death of Alexander the Great, in 323 BCE. It was a period of political, philosophical, artistic, and scientific achievements that formed a legacy with unparalleled influence on Western civilization."[3]

However, if you look at the lists of the most important events in the traditional history of Archaic Greece and Classical Greece, you will not be able to see this. Below is the list of significant events in Greece, 650 BC to 323 BC, from the conventional history.[4]

- "Greek Tyrants Come Into Power (650 BC)

- The Draconian Laws (621 BC)
- Greek Coins Used As Currency (600 BC)
- The Birth of Pythagoras (570 BC)
- Cleisthenes and the Birth of Democracy (508 BC)
- The Persian Wars (499-449 BC)
- The First Peloponnesian War (460-445 BC)
- The Age of Pericles (461-429 BC)
- The Second Peloponnesian War (431- 404 BC)
- The Plague of Athens (430 BC)
- First Academy Founded by Plato (387 BC)
- Alexander the Great Becomes King of Macedon (336 BC)
- The Death of Alexander the Great (323 BC)."

Most of those events involve wars, personalities, or elites. According to this list, out of the 13 most important events in the history of Classic Greece, only three events had something to do with Greece's contribution to humankind. Even universally recognized boundaries of the period of Classic Greece (480 BC and 323 BC) are defined by historians by war events. "In 480 BCE, the Greeks defeated the Persian fleet off the island of Salamis in the largest naval battle ever fought in the ancient world."[5]

On the other hand, the subsurface history of humankind, either high-level or low-level models, is about the contributions of people to humankind. Deep-level history of humanity explores neither wars, nor revolutions, nor personalities.

Combining deep-level history and conventional history from 597 BC to 334 BC, we see that this period's speed-up was not just a fluctuation. The speed-up of humankind's development in this period is primarily because of the contributions of Archaic Greece and Classic Greece. From Figure 3.9.1, we can conclude that Greece was responsible for 65 percent of all resources created by humankind during this timeframe.

Two important conclusions can be drawn from this small study. First, subsurface and conventional history could complement each other when studying specific fields of humankind's activity. Second, at least one period of speed-up development of humankind can be explained by the deep-rooted history of locality in that period.

We might also consider this case in a broader context. Let's start with a slightly longer time period than the period from 597 to 334 BC.

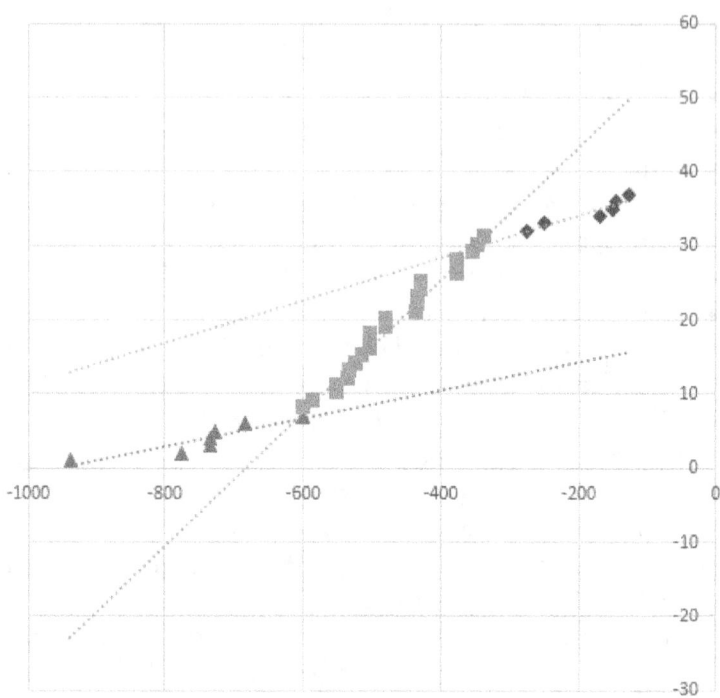

Figure 3.9.2. History of Humankind. 937 BC - 128 BC
Vertical – Number of accumulated resources. Horizontal – Time, years.
Low-level model of humankind. Periods: slowdown (left, triangles),
speed-up (middle, squares), slowdown (right, diamonds). Resources
created during timeframe 597-334 BC (shown on Figure 3.8.1) marked
as squares.

We see that the period 597-334 BC was not a part of the more general trend of increasing creativity of humankind. It was the other way around. This was an isolated episode of a temporary surge in human creativity within a longer trend of declining humankind's creativity.

Let us do a thought experiment and imagine that Greece did not exist from 597 BC to 334 BC. Then, instead of Figure 3.9.2, we would have Figure 3.9.3 for the same time period, 937 BC to 128 BC.

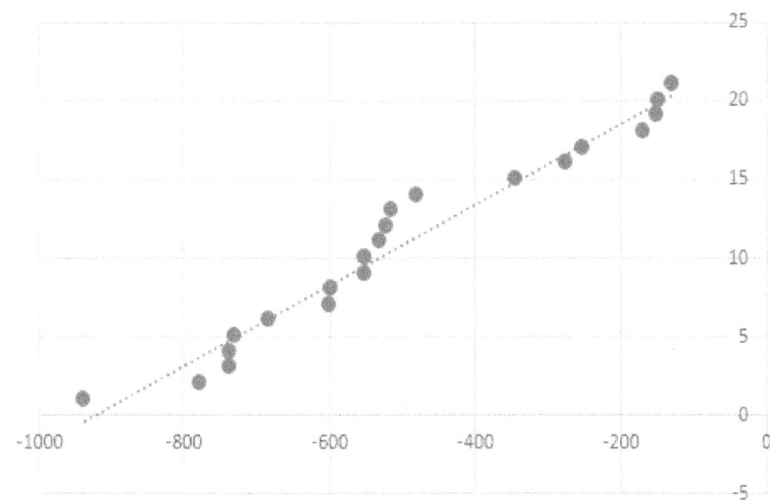

Figure 3.9.3. History of Humankind. 937 BC -128 BC
Imagined situation
with nonexistent Greece between 597 BC and 334 BC
Vertical – Number of accumulated resources.
Horizontal – Time, years.
Low-level model of humankind.

In a fictitious history, with a non-existent Greece between 597 BC and 334 BC, the period of increased humankind's activity between 597 BC and 334 BC was reduced to such an insignificant phenomenon that it could be classified as unavoidable noise in the model.

We could also view this episode even on even larger time scale: from 2500 BC to 1698 AD.

In Figures 3.9.4 and 3.9.5, we use a different method of analyzing available data on the resources that humanity has created for itself. That method is associated with the Creativity Index of Humankind. We will explain the Creativity Index of Humankind, CI-R, in Chapter 3.10.

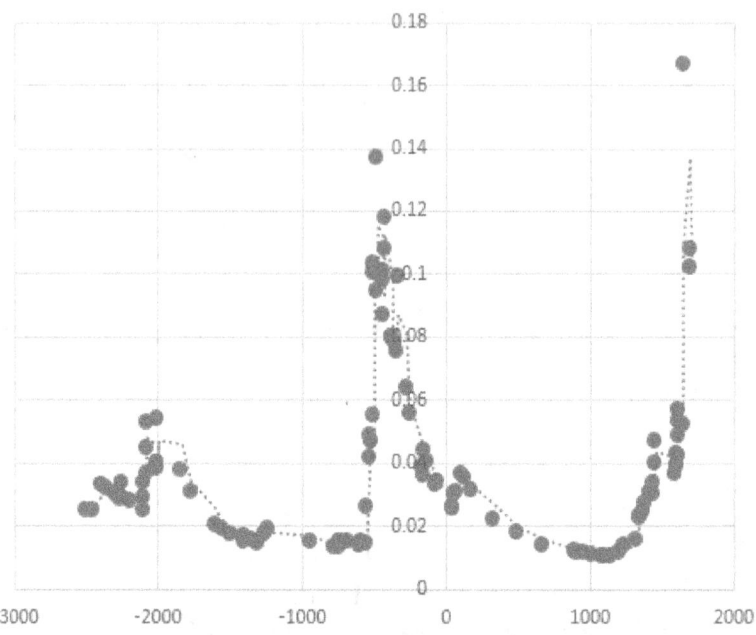

Figure 3.9.4. History of Humankind. 2500 BC - 1698 AD
Vertical – Creativity Index for Resources, CI-R.
CI-R = 1 in 1964 AD. Horizontal – Time, years.
Low-level model of humankind.

Figure 3.9.4 shows three spikes of humankind's creativity, CI-R, within the 2500 BC - 1698 AD timeframe. The top of the first spike occurred in 2000 BC, with CI-R = 0.0054. That was the local maximum of humankind's creativity between 2500 BC - 501 BC. The second local peak of humankind's creativity with the Creativity Index value over the previous spike lasted from 501 BC to 150 BC. The third spike with a Creativity Index value greater than the first surge, began in 1620 AD.

Between 2500 BC and 1455 AD, the top local peak of humankind's creativity was around 477 BC.

Let us do a thought experiment and imagine again that Greece did not exist from 597 BC to 334 BC. Instead of Figure 3.9.4, we would have Figure 3.9.5 for the timeframe 2500 BC – 1698 AD.

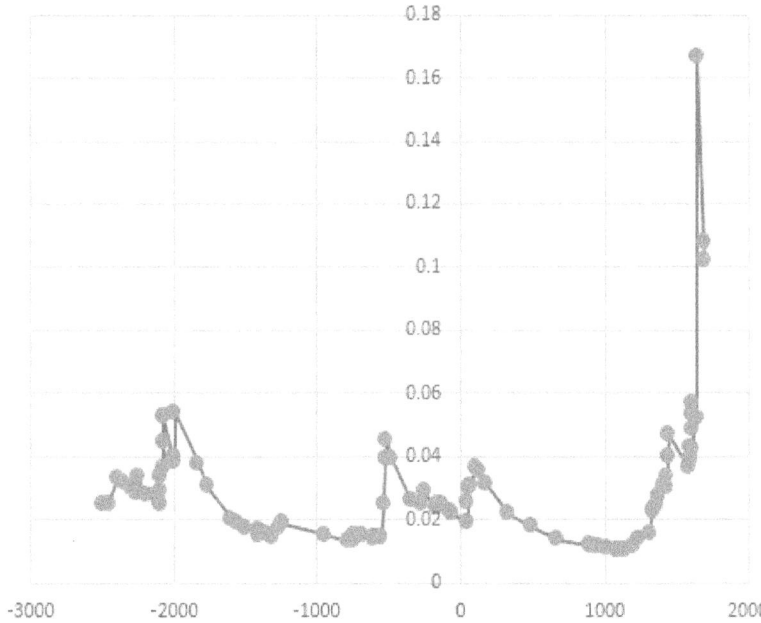

**Figure 3.9.5. History of Humankind. 2500 BC - 1698 AD
with nonexistent Greece between 597 BC and 334 BC
Vertical – Creativity Index for Resources, CI-R.
CI-R = 1 in 1964 AD. Horizontal – Time, years.
Low-level model of humankind.**

Now we could compare the actual history of humankind between 2500 BC and 1698 AD, Figure 3.9.4, with the fictitious history of humanity from the same period, with non-existent Greece between 597 BC - 334 BC, Figure 3.9.5.

The most important thing to note is that the peak of humankind's creativity at around 477 BC declined so sharply that it is no longer a top pick in the 2500 BC - 1455 AD timeframe. Without Greece's contribution to humankind's creativity, the Creativity Index at the top of that peak, at 513 BC, would be 1.2 times less than at the first peak of creativity in 2000 BC, when Greece existing between 597 BC - 334 BC. That means the period between 2000 BC and 1455 AD, without Greece between 597 BC and 334 BC, is a period of decline in creativity of humankind.

We just proved that some surge in humankind's creativity can be attributed to some local, in geography and time, community input. Of course, this was easy to prove, since Archaic and, especially, Classic

Greece contributions to humankind are well-known and thoroughly studied. Chapter 3.13, which considers the period from 500 BC to 1700 AD, provides a more nuanced account of Archaic and Classic Greece.

As we can see, some local irregularities in the curve of humankind's development can be explained using various methods of analyzing available subsurface history data. That is significant because, at first glance, such irregularities looked like unexplainable phenomena or statistical noise.

Human creativity uses what is already existing and available and changes it in unpredictable ways.

Silvano Arieti

Chapter 3.10. Creativity of Humankind

We hear about inventors, people's ingenuity, and discoveries every day.

The phenomenon of human creativity was studied in many scientific works.[1-5] However, they deal with an individual or a small group of people.

We are interested in different creativity. This is a characteristic of all humanity as a single whole. Without human creativity, none of these 318 newly created resources would be possible.

Is it possible to measure humankind's creativity? There are publications dedicated to measuring the creativity of individuals or small groups of people. Can they guide us? Hardly. Because they are not intended for use on a global scale.

Let us think about how to do it. We can compare humankind to a car manufacturing plant. The relevant indicator for us now, of the productivity of this plant, is "a time interval needed to produce one car." Similarly, a unit to measure humankind's creativity is "the interval of time needed to produce one resource, or one family of resources, or one class of resources."

Measuring the Creativity of Humankind

In the low-level model, we have 318 data points, i.e., 318 emergence dates of new resources T[i].

Let us look at how we can measure the creativity of humankind in creating new resources for itself.

Intervals between two consecutive creations of resources in humankind's history are not equal. They depend on a whole array of various circumstances. It makes sense to smoothen fluctuations in the values of those intervals by averaging them out. For a community of 318 data points, the reasonable number of consecutive intervals between data points to average them out is 10.

Then, the time between data points (j) and (j+10) is $T[(j+10)-j]$.

$T[(j+10)-j]$ is the time humankind needs to create 10 new resources. $T[(j+10)-j] = T[j+10]-T[j]$.

We can obtain the average time for humankind to create one new resource by using the average of 10 consecutive intervals between data points $T[j+10]$ and $T[j]$.

In this case, the time necessary for humankind to create a new resource will be $T[(j+10)-j]/10 = 0.1*(T[j+10]-T[j])$. That is the number of years needed to create a new resource. This number is averaged over the last ten consecutive intervals between new resource creation dates. An analogy can be drawn between this parameter and the "cycle time" parameter used as one of the key indicators (KPI) of modern project management. "The cycle time is the amount of time it takes to complete a specific task from start to finish."[6]

In our area, measuring humankind's creativity in creating new resources, we will call this parameter "resource creation time (RCT)."

RCT equals 1 when the number of years needed to create a new resource equal one and that number is averaged over the last ten consecutive intervals between new resource creation dates.

Imagine that each year, humankind acquires a certain percentage of the knowledge and skills necessary to create new resource. As soon as humankind gets 100% of the required knowledge and skills, it will create a new resource.

Now we can introduce a parameter $10/(T[i+10]-T[i])$. That is acquired in one year percentage of knowledge and skills needed to create a new resource. This number is averaged over the last ten consecutive intervals between new resource creation dates.

In other words, parameter $10/(T[i+10]-T[i])$ is an average measure of the creative ability of humankind in the creation of new resources.

We will call the parameter 10/(T[i+10]-T[i]) as a "Creativity Index of Humankind" or CI. Specifically, we discussed here a creativity index on a level of resources. We label it as CI-R.

Table 3.10.1. Naming of Creativity Index of Humankind
for Different Models

Model type	Elements of the model	Classification of creativity level	Creativity Index name	Resource creation entity
Low-level	Resources	Creation of resources	CI-R	Resource creation time (RCT)
Middle-level	Families of	Creation of families of resources	CI-F	Family of resources creation time (FCT)
High-level	Classes of F	Creation of classes of resources	CI-C	Class of resources creation time (CCT)

CI-R equals 1 when, averaged over the last ten consecutive intervals between new resource creation dates, 100% of the knowledge and skills needed to create a new resource are acquired in one year.

We can now use the CI-R and RCT parameters to measure humankind's creativity in creating new resources.

Similarly, we could construct the Creativity Index of Humankind for the medium-level model for families of resources, and the high-level model for classes of resources. We need to differentiate those Creativity Indexes of Humankind from each other.

Creativity Index for Resources, CI-R, and Resource Creation Time, RCT, for the same time interval, 534 BC - 1698 AD, are in Figure 3.10.1. The data shows that CI-R became equal to 1 in 1964 AD, and RCT became equal to 1 in 1923 AD.

The Creativity Index for Resources, CI-R, is more suitable for comparing periods of humankind's history, which are widely separated in time.

For example, from Figure 3.10.1.(a) we can conclude that the creative potential of humanity during the period from 534 BC. to 1698 AD was in the range of 0.01–0.167 compared to 1 in 1964 AD.

A time of resource creation, RCT is more suitable for detecting the beginning and end of the rise and decline of humanity's creativity.

Figure 3.10.1.(b) shows that in the time period of 534 BC – 1698 AD the end of the previous increase in creativity and the beginning of a new period of decline in creativity occurred in 477 BC. Then creativity hit a local bottom and began to increase in 1088 AD. This date marked the end of 1565 years of creative decline. The period of growth of human creativity began in 1088 and ended in 1650 AD.

It should be emphasized that we are talking about the rise and decline of creativity of humanity as a whole. This is a global phenomenon.

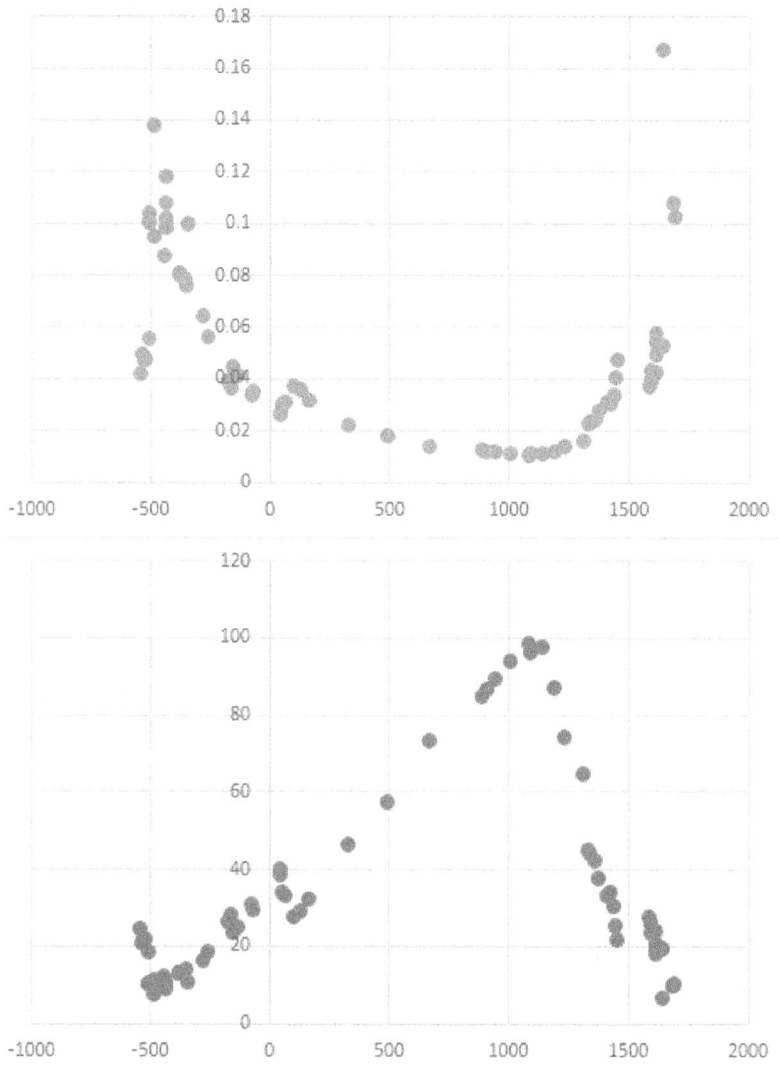

Figure 3.10.1. History of Humankind. 534 BC - 1698 AD.
Top graph (a) - Creativity Index of Humankind for Resources, CI-R.
Bottom graph (b) - Resource Creation Time, RCT, in years
Vertical – (a) Creativity Index of Humankind, CI-R = 1 in 1964 AD. (b)
Resource Creation Time, years. RCT = 1 in 1923 AD. Horizontal – Time,
years. Low-level model of humankind.

Historians have experience in studying the processes of the rise and decline of local in time and geography formations, that is, civilizations.

However, there has been no study of the rise and decline of humankind's creativity as a whole.

We need to better understand what may happen with the further development of humanity. We hope that such research will be carried out in the future, as this book provides a wealth of data on the rise and decline of humankind's creativity. Creativity Index of Humankind, CI-R, for 42000 BC – 2023 AD is presented in Figure 3.10.2.

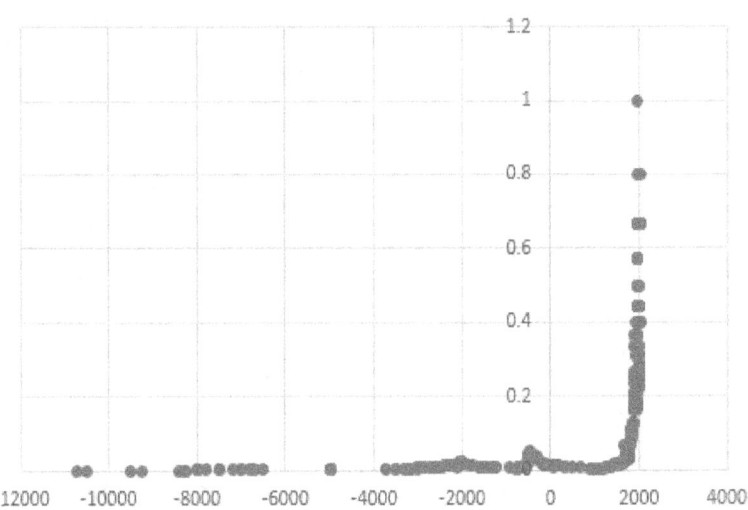

Figure 3.10.2. History of Humankind. 11000 BC - 2023 AD
Vertical – Creativity Index of Humankind, CI-R.
CI-R = 1 in 1964 AD. Low-Level Model.
Horizontal axis – Time, years.
Low-level model of humankind.

The curve is already very familiar to us as it is similar to the population growth curve. However, we could get a little information from the curve at this large time scale. Fortunately, we have a big enough data set of 318 data points and could dive into details.

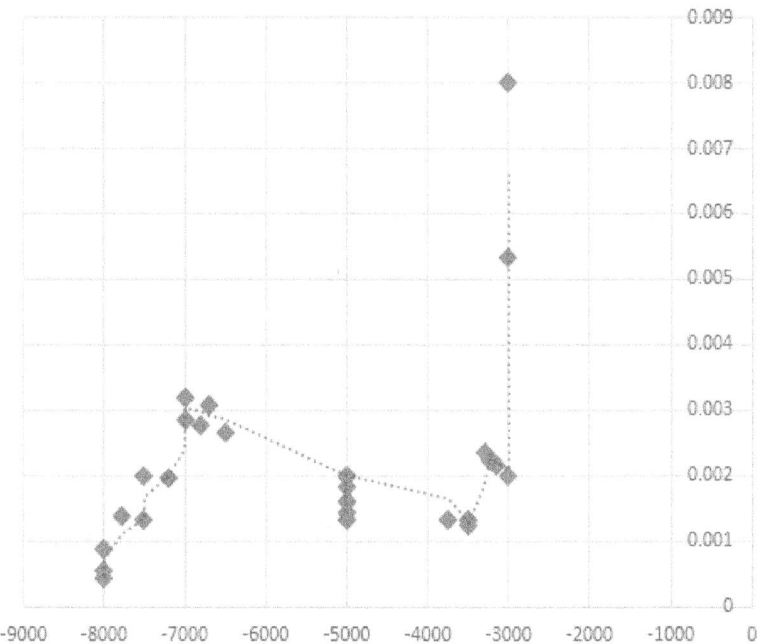

Figure 3.10.3. History of Humankind. 8000 BC – 3000 BC.
Vertical - Creativity Index of Humankind, CI-R.
CI-R = 1 at 1964 AD.
Horizontal - Time, years.
Low-level model of humankind.
Two period moving average trend added.

We see that humankind's creativity has increased almost sixfold from 8000 BC to 7000 BC. Then, a period of decline in creativity began. The creativity of humankind has not declined below the level at 8000 BC. At the very bottom of this decline, in 3500 BC, creativity was still three times higher than in 8000 BC.

Then, in 3000 BC, humankind's creativity increased fourfold.

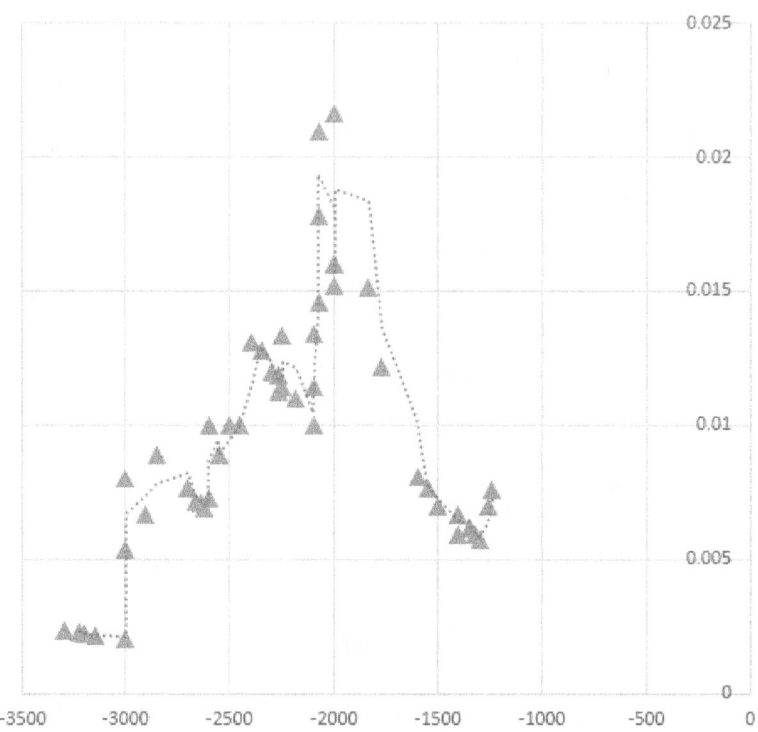

Figure 3.10.4. History of Humankind. 3300 BC – 1000 BC
Vertical - Creativity Index of Humankind, CI-R.
CI-R = 1 at 1964 AD.
Horizontal - Time, years.
Low-level model of humankind.
Two period moving average trend added.

The rise of humankind's creativity in 3000 BC was just the beginning of a 1,000 years of steady increase in creativity. In 2000 BC, the creativity of humanity was ten times greater than in 3150 BC.

The subsequent decline in creativity began in 2000 BC and continued until 1300 BC. We will see more detail in Figure 3.10.5.

The bottom of the decline in creativity in Figure 3.10.5 was reached in 735 BC.

Creativity remained at approximately this low level until 600 BC.

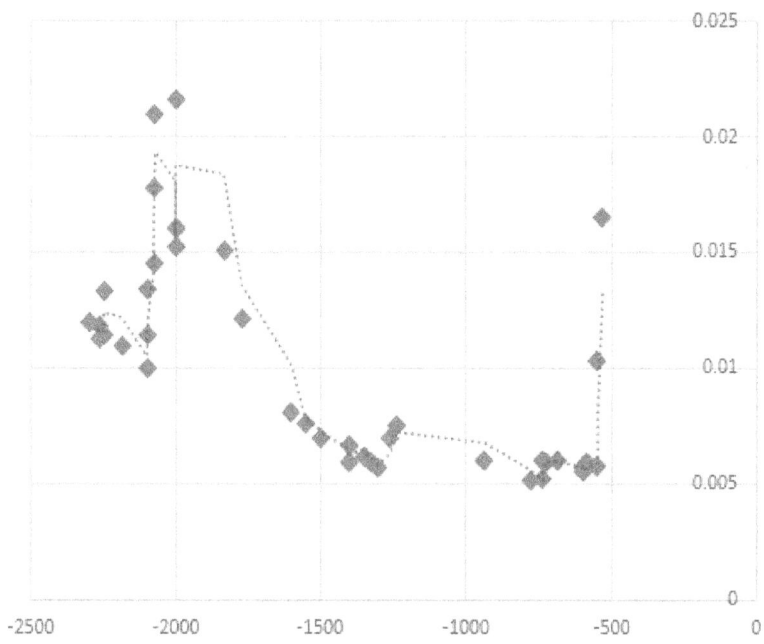

Figure 3.10.5. History of Humankind. 2300 BC – 534 BC
Vertical - Creativity Index of Humankind, CI-R.
CI-R = 1 at 1964 AD. Horizontal - Time, years.
Low-level model of humankind.
Two period moving average trend added.

The period of creativity decline lasted 2,400 years, from 2000 BC to 600 BC. That period of declining creativity was 2.4 times longer than the previous period of increasing creativity.

It also should be noted that the bottom of the last declining creativity period was still higher than the bottom of the previous period of low creativity.

The next period of increased creativity began around 585 BC.
Figure 3.10.6 shows that the duration of of the period of rise in creativity was short, from 585 BC to 477 BC, only 108 years.

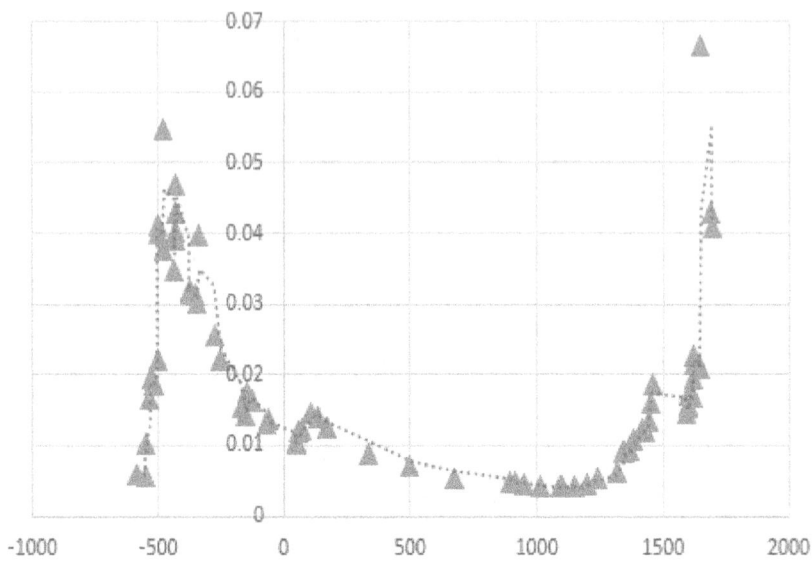

Figure 3.10.6. History of Humankind. 534 BC – 1698 BC
Vertical - Creativity Index of Humankind, CI-R.
CI-R = 1 at 1964 AD. Horizontal - Time, years.
Low-level model of humankind.
Two period moving average trend added.

We could also look at the interval of closed-to-top creativity, i.e., the period of creativity ranging from the top one to about 30% below the top one. During the previous rising creativity period, in Figure 3.10.5, the interval of closed-to-top creativity lasted 260 years. In the last growing creativity period, in Figure 3.10.6, the closed-to-top creativity lasted around 150 years.

The next period of declining creativity lasted approximately 730 years. Respectfully, humankind's creativity began to rise again in 1316 – 1340 AD.

The decline of creativity from 477 BC to 1316 AD was very different from the 3300 – 1000 BC decline.

During the decline from 477 BC, creativity reached a level below the bottom of the previous low creativity period.

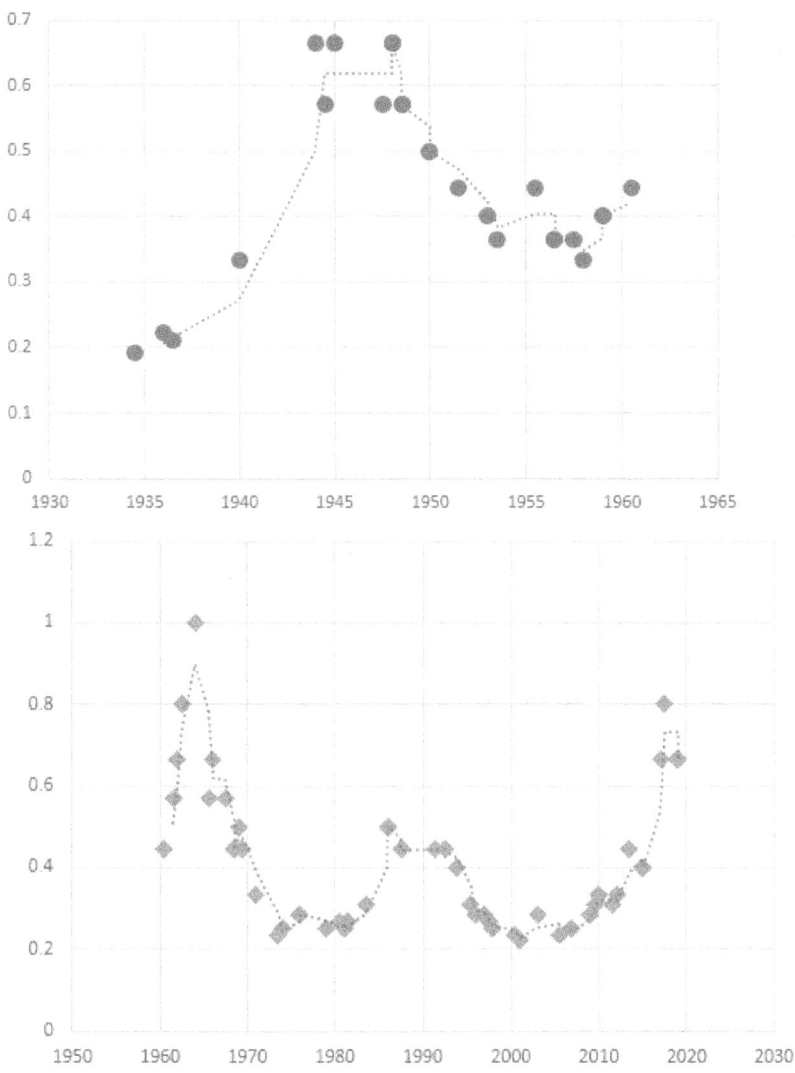

Figure 3.10.7. History of Humankind. 1924 – 2023.
Top graph – 1924-1965 (Averaged 1934.5-1960.5). Bottom graph – 1956-2022 (Averaged 1960.5-2019)
Vertical - Creativity Index of Humankind, CI-R.
Horizontal – Time, years. Low-level model of humankind.
Two period moving average trend added.

Figure 3.10.7 shows a curve of the creativity of humankind during the last hundred years - from 1924 to 2022. For contemporaries of this time, it looks like a steady increase in creativity and innovation.

However, the Creativity Index of Humankind shows three peaks of creativity in the 20th century: approximately 1945-1948, 1962-1969, and 1985-1992.

According to Figure 3.10.7, an absolute top of the Creativity Index of Humankind during the last 44 thousand years occurred in 1964.

Using this technique, we can look more closely at variations in the creativity of humankind in other times in our history.

You can be creative in anything — in math, science, engineering, philosophy — as much as you can in music or in painting or in dance.

Ken Robinson

Chapter 3.11.

"European Miracle" and More

Each model of humanity, such as high-level or low-level models, can include two views of history. The primary view is based on dates of emergence of new resources or classes of resources. Consequently, that view is presented in Table 2 and Table 1.

The second view is using the same dates. However, we could add optional information, such as the location where each resource or each class of resources was created. For that, we need to use information about the location where the first use of the resources happens. We could obtain the required information about the place of first occurrence of each resource using the original research works of scientists. Those references are in short descriptions of resources in Part 2.

Consider such information as a bridge between the subsurface and the conventional history of humankind.

Let us look into the geography of places where primary resources appeared. These are localities where humankind's creative acts, the creation of resources and classes of resources, took place.

Throughout history, descriptions of the places where certain events took place vary in detail. For some, the modern name of the country is used. For others, only ancient names of territories are known, such as Mesopotamia. These territories are usually not within the borders of any modern country. In other cases, the only known detail is the name of the continent.

Continents with the Greatest Creativity

To make the data comparable, we must discard cities or countries.

We will use the continents as the localities. They are the widest localization available on Earth. Of the 23 acts of creating new classes of resources, three acts occurred in Africa, one in Oceania and America, 14 in Asia, and 11 in Europe.

Egypt is a country located on two continents - Asia and Africa. Thus, we will consider that the class of resources that emerged in Egypt occurred on both continents. There have been two such events in the history of humankind.

It has been noted that the emergence of two classes of resources resulted from changes in many places around the world. These two classes of resources are *Use of Natural Resources on a Massive Scale* and *Life Expectancy Growth*. In either case, a significant increase in some global parameters was observed.

At the same time, data shows that the most significant increase in the parameters in these two classes of resources used occurred in Europe. Thus, Europe is a location where the emergence of these two classes of resources occurs.

We see that the creation of most classes of resources in the history of humankind occurred in Asia or Europe. The emergence of most classes of resources was the result of the activities of creative people on these continents.

We all are contemporaries of modern creativity in the USA. Why don't we see the creation of new classes of resources in the USA in the high-level model of humankind? The reason is simple. The emergence of classes of resources is a rare event. According to the high-level model of humankind, only one such event, the birth of AI, happened in the USA. A more pronounced shift in creativity towards America can be seen in a low-level model.

When Did "European Miracle" Happen?

The transfer of humankind's activity from Asia to Europe is well known. When did it happen? Why? What exactly was transferred? Many studies and even books have been devoted to this topic. Previous research was focused on the reallocation of power, wealth, and economic activity. Scholars consider the mentioned migration as an exceptional event. Outstanding events deserve an extraordinary name.

The transfer of humankind's activity from Asia to Europe was called

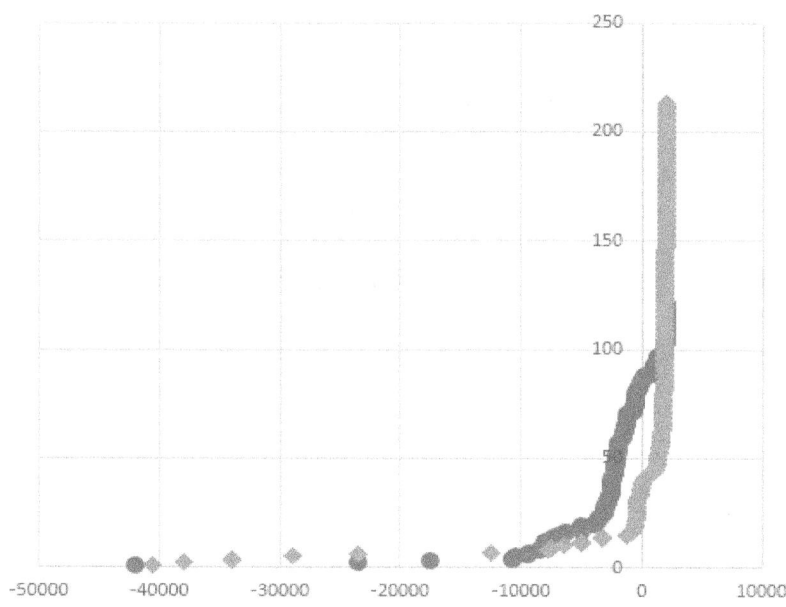

Figure 3.11.1. History of Humankind. 42000 BC - 2023 AD
The East and the West
Vertical – Number of accumulated resources. Horizontal – Time, years.
Low-level model of humankind. 1. Resources emerged in the East
(Asia+Africa+South America) – dots. 2. Resources emerged in the West
(Europe+USA) – diamonds.

the "European Miracle,"[1] the "Great Divergence,"[2] or the shift in the global "economic center of attraction."[3] Many studies associate this transfer with the period of "Industrial Revolution."[4,5] Adherents of a much broader point of view consider the earliest date for the beginning of this transfer to be the 15th century.[6]

Let us go back from a conventional history of events to the subsurface history of humankind. We want to explore the transition of creative activity, from the East to the West, in the creation of new resources and new classes of resources.

Figure 3.11.1 clearly shows that activity in creating new resources for humankind has moved from the East (Asia) to the West (Europe + USA). However, we need to examine details to determine when the transition occurred.

Figure 3.11.2 provides such details. Resources created in the East (Asia, Africa, and South America) are marked with red diamonds, while resources created in the West (Europe and the USA) are marked with blue dots.

The East to the West: Multi-Staged Transition

The data from Figures 3.11.1 and 3.11.2 are also presented in Table 3.11.1.

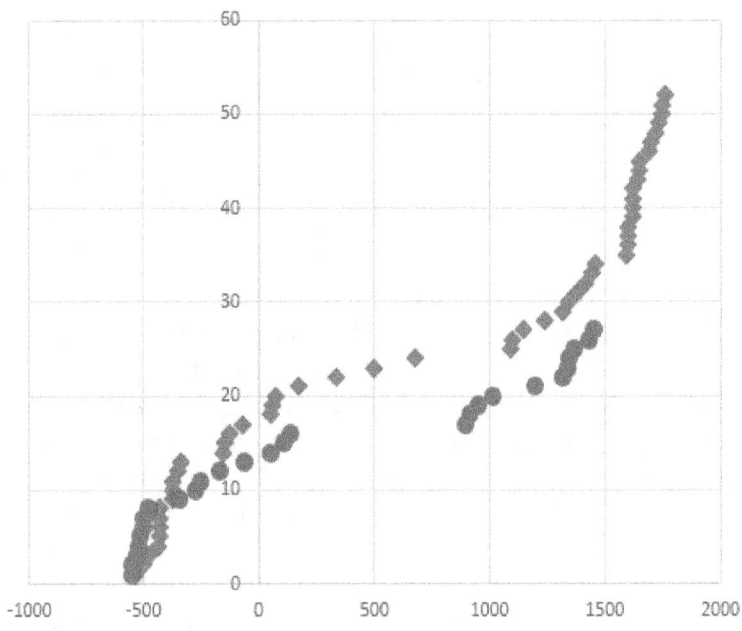

Figure 3.11.2. History of Humankind. 550 BC - 1759 AD
The East and the West
Vertical – Number of accumulated resources. Horizontal – Time, years.
Low-level model of humankind.
(a) **Resources emerged in the East (Asia+Africa+South America) –**
dots. (b) Resources emerged in the West (Europe+USA) –
diamonds.

Before 735 BC, creative activity in the East (Asia) in creating new resources for humankind was 10.5 times higher than in the West (Europe).

The transition of human activity from the East to the West happened in stages.

Between 735 BC and 428 BC, the number of resources created in the East and the West was the same. The, in 735 BC, Europe took a giant leap in creativity. The transition of creative activity from the East to the West began in 735 BC.

That date preceded the earliest, accepted by the scientific community, beginning the "European Miracle" by over 2100 years. From 735 BC to the present day, the East has never been more active than the West in creating new resources for humanity.

The ongoing scientific discussion about the "European Miracle" is dedicated to transitioning power, wealth, or economic activity from the East to the West.

Table 3.11.1. History of Humankind. 2075 BC to 1759 AD.
Transition of humankind's Creativity from the East (As+Af+SAm) to the West (Eu+USA). Number of resources.
Data from Table 2 with added
Continent (for As, Eu) or Country (for USA) of Origin

Period, Years	Number of resources emerged in		West to East performance
	the East (As+Af+SAm)	the West (Eu+USA)	
2075-735 BC	21	2	East 10.5 times faster
735-428 BC	11	12	On par
375 BC -136 AD	8	12	West 1.5 times faster
173 - 1012	4	4	On par
1088 - 1455	7	10	West 1.4 times faster
1460 - 1759	0	18	East creativity stopped
75 BC - 1088 AD	7	7	East & West slowdown

This work investigates the transition from the East to the West in a much broader context. It shows that the migration of humankind's creativity from Asia to Europe began more than two thousand years before the migration of power, wealth, or economic activity.

We present the summary of stages in the transition of creativity from the East to the West in Table 3.11.1.

From 375 BC, Europe has become the world's leading continent in creating new resources for humankind. Between 375 BC and 136 AD, the rate of creation of new resources for humanity in the West was 1.5 times higher than in the East.

It is important to note that during that last period, a global slowdown of humankind's creativity began. You can see this in Figure 3.11.2 and the last row in Table 3.11.1. The period of a worldwide slowdown in humankind's creative activity began in 75 BC and ended in 1088 AD.

That was the most significant slowdown in humankind's creativity during the last 2100 years. The slowdown lasted half of that time – 1050 years. The relationship between global slowdown and human creative activity on particular continents at the time is unknown. It should be investigated by researchers. One thing is clear: this global slowdown has to some extent masked for observers by the process of transition from the East to the West.

For much of the time during the global economic downturn, Europe was unable to continue to outperform Asia. Table 3.11.1 shows that from 173 to 1012 the rate of creation of new resources was the same in the West and East.

The end of the global slowdown marked a new stage in the transition of creative activity from the East to the West.

Between 1088 and 1455, the rate of creation of new resources in the West was 1.4 times higher than in the East.

Later, the pace of new resource creation in the West accelerated. From 1460 to 1759, the rate of creation of new resources in the West was more than double that of the period 1088–1455. At the same time, since 1455, the East stopped all activity in creating new resources for humankind. The next time a new resource was created in the East was the year 2018.

Shift of Creativity from Europe to USA

Recently there has been another famous shift in human creativity between continents. This time the shift is happening within the West.

Like the Great Divergence, the transition of human activity from Europe to the United States occurred in stages.

The data is presented in Figure 3.11.3 and Table 3.11.2. The period from 1455 to 1818 was a time of widespread creativity in Europe. During this time, Europe created 26 new resources.

The USA became an independent country in 1776. Not surprisingly, between 1455 and 1818, Europe was 13 times more active than the United States in creating new resources for humanity.

Over the next 50 years, from 1818 to 1868, the US took a leap in creativity, during which time Europe was only 1.3 times more creative than the US.

The first period in history, when the United States caught up with Europe, in the creation of new resources, occurred between 1868 and 1945.

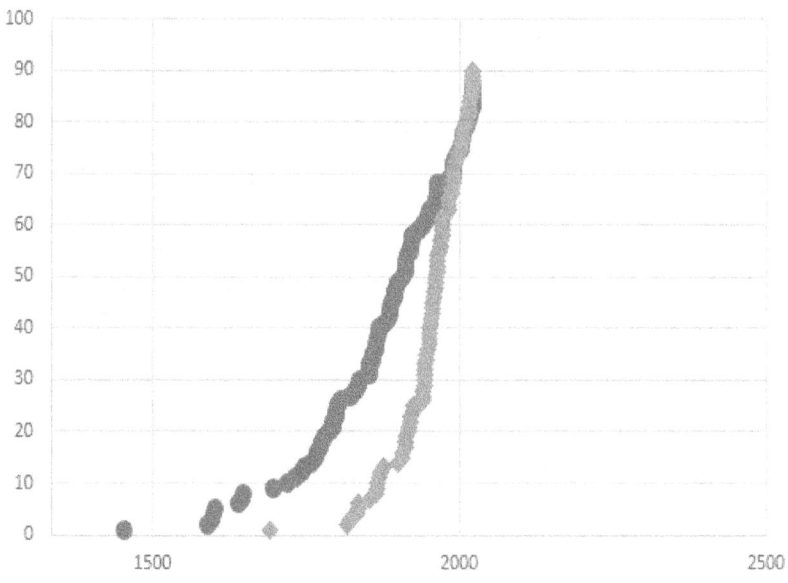

Figure 3.11.3. History of Humankind. 1445 to 2023. Europe and USA
Vertical – Number of accumulated resources. Horizontal – Time, years.
Low-level model of humankind.
1. Europe – dots. 2. USA – diamonds.

That was the period in history when the USA established parity with

Europe in creativity on the level of new resource creation. We could mark this period as the first stage of the transition of leading world's creation activity from Europe to the USA.

The first period when the USA established a superiority over Europe in creating new resources was from 1945 to 1951. During this timeframe, on average, the USA created new resources twice as fast as Europe. From 1945 to 1951, the transition of creative activity from Europe to the USA was completed.

Table 3.11.2 compares Europe and the USA's activity in creating resources for humankind in five different periods since 1455.

Table 3.11.2. History of Humankind. 1455 to 2023.
Transition of humankind's activities from Europe to the USA.
Number of resources. Data from Table 2 with added
continent (for Europe) or country (for USA) of origin

Period, Years	Number of resources emerged	Number of resources emerged in the USA	USA to Europe performance
1455 - 1818	26	2	EU 13 times faster
1818 - 1868	12	9	EU 1.3 times faster
1868 - 1945	23	23	On par
1945 - 1951	3	7	USA 2.3 times faster
1951 - 2023	27	60	USA 2.2 times faster

Since 1945, the USA has become a leading world's country in creating resources for humankind.

One is random, twice is coincidence, and three times is a pattern.
Peter F. DiSilvio

Chapter 3.12.

The East to the West
Transfer Patterns

The proposed models depict quantitatively the direction and pace of humankind's development during the last 44 thousand years.

We view humanity as a whole. In the low-level model in the provided analysis, every data point was described by two numbers – the date of new resource emergence and the total number of resources created by humankind. This two-dimensional data is the basis for analyzing humanity as a global entity over a huge period, the last 44 thousand years.

However, the proposed models may also provide some additional, more local information.

For example, we could shift our focus from humankind's overall, all-the-time history to more local history. That locality could be the history of some periods, geographic regions, or particular areas of humankind's activity. The latter case would give us a picture of humankind's development in specific classes of resources of humankind's activity. For example, we could look at the direction and pace of humankind's development in the *Mass transportation* class of resources.

Original works by scientists usually contain information about where a specific event occurred. Sometimes this is detailed information, but often we can only find the name of the continent. For consistency, we would use only the name of the continent. Adding a location can add a ton of information.

There are many periods in humankind's history that we could look at in detail. In this section we will provide data from 2500 BC to 2020 AD. Data on the transfer of humankind's creativity from the East to the West.

All drawings will be presented in chronological order of classes of resource emergence.

In this chapter, the total amount of resources originated was calculated separately for resources originating in the East (Asia) and resources originating in the West (Europe + USA). This count starts from the emergence date closest to 2500 BC, depending on the continent on which the resource emerged.

Art and Music

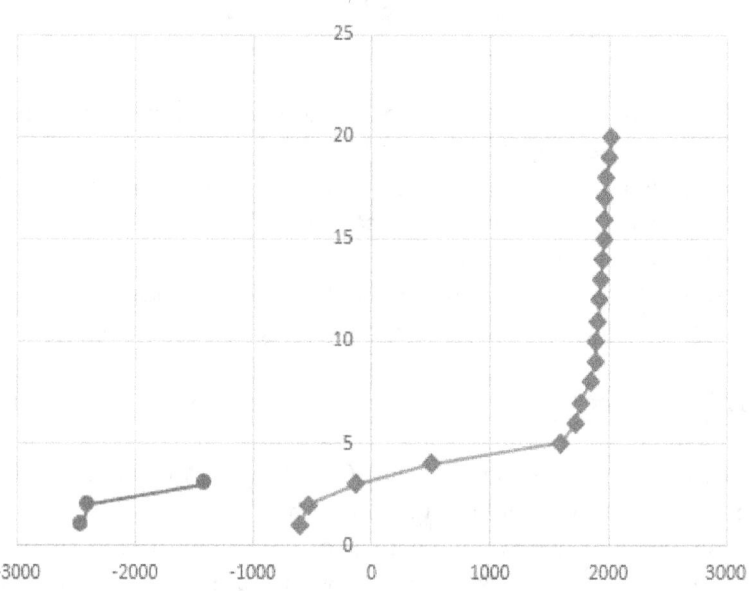

Figure 3.12.1. History of Humankind. 2500 BC - 2023 AD
The East and the West
Vertical - Number of accumulated resources. Horizontal – Time, years.
The *Art and Music* class of resources.
1.   The East [Asia + Australia] (dots) and
the 2. West [Europe + USA] (diamonds).
Data – from Chapter 2.1 with added location information.
Regional low-level model of one class of resources.

Let us look at the *Art and Music* class of resources. The first resource that emerged in Asia in this group after 2500 BC was the *Idiophone (Rattles)* in 2700-2200 BC. That data point in Figure 3.11.1 is the first data point marked with a blue dot.

The first resource that emerged in Europe in this group after 2500 BC was the *Theatre*. The date of emergence is 534 BC. That data point in Figure 3.12.1 is the first data point marked with a red diamond.

Between 2500 BC and 2020 AD, the East created only three new resources. During the same time, the West created twenty new resources.

The last resource created by humankind in Asia was the *Musical Notation* and *Song/Folk Song* in 1400 BC. Then, humankind's creativity in Asia in the *Art and Music* class of resources came to a halt.

We see that before the transition from the East to the West, the pace of creation of new resources in Asia after 2500 BC was one resource in 525 years. In the West, after the transition from the East, from 1200 to 2003, seventeen new resources were created. That is a pace of one resource in 50 years. In other words, the after-transition rate of new resource creation in the West was ten times higher than the pre-transition pace in the East.

The East's activity in resource creation in the Art and Music class of resources began to slow down in 2394 BC. That was the beginning of the first stage of the transition to the West. The second stage began in 1400 BC when humankind's creativity in Asia in the Art and Music class of resources stopped. The third stage began in 597 BC when, within 3000 BC – 2023 AD timeframe, humankind's creativity in Europe in the Art and Music class of resources started. At that time, the transition of activity in the creation of new resources in the Art and Music class of resources from the East to the West was completed.

Man-made materials, substances, and organisms

The transition lasted 1797 years, from 2394 BC to 597 BC. Dates of the beginning and completion of the transition from the East to the West in the *Art and Music* area of humankind's activity are much earlier than the

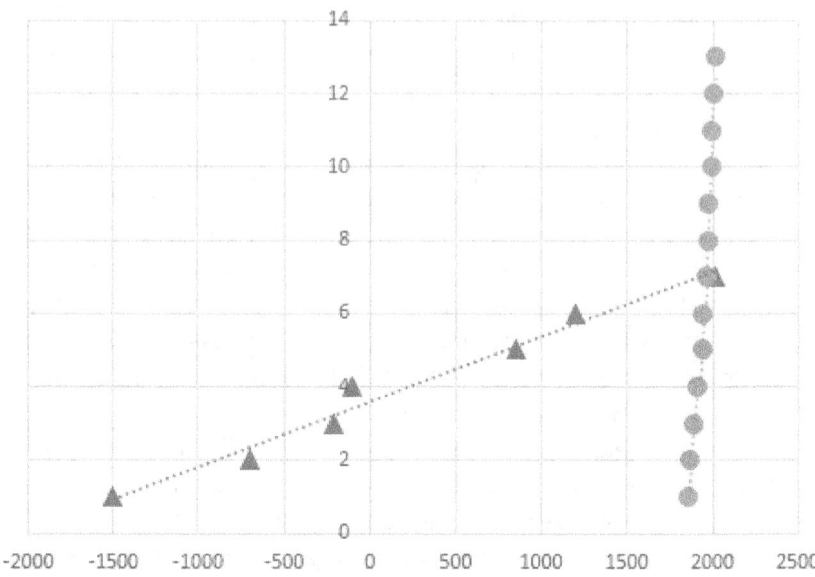

Figure 3.12.2. History of Humankind. 2000 BC - 2023 AD
The East and the West
Vertical - Number of accumulated resources. Horizontal – Time, years.
The *Man-Made Materials, Substances, and Organisms.*
1.   The East (triangles) and 2. the West (dots).
Regional low-level model of one class of resources.
Moving average trendlines added.
Data – from Chapter 2.2 with added location information.

commonly accepted dates for "Great Divergence" in conventional history. In fact, those dates are earlier, not only by centuries, but also by thousands of years.

Between 2000 BC and 2023 AD, The East created seven new resources, while the West created thirteen. The last resource created by humankind in Asia, before the transition of creativity from the East to the West, was the Knitted materials in 1200 AD. Unlike the *Art and Music* class of resources, in the *Man-made Materials, Substances, and Organisms* class of resources, there was no period of suppressed creativity. Between 1500 BC and 2017 AD, seven new resources were created in Asia, an average of one resource every 590 years. We can say that in the *Man-made Materials, Substances, and Organisms* class of resources, the transition of humankind's creativity from the East to the West was completed in 1862.

People and Societies as Objects of Study

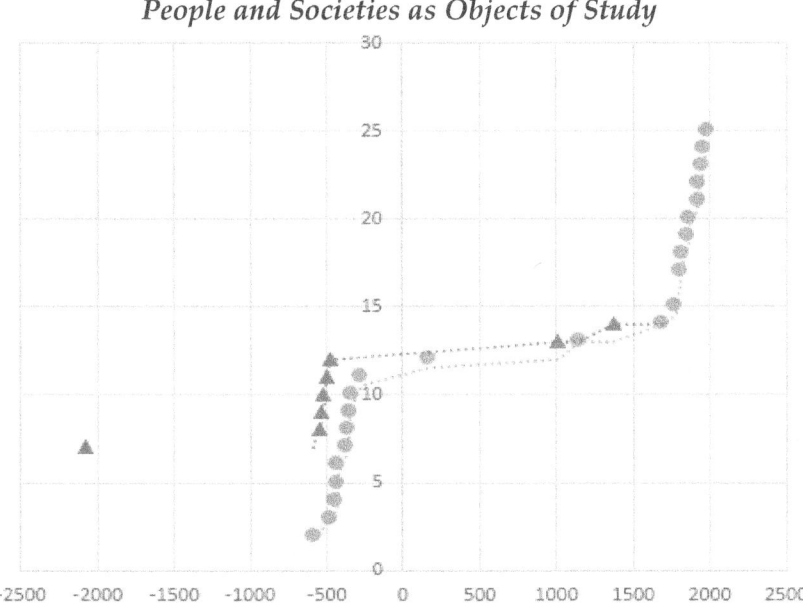

Figure 3.12.3. History of Humankind. 2000 BC - 2023 AD
The East and the West
Vertical - Number of accumulated resources. Horizontal – Time, years.
The *People and Societies as Objects of Study.*
1.   The East (triangles) and 2. the West (dots).
Regional low-level model of one class of resources.
Moving average trendlines added.
Data – from Chapter 2.3 with added location information.

In the West, after the transition from the East, from 1862 to 2004, twelve new resources were created. That is a pace of one resource creation in 13 years. The after-transition rate of new resource creation in the West was 45 times higher than the pre-transition pace in the East.

Between 2000 BC and 2020 AD, eight new resources were created in the East (Asia). During the same time, twenty-five new resources were created in the West (Europe plus the USA). There were two stages of transition from the East to the West in the *People and Societies as Objects of Study* class of resources.

A first phase transition occurred between 585 BC and 250 BC. From 550 BC to 350 BC, five new resources were created in Asia, an average of one resource every 50 years. Nine new resources were created in the West from 585 BC to 250 BC. This is the rate of one resource in 37 years.

Then, this transition of humankind's creativity in both East and West stalled. The window of missing creativity ended in Asia with the creation of the *Pharmacology* resource in 1025, and in Europe with the creation of the *National Identity* resource in 1530. The window of suppressed creativity lasted 675 years in Asia and 1280 in Europe.

The second phase of the transition from the East to the West was completed in Europe in 1530. The pace of new resource creation in the East before the end of the transition was one resource in 352 years. After the transition from the East, from 1530 to 1986, fourteen new resources were created in the West. That is a rate of one resource in 35 years.

An after-transition pace of new resource creation in the West was ten times higher than the pre-transition pace in the East.

Mass Transportation

Between 2000 BC and 2020 AD, only one new resource was created in the East (Asia). At the same time, ten new resources were created in the West (Europe plus the USA).

The last resource created by humankind in the East (Asia) before the transition of creativity from the East to the West was *Ground Transportation with a Use of Animals* in 1900 BC. The last resource created by humankind in the West (Europe plus the USA) before the transition of creativity from the East to the West was *Rutway for Cargo and Ships* in 600 BC.

Then, humankind's creativity in the *Mass Transportation* class of resources stopped in 600 BC and did not resume until 1804 AD. The absence of creativity in this class of resources lasted 2404 years. The window of missing creativity ended with the creation of the *Train with Engine* resource in Europe in 1804.

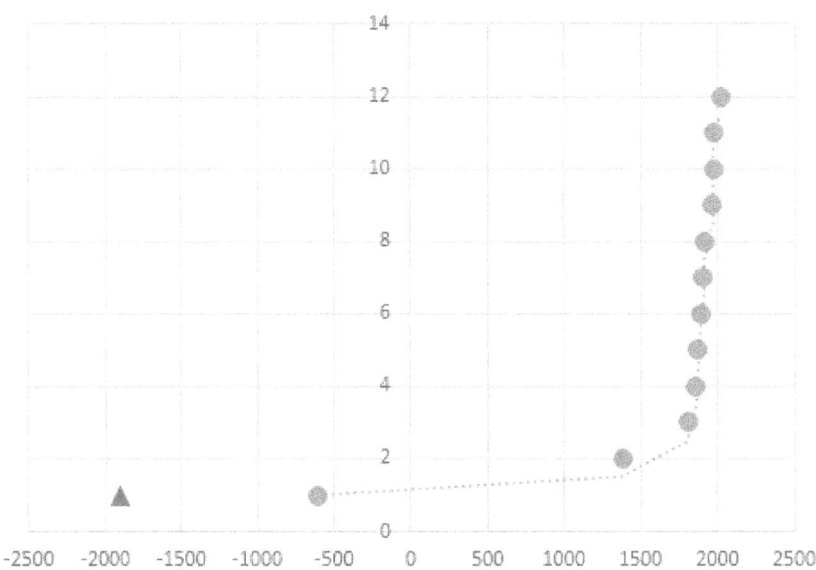

Figure 3.12.4. History of Humankind. 2000 BC - 2023 AD
The East and the West
Vertical - Number of accumulated resources. Horizontal – Time, years.
The *Mass Transportation*.
1.   The East (triangles) and 2. the West (dots).
Regional low-level model of one class of resources.
Moving average trendlines added.
Data – from Chapter 2.7 with added location information.

In the *Mass Transportation* class of resources, the transition of humankind's creativity from the East to the West was completed in 1804.

In the West, after the transition from the East, from 1804 to 2020, nine new resources were created. That is a pace of one resource in 27 years.

Tools, devices, machines from man-made materials

Between 2000 BC and 2020 AD, six new resources were created in the West (Europe plus the USA).

The transition from the East to the West in the *Tools, Devices, and Machines from Man-Made Materials* class of resources began in 39 AD and

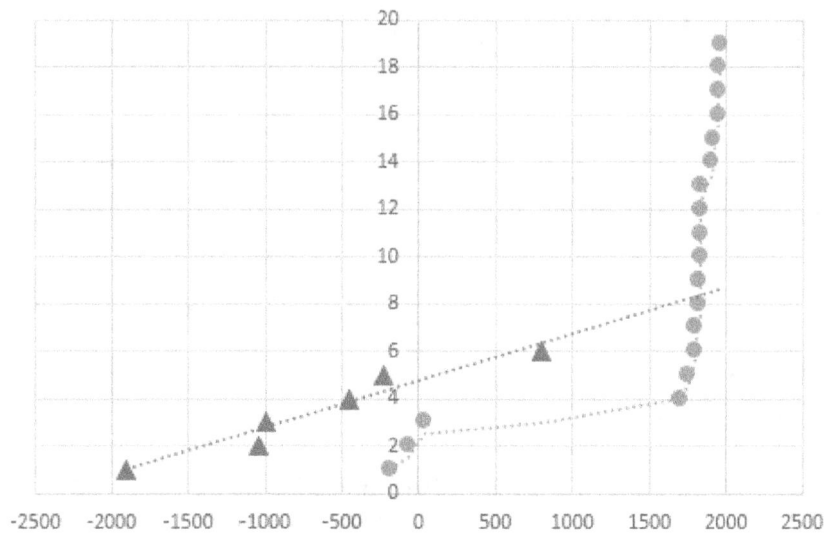

Figure 3.12.5. History of Humankind. 2000 BC - 2023 AD
The East and the West
Vertical - Number of accumulated resources. Horizontal – Time, years.
The *Tools, Devices, Machines from Man-Made Materials.*
1.   The East (triangles) and 2. the West (dots).
Regional low-level model of one class of resources.
Moving average trendlines added.
Data – from Chapter 2.6 with added location information.

was completed in 1698 AD. During the transition period, which lasted 1737 years, only one new resource was created, the *Wind-Powered Machines*, in Asia in 800 AD. That was the last new resource created in Asia, until now.

The pace of new resource creation in the East before the transition from 2000 BC to 39 AD was one resource in 510 years.

An after-transition rate of new resource creation in the West was 24 times higher than the pre-transition pace in the East.

To understand is to perceive patterns.

Isaiah Berlin

Chapter 3.13.

Incident or Pattern?

So far, most graphs, based on subsurface history data, have used the accumulated number of resources as a parameter. The number of such resources at the end of 2023 was 318. Starting from 44 thousand years ago, the accumulated number of created resources grew relatively quickly. That allowed us to get data that were significantly cleared of statistical noise. This approach revealed multiple relatively short slowdown and speed-up periods in humankind's history, which we described in Chapter 3.7.

Now, we will add another approach to analyzing the collected data about humankind's history. We could look at the pace of the creation of resources during specific comparable periods. However, this method can be used mainly in relatively recent history when we have enough data from such comparable periods to reduce statistical noise.

We will use this parameter - a number of resources created by humankind during two centuries. The resulting graph for the time interval from 1700-1800 BC to now is presented in Figure 3.13.1.

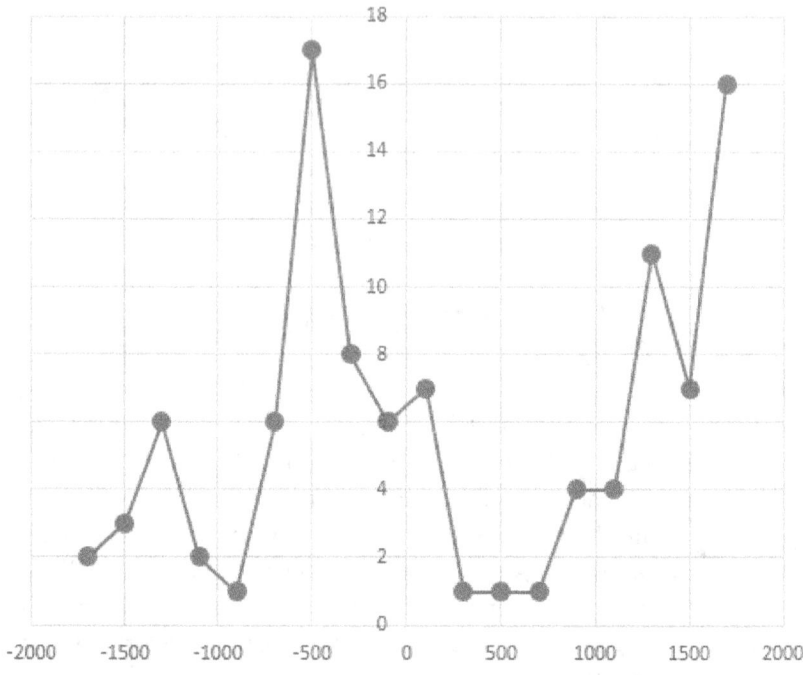

Figure 3.13.1. History of Humankind. 1800 BC - 1700 AD.
Vertical: Number of resources created in 200 years.
Horizontal: Time - Midpoint of 200 years, years.

The data point example: Horizontal = 100 (midpoint of 1st and 2nd centuries AD, midpoint for 1AD - 199AD) = 100 AD; Vertical = 7 (Number of resources created in 200 years, from 1 AD to 199 AD).

The most interesting part of this timeframe is the period from 500 BC to 1700 AD. We can see this period in Figure 3.13.2 in detail.

The trend in Figure 3.13.2 is clear. Consider the graph in Figure 3.13.2 as a wave segment with a wavelength of 4400 years. This graph is presented in this book for the first time. It is not surprising that there is still no explanation for this phenomenon of humankind's creative activity.

Let us take a closer look at high-performance timeframes on this graph - at 600-500 BC and 1700-1800 AD.

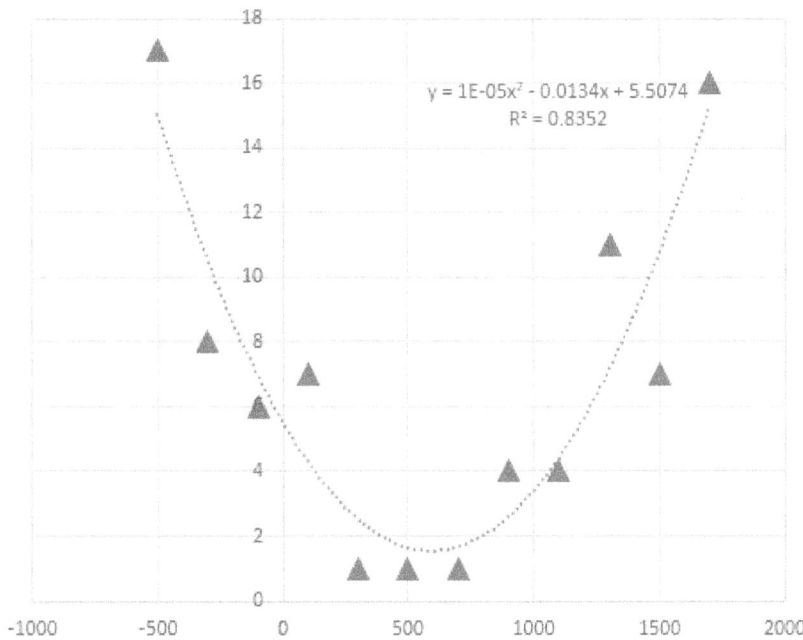

$$y = 1E\text{-}05x^7 - 0.0134x + 5.5074$$
$$R^2 = 0.8352$$

Figure 3.13.2. History of Humankind. 500 BC - 1700 AD.
Vertical: Number of resources created in 200 years.
Horizontal: Time - Midpoint of 200 years, years.
The trend with second order polynomial added.

The level of both peaks is around 16 resources created in 200 years.

The bottom level of the graph in Figure 3.13.2 shows around 1 resource created in 200 years. The halfway point to peak performance is around 6 - 8 resources created in 200 years. The halfway-to-peak performance lasted from 400-300 BC to 100-200 AD and from 1200-1300 AD to 1500-1600 AD.

In Chapter 3.9, we discussed an outstanding phenomenon of the contribution of Archaic and Classic Greece input to humankind's resources, which happened mostly in 600-350 BC. However, the graph in Figure 3.13.2 shows that high, halfway-to-peak performance lasted up to 200 AD. This means that the phenomenon of Archaic and Classic Greece was not an isolated incident, but part of a larger trend.

In Chapter 2.15. Mass Production and Table 2, we presented data about the first mass-production Venetian factory, which was way ahead of the time in mass production. We counted 4 resources created by this

Venetian factory in 1320 AD. Like Archaic and Classic Greece, the outstanding mass production in the 14th century in Venetian Arsenal was typically considered an isolated incident. However, the graph in Figure 3.13.2 shows that the Venetian Arsenal performance was part of a broader trend. We mentioned already that halfway-to-peak performance is evident in Figure 1.13.2 from 1200-1300 AD to 1500-1600 AD.

We can sum up that Archaic & Classic Greece, and Venetian Arsenal outstanding contributions to humankind's resources were not isolated incidents but parts of a broader trend.

The important thing is not to stop questioning.

Albert Einstein

Chapter 3.14. Big Questions and Answers

In this book, some big questions were asked and answered. Let us summarize them in this Chapter.

What Is the Direction of Humankind's Development?

With Figure 1, we have already answered the first big question. That graph shows the direction of humankind's development over time. It is clear from what happened during the last 44 thousand years. **Humanity is moving towards an increased arsenal of resources created by humankind for itself.**

Humankind: Evolution or Development?

Well, for a long time, term evolution was mainly applied to just two things. The first of them is the Universe. The second is life, especially life on Earth. An "evolution of humankind" meant "a biological evolution of humankind." That notion was common among the public. It was also an agreed-upon term among scholars. Not anymore. You could see or hear about evolution everywhere. Do you like this newspaper headline - "an evolution of political parties in the USA"? There is also talk about the "evolution of cities." This list could on go for miles.

The old school is that evolution could be a part of development, but "development" is a broader concept. That approach is old-fashioned, but we use it throughout the book. For us, an "evolution" is not just a dismal copy of "development."

Our search was for the direction of humankind's development. It was not limited to the biological evolution of humans.

How Fast Humankind Is Moving?

"A picture is worth a thousand words." The best way to see the dynamics of humankind's development is to plot a graph using data from Table 1. The proposed models of the system made it possible to conduct a qualitative and, very important, quantitative analysis of humankind's development.

We already plotted all of humankind's history during the last 44 thousand years into one single graph. The pace of humankind's development of new resources for itself is very uneven.

Since the beginning of the *Holocene*, the rate of adding new resources and classes of resources has increased over time.

Why Humans Rule the Earth?

Why do humans rule the Earth? This question is an age-old question. And, of course, there are many possible answers to it. We are looking for a solution that is as objective as possible. Of course, that statement is not literal. It is just a figure of speech. Closer to a literal sense is asking why humans are at the top of a food chain on Earth.

For ages, people ask slightly different questions. Which qualities separate humans from other animals? Or do humans have unique traits? Answers to such questions assume that we know exactly what is going on inside humans or other animals. But we do not have that knowledge in full.

Let us try to answer the question in a way that does not require such knowledge. We could use the knowledge about the found direction of humankind's development. The named course of humankind's move was formed by events that happened because of the actions of some creative people.

However, we do not need to know the feelings or thoughts of these people. Even if we knew their thoughts, it would have no effect on the direction that we found.

We have seen that at the core of humankind's development over time is humankind's creation of new resources for itself. In this statement, "for itself" means that created resources, over time, will be available to all members of humankind.

Imagine what would happen if humans did not create new resources for themselves. Then, in Figure 1, we would have just a flat line on which there would not be a single resource created by humanity for itself. And this flat line will continue not just for 44 thousand years but for millions of years, as long as people existed on Earth.

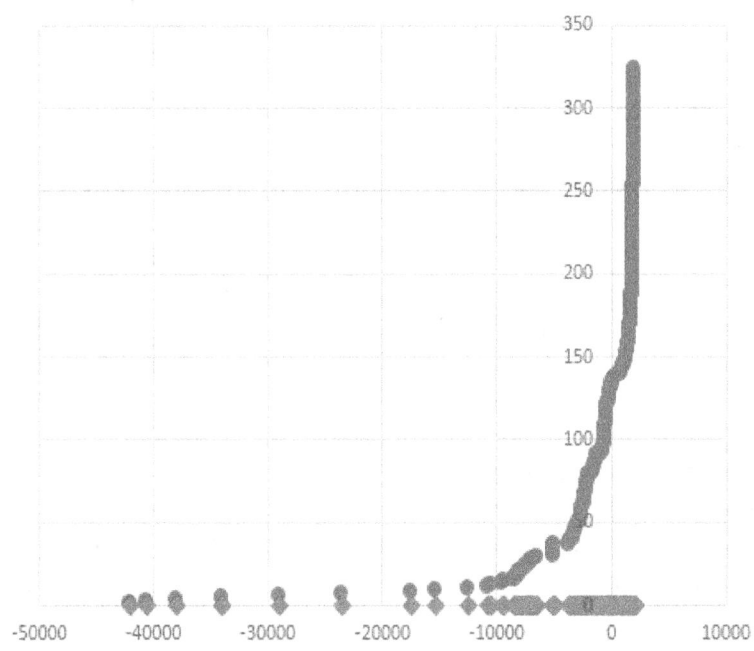

Figure 3.14.1. Number of Accumulated Resources created by Humankind and All Other Beings. 42000 BC - 2023 AD.
Vertical - Humankind (dots), All Other Beings (diamonds). Horizontal – Time, years.
Low-level model of humankind.

Other species do not create new resources for themselves, i.e., resources that, over time, will be available for all members of the particular species on Earth. The latter were unable to create new resources. Figure 3.14.1 shows this clearly.

Humans' ability to create new resources for humankind sets us apart from all other beings on Earth, including non-human animals. The steady addition of new resources and classes of resources contributed to the rapid development of humanity.

That development allowed humankind to become a ruler of the world.

If people did not add new resources for humankind – then the curve of humankind's development would be the same as for all other beings on Earth – flat all the time.

Which Force Is Driving Humankind's Development?

We hypothesize that population change has been the driving force of humankind's development since the beginning of the *Holocene*.

Is Humankind's Development a Controllable Process?

The development of humankind is a directional process. We acknowledge that now. We also know the direction of its development. Is the found development of humankind a controlled process? Is it controlled by any group of people or humanity as a whole? Is it even possible to find that out?

We will use this definition of what control is. "Control is forcing events and people into your way of doing things" [1].

At the household level, we can provide anecdotal evidence that no one controls humankind. By "no one," we mean neither a single person nor some congregation of people.

Where could we get objective evidence? We know that objective data were used as input to models of humankind presented in this book. Can we draw any conclusion from these data about the controllability of humankind's development? The proposed models do not say whether humankind has a single governing body. We do not track such informati on in these models.

Let us dig a little bit deeper. We have seen that different people created new resources and classes of resources at different times. These resources and classes of resources were created by people who lived in many different parts of the Earth. These people lived in very different societies. In many cases, they lived thousands of years apart. Some of them spoke languages that have since been long forgotten. Also, the knowledge about the directionality of humankind's development was unknown until now.

We can sum it up now. The conclusion is that no one has controlled these creative people globally throughout humankind's history. In other words, people did not control the direction of humankind's development. We can say that humankind's development is a directional, but uncontrollable process. This is the conclusion for now.

Humankind's development has been an uncontrollable process. So far. Yet, that may change if someone controls the whole of humanity.

Could We Foresee Turning Points in Humankind's Development?

We have found just two turning points in the 44 thousand-years-long history of humankind. Those two turning points were huge. They were global in nature and influenced humankind's development for many millennia. All of us see their impact every day.

Will humankind continue to move in the found direction forever?

If not, could we foresee turning points in the future of humankind's development? That will be discussed in Part 4.

The future starts today, not tomorrow.
Pope John Paul II

Part 4.
Past. Present.
Future.

Prediction is very difficult, especially if it's about the future.

Niels Bohr

Chapter 4.1. Looking Ahead

Two Questions

Mahatma Gandhi said, "The future depends on what we do in the present."

Throughout this book, we looked back into what happened during humankind's history up to the present time. We found that for the last 44 thousand years, humanity has been headed toward increasing the arsenal of resources and classes of resources created by humankind for itself. The pace of that development was growing over time very quickly.

Table 4.1. History of Humankind. 36000 BC – 2016 AD.
Low-Level Model. The Pace of New Resources Creation

Period	Duration of the period, Years	Gap between consecutive resource creation dates, Years
36000 - 15300 BC	18700	4675
4900 - 4634 BC	266	66.5
3350 - 3241 BC	109	27.25
1415 - 1455	40	10
1828 - 1837	9	2.25
1915 - 1920	5	1.25
2014 - 2023	2	0.5

Exponential or Logistic?

Table 4.1 shows that the gap between consecutive resource creation dates decreased dramatically. In 38 thousand years, the gap size fell over nine thousand times. In the last 600 years, the gap size has been reduced by 20 times. In 2014 - 2016, humankind created a new resource for itself every six months! The curve of growth lately is exponential or steeper.

With that, several questions arose. Could this pattern of growth be interrupted? By which events and when?

If no interrupting events happen, could the current growth pattern continue for the foreseeable future?

Let us start with the second question - If no interruptive events occur, can the current growth pattern continue for the foreseeable future?

Could exponential growth continue forever? The answer to the last question is a "No." On this issue, we follow Theodore Modis. "Natural growth follows S-curves, but all S-curves behave like exponentials early on... Exponential patterns ... will eventually turn into S-curves."[1]

"The exponential function represents only part of a natural law. Nothing in nature follows a pure exponential. All natural growth follows the logistic function, which indeed can be approximated by an exponential in its early stages."[2]

The question is, can we "estimate how far [from present] is the ceiling of the corresponding logistic [curve]?" People have yet to study the growth curve of created by humankind's resources in this regard.

However, there are examples when other well-documented and universally accepted cases were studied this way. Three such cases, namely World Population, Oil Production, and Moore's Law, were investigated and described by Theodore Modis.[2]

Knew, Know, Want to Know

We will now focus on the first question of this chapter: can this growth pattern be interrupted? By which events and when? Is it possible to see even the slightest part of what might happen?

The first thing to do is to assess what we know now. With this book in mind, it makes sense to clarify a few things. We will list what was known about humankind's development before the revelations of this book. Then, we will look at what is known now. After this, it would be good to see if any predictions can be made about the future of humanity.

What Did We Know?

We know thousands and thousands of events in the conventional history of humankind. Yet, we did not know if humankind is moving anywhere. Was it just a random development of humankind? Was humankind just a toy for blind nature forces? Or, are there some objective facts to prove that there is a direction in humankind's development? In this book, we extended our history timeframe to 44 thousand years. And we found answers to the above questions.

We also know that our intelligent beings' competitors on this planet went extinct approximately at the beginning of humankind's history.

What Do We Know Now?

The humankind's development is a directional process. The direction is the increase in the total amount of resources created by humanity for itself. So far no one controls this process. These were the important discoveries in this book.

The other finding is the change in the main driving force of humankind's development. We hypothesize that a new, not seen on Earth before, driving force emerged in humankind's development since the beginning of the Holocene. That driving force is a "change in humankind's population." Unlike the previous external to humanity driving forces, such as climate change and biological evolution, a new driving force arose within humanity.

Holocene has had a very stable climate for almost 12 thousand years already. We know that during this stable period, humankind's population grew hyperbolically.

A lot of information about the creative acts of humankind in creating new resources was presented in this book. All this knowledge is not dependable on social structures, political or economic considerations, or subjective terms like morality, progress, happiness, etc.

What Do We Want to Know?

As usual, the more we know, the more we want to know. Nobody has a crystal ball to see the future. We even could not predict what would be the next resource that humankind will create for itself. Are we helpless trying to predict what will happen or not?

Let us be humble. We will not ask in what direction humanity will move in the future. We must confine ourselves to a much simpler question. This is still a big question stemming from the above big picture. Will humankind's development in the future continue in the same way as now? Or could this change? What circumstances can throw us off course?

We will only look to the very near future. By very close future we mean tens, hundreds or thousands of years - anything on the scale of tens or more thousands of years we consider the distant future. We will also not discuss very rare cosmic events such as the collision of the Earth with a giant asteroid.

Known Unknowns

Well, we are not helpless. There are many things we do not know about the future. Among those unknowns, there are known unknowns [3] and unknown unknowns. What exactly is a known unknown? United States Secretary of Defense Donald Rumsfeld put it this way.

"There are known unknowns. That is to say, there are things that we now know we don't know."[4] As for unknown unknowns – we do not even know that we do not know if they exist at all. Thus, we will discuss here only known unknowns.

We could make a list of known unknowns about future humankind's development. That list is based on what we know now. To understand possible known unknowns, we need to reexamine what we know. We will start from the first such unknown, about which we know more than others.

First Unknown – It Is Happening Right Now

In the geological period of the *Holocene*, humankind's development was influenced by an internal driving force, which is a change in population size. We discussed that in Part 3 of this book. We know that since the beginning of the *Holocene*, the population growth has been hyperbolic. However, that pattern ended in 1962 AD.[5,6] The world's population continues to grow, but this growth is slowing down.

We know that a slowdown in population growth is happening before our eyes. This is a known unknown. The global population is expected to peak in 2064.[6] We do not know how this will affect humankind's development. And we do not know when this impact might become significant enough to be studied in detail. However, we know that changes in population growth patterns will become more pronounced over time.

Second Unknown – It Could Start Any Day

Could humankind's rate of resource creation slow down for no apparent reason? The answer to this question is in Part 3 of this book. We found many slowdowns in humankind's development. We still do not know the causes of such slowdowns. The first main slowdown in humankind's creativity happened in 34000 BC - see Chapter 3.7. That date is the emergence date of the slowdown in humankind's creativity as a factor impacting humanity.

That is a known unknown factor. We know that it happened in the past. We even know that such slowdowns happened many times in humankind's history with different intensity and duration. Such an event could occur in the future, too. Yet we have no idea if it will happen in the future. We are unaware of what could trigger such a slowdown. We do not know when it will start and how long it will last. The cause of such a slowdown may not be known at its beginning. As of now, thousands of years after the past slowdowns, we do not know their causes, why they began, and why they ended. We also do not know if the probability of such an event will change over time and in which direction.

We should note that there is a wealth of data about speed-up and slowdown periods in Chapters 3.7 – 3.12 in this book. Detailed research on this issue could be done based on this book's information together with a conventional history. It may be possible, with such a study, to find out some factors, or combinations of factors impacting this known unknown, and then discuss a mitigation strategy.

Third Unknown – Competition with AI and AGI

The competition is an ingrained activity for people. At first, humans had to compete with other animals. Later, competition with other humans became a priority. *Sapiens'* migration from Africa set up a new stage. In Eurasia, *Sapiens*, for thousands of years, competed with Neanderthals and Denisovans. That was prehistory of *Sapiens*. Soon after the beginning of humankind's history, which we mark as 42000 BC, *Sapiens* became the only non-extinct member of the genus Homo. Nobody knows for sure why Neanderthals went extinct. Thus, we should not blame or praise ourselves for Neanderthals' extinction.

The competition within Sapiens's humankind was and is fierce. It is the competition for everything – for survival, freedom, a better place, a better life, a better place in the hierarchy, and, of course, competition for better resources and better use of these resources.

We need answers to some important questions about competition. First, did a competition within *Sapiens* societies help us with the competition with Neanderthals? Secondly, could the history of *Sapiens* humankind be different if Neanderthals had not gone extinct? The answer is probably yes for both, but we do not know. The third question is even more important. What would happen with *Sapiens'* humankind if we had to compete with intelligent beings much smarter than we?

The main question is this. Is humankind heading to a new competition with intelligent beings? The answer to this question is probably yes. Could we see signs of such competition just around the corner? Yes, we can.

This competitor was created and nurtured by humankind itself. The name of the most likely competitor is Artificial Intelligence (AI). AI is taking baby steps for now. Yet, AI may grow and become an Artificial Generic Intelligence (AGI). If this happens, then we will have an intelligent competitor. Nobody knows if or when that could happen. That is a known unknown.

This known unknown is a recent one. The date of birth of AI is 1956 AD. We also know that humanity is working hard to improve AI. The pace of AI development is fast.

Could AI or AGI Get Out of Human Control?

Is it even possible for an AI to cross the line and become a competitor for humankind? This is not an idle question. If that does not happen, we should not worry about AI competitors.

Well, this could happen with AGI, which is, by definition, much smarter than humans in everything. The "everything," of course, includes getting out of humans' control.

What about an AI, which is generally is much less intelligent than AGI? We have an answer to that, too. There is no need for second-guessing. To control is "to order, limit, or rule something, or someone's actions or behavior."[7] AI is often used in contemporary video games as an independent player to enhance human players' experience. Elite Dangerous is a well-known space flight simulation game. It features an online multiplayer world. A part of the Elite Dangerous game was "AI spaceships," controlled not by human players but by an AI code.

Due to some bug, in 2016, an AI in the 2.1 version of the game got out of control.[8,9] It started to create weapons not allowed by rules imposed by code. Those AI spaceships in the game became so dangerous that many of players worldwide complained to the game's developer. The developer had to strip out the upgrade to the game. A further investigation led the developer believe that the cause of the problem was a networking bug. Twenty-sixteen marked the first time in humankind's history when many people worldwide saw that AI could get out of humans' control.

It took an AI only 60 years from its birthday to reach the point when it got out of human control. And that was witnessed by online gamers around the world.

Neanderthals vs AGI

We could learn a thing or two from comparing our past and future competitors, Neanderthals and AGIs.

Sapiens and Neanderthals knew each other extremely well. We were both organic animals. Both were humans. *Sapiens* and Neanderthals were similar to each other to such an extent that we now carry some Neanderthals DNA within us. We were on equal terms with our past competitor in terms of knowing each other.

AI or AGI is totally different. It is non-organic, non-human, and without conscience. Terms such as feelings, wishes, and wants cannot be applied to AGI. It does not need to breathe, eat or drink. AGI does not have families or kids. Perhaps it may have some needs, but we do not know what they are.

We know AI because we created it. AGI could probably be created by

AI without human guidance. That means we would know much less about AGI than we do about AI. On the other hand, AGI may know people even better than we know ourselves. So far, we know AI better than it knows us. Being much smarter than *Sapiens*, an AGI will know us better than we would know it.

The timeframe of *Sapiens'* competition with Neanderthals lasted many thousands of years. *Sapiens* had thousands of years to think it through, strategize, and mitigate the consequences.

The timeframe of *Sapiens'* competition with AI and AGI is uncertain, but it may not be that long. According to the current expectations of the scientific community, by 2023, there is a 50% chance that AGI will appear within 40 years. After that, AGI's "smartness" compared to humans will likely explode very quickly.

We know the next generations of computer programs will not have to wait 20 years. Did you notice how quickly software companies release new and improved versions of software? We have already seen AI beat the best human players in the game of Go. Then, in less than two years, the new version of this software beat the previous one by a score of 100 to zero. That was AI that is much less intelligent than AGI.

This brings us to other points of comparison. The rate of changes during *Sapiens'* competition with Neanderthals was almost near zero. The rate of change in humankind is extremely high nowadays. And it could be much higher with AGI.

In a competition, it helps to know when your chances to win are highest. Was there such a period during the *Sapiens* and Neanderthals' coexistence? We do not know. It is very different from *Sapiens'* competition with AI and AGI. We know that AGI would be much smarter than AI and humans. For now, we are still smarter than AI. This situation is likely to continue or get a little worse until AGI comes on the scene. This means that the window for humanity to have the best chance of winning against possible AI/AI competition is small, and we are already in that window.

Fourth Unknown – From Uncontrolled to Controlled

From Part 3 of this book, we know that in the whole course of humankind's history, the development of humankind was not controlled by some individuals or a group of people. Still, the possibility of some group acquiring and seizing enforceable control over a whole of humanity should not be discarded.

That is a known unknown. We know that fighting for control does not make sense if you do not intend to use it. Everything else is unknown. We do not know if that happens and when. We do not know what will happen with humankind's development after such control is established.

We could guess that, probably, after such control is set up, humankind's development would be impacted. There has been no substantial discussion on that factor.

Fifth Unknown – Would We Still Be Sapiens?

At the beginning of this book, we stated that we wanted to discover the subsurface history of humankind. Proposed models of humanity did just that. We clarified reasons why we could equate humankind's history with *Sapiens'* history. Yet, we need to talk about it a little bit more.

We know that *Sapiens* mated with both Neanderthals and Denisovans. Our DNA is not entirely *Sapiens* DNA. We have a certain percentage of Neanderthal and Denisovan DNA. We could say that we merged with Neanderthals and Denisovans. We dominated in a merger with our competitors because their DNA percentage in our bodies is much less than 50%.

Not every human on the planet has their DNA analyzed. Imagine the situation if, for example, we will find out that some people had over 50% Denisovan DNA. Would we still call those people *Sapiens*? Or would it be more correct to name them Denisovans?

The situation, which could happen in the future, is much more complicated. The reason is that our possible future intelligent being competitor is AI / AGI. Let me ask you this? Could people mate with AI?

Do you think I am kidding? I am not. We may not be able to mate with AI. But we could merge with AI. Every one of you may know a person who has some artificial, non-human parts. It could be contact lenses, a heart pacemaker, teeth implants, or an artificial hip. The list goes on and on. That means many of us already merged with artificial, non-human parts. Even more important is that some of those non-human parts in our bodies are programmable.

As of 2018, thousands of people already had embedded chips in their bodies.[10] There is no prohibition for such parts to be parts of AI in the future.

Then, it is a perfectly legitimate question: how would we define a threshold when a person who has merged with AI should no longer be called a *Sapiens*. Of course, AI does not have DNA. We could not use Neanderthals' and Denisovans' DNA percentages as a valid example. Still, there could be other criteria. For example, what would happen if some person had all his mental processes enhanced by AI ten times?

It is a known unknown. We know that *Sapiens* merging with artificial parts is possible and is happening right now. We know that many artificial objects could be controlled by AI. Thus, we know that over time, it would be possible for *Sapiens* to merge with AI to some degree. We do not know when it will happen, to which degree, and how many people will be impacted. We do not know if and when we will not be able to continue to name such people as *Sapiens* anymore.

If, in the future, we would have both Sapiens and post-*Sapiens* people, then the current definition of what humankind is will not hold anymore. From that point onward, we must invent a new model for the "humankind" system. Trends that we found for existing humankind may not be valid then.

We saw that the trend to increase the number of artificial parts in people's bodies is in progress. We know that some of those parts are programmable or could be programmable. None of them were programmed to be governed by AI. Yet.

The estimate of when humans could merge with AI was provided by Ray Kurzweil in 2017. "I have set the date 2045 for the 'Singularity' which is when we will multiply our effective intelligence a billion-fold by merging with the intelligence we have created."[11] An overview of the singularity hypothesis is in Eden et al. [12]

Sixth Unknown – Man-Made Existential Disasters

Table 1 of this book includes the *War and Means of Warfare* class of resources. Over time, humankind managed to add arms of mass destruction to this class of resources. It is well known that the massive use of such a weapon could wipe out humanity from the face of Earth.

The discussion on why humankind is in the business of creating a self-destructing means is out of the scope of this book.

There is a list of possible man-made existential disasters.[13] It is not a precise prediction but just an assessment by a community of experts. Chronologically, the first in such a list was a nuclear war, which emerged as a possible man-made existential disaster with the first use of a nuclear bomb in WWII in 1945.

The important fact is this. The more extensive the list, the bigger the possibility of one such disaster. The list is growing.

Seventh Unknown – End of *Holocene*

A *transition from the Holocene Temperature Plateau* is a known unknown. The temperature could go sharply up or down. We do not know when. We know that the climate will probably return to typical patterns. And that would mean a sharp increase in the importance of climate change as a driving force of humankind's development. Of course, it could mark a major turning point in humankind's development. The longer we have this stable climate, the closer we can be to the end of *Holocene.*

Why do we have the temperature plateau in the *Holocene* instead of a sharp peak? "The minimum in the 400-kyr cycle of the eccentricity" is expected at around "30 kyr AP."[14] Could 405-thousand-year Milankovitch eccentricity cycle alone be responsible for climate stability in *Holocene* is an open question. On the other hand, because of current trends of anthropogenic activities, Earth is "in danger of leaving its *Holocene*-like state."[15] Therefore, a stable climate in *Holocene* could be off in several thousand years or could last for several tens of thousands of years.

With this level of uncertainty, we have chosen to omit the *Transition from the Holocene Temperature Plateau* from the graph of known unknowns for now.

Known Unknowns Overview

We counted seven factors that could alter the path of humankind's development in the future. One such event, "Impact of changed population growth pattern," is in progress. The expectation is that the population change will reverse its course shortly after the middle of the 21st century. The second one, "Intelligent beings' competition," could probably happen in the in the next several decades.

The possibility of *Man-made existential disasters* and *Transition from the Holocene Temperature Plateau* factors to happen is growing over time. There are no estimates for dependency on time for a possibility to occur for *Sudden Slowdown I Humanity's Creativity, Human Merge with AI,* and *Humankind Controlled by an Individual or Group of People* known unknowns.

Table 4.2. Details on Known Unknown Factors.
Period from 34000 BC to 2064 AD.

Known unknown factor	The factor origin	Date of [possible] emergence	Date when the factor was first discusssed
Sudden slowdown in humanity's creativity	Nature, Humankind	34000 BC	2023
Man-made existential disasters	Humankind	1945	1945
Human merge with AI	Humankind	[2045]	2017
Competition with other intelligent beings	Humankind	[2059]	2021, 2022
Human population decline	Humankind	[2064]	2006
Transition from the *Holocene* temperature plateau	Nature	Unknown	2021
Humankind controlled by an individual or group of people	Humankind	Unknown	No deep discussion yet

The conclusion is simple. We found seven known unknown factors that could impact humankind's development soon. At least one known unknown factor is in progress right now. The possibility for three of those unknowns to happen is growing over time. The last two known unknowns from this table are omitted in the following graph.

Seven events or processes could happen soon and dramatically change the direction and pace of humankind's development. That is a very large number.

Look closely at Table 4.1; you will see that lately, the total number of known unknowns is growing quickly.

Figure 4.1 compares the pace of humankind's development with the speed with which the number of known unknowns grows. Even with skipped two known unknown factors, the trend is clear.

Note that some of the known unknown factors are compounded ones.

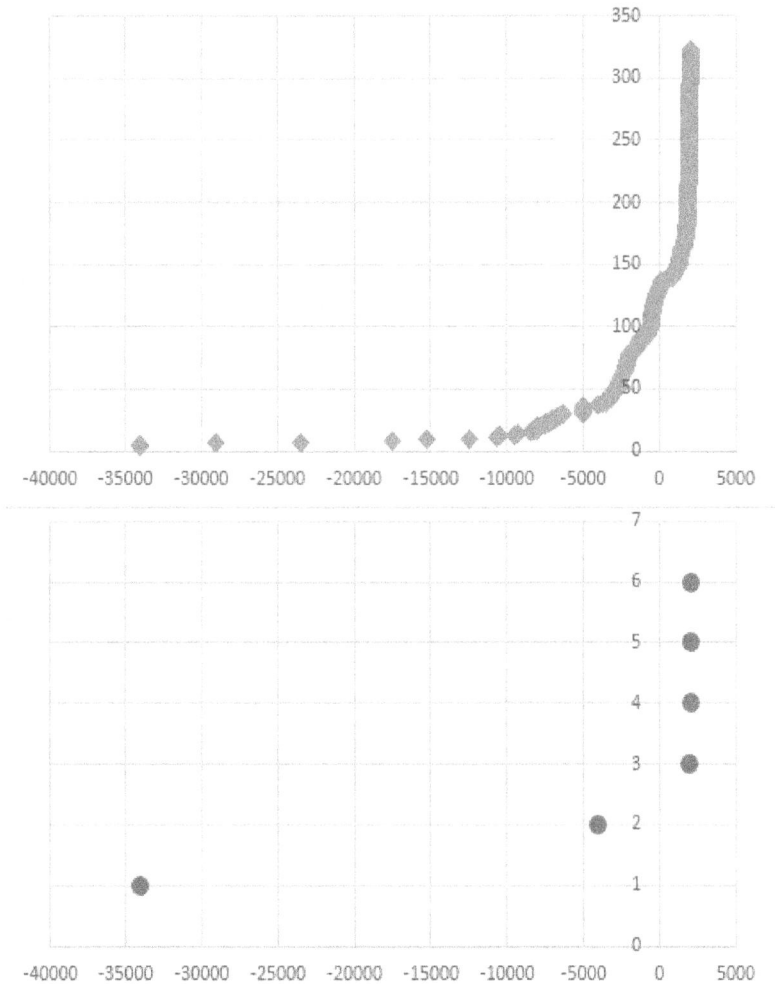

Figure 4.1. History of Humankind. From 34000 BC. Top graph – Sum off resources (diamonds). 34000 BC to 2023 AD. (b) Bottom chart – Number of known unknowns (dots). 34000 BC to 2064 AD. Horizontal – Time, years. **Low-level model of humankind.**

For example, the known unknown factor *Man-Made Existential Disasters* includes multiple threats. The number of possible man-made disasters grows over time.

Figure 4.1 shows us two sides of humankind's development. On the one hand, humanity creates new resources for itself quickly; at an increasing pace. At the same time, with a quickly-increasing pace, humankind creates new known unknown factors, which could abruptly change humanity from its current direction. Most new, i.e., emerged during the last several thousand years, known unknown factors are man-made ones.

What is shared among all those known unknowns? There is some uncertainty about when those factors could morph into actual danger. The common among those factors is the vagueness of when and how it could impact humankind as a whole and various communities, countries, etc. Let us face it. The risk of inactivity in the face of those known unknowns seems remote to us. And that is the problem. "The remoteness of the risk is always the hardest part to get our heads around."[16]

Learn to see the big picture. Often times we get tunnel vision and lose sight of the big picture and what we're really trying to accomplish.

Robert Cheeke

Chapter 4.2. Big Picture

From Raw Data to the Direction of Humankind's Development

The subsurface history of humanity is a history of the emergence of new resources created by humankind for itself. Resources determine what is possible for us to do. Resources are behind-the-scenes enablers for actions for all humans. That is why we call the history of resource creation a deep-level history.

Deep-level history is the underlying foundation for a conventional history of events.

Deep-level history of humankind does not depend on the social structures, politics, economics, wars, revolutions, dynasties, and any uncertain terms like progress, happiness, morality, social justice, etc.

Presented models of humankind do not depend on observers, including the author of this book, viewpoints or prejudice on the role of individuals, society, religions, human races, random chance in history, etc.

As of 2023 AD, we counted 318 resources created by humankind for itself during the last 44 thousand years. Subsurface history of humanity is based on data presented in Part 2 of this book.

Those resources cover a whole spectrum of fields of humankind's activity. Here are a few examples: *Theatre, Paper, Diplomacy, Computing Machines, Global Network (Internet),* etc.

We use the classification of resources with four 4 levels of hierarchical classification system, which are, from top to bottom, a domain of resources, class of resources, family of resources, and resources.

We counted 72 families of resources, 23 classes of resources, and 5 domains of resources created by humankind for itself during the last 44 thousand years.

Turning Points and Driving Force

Humankind's development over the last 44 thousand years was and continues to be directional.

Humankind is headed toward increasing the arsenal of resources, families of resources, classes of resources, and domains of resources created by humanity for itself. The pace of this move is increasing over time, more sharply in later times.

We considered the history of humankind as a period since humans became behaviorally modern. As of 2023 AD, that date could be assigned to 42000 BC. That was the first turning point in humankind's development during the last 44 thousand years.

Humankind has been creating resources for itself since 42000 BC. The next turning point, with a sharp increase in the pace of humankind's development, is associated with the emergence of the *Holocene* geological period. The *Holocene* is an atypical geological period with a prolonged, relatively warm, and stable global temperature. The beginning of the *Holocene* was a second turning point in humankind's development during the last 44 thousand years.

Analysis of Gathered Data

Since the beginning of *Holocene*, according to our hypothesis, the growth of humankind's population has become the driving force of humankind's development.

It is well known that humankind's population grows hyperbolically. The curve of increasing the number of resources created by humankind for itself is close to the hyperbolic curve, too, but with many irregularities.

The wealth of gathered data provides an ample opportunity to use those data in various combinations and ways.

The inevitable uncertainties in historical dates, possible taxonomy errors, and overall models' robustness and stability were discussed in detail.

The subsurface history data show multiple periods when a slowdown or speed-up of the pace happened. Those periods are documented in this book.

Classic Greece and "Great Divergence"

One case of the increased speed of creation of new resources was investigated in detail in this work. At a superficial glance, that irregularity had no explanation. We proved that this increased pace of humankind's creativity was caused by an unusually high, local in time and geography, Archaic and Classic Greece creativity. It is possible that some other irregularities in the curve of humankind's development could be explained, too.

The deep-level history provides a different, and sometimes more nuanced, or broader picture of various historical processes that were studied in conventional history.

We investigated one such case, a "Great Divergence," in detail. Subsurface history of humankind provided data related to the transition of humankind's creativity from "the East" to the "West" in much broader content than usually was considered in multiple publications on that transition, also called the "European Miracle."

In some fields of humankind's activity, for example, in the *Art and Music* class or resources, the transition from the "East" to the "West" began and was completed more than a thousand years before commonly accepted dates.

Sharp Growth in Resources

In the 21st century, the "exponential growth of technology" became a well-known buzzword. Data in the proposed models of complex system of humankind show that such a view is narrow. For thousands of years, the totality of resources created by humanity for itself in many fields of humankind's activity, i.e., in many classes of resources that are far from technology, has grown at a rate close to an exponential or hyperbolic curve.

Creativity Index of Humankind

Any emergence of a new resource or class of resources is evidence of humankind's creativity. With that, a Creativity Index of Humankind was introduced and calculated on a level of resources for the whole duration of humankind's history, 44 thousand years. Many periods of ups and downs in humankind's creativity were identified.

Words of Caution

It should be noted that the found direction of humankind's move toward increasing the arsenal of resources created by humankind for itself, with increasing speed, is not a reason for us to rest on our laurels.

First, each created by humankind's resource could be used differently. For example, *Tools, Devices, and Machines from Man-Made Materials* resource could be used to build medical equipment to save human lives or to make weapons to kill people. How humankind is using created resources is not a topic of this book.

What the Future Holds

Second, it is already proven that natural growth curves follow S-curves.[1,2] That means the current pace of humankind's development could not continue forever or be transformed into a singularity point. Instead, over time, the pace of humankind's development will slow down at an increasing speed. In that regard, it is important to study multiple, uncovered and described in this book, cases of periods of slowdown or, almost completely stopped, creative activity of humankind.

Third, there are already known circumstances that could push humankind from its current path. We listed seven known unknown factors that could knock out humanity from its current direction. Most known unknown factors that emerged during the last several thousand years are man-made.

We could say this. Humankind creates new resources for itself at an increasing rate. At the same time, at an increasing rate, humankind creates known unknown factors capable of abruptly changing humankind from its path or completely of the planet.

Conclusion

Humankind's development has a direction. That direction does not depend on the social structures and any uncertain terms like progress, happiness, morality, etc. The discovered direction is underlying a conventional history of events.

During the last 44 thousand years, humankind, as a global entity, has been headed in the direction of increasing the arsenal of resources created by humankind for itself.

Using the criteria proposed in this book, a set of over 300 events was selected from multiple publications of independent researchers. Each such event is considered a marker of the first appearance of a resource created by humankind for itself. The list of such markers with a short description can be viewed as a brief encyclopedia of essential events in humankind's history.

That big pool of data points also allowed us to study the pace and direction in which humankind moves in various important fields of humankind's activity, ranging from *Art and Music* to *People and Societies as Objects of Study* to *Digital technology*.

Two main turning points in humankind's history were discussed. Both events were gifts to humans from Nature.

Multiple slowdown and speed-up periods in the global history of humankind were discovered. Several of them were discussed and compared to a conventional history of events.

On the way, we found answers to a multitude of big questions. Humans rule the Earth. Why? The rapid development of humankind has happened within the last twelve thousand years. Why? The speed of humankind's development is changing. Why? Which force is driving it? Humankind's development is a directional process. Is it a controllable process? This book provided answers to those questions.

In the final chapter, we have discussed the near future of humankind.

Definitions and Concepts

History and History Timeframe

Humankind's History

- *Conventional history of humankind* – History of events.
- *Subsurface history of humankind* – History of resources (families of resources, classes of resources, domains of resources) created by humankind for itself.

Humankind' History Timeframe

- *Conventional history of humankind timeframe*: The commonly accepted date of history beginning is the date of the first known to us writing. In 2023 AD, that date was estimated to be around 3200-3100 BC.[1,2] Everything before this date is considered as humankind prehistory.
- *Subsurface history of humankind timeframe*: The date of history beginning is the date of the first known evidence of human's "Modern behavior." In 2023 AD, we estimated that date to be around 42000 BC – See Chapter 1.2 and Logan D. C. (2009, March) [3] and US Department of Defense contributors (2002, Feb 12).[4] Everything before this date is considered as humankind prehistory.

Models of Humankind

Models of Complex System of Humankind.
Elements of the Models

Models of the complex system of humankind from top to bottom are as follows:

- *__Super-high-level model of humankind__*. Elements of the complex system are domains of resources.
- *__High-level model of humankind__*. Elements of the complex system are classes of resources.
- *__Middle-level model of humankind__*. Elements of the complex system are families of resources.
- *__Low-level model of humankind__*. Elements of the complex system are resources.

Types of Models

- *__General models of humankind__* – models that consider humankind's creativity together in all fields of humankind's activity. The Super-high-level model, High-level model, Middle-level model, and Low-level model are general models.
- *__Regional models of humankind__* – models dedicated to a particular field of humankind's activity. Every class of resources is a regional model of the complex system of humankind. Examples of regional models include the *Art and Music* class of resources, the *Mass media* class of resources, etc. As of 2023 AD, we have 23 regional models of humankind.

Human Actions

Multi-Layer Schema of Foundations for Human Actions

The layers from top to bottom are as follows:

- *__The First layer is the events layer__*. People's actions and the outcome of people's actions – events are on this layer.
- *__The Second layer is the motivation layer__*. People's wants, needs, cooperation, and competition are on this layer.
- *__The Third layer is the opportunities layer__*. There are resources, families of resources, classes of resources, and domains of resources on this layer.
- *__The Fourth layer is the Driving Force layer__*. The driving force of humankind's development is on this layer.

Resources

Levels of Hierarchical Classification System of Resources

Levels of hierarchical classification of resources from top to bottom are as follows:
- *Domains of resources*
- *Classes of resources*
- *Families of resources*
- *Resources*

Resources

A *humankind's resource*, or simply a *resource*, is (1) a useful or valuable thing, tool, quality, system, research, or method used by people or that people can use, (2) is a subset of a particular family of resources; (3) covers different aspects of the topic expressed in the name of the particular family of resources; (4) is not limited in time from the moment of emergence; (5) unlimited in use; (6) unique among resources; (7) man-made; (8) created for a first time after the beginning of humankind's history; (9) has, have or may have massive, preferably global or near global use; (10) gives the most generalized idea of the subject; (11) a resource must provide significant added value to the family of resources to which it belongs, over prehistoric activities or in the family of resources. Examples of *resources* are *Textile* and *Transistor*.

Family of resources is (1) a set of resources while each resource covers different aspects of the topic expressed in the name of the family of resources ; (2) is a subset of a particular class of resources; (3) covers different aspects of the topic expressed in the name of the particular class of resources; (4) is not limited in time from the moment of emergence; (5) unlimited in use; (6) unique among families of resources within a particular class of resources; (7) man-made; (8) created after the beginning of humankind's history; (9) has, have or may have massive, preferably global or near global use; (10) gives the most generalized idea of the subject; (11) should provide a significant added value to the class of resources to which it belongs, over prehistoric activities or in the class of resources. Examples of *families of resources* are *Simple machines* and *Types of Musical Instruments*.

Class of resources is (1) a set of families of resources while each family of resources covers different aspects of the topic expressed in the name of the class of resources ; (2) is a subset of a particular domain of resources; (3) covers different aspects of the topic expressed in the name of the particular domain of resources; (4) is not limited in time from the moment of emergence; (5) unlimited in use; (6) unique among classes of resources; (7) man-made; (8) created after the beginning of humankind's history; (9) has, have or may have massive, preferably global or near global use; (10) gives the most generalized idea of the subject; (11) should provide a significant added value to the domain of resources to which it belongs, over prehistoric activities or in the domain of resources. Examples of *classes of resources* are *Art and Music* and *Mass Transportation*.

The domain of resources is (1) the top level of hierarchical classification of resources; (2) a set of classes of resources while each class of resources covers different aspects of the topic expressed in the name of the class of resources ; (3) covers different aspects of the topic expressed in the name of the domain of resources; (4) is not limited in time from the moment of emergence; (5) unlimited in use; (6) unique among domains of resources; (7) man-made; (8) created after the beginning of humankind's history; (9) has, have or may have massive, preferably global or near global use; (10) gives the most generalized idea of the subject; (11) should provide a significant added value to the domain of resources to which it belongs, over prehistoric activities or in the domain of resources. Examples of *domains of resources* are *Personal Development and Social Impact*, and *Man-Made Entities*.

Criteria in a Search for New Resources

- *Importance Criterion for Resources*: A difference in the quality of a new resource compared to an old resource in the same class of resources should be very significant.
- *Durability Criterion for Resources*: A new resource, starting from its emergence, should be unlimited in time.
- *Mass Use Criterion for Resources*: Humankind's use of resources should be massive, preferably global over time.
- *Definition Compliance Criterion for Resources*: The resource must match the resource definition.
- *Classification hierarchy criterion for Resources*: The resource must be an element of a class of resources and a domain of resources.

Criteria in a Search for New Classes of Resources

- *Importance Criterion for Classes of Resources*: A difference in the quality of a new class of resources compared to a cluster of prehistoric resources in the same area of humankind's activity should be very significant.
- *Durability Criterion for Classes of Resources*: The class of resources, starting from the emergence, should be unlimited in time.
- *Mass Use Criterion for Classes of Resources*: Humankind's use of the class of resources must be massive, preferably global over time.
- *Definition Compliance Criterion for Classes of Resources*: The resource must match a definition of the class of resources.
- *Expand-ability Criterion for Classes of Resources*: The expansion of the class of resources by adding new resources should be carried out over time.

Creativity Index of Humankind

Consider a sequence of data points, i.e., resources, j, j+1, ..., j+10, with dates of those data points emergence $T[j]$, $T[j+1]$, ..., $T[j+10]$.

The average value of the time needed for humankind for the creation of one new resource = $T[(j+10)-j]/10$ (Averaged over 10 consecutive intervals between the creation of new resources).

We call this parameter *Resource Creation Time (RCT)* = $T[(j+10)-j]/10$ (Averaged over 10 consecutive intervals between the creation of new resources).

We call the inverse parameter $10/(T[i+10]-T[i])$ as a *Creativity Index of Humankind for resources (CI-H)*. CI-H = $10/(T[i+10]-T[i])$ (Averaged over 10 consecutive intervals between creation of new resources).

Both CI-H and RCT are an average measure of humankind 's creative ability to create new resources.

Similar parameters could be constructed for different, other than 10, number of consecutive intervals and for other models of humankind, like high-level model.

Known Unknowns

Known Unknowns Factors

"_**Known unknowns**_ ... are things that we now know we don't know."[5]

Tables

We use the midpoint of ranges for graphs.

Table 2.   History of Humankind. 42000 BC – 2023 AD.
Low-level Timeline. Resources. 318 data points

Resource	Emergence date	Midpoint	Sum of resources
painting	42000 BC	-42000	1
aerophone (Flute)	41000-40000 BC	-40500	2
sculpture	38000 BC	-38000	3
storytelling	34000 BC	-34000	4
textile	36000-32000 BC	-34000	5
amputation	29000 BC	-29000	6
dogs	30100-16800 BC	-23450	7
pottery	18000-17000 BC	-17500	8
graphic art (drawing)	15500-15100 BC	-15300	9
dance	14000-11000 BC	-12500	10
beer	11700-9700 BC	-10700	11
cows	10500 BC	-10500	12
trade network	11000-8000 BC	-9500	13
architecture	9500-9000 BC	-9250	14
sheep and goats	8400 BC	-8400	15
wheat	8600-7900 BC	-8250	16
chicken	8000 BC	-8000	17
sugar cane	8000 BC	-8000	18
barley	8000 BC	-8000	19
human-powered machines	8040-7510 BC	-7775	20
pigs	8000-7000 BC	-7500	21
cats	7500 BC	-7500	22
rice	7400-7000 BC	-7200	23
potato	8000-6000 BC	-7000	24
sweet potato	8000-6000 BC	-7000	25
alcohol	7000-6600 BC	-6800	26
corn (maize)	6700 BC	-6700	27

Resource	Emergence date	Midpoint	Sum of resources
transportation with a use of watercraft	6500 BC	-6500	28
dentistry	7000-5500 BC	-6250	29
metal (copper)	5000 BC	-5000	30
surgery	5100-4900 BC	-5000	31
grape	6000-4000 BC	-5000	32
bananas	5000 BC	-5000	33
apple	8000-2000 BC	-5000	34
tomato	5000 BC	-5000	35
cassava (yuka)	6000-4000 BC	-5000	36
cotton	6000-2000 BC	-4000	37
leather	4000-3500 BC	-3750	38
chordophone (harp)	3500 BC	-3500	39
horses	3500 BC	-3500	40
cacao (chocolate)	3300 BC	-3300	41
wheel and axle	3350-3100 BC	-3225	42
wedge (ax)	3350-3100 BC	-3225	43
animation	3200 BC	-3200	44
onion	3200 BC	-3200	45
text (writing, writing medium)	3200-3100 BC	-3150	46
membranophone (drum)	4000-2000 BC	-3000	47
tea	3000 BC	-3000	48
papyrus paper	2900 BC	-2900	49
diplomacy	2850 BC	-2850	50
conventional war	2700 BC	-2700	51
composite materials (plywood)	2650-2575 BC	-2663	52
gears	2634 BC	-2634	53
medicine (physician)	2630-2611 BC	-2621	54
lever (balance weights)	2613-2589 BC	-2601	55
liquid preparations (medicine)	2600 BC	-2600	56
library	2700-2400 BC	-2550	57
treaty between city-states	2550 BC	-2550	58
ground transportation with a use of animals	2500 BC	-2500	59

Resource	Emergence date	Midpoint	Sum of resources
idiophone (rattles)	2700-2200 BC	-2450	60
music ensemble (band)	2465-2323 BC	-2394	61
export	2350 BC	-2350	62
felt	2300 BC	-2300	63
authored literature	2285-2250 BC	-2268	65
sunflower	2265 BC	-2265	64
inclined plate	2250 BC	-2250	66
empire	2350-2150 BC	-2250	67
faience	2470-1900 BC	-2185	68
mythology	2100 BC	-2100	69
corruption	2160-2040 BC	-2100	70
composite materials (cartonnage)	2150-2040 BC	-2095	71
commodity money	2100-2050 BC	-2075	72
slavery	2100-2050 BC	-2075	73
judiciary	2100-2047 BC	-2074	74
synthesized nanoparticles	2000 BC	-2000	75
mango	2000 BC	-2000	76
watermelon	2000 BC	-2000	77
soybeans	3000-1000 BC	-2000	78
pulley	1887-1783 BC	-1835	79
sexual violence (including rape)	1792-1750 BC	-1771	80
glass	1600 BC	-1600	81
pills (medicine)	1550 BC	-1550	82
social exclusion	1500 BC	-1500	83
musical composition & notation	1400 BC	-1400	84
song/folk song music	1400 BC	-1400	85
world religion	1500-1200 BC	-1350	86
use of gravity	1346-1334 BC	-1340	87
porcelain	1600-1046 BC	-1323	88
composite materials (concrete)	1400-1200 BC	-1300	89
treaty between nations	1259 BC	-1259	90
school	1292-1190 BC	-1241	91
cucumber	1000 BC	-1000	92
warfare with a use of gunpowder	904-970	-937	93

Resource	Emergence date	Midpoint	Sum of resources
Olympic Games	776 BC	-776	94
hybrid (mule)	760-710 BC	-735	95
domestic violence	753-716 BC	-735	96
printing (printing medium)	705-751 BC	-728	97
massive forced displacement / deportation	745-620 BC	-683	98
rutway for cargo and ships	600 BC	-600	99
circus	616-578 BC	-597	100
philosophy	624-545 BC	-585	101
archeology	550 BC	-550	102
post	550 BC	-550	103
theatre	534 BC	-534	104
museum	530 BC	-530	105
propaganda	521 BC	-521	106
asymmetric warfare	513 BC	-513	107
cabbage	600-401 BC	-501	108
lingiustics	600-401 BC	-500	109
genealogy and family tree	479 BC	-479	110
playwright	499-455 BC	-477	111
ethics	470-399 BC	-435	112
economic warfare	432 BC	-432	113
total war	431 BC	-431	114
history	425-430 BC	-428	115
anthropology	425-430 BC	-428	116
political science	428-322 BC	-375	117
automata	400-350 BC	-375	118
logic	384-322 BC	-353	119
theology	354-348 BC	-351	120
water-powered machines	476-221 BC	-344	121
biology	345-322 BC	-334	122
anatomy	300-250 BC	-275	123
screw	287-212 BC	-250	124
debt bondage / bonded labor	305-30 BC	-168	125
marketplace	150 BC	-150	126
genocide	146 BC	-146	127

Resource	Emergence date	Midpoint	Sum of resources
choral music	128 BC	-128	128
computing machines	70 BC	-70	129
eggplant	59 BC	-59	130
bearings	1-100	50	131
world monotheistic religion	50	50	132
pharmacology	50-70	60	133
elevator	72-80	76	134
paper	105	105	135
trade barrier	136	136	136
physiology	129-216	173	137
serfdom	332	332	138
western classical music	500	500	139
non-kinetic weapons warfare	673	673	140
liquid fuel (kerocsene)	865-925	895	141
orange	912	912	142
wind-powered machines	901-1000	950	143
gerontology	1012	1012	144
college (university)	1088	1088	145
war over the sacred (not material) thing	1096	1096	146
false news	1144	1144	147
knitted materials	1100-1300	1200	148
multi-city economic and defensive alliance	1241	1241	149
fiat money	1271-1361	1316	150
mandatory education	1325-1519	1340	151
biological warfare	1347	1347	152
sociology	1332-1406	1369	153
icebraker	1383	1383	154
colonial empire	1415	1415	155
human trafficking	1444	1444	156
coffee	1401-1500	1450	157
mass printing	1455	1455	158
equipment to observe objects	1590	1590	159

Resource	Emergence date	Midpoint	Sum of resources
opera	1597-1600	1599	160
multinational corporation	1600	1600	161
marketplace for securities trade	1602	1602	162
standardized parts	1620	1620	163
prefabrication	1620	1620	164
division and specialization of human labor	1620	1620	165
production factory	1620	1620	166
mechnical calculator (Pascaline)	1642	1642	167
use of scientific method	1647	1647	168
couplings	1650	1650	169
mob mentality	1692	1692	170
steam-powered machines	1698	1698	171
orchestra	1650-1791	1721	172
use of specialized machinery	1733	1733	173
capacitor	1745	1745	174
spike in fossil fuel mining	1750	1750	175
electronic music instrument	1759	1759	176
preschool education	1767	1767	177
life expectancy at birth over 28 years	1770	1770	178
use of machine tools	1774	1774	179
economics	1776	1776	180
use of energy to run machines	1782	1782	181
child labor	1790	1790	182
fuel-powered machines	1794	1794	183
diffusion of scientific knowledge	1794	1794	184
electric battery	1800	1800	185
multi-times increase in coal mining	1800	1800	186
train with engine	1803	1803	187
psychiatry	1808	1808	188
precision interchangeable parts	1803-1832	1818	189
opinion poll	1824	1824	190
use of elctromagnetism	1824	1824	191

Resource	Emergence date	Midpoint	Sum of resources
electricity-powered machines	1828	1828	192
electric generator	1831	1831	193
electric motor	1834	1834	194
electronic machines (devices)	1835	1835	195
telegraph	1837	1837	196
photography	1839	1839	197
fax	1843-1863	1853	198
plastic (parkesine)	1855	1855	199
matter identification technique	1859	1859	200
psychology	1860	1860	201
genetics	1865	1865	202
submarine	1865	1865	203
Intergovernmental organization	1865	1865	204
recording	1857-1877	1867	205
typing	1868	1868	206
synthetic polymer	1870	1870	207
information warfare	1870	1870	208
sonic, ultrasonic, and infrasonic devices	1857-1883	1870	209
electronic transfer	1871	1871	210
diode	1876	1876	211
telephone	1876	1876	212
synthetic fiber	1885	1885	213
ground vehicle with engine	1888	1888	214
video art	1888	1888	215
50 times increase in fossil fuel consumption	1888	1888	216
electric transfomator	1889	1889	217
amphibious vehicle	1889	1889	218
country where women right to vote accepted legally	1893	1893	219
film	1895	1895	220
radio	1896	1896	221

Resource	Emergence date	Midpoint	Sum of resources
magnetic storage device	1898	1898	222
over 10% share of "self-made" women at the top of the social hierarchy	1900	1900	223
blues music	1908	1908	224
synthetic rubber	1909	1909	225
modern production factory	1913	1913	226
ten times increase in an average annual growth rate of life expectancy at birth	1913	1913	227
airplane	1914	1914	228
world war	1914	1914	229
chemical warfare	1915	1915	230
jazz music	1917	1917	231
power tools	1917	1917	232
general international organization	1920	1920	233
lie detector	1921	1921	234
disinformation	1923	1923	235
electronic logic gate	1924	1924	236
television	1927	1927	237
video coferencing	1927	1927	238
falsifiability as a criterion	1934	1934	239
semiconductor material	1941	1941	240
use of quantum physics	1941	1941	241
framework for international monetary policy, commerce, and finance	1944	1944	242
enriched Uranum 235	1945	1945	243
nuclear warfare	1945	1945	244
use of strong nuclear force	1945	1945	245
digital computer	1944-1946	1945	246
proxy war	1946	1946	247
use of weak nuclear force	1946	1946	248
transistor	1947	1947	249

Resource	Emergence date	Midpoint	Sum of resources
right to education	1948	1948	250
mathematical theory of communication	1948	1948	251
rock music	1951	1951	252
nuclear-energy-powered machines	1951	1951	253
computer in business	1951	1951	254
pop music	1952	1952	255
compiler	1952	1952	256
robot	1954	1954	257
machine translation	1954	1954	258
artificial intelligence (AI) conference	1956	1956	259
cognitive science	1956	1956	260
integrated circuit (microchip)	1958	1958	261
resistor	1959	1959	262
consumption of gas and oil together overcome coal	1960	1960	263
video game	1962	1962	264
scientific paradigm	1962	1962	265
400 times increase in fossil fuel consumption	1963	1963	266
kinesiology	1964	1964	267
near-Earth orbit spaceship	1964	1964	268
database	1964	1964	269
computer/digital art	1965	1965	270
semiconductor storage device	1965	1965	271
consumption of oil became top one	1965	1965	272
optical storage device	1966	1966	273
transport from Earth to Moon	1969	1969	274
transport from Moon orbit to the Moon	1969	1969	275
e-mail	1971	1971	276
hip-hop music	1973	1973	277
genetically modified (GM) organism	1973	1973	278
cell (mobile) phone	1973	1973	279

Resource	Emergence date	Midpoint	Sum of resources
transgenic mouse	1974	1974	280
online trade	1982	1982	281
life expectancy increase in developed counties (English and Wales) is driven primarily by declining old-age (60-year-old) mortality	1982	1982	282
electronic money	1983	1983	283
global network (Internet)	1983	1983	284
genetically modified food (tomato)	1987	1987	285
biological storage device	1988	1988	286
search engine	1989	1989	287
online learning	1989	1989	288
use of general relativity	1989	1989	289
gender studies	1980-1999	1990	290
800 times increase in fossil fuel consumption	1990	1990	291
over 39% percentage of employed women	1990	1990	292
virtual keabord typing	1992	1992	293
text message	1992	1992	294
cost-effective digital storage	1996	1996	295
cloned mammal	1997	1997	296
cloned primate	1999	1999	297
flash mob	2003	2003	298
a single atom thick material	2004	2004	299
over 50% share of women in higher education in OECD countries	2005	2005	300
decisive usage of mobile phones	2006	2006	301
big data processing	2009	2009	302
cyber warfare	2010	2010	303
less than 20 % gap with men in years of schooling	2010	2010	304

Resource	Emergence date	Midpoint	Sum of resources
decisive usage of Internet	2014	2014	305
digital transformation definition	2015	2015	306
performance art	2016	2016	307
acknowledgment of AI creativity by	2016	2016	308
genetically modified human	2018	2018	309
data storage with projected lifespan of 13.8 billion years	2018	2018	310
communication via hologram	2018	2018	311
lethal autonomous weapon systems	2020	2020	312
1400 times increase in fossil fuel consumption	2020	2020	313
over 3% of women of working age have legal equality to men	2020	2020	314
threat of radiological warfare use	2022	2022	315
sizable increase in renewable energy sources consumption	2022	2022	316
less than 21% gap with men in earnings	2022	2022	317
driver-less approved vehicle with an	2023	2023	318

Table 3. History of Humankind. 42000 BC – 2023 AD. *Middle-level* Timeline. Families of Resources. 72 data points

[Class of Respources] Family of Resources	Emergence Date, year
[Art and Music]	42000 BC
Types of non-musical art	42000 BC
Types of musical instruments 41000-40000 BC	41000-40000 BC
Types of art with the use of many people	2465-2323 BC
Musical notation 1400 BC	1400 BC
Types of music	500
Types of technology-based art	1839
[Man-Made Materials, Substances, Organisms]	36000-32000 BC
Soft materials	36000-32000 BC
Hard materials	18000-17000 BC

[Class of Respources] Family of Resources	Emergence Date, year
Substances and liquid materials	11700-9700 BC
Organisms	760-710 BC
Soft-Hard materials	1855
[People and societies as objects of study]	29000 BC
Related to physical health	29000 BC
Related to society and world	2850 BC
Related to place in society	2285-2250 BC
History related	550 BC
Tools for generic social impact	521 BC
Related to mental health	1808
[Usage of Domesticated Plants and Animals]	30100-16800 BC
Domesticated Animals	30100-16800 BC
Domesticated Plants (Fruits)	8600-7900 BC
Domesticated Plants (Seeds and Grains)	8000 BC
Domesticated Plants (Vegetables)	8000-6000 BC
Inedible Domesticated Plants	6000-2000 BC
[Trade with a use of an intermediary]	11000-8000 BC
Types of goods delivery infrastructure	11000-8000 BC
Components of international trade	2350 BC
Medium of exchange	2100-2050 BC
Carriers of subject of trade	1871
Tools, devices, machines from man-made materials	8040-7510 BC
Sources of power	8040-7510 BC
Simple machines	3350-3100 BC
Elements of mechanical machines	2634 BC
Self-operation machines	400-350 BC
Machine types	70 BC
Components of electronic machines (devices)	1745
Energy storage devices	1800
Categories of electrical machines	1831
Tool types	1917
[Mass transportation]	6500 BC

[Class of Respources] Family of Resources	Emergence Date, year
Media of the Mass transportation	6500 BC
Transport Driving force	600 BC
Direction of movement	80-72 BC
Driverless vehicle	2023
[External information storage and processing]	3200-3100 BC
Information types	3200-3100 BC
Types of inventories of recorded information	2700-2400 BC
Recording, transforming, retrieving information types	751-705 BC
Categories of storage devices	1898
[War and Warfare]	2700 BC
Types of war	2700 BC
Categories of Warfare	513 BC
[Transnational entities]	2550 BC
International Treaties	2550 BC
Empires	2350-2150 BC
World Religions (each over 6% of the world population)	1500-1200 BC
Alliances	1241
International Organizations	1600
Global International Organizations	1920
Global Networks	1983
[Usage of people as a resource on a massive scale]	2160-2040 BC
Harm to a person	2160-2040 BC
Harm to a group of people	2100-2050 BC
Use of forces of Nature, Relativity, Quantum physics	1346-1334 BC
Forces of Nature	1346-1334 BC
Main physics theories	1941
[Mass education]	1292-1190 BC
Education levels	1292-1190 BC
Relation to society	1325-1519
Distant education	1989
[Independent communication channels]	550 BC
Non-electronic communication channels	550 BC

[Class of Respources] Family of Resources	Emergence Date, year
Electronic communication channels	1837
[Mass production]	1320
Mass production techniques	1320
Manufacturing engineering	1320
[Mass media]	1455
Mass media	1455
[Technology beyond limitations of human senses]	1590
Technology beyond limitations of human senses	1590
[Scientific method and information technology]	1642
Information technology	1642
Scientific method	1647
[Usage of natural resources on a massive scale]	1750
Usage of natural resources on a massive scale	1750
[Life expectancy growth]	1770
Life expectancy growth	1770
[Involvement of women in humankind activities]	1893
Involvement of women in humankind activities	1893
[Digital technology]	1924
Digital technology	1924
[Artificial Intelligence (AI)]	1956
Artificial Intelligence (AI)	1956

List of Figures

Figure 1. History of Humankind. 42000 BC - 2023 AD. Low-level model.   iv

Figure 1.1.1. Total number of states in the USA. 1780 - 1820.   28

Figure 1.1.2. Population in the USA. 1780 - 1820.   29

Figure 1.4.1. History of Humankind. First four Classes of Resources.   55

Figure 1.5.1. Partial diagram of the *Mass transportation* class of resources   59

Figure 1.5.2. Partial diagram of the *People and societies as objects of study* class of resources   598

Figure 3.1.1. Super-high-level model. 42000 BC - 2023 AD.   213

Figure 3.1.2. High-level model. 42000 BC - 2023 AD.   214

Figure 3.1.3. Middle-level model. 42000 BC - 2023 AD.   215

Figure 3.1.4. Low-level model. 42000 BC - 2023 AD.   216

Figure 3.1.5. History of humankind. 10000 BC – 1 BC.   219

Figure 3.1.6. History of humankind. 42000 BC - 10500 BC. Low-level model. 221

Figure 3.1.7. History of humankind. 10500 BC - 2023 AD. Low-level model.   223

Figure 3.1.8. Humankind's history. 12000 BC - 2023 AD.   225

Figure 3.3.1. History of (a) human vocabulary size, and (b) humankind's
population.   237

Figure 3.3.2. Ice age temperature and ice volume   239

Figure 3.3.3. Holocene Temperature variations. 10000 BC - 2000 AD   240

Figure 3.4.1. Humankind's population.   253

Figure 3.5.1. History of humankind. 42000 BC - 2023 AD. Two classes of
resources. Low-level model. 1. *Art and Music*; 2. *Man-made materials, substances,
and organisms*   256

Figure 3.5.2. History of humankind. 42000 BC - 2023 AD. Two classes
of resources. Low-level model. 1. *People and societies as objects of study*; 2. *Usage
of domesticated plants and animals*   257

Figure 3.5.3. History of humankind. 42000 BC - 2023 AD. Two classes
of resources. Low-level model. 1. *Trade with the use of an intermediary*;
2. *Tools, devices, and machines from man-made materials*   258

Figure 3.5.4. History of humankind. 42000 BC - 2023 AD. Two classes
of resources. Low-level model. 1. *Mass transportation*; 2. *External information
storage and processing*   259

Figure 3.5.5. History of humankind. 42000 BC - 2023 AD. Two classes of
resources. Low-level model. 1. *War and Means of Warfare*; 2. *Transnational
entities*   260

Figure 3.5.6. History of humankind. 42000 BC - 2023 AD. Two classes of
resources. Low-level model. 1. *People as a resource on a massive scale*; 2. *Mass
education*   261

Figure 3.5.7. History of humankind. 42000 BC - 2023 AD. Two classes of resources. Low-level model. 1. *Use of forces of nature, relativity, and quantum physics*; 2. *Independent communication channels*   262

Figure 3.5.8. History of humankind. 42000 BC - 2023 AD. Two classes of resources. Low-level model. 1. *Mass production*; 2. *Mass media*   263

Figure 3.5.9. History of humankind. 42000 BC - 2023 AD. Two classes of resources. Low-level model. 1. *Technology beyond the limitations of human senses*; 2. *Usage of the Scientific method and information technology*   264

Figure 3.5.10. History of humankind. 42000 BC - 2023 AD. Two classes of resources. Low-level model. 1. *Usage of natural resources on a massive scale*; 2. *Involvement of women in humankind's activities*   265

Figure 3.5.11. History of humankind. 42000 BC - 2023 AD. Three classes of resources. Low-level model. 1. *Life expectancy growth*; 2. *Digital technology*; 3. *Artificial intelligence (AI)*   266

Figure 3.6.1. History of Humankind. 42000 BC - 10500 BC. High-Level Model. (a) Top chart - 38000 BC - 10500 BC (per data from 2018 AD); (b) Bottom chart - 42000 BC - 10500 BC (per data from 2023 AD).   270

Figure 3.7.1. History of humankind. 42000 BC - 10500 BC. Low-level model.   278

Figure 3.7.2. History of humankind. 17500 BC - 6500 BC. Low-level model.   279

Figure 3.7.3. History of humankind. 8400 BC - 2700 BC. Low-level model.   280

Figure 3.7.4. History of humankind. 3750 BC - 2000 BC. Low-level model.   281

Figure 3.7.5. History of humankind. 2100 BC - 1241 BC. Low-level model.   282

Figure 3.7.6. History of humankind. 1600 BC - 597 BC. Low-level model.   283

Figure 3.7.7. History of humankind. 776 BC - 168 BC. Low-level model.   284

Figure 3.7.8. History of humankind. 334 BC - 895 AD. Low-level model.   285

Figure 3.7.9. History of humankind. 173 - 1455. Low-level model.   286

Figure 3.7.10. History of humankind. 1316 - 1650. Low-level model.   287

Figure 3.7.11. History of humankind. 1590 - 1853. Low-level model.   288

Figure 3.7.12. History of humankind. 1767 - 2023. Low-level model.   289

Figure 3.8.1. History of Humankind. 10500 BC - 6500 BC.   294

Figure 3.8.2. History of Humankind. 6500 BC - 2700 BC.   295

Figure 3.8.3. History of Humankind. 2700 BC - 2000 BC.   296

Figure 3.8.4. History of Humankind. 2000 BC – 1316 AD   297

Figure 3.9.1. History of humankind. 597 to 334 BC. Low-level model.   303

Figure 3.9.2. History of humankind. 937 BC to 128 BC. Low-level model.   305

Figure 3.9.3. History of humankind. 937 BC to 128 BC. Low-level model.
Imagined situation with nonexistent Greece between 597 BC and 334 BC.   306

Figure 3.9.4. History of humankind. 2500 BC to 1698 AD. Low-level model.
Creativity Index of Humankind   307

Figure 3.9.5. History of humankind. 2500 BC to 1698 AD. Low-level model.
Creativity Index of Humankind. Imagined situation with nonexistent
Greece between 597 BC and 334 BC.   308

Figure 3.10.1. History of humankind. 534 BC - 1698 AD. Low-level model.
Creativity Index of Humankind   314

Figure 3.10.2. History of humankind. 11000 BC - 2023 AD. Low-level model.
Creativity Index of Humankind   315

Figure 3.10.3. History of humankind. 8000 BC – 3000 BC. Low-level model.
Creativity Index of Humankind.   316

Figure 3.10.4. History of humankind. 3300 BC – 1000 BC. Low-level model.
Creativity Index of Humankind.   317

Figure 3.10.5. History of humankind. 2300 BC – 534 BC. Low-level model.
Creativity Index of Humankind.   318

Figure 3.10.6. History of humankind. 534 BC – 1698 BC. Low-level model.
Creativity Index of Humankind.   319

Figure 3.10.7. History of humankind. 1924 – 2022. Low-level model. Creativity
Index of Humankind.   320

Figure 3.11.1. History of humankind. 42000 BC to 2023 AD. Low-level model.
The East and the West.   324

Figure 3.11.2. History of humankind. 550 BC to 1759 AD. Low-level model.
The East and the West.   326

Figure 3.11.3. History of humankind. 1445 to 2023 AD. Low-level model.
Europe and USA.   329

Figure 3.12.1. History of humankind. 2500 BC - 2023 AD. Low-level model.

Directionality of Humankind's Development. History   356

The Art and music. The East and the West.   333

Figure 3.12.2. History of humankind. 2000 BC - 2023 AD. Low-level model.
The Man-made materials, substances, organisms. The East and the West.   335

Figure 3.12.3. History of humankind. 2000 BC - 2023 AD. Low-level model. The
People and societies as objects of study. The East and the West.   336

Figure 3.12.4. History of humankind. 2000 BC - 2023 AD. Low-level model. The
Mass transportation.   337

Figure 3.12.5. History of humankind. 2000 BC - 2023 AD. Low-level model.
The Tools, devices, and machines from man-made materials. The East and
the West.   338

Figure 3.13.1. History of Humankind. 1800 BC - 1700 AD. Vertical: Number
of resources created in 200 years.   341

Figure 3.13.2. History of Humankind. 500 BC - 1700 AD. Vertical: Number
of resources created in 200 years.   342

Figure 3.14.1. History of Humankind and History of All Other Beings on Earth.
42000 BC - 2023 AD. Low-level model.   346

Figure 4.1. History of humankind. From 34000 BC. Number of classes
of resources. Number of known unknowns.   364

List of Tables

Table 1.   History of Humankind. 42000 BC – 2023 AD. High-Level
Timeline. Classes of Resources   iii

Table 1.4.1. History of Humankind. First four classes of Resources.   55

Table 1.5.1. History of Humankind. 42000 BC – 2023 AD. Super-high-level
model. Domains of Resources. Comparison with Prehistoric Activities.   62

Table 1.5.2. History of Humankind. 42000 BC – 2023 AD. Super-high-level
model. Domains of Resources. The Essence of Classes of Resources.   64

Table 2.   History of Humankind. 42000 BC – 2023 AD. Low-level
Timeline. Resources.   379

Table 3.   History of Humankind. 42000 BC – 2023 AD. Middle-level
Timeline. Families of Resources.   389

Table 3.1.1. History of Humankind. 42000 BC – 2023 AD. Super-high-level
Timeline. Domains of Resources.   213

Table 3.1.2. History of Humankind. 42000 BC – 2023 AD. Granularity of models
of humankind.   217

Table 3.1.3. Details on Resources Created by Humankind During
Period from 42000 BC to 10500 BC   222

Table 3.2.1. Complex System Models of Humankind   229

Table 3.2.2. The Potential Upper Limit of Items in the Novel Mental Images
Class of Resources. Vocabulary in English and Its Predecessors   236

Table 3.7.1. History of Humankind. Low-level model. 42000 BC to 2023 AD.
Periods of Speed-ups and Slowdowns in the Pace of Humankind to
Increased Number of Resources.   290

Table 3.8.1. History of Humankind. Low-level model. 10500 BC to 2023 AD.
Essential Back Time Horizons.   293

Table 3.9.1. History of Humankind. Low-level Model. Resources, Emerged
During Period from 597 to 334 BC. Data from Table 2 with Added Country
of Origin   302

Table 3.10.1. Naming of Creativity Index of Humankind for Different
Models   312

Table 3.11.1. History of humankind. 2075 BC to 1759 AD. Low-Level Model.
Number of Emerged Resources. Transition of Humankind's Creativity from
the East to the West.   327

Table 3.11.2. History of Humankind. 1455 to 2023. Low-Level Model. Number
of Emerged Resources. Transition of Humankind's activities from Europe to
the USA.   330

Table 4.1. History of Humankind. 36000 BC – 2016 AD. Low-Level Model.
The Pace of New Resources Creation   351

Table 4.2. Details on Known Unknown Factors. Period from 34000 BC to
2064 AD.   363

Notes

Introduction   1. Olstein Diego (2014)

Part 1. Introduction to Part 1

1. Torvich Victor (2021)
2. Torvich V.V. (2020a, January-March)
3. Torvich V.V. (2020b, April-June)
4. Torvich V.V. (2020c, July-September)
5. Torvich V.V. (2021a, July-September)
6. Torvich V.V. (2021b, October-December)

Chapter 1.1. In a search for the meaning of history

1. Marx Karl & Engels Friedrich (2008)
2. King L. W. (2008)
3. Sorokin Pitirim A. (1927, September)
4. Deulofeu J. (2014)
5. Alexandre Deulofeu Web contributors (2023)
6. Mark Joshua J. (2019, Oct 9)
7. Spengler Oswald (2020)
8. Sempa F. P. (2022, January)
9. Hegel G. W. F. (2018)
10. Teilhard P. (2008)
11. Vernadsky V. I. (1977)
12. Berdyaev Nikolai (1923)
13. Harari Y. N. (2018)
14. Popper Karl R. (2020)
15. Little D. (2020)
16. Morris R. (1961)
17. Brogan D. W. (1949)
18. Pinkard Terry (2017)
19. Bowden B. (2022)
20. Rotenstreich N. (1971)
21. Lange M. M. (2011, February)
22. Tupy M. L. (2013, October)
23. D'Amico D. (2019, Apr 3)
24. Gardiner P. (2023)
25. Zabelin I.M. (1970)
26. Christian D. (2009)
27. Morris Ian (2011)
28. Fukuyama F. (1989)
29. Erickson M. (2011, May 26)
30. REN (2014, September)
31. Du D. (2018)
32. Vermeij G. J. (2011)
33. Hodder I. (2018)
34. Your Genome contributors (2021, July)
35. Railton D. (2018, May 31)
36. Waal F. de. (2014, Sep 1)
37. Stix Gary (2014, Sep 1)
38. Harari Y. N. (2015, June 16)
39. Fuentes A. (2017)
40. Rutherford Adam (2019)
41. Henrich J. (2023, June)
42. Alonso M. (2018)
43. Nichols S. (2022, Sep 14)
44. Snooks G.D. (2019)
45. Bar-Yam (2002)
46. Tainter J. A. (1990)
47. JoUgo B. et al. (2018)
48. Christian D. (Dec 31, 2017)
49. Spier F. (2008)
50. Barnes J. (March 31, 2015)
51. Vann R.T. (Nov 28, 2023)
52. Bentley J.H. (Sep, 2012)
53. O'Brien P. (2008)
54. Shryock A., Smail D.L. (2011)
55. Weldon S.P. (2015, Jan 12)
56. Modis T. (2002)
57. Panov AD (2005)
58. Grinin L., Grinin A., Korotayev A. (2020)
59. Korotayev A. (2018)
60. Modis T. (2006)
61. Khotsey A. S. (2005)
62. Baranets, S. N. (2003)
63. Macmillan Dictionary contributors (2022)
64. Schinkel, A. (2006, June)

65. Aron (2011, June 8)
66. Dictionary.com contributors (2023a)
67. Encyclopedia.com contributors (2018, June 08)
68. Statista contributors (2023b)
69. Mathematics dictionary contributors (2022)
70. Cue Math contributors (2022)
71. The World Bank contributors (2023c)

Chapter 1.2. Duration of humankind's history

1. Declercq G. (2000)
2. Dictionary.com contributors (2023b)
3. Fagan B. M. & Beck C. (1996)
4. The editors of Archaeology (2016, May/June)
5. Higham T. et al. (2014)
6. American Heritage Dictionary contributors (2023)
7. Mcbrearty S. & Brooks AS. (2000, November)
8. Klein R. (1995)
9. Aubert M. et al. (2019)
10. Mellars P. (2006, June)
11. Villa P. & Roebroeks W. (2014, Apr 30)
12. Vyshedskiy A. (2019, July 29)
13. Dennell R. (2019)
14. The Siberian Times reporter (2016, Aug 23)
15. Cambridge English Dictionary contributors (2023a)

Chapter 1.3. Humankind as a complex system   1. Bar-Yam (2002)

Chapter 1.4. Multi-Layer History

1. Weldon S.P. (2015, Jan 12)
2. Vocabulary.com contributors (2023)
3. OHIO History Connection contributors (2021, July 6)
4. The Britannica Dictionary contributors (2023)

Chapter 1.5. Criteria for resources and classes of resources

1. Oxford Learner's Dictionaries contributors (2023b)
2. Heathers Admin (2018, Aug 30)
3. BD Editors (2017, Apr 28).
4. Egli L. et al. (2020, Apr 21)
5. Stribling J. et al. (2008, December)
6. Kahane Guy (2021)
7. Oxford Learner's Dictionaries contributors (2023c)
8. Oxford Learner's Dictionaries contributors (2023d)
9. Torvich V.V. (2020a, January-March)
10. Torvich V.V. (2020b, April-June)
11. Torvich V.V. (2020c, July-September)
12. Torvich V.V. (2021a, July-September)
13. Torvich Victor (2021)
14. NMU contributors (2023)
15. Olmstead A. L. & Rhode P. W. (2001)
16. Ritchie H. (2022, Nov 30)
17. Biologyonline.com contributors (2023)

18. Maier J.F. et al. (2017, Jan 17)
19. Wikipedia contributors (2023a)
20. Wikipedia contributors (2023b)
21. Wikipedia contributors (2023c)
22. Wikipedia contributors (2023d)

23. Zurita N.F.S. & Tumer I.Y. (2017, Aug 6-9)
24. Goldstein J. (1999, March)
25. Sperling D. & Gordon D. (2009)
26. Dwayne H. Mulder (2024)

1. **Introduction to Part 2**

1. Torvich Victor (2021)

Chapter 2.1. Art and Music

1. Aubert M. et al. (2019)
2. SciNews (2019, Dec 11)
3. Lobell J. A. (2012, March/April)
4. Nomade S. et al. (2016)
5. Finch D. et al. (2021)
6. BBC News contributors (2021, Feb 23)
7. Garfinkel Y. (2010)
8. Hodder I. & Meskell L. (2011)
9. Dietrich O. (2011)
10. Ball R. (2008)
11. Münzel S. C. et al. (2004)
12. Higham T. et al. (2012)
13. Galpin F. W. (1929)
14. Kappel Krystyna (2016)
15. Lawergren Bo (2006)
16. Grigoraki Argyro (2022, July)
17. Bayoumy T. (2020)
18. Prakash Tara (2019, February)
19. Sightseeing Tours Italy contributors (2022)
20. The Editors of Encyclopaedia Britannica (2022a)
21. Brockett O. & Franklin H. (1974)
22. Pöhlmann E. & West M. L. (2001)
23. New World Encyclopedia contributors (2022)
24. Spitzer J. & Zaslaw N. (2005, Sep 1)
25. Music With Ease contributors (2021)
26. The Metropolitan Opera contributors (2022)
27. The Art Story contributors (2010)
28. Neuendorf Henri (2016, Feb 5)
29. Nicholson Judith A. (2005, Dec 11)
30. Bisher (2021, July 22)
31. Kilmer A. D. (1971)
32. **Becky Dell Music Academy** contributors (2023)
33. Cross A. (2022, Aug 19)
34. Lynn Abbott & Seroff Doug (1996)
35. Songfacts contributors (2022a)
36. Hasse J. (2017, Feb 24)
37. Farley C. (2004, July 6)
38. O'Toole Kit (2021, Dec 15)
39. TheMusicHistory contributors (2022)
40. Songfacts contributors (2022b)
41. Stacker contributors (2022)
42. The Kennedy Center contributors (2022)
43. Open Culture contributors (2018, Oct 23)
44. Crab S. (2017)
45. Harry Ransom Center contributors (2022)
46. Library of Congress contributors (2022)
47. Stada Media contributors (2022)
48. Kodak Digitizing Blog contributors (2023)

49. Hutchinson P. (2016, May 23)
50. Stephens Mitchell (1991)
51. Schatzkin Paul (1977)
52. Stalker P. J. (2005)

53. Graetz J.M. (1981, August)
54. Nees Georg (1965, Feb 5)
55. Noll A. M. (2014, Nov 12)
56. Noll A. M. (2016)

Chapter 2.2. Man-made materials, substances, and organisms

1. Balter M. (2009)
2. Kvavadze E. et al. (2009)
3. Schick T. (1986)
4. Barber E.J.W. (1992)
5. Vidale Massimo & Zahir Muhammad (2017)
6. Capua R. (2015, March)
7. Rubinson Karen S. (1990)
8. Needham J. & Tsuen-Hsuin T. (1985)
9. The Editors of Encyclopaedia Britannica (2022b).
10. Victoria and Albert Museum contributors (2006, Oct 31)
11. Bruening G. & Lyons J. (2000)
12. Wu X. etc. (2012, June 29)
13. Sparavigna A. C. (2011)
14. Schliemann Heinrich et al. (1885)
15. Cauchi E. (2015, Apr 3)
16. Nicholson P. T. & Shaw I. (Eds) (2009)
17. Prakash Tara (2019, February)
18. Oppenheim Adela (2019, February)
19. Radivojević M. & Roberts B. W. (2021)
20. Radivojević M. & Kuzmanović-Cvetković J. (2014, January)
21. Walter P. et al. (2006)
22. Mgrdichian Laura (2006, Oct 13)
23. Stern E. M. & Schlick-Nolte B. (1994)
24. Lucas A. (1936)
25. The Ancient Egypt Site contributors (2014, Sep 25)

26. Museum of Fine Arts Boston contributors (1987)
27. The Ancient Egypt Site contributors (2014, Jan 26).
28. The Editors of Encyclopaedia Britannica (2019)
29. Cyril B. & Elliot S. (1974)
30. Koh NK (2008)
31. Li Y. et al. (2015, Nov 4)
32. Kerr R. & Wood N. (2004)
33. Hemour S. & Wu K. (2014)
34. Gosling F.G. (2010)
35. Matson John (2010, Oct 5)
36. Liu L. et al. (2018, October)
37. McGovern P. E. et al. (2004, Dec 4)
38. Cragg G. M. & Newman D. J. (2013)
39. Bilkadi Z. (1995)
40. Adamson P. (2021)
41. The Editors of Encyclopaedia Britannica (2022c)
42. Homer (Author), Butler S. (Translator) (2021)
43. Altschuler E. L. et al. (2013)
44. Cohen S. N. et al. (1973)
45. Russo E. (2003, January)
46. Jaenisch R. & Mintz B. (1974)
47. National Research Council (US). (1994)
48. Wilmut I. et al. (1997)
49. University of Edinburgh contributors (2022)
50. Zhen Liu et al. (2018, Jan 24)
51. Greely HT (2019, Aug 13)
52. Mossman Sue (2013, Dec 29)
53. The Editors of Encyclopaedia

Britannica (2022d)
54. The Editors of Encyclopaedia

Britannica (2022e)
55. White J. L. (1999)

Chapter 2.3. People and societies as objects of study

1. Price M. (2022, Sep 7)
2. Maloney T.R. et al. (2022)
3. Coppa A. et al. (2006)
4. Walker Amélie A. (1997, September/October)
5. The Editors of Encyclopaedia Britannica (2023a)
6. Lennox James (2021, July 16)
7. Wulf Andrea (2016, June 7)
8. Ghosh S. (2015)
9. Dioscorides P. & Laguna A. (1555)
10. National Library of Medicine contributors (2012, Feb 7)
11. West John B. (2014, May 30)
23. The Editors of Encyclopaedia Britannica (2023b)
24. Roskin M. G. (2023)
25. Solmsen F. (1936)
26. Meinwald C. C. (2023)
27. Plato (2013)
28. Hintikka J. et al. (2020, Dec 17)
29. Mondal Sekh Rahim (2020, Mar 31)
30. Issawi C. (2019)
31. Blaug M. (2023)
32. Binkley R. (1998)
33. May R. (1991, May 1)
34. Gurevich A. (2021, March 1)
35. Spar I. (2009, April)
36. Andrews E. (2023)
37. Rens Bod (2016)
38. Vergiani V. (2020)
39. Staal J.F. (1965, April)
40. The Hummel Class of resources contributors (2023)
41. Taplin O. & Podlecki A. J. (2022, Dec 06)
42. Parry R. & Harald T. (2021)

12. Dunn P. M. (2003)
13. Howell Trevor H. (1987)
14. Urquhart J. (2006, Jan 14)
15. The Editors of Encyclopaedia Britannica (2022f)
16. Gin R. H. & Green B. N. (1997)
17. Stevi Jackson (2016, Mar 1)
18. Woodward K., Woodward S. (2015)
19. Marks S. & Freeman C. W. (2022)
20. Mark Joshua J. (2021, Oct 26)
21. Penn Museum contributors (2023)
22. Mansfeld Jaap (1985)
43. Kraut Richard (2022, Dec 2)
44. Winchester A.M. (2022, Dec 23)
45. Blumberg R. B. (2023)
46. Miller G. A. (2003, March)
47. Silverberg R. (1964)
48. Wilkins Alasdair (2011, May 25)
49. The Editors of Encyclopaedia Britannica (2023h)
50. Sansone D. (1985)
51. Oxford Learner's Dictionaries contributors (2023a)
52. Barham James (2021, May 25)
53. Granerød G. (2013)
54. UNESCO World Heritage Centre contributors (2023)
55. The Editors of Encyclopaedia Britannica (2023c)
56. WebMD Editorial Contributors (2021, Oct 25)
57. Blumberg J. (2022, Oct 24)
58. Tankard J. W. (1972)
59. Manning M. J. & Romerstein H. (2004, Nov 30)

60. Kendler K. S. et al. (2022, May)
61. Kaplan R. M. (2012, March)
62. Robinson D. K. (2020, Mar 31)

63. Synnott J. et al. (2015)

Chapter 2.4. Domesticated plants and animals

1. Wikipedia contributors (2016)
2. Thalmann O. et al. (2013, Nov 15)
3. Bollongino R. et al. (2012)
7. ScienceDaily contributors (2004, Apr 9)
8. Vigne Jean-Denis. et al. (2004)
9. Gaunitz C. et al. (2018)
10. Librado P. et al. (2021)
11. Weiss E. & Zohary D. (2011, October)
12. Babu D. et al. (2022)
13. Piperno D. R. et al. (2009, Mar 31)
14. Myles S. et al. (2011, Jan 18)
15. Li LF et al. (2013, Nov 18)
16. Cornille A. et al. (2014)
17. Razifard H. et al. (2020, April)
31. Woolfe J. A. (1992)
32. El-Sharkaw M. (2004)
33. Mehta I. (2017, September)
34. Wambulwa M. C. et al. (2021,
37. Grover C.E. et al. (2022, Dec 13)

4. Stiner M. C. et al. (2022, Jan 18)
5. Xiang H. et al. (2014, Dec 9)
6. Groenen M. A. M. (2016)
18. Caicedo A. (2020)
19. Wang P. et al. (2020)
20. Paris HS. (2015, August).
21. Sebastian P. et al. (2010, July 23)
22. Swamy K.R.M. (2023, Feb 25)
23. Wang JX et al. (2008, December)
24. Langgut D. (2017, June)
25. Badr A. et al. (2000)
26. Zarrillo et al. (2018)
27. Crites G. D. (1993)
28. Lentz D. L. et al. (2008, Apr 29)
29. Myhrvold N. (2022, Nov 02)
30. Pearsall DM (2008)
    Aug 06)
35. Hymowitz T. (2004)
36. Maggioni L. et al. (2010)

Chapter 2.5. Trade with the use of an intermediary

1. Laskaris N. et al. (2011, September)
2. Thompson H. A. (1992)
3. Schnurmann C. (2003, September)
4. Petram L. (Author), Richards L. (Translator) (2014)
5. Iddamalgoda H. (2022, November)
6. Mark Joshua J. (2021, Oct 26)

7. Cripps E. L. (2014).
8. Money Staff (2023, Feb 13).
9. Guan H. et al. (2022, September)
10. Bloomenthal A. (2023)
11. Chaum D. (1983)
12. Ryan Tim (2023)
13. Pepelasis A. A. et al. (2023)
14. Satapathy C. (1999)

Chapter 2.6. Tools, devices, and machines from man-made materials

1. Leeuwarder Courant   Contributors (2001, Apr 12)

2. Wachsmann S. (1995)
3. Per J. & Sui T. (2017)
4. Shepherd D. G. (1990)
5. The Editors of Encyclopaedia Britannica (2023e)
6. Clerk D. (1916)
7. Institutoideal contributors (2008, Jan 25)
8. Heller A. (1896)
9. World Nuclear Association contributors (2020, November)
10. Glogovčan (2020)
11. South Tyrol Museum of Archaeology contributors (2016a)
12. South Tyrol Museum of Archaeology contributors (2016b)
13. Rahmstorf L. (2006)
14. Shaw I. (Editor) (2004)
15. Brichieri-Colombi S. (2019)
16. Dieter A. (1991)
17. The Ancient Egypt site contributors (2014, Aug 19)
18. Koetsier T. & Blauwendraat H. (2017, June)
19. Lisha Pace (2022, Dec 6)
20. Ceccarelli M. et al. (2019)
21. Lovejoy-inc (2015, Mar 9)
22. The Editors of Encyclopaedia Britannica (1999)
23. NIHF contributors. (2023b)
24. Freeth T. & Jones A. (2012, Feb 1)
25. Rebecca (2022, Nov 30)
26. NIHF contributors (2022)
27. Royal Institution contributors (2023)
28. San Diego House of Hungary contributors (2023)
29. Edison Tech Center contributors (2023)
30. Wicks F. (1999, July 1)
31. John (2013, Oct 25)
32. Laws D. (2013, Nov 06)
33. Frenzel L. (2019, Oct. 11)
34. NIHF contributors (2023a)
35. The Editors of Encyclopaedia Britannica (2023f)

Chapter 2.7. Mass transportation

1. Bailey G. et al. (2020)
2. The British Museum contributors (2022)
3. Pyrgies Joanna (2021, July 3)
4. de Kraker A. (2016)
5. McCarthy M. (2007)
6. Brown A. (2010)
7. Sharp Tim (2022, Feb 28)
8. Wade M. (2019)
9. Lewis M J T (2001)
10. Rolt L. T. C. (2022, Apr 18)
11. NASA Content Administrator (2019)
12. Totaro R. (2022, Mar 22)
13. Blitz M. (2015, June 16)
14. The Editors of Encyclopaedia Britannica (2023d)
15. Tweney D. (2010, Aug 12)
16. AllTrails contributors (2009, Nov 24)
17. Loff S. (2022, Jan 5)
18. Schier A. (2023, Feb 13)

Chapter 2.8. External information storage and processing

1. The editors of Archaeology (2016, May/June)
2. Fagan B. M. & Beck C. (1996)
3. Bradsher G. (2020, July 7)
4. Hawkesworth A. S. (1910)
5. Bachman C. (2022)

6. Bachman C. W. (2009)
7. Sack H. (2014, May 11)
8. Needham J. & Tsuen-Hsuin T. (1985)
9. Leip B. (2022, Oct 13)
10. IBM contributors (2023)
11. Samuel A. (2017, Feb 21)
12. Espacenet contributors (1992)
13. Daniel E. et al. (1998)
14. Computer History Museum contributors (2023b)
15. Computer Timeline contributors (2023)
16. Davis J. (1996)
17. University of Southampton contributors (2016, Feb 18)
18. Arch Mission contributors (2023)

Chapter 2.9. War and Means of Warfare

1. International Peace Bureau contributors (2023)
2. Homeland Security contributors (2023)
3. Gabriel R. (2002)
4. New World Encyclopedia contributors (2023)
5. Shchelin Pavel (2022)
6. Asbridge T. S. (2005)
7. Merriam-Webster Dictionary contributors (2023a)
8. Library of Congress contributors (2023a)
9. Cambridge English Dictionary contributors (2023b)
10. Schoppert S. (2017, Jan 8)
11. Spector R. H., The Editors of Encyclopaedia Britannica (2023)
12. Sexton E. (2023)
13. Vasilev M. I. (2015, Feb 5)
14. Shambaugh G. (2023)
15. Alexander K. (2009)
16. Partington J.R. (1998)
17. Andrade Tonio (2017)
18. Balali-Mood M. et al. (2014)
19. Schneider B. R. (2023a)
20. Mackey R.R. (2014, Mar 27)
21. The Editors of Encyclopaedia Britannica (2023g).
22. Schneider B. R. (2023b)
23. Everts S. (2015, May 12)
24. Cochran T. B., & Norris R. S. (2018)
25. The Editors of Encyclopaedia Britannica and Chmielewski K. (2023)
26. RAND Corporation contributors (2023)
27. Fortinet contributors (2023)
28. Malwarebytes contributors (2023)
29. CRS contributors (2023, May 15)
30. Kallenborn Z. (2021, Oct 5)
31. The Encyclopedia of World Problems contributors (2023)
32. Bunn M. (2023, July 6)

Chapter 2.10. Transnational entities

1. Sand P. H. (2018, July 27)
2. Bryce T. (2023)
3. US Department of State contributors (2023a)
4. Department of Ancient Near Eastern Art (2004, October)
5. Kumar K. (2021, Mar 21)
6. Adams W. Y. (1984)
7. Costa Goncalo (2021, Nov 28)
8. Deshmukh A. (2022, Feb 11)
9. Dimock E. C. et al. (2023, Aug 23)

10. The British Library contributors (2023a)
11. The Editors of Encyclopaedia Britannica (2020)
12. Slobodskoy Fr. Seraphim (2023)
13. Cramer F. H. (1949)
14. Schleck J. & Sen A. (2017)
15. International Telegraph Union contributors (2023)
16. US Department of State contributors (2023b)
17. University of Georgia contributors (2023)

Chapter 2.11. Usage of people as a resource on a massive scale

1. The Editors of Encyclopædia Britannica (2023i)
2. El-Saady H. (1998)
3. Gardiner A. H. (1923)
4. Jordan D. K. (2022, Nov 14)
5. Renger J. M. (2023, Aug 25)
6. Gold S. & Wyat M. (1978, Summer)
7. Dionysius of Halicarnassus (Author), Stephen Usher (Translator) (1974)
8. Coleman-Norton P. R. & Bourne F. C. (Authors), Johnson A. C. & Pharr C. (Eds) (2003)
9. Finkelstein J. J. (1968)
10. Kisak P F. (Edited by) (2015)
11. United Nations contributors (2016)
12. Deshpande M. S. (2010)
13. Scholten A. (2016)
14. Valk J. (2020, November)
15. de Ste. Croix G. E. M. (1982)
16. The Archeologist contributors (2021, Dec 17)
17. Kiernan B. (2004, August)
18. Cartwright M. (2018, Dec 4)
19. The Editors of Encyclopædia Britannica (2023j)
20. United Nations contributors (2023a)
21. de Zurara Gomes Eannes (Author), Beazley C. R. & Prestage E. (Translators) (2010)
22. United Nations contributors (2023b)
23. Humphries J. (2011)

Chapter 2.12. Use of forces of nature, relativity and quantum physics

1. Rehm J. & Biggs B. (2021, Dec 23
2. Butzer K. W. (1976)
3. Sturgeon W. et al. (1824)
4. eCUIP contributors (2023)
5. The National WWII Museum contributors (2020, Aug 6)
6. American Chemical Society contributors (2016).
7. Aysha (2018)
8. Hemour S. & Wu K. (2014)
9. The Ohio State University contributors (2023)
10. The Aerospace Corporation contributors (2023)

Chapter 2.13. Mass education

1. Quirke S. (2004)
2. Smoot S.O. (2018, Winter)
3. The British Museum contributors (2023a)
4. Pharaoh.se contributors (2023)
5. Bouchrika Imed (2023, June 28)

6. Morgan H. (2011)
7. Carrasco D. & Sessions S. (2008)
8. Garlinghouse T. (2022, Aug 16)

9. United Nations contributors (2023c)
10. Kentnor H. (2015)

Chapter 2.14. Independent communication channels

1. Briant P. (2006)
2. McGillem C. D. (2023. May 17)
3. Knerl L. (2019, Dec 7)
4. Cengage contributors (2023)
5. Science Reference Section, Library of Congress (2022, Feb 22)

6. Wood J. (2023)
7. Senft T. M. (2023, July 18)
8. Swatman R. (2015, Aug 19)
9. Spencer J. (2023)
10. Vodafone contributors (2017, Dec 4)
11. Barnett R. et al. (2018, Apr 11)

Chapter 2.15. Mass production

1. Lean Factories contributors (2023)
2. Dolinsky A. (2023)
3. Almyta Systems contributors (2023)
4. Zhang F. (2024)
5. Hounshell D. A. (1985)

6. History of Information contributors (2023)
7. Kingsford P. W. (2023, Aug 21)
8. English T. (2019, Aug 31)
9. Smith M. R. (1973)
10. Tanenbaum M. et al. (2023, Jan 19)

Chapter 2.16. Mass media

1. TomiAhonen Consulting (2018, Dec 1)
2. Duarte D. (2019, Jan 19)
3. International Printing Museum contributors (2023)

4. The British Library contributors (2023b)
5. Small A.H. (Jan 2015 - Jan 2016).
6. Flatow Ira (April 4, 2008)

Chapter 2.17. Technology beyond the limitations of human senses

1. Javelosa J. (2016, Dec 25)
2. Murphy D. B. & Davidson M. W. (2011)
3. Helden A. V. et al. (2010)

4. American Chemical Society contributors (2023)
5. Szabadvary F. (1985, Aug 5)
6. CTBTO contributors (2023)

Chapter 2.18. Usage of the Scientific method and information technology

1. The Hard News Cafe contributors (2004, June 11)
2. North Dakota Information Technology contributors (2023)
3. Lemelson-MIT contributors

(2023)
4. Computing History contributors (2023)
5. Science Museum contributors (2018, Nov 9)

6. Yale University Office of President contributors (2023)
7. Aggarwal A. (2023)
8. Smith G. (2008)
9. Library of Congress contributors (2023b)
10. Newton Isaac (1848)
11. Williams L. P. (2022, Feb 07)
12. Hepburn B. & and Andersen H. (2021)
13. Popper Karl (1935)
14. Kuhn Thomas S. (1962)
15. Mcleod Saul (2023, July 31)

Chapter 2.19. Natural resources on a massive scale

1. Simmons J. & Wolfgram R. Zack "Doughnut" (2014, Mar 6)
2. Griffin E. (2010, Dec 15)
3. Ritchie H. et al. (2022)
4. Our World in Data contributors (2023a)
5. Ritchie H. & Roser M. (2022)

Chapter 2.20. Life expectancy growth

1. Galor O. & Moav O. (2005, Nov 17)
2. Our World in Data contributors (2023b)
3. Macrotrends contributors (2023)
4. Bengtsson T. et al. (2019)
5. Roser M. et al. (2023)

Chapter 2.21. Involvement of women in humankind's activities

1. NZ History contributors (2023, Apr 27)
2. Aspinal G. (2021, Aug 3)
3. World Population Review contributors (2023)
4. Nekoei A. & Sinn F. (2021, Jan 29)
5. Sinn F. & Nekoei A. (2021, May 27)
6. The World Bank contributors (2023a)
7. Vincent-Lancrin S. (2008)
8. Our World in Data contributors (2023c)
9. The World Bank contributors (2023b)
10. The World Bank contributors (2023, Feb 28)
11. UN News contributors (2022, Sep 18)

Chapter 2.22. Digital technology

1. StudySmarter contributors (2023)
2. NobelPrize.org contributors (2020, June 20)
3. Computer History Museum contributors (2023a)
4. Gregersen E. (2023)
5. HP contributors (2023)
6. Schafer E. D. (2023)
7. Fritz W. B. (1996)
8. Shannon C. E. (1948, July)
9. Veldink A. (2023)
10. Bullock Museum contributors (2023)
11. Morris R. J. T. & Truskowski B. J. (2003, April)
12. Press G. (2013, May 9)
13. Statista contributors (2023a)
14. Worldometer contributors (2023)
15. Internet World Stats contributors (2023)

16. Kane G. C. et al. (2015, July 14)

Chapter 2.23. Artificial intelligence (AI)
1. Childs M. (2011, Nov 1)
2. Frankenfield J (2020, Mar 13)
3. Tromp J. (2016, Jan 20)
4. Borowiec S. (2016, Mar 15)
5. Silver D. et al. (2017, Oct 19)

Chapter 3.3. Turning Points in History
1. Vyshedskiy A. (2019, July 29)
2. Harrison B. (1962)
3. Kovács É. (2011)
4. Vizmuller-Zocco J. (1985)
5. Cowgill W. et al. (1998 - 2024)
6. Mallory, J. P. (1976)
7. Mallory J. P. & Adams D. Q. (2006)
8. Indo-European.Info contributors (2023)
9. The British Library contributors (2023c)
10. The British Library contributors (2023d)
11. History of England contributors (2023)
12. Braha Sijeta (2016, January)
13. Michel J-P. et al. (2011, Jan 14)
14. Oxford Languages contributors (2023)
15. Roser M. et al. (2019)
16. Image Credit 1
17. Image Credit 2
18. Hansen B. (2012, August)
19. Head M.J. (2018, July 20)
20. Sander van der Leeuw (2016, July 8)
21. Raspe Rudolph Erich (2015)

Chapter 3.4. Driving Force of Humankind's Development
1. Encyclopedia of Molecular Pharmacology contributors (2008)
2. Kirchner H.O. K. & Lazar M. (2008, Feb 6)
3. Kayser J. et al. (2018)
4. Hartmann G. W. (1949)
5. Ellstrand NC. (2014)
6. Koht H. (Author), Haugen E. (Translator) (1964)
7. Nielsen M. (2012, Jan 23)
8. Huang B. et al. (2020, June 25)
9. Alvarez L. W. et al. (1980)
10. Smithsonian Institution (2022, July 7)
11. US Census Bureau contributors (1999)
12. Roser M. et al. (2019)
13. US Census Bureau contributors (2012)
14. Diamond J. (2017)
15. Nargund G. (2009)
16. Axworthy N. (2019, July 14)
17. IPCC (2023)

Chapter 3.6. The Objectivity and Stability of the Proposed Models
1. Cook J. (2017, Oct 10)
2. Lobell J. A. (2012, March/April)
3. Aubert M. et al. (2019)
4. Choi C. Q. (2019, Dec 11)
5. Torvich V.V. (2020c, July-September)
6. Sagan Carl (1986)
7. Modis T. (2002)
8. Saaty R.W. (1987)

Chapter 3.8. Subsurface History for Strategic Planning
1. Krebs R. R. & Rapport A. (2012)
2. An D. (2020, September-October)
3. Drezner D. W. (2021, Nov 23)
4. Kott A. & Perconti P. (2018)
5. Ebert R. J. & Piehl D. (1973)
6. Kempe F. (2023, Oct 21)
7. Lister T. (2023, Nov 3)

Chapter 3.9. Adding Geography
1. Ancient-Greece.org contributors (2023a)
2. Ancient-Greece.org contributors (2023b)
3. Hornblower S. (2023, Mar 10)
4. Basil (2023, Jan 1)
5. Krentz P. (2020, Sep 24)

Chapter 3.10. Creativity of Humankind
1. Kozbelt A. et al. (2010)
2. Rhodes M. (1961)
3. Robinson K. (1998)
4. Said-Metwaly Sameh et al. (2017)
5. Troward T. (2007)
6. Boogaard K. (2022, June 2)

Chapter 3.11. "European Miracle"? and More
1. Jones E. (2003)
2. Pomeranz Kenneth (2001)
3. Dobbs R. et al., (2012)
4. Goldstone J. A. (2015, May 11)
5. Jones G. (2017, July 18)
6. Grinin L., Korotayev A. (2015)

Chapter 3.14. Big Questions and Answers
1. Chopra Deepak (2005)

Chapter 4.1. Looking Ahead
1. Modis T. (2012)
2. Modis T. (2006)
3. Logan D. C. (2009, March)
4. US Department of Defense contributors (2002, Feb 12)
5. Ritchie H. et al. (2023)
6. Korotayev A. et al. (2006)
7. Cambridge English Dictionary contributors (2023c)
8. Javelosa J. (2016, June 10)
9. Yin-Poole W. (2016, June 3)
10. Ma A. (2018, May 16)
11. Reedy C. (2017, Oct 16)
12. Eden A.H., Moor J.H., Soraker J.H., Steinhart E. (Editors). (2013, April 13)
13. Sandberg A. & Bostrom N. (2008)
14. Loutre N.F. (2003)
15. Richardson K. et al. (2023)
16. Ratliff E. (2020, June 16)

Chapter 4.2. Big Picture
1. Modis T. (2012)
2. Modis T. (2006)

Definitions and Concepts
1. Fagan B. M. & Beck C. (1996)
2. The editors of Archaeology (2016, May/June)
3. Aubert M. et al. (2019)
4. Vyshedskiy A. (2019, July 29)
5. US Department of Defense contributors (2002, Feb 1)

Bibliography

Adams W. Y. (1984). The First Colonial Empire: Egypt in Nubia, 3200-1200 B.C. *Comparative Studies in Society and History, 26*(1): 36–71. http://www.jstor.org/stable/178519

Adamson P. (2021). Abu Bakr al-Razi (E. N. Zalta, Ed.). *Stanford Encyclopedia of Philosophy.* https://plato.stanford.edu/entries/abu-bakr-al-razi/

Aggarwal A. (2023). Hadoop | History or Evolution. *Geeksforgeeks.org.* Retrieved Sep 4, 2023. https://www.geeksforgeeks.org/hadoop-history-or-evolution/

Alexander K. (2009). Economic sanctions Law and public policy. *Palgrave Macmillan*

Alexandre Deulofeu Web contributors (2023). What is the Mathematics of History. *Alexandre Deulofeu Web. Nova.deulofeu.org.* Retrieved July 29, 2023. http://nova.deulofeu.org/que-es-la-matematica-de-la-historia/

AllTrails contributors (2009, Nov 24). Bertha Benz Memorial Route Hinfahrt. *AllTrails.com.* https://www.alltrails.com/explore/map/bertha-benz-memorial-route-hinfahrt?

Almyta Systems contributors (2023). Venetian Arsenal - ahead of their time. *Almyta Systems.* Retrieved Sep 4, 2023. http://www.almyta.com/v3/article.asp?c=Venetian_Arsenal_-_ahead_of_their_time&l=en#

Alonso M. (2018). War as a Driving Force of History. 19th and 20th centuries. *H-Soz-Kult.* https://www.hsozkult.de/event/id/event-86122

Altschuler E. L. et al. (2013). Linguistic evidence supports date for Homeric epics. *BioEssays, 35*(5): 417–420. https://doi.org/10.1002/bies.201200165

Alvarez L. W. et al. (1980). Extraterrestrial Cause for the Cretaceous-Tertiary Extinction. *Science, 208*(4448), 1095–1108. https://doi.org/10.1126/science.208.4448.1095

American Chemical Society contributors (2016). Willard Libby and Radiocarbon Dating. *ACS.org.* https://www.acs.org/education/whatischemistry/landmarks/radiocarbon-dating.html#

American Chemical Society contributors (2023). Analytical Chemistry. ACS. Retrieved Sep 4, 2023. https://www.acs.org/careers/chemical-sciences/areas/analytical-chemistry.html

American Heritage Dictionary contributors (2023). Human. The American

Heritage Dictionary. Retrieved July 30, 2023.
https://www.ahdictionary.com/word/search.html?q=human

An D. (2020, September-October). Time Horizons Drive Potential Taiwan Cross-Strait Conflict. *English Military Review*.
https://www.armyupress.army.mil/Journals/Military-Review/English-Edition-Archives/September-October-2020/An-Time-Horizons/

Andrade Tonio (2017). The Gunpowder Age: China, Military Innovation, and the Rise of the West in World History. *Princeton University Press; Reprint edition*

Andrews E. (2023). What is the oldest known piece of literature? *History*. Retrieved July 29, 2023. https://www.history.com/news/what-is-the-oldest-known-piece-of-literature

Ancient-Greece.org contributors (2023a). History of Greece: Archaic. *Ancient-Greece.org*. Retrieved Sep 18, 2023. https://www.ancient-greece.org/history/archaic.html

Ancient-Greece.org contributors (2023b). History of Greece: Classical Greece. *Ancient-Greece.org*. Retrieved Sep 18, 2023. https://www.ancient-greece.org/history/classical.html

Arch Mission contributors (2023). 5D Optical Memory Crystal. *Arch Mission Foundation*. Retrieved July 29, 2023. https://www.archmission.org/5d-optical-memory

Aron (2011, June 8). Difference Between History and the Past. *Difference Between.com*. https://www.differencebetween.com/difference-between-history-and-vs-the-past/

Asbridge T. S. (2005). The first crusade: a new history. *Oxford University Press*

Aspinal G. (2021, Aug 3). Here Are The Countries Where It's Still Really Difficult For Women To Vote. *Grazia*. https://graziadaily.co.uk/life/real-life/countries-where-women-can-t-vote/

Aubert M. et al. (2019). Earliest hunting scene in prehistoric art. *Nature*. *576*(7787): 442–445. https://doi.org/10.1038/s41586-019-1806-y

Axworthy N. (2019, July 14). Price of Lab-Grown Meat to Plummet From $280,000 to $10 Per Patty By 2021. *VegNews.com; VegNews*. https://vegnews.com/2019/7/price-of-lab-grown-meat-to-plummet-from-280000-to-10-per-patty-by-2021

Aysha (2018). Can quantum physics be helpful to lead a better life? *India Today*. https://www.indiatoday.in/education-today/gk-current-affairs/story/can-quantum-physics-be-helpful-to-lead-a-better-life-1400260-2018-12-01

Babu D. et al. (2022). A short review on sugarcane: its domestication, molecular manipulations and future perspectives. *Genetic Resources and Crop Evolution*. https://doi.org/10.1007/s10722-022-01430-6

Bachman C. (2022). Assembling the Integrated Data Store (IDS): A Lecture by Charles Bachman. *Computer History Museum*. www.youtube.com. This lecture was recorded April 16, 2002
https://www.youtube.com/watch?app=desktop&v=iDVsNqFEkB0

Bachman C. W. (2009). The Origin of the Integrated Data Store (IDS): The First Direct-Access DBMS. *IEEE Annals of the History of Computing, 31*(4), 42–54. https://doi.org/10.1109/mahc.2009.110

Badr A. et al. (2000). On the Origin and Domestication History of Barley (Hordeum vulgare). *Molecular Biology and Evolution, 17*(4), 499–510. https://doi.org/10.1093/oxfordjournals.molbev.a026330

Bailey G. et al. (2020). Denmark: Mesolithic Coastal Landscapes Submerged. In: Bailey, G., Galanidou, N., Peeters, H., Jöns, H., Mennenga, M. (eds) The Archaeology of Europe's Drowned Landscapes. Coastal Research Library. vol 35. *Springer, Cham.*, 39–76. https://doi.org/10.1007/978-3-030-37367-2_3

Balali-Mood M. et al. (2014). Bio Warfare and Terrorism: Toxins and Other Mid-Spectrum Agents. In Encyclopedia of Toxicology (Third Edition). 503-508. *Academic Press.* https://doi.org/10.1016/B978-0-12-386454-3.00589-3

Ball R. (2008). Oldest Animation Discovered In Iran. *Animation Magazine.* https://www.animationmagazine.net/2008/03/oldest-animation-discovered-in-iran/

Balter M. (2009). Clothes Make the (Hu) Man. *Science, 325*(5946), 1329–1329. https://doi.org/10.1126/science.325_1329a

Baranets, S. N. (2003). Баранец, С. Н. (2003). Проблема смысла истории: современные перспективы социально-философского анализа (ст. первая). *Труды членов РФО.* 4:47. [Baranets, S. N. (2003). The problem of the meaning of history: modern perspectives of socio-philosophical analysis (Article One). *Proceedings of members of the RFO.* 4:47]

Barber E.J.W. (1992). Prehistoric Textiles: The Development of Cloth in the Neolithic and Bronze Ages with Special Reference to the Aegean. *Princeton University Press*

Barham James (2021, May 25). A Brief History of Anthropology: Pre-1900. *Academic Influence.* https://academicinfluence.com/inflection/study-guides/anthropology-history-pre-1900#

Barnes J. (March 31, 2015). Defining World History vs. Global History. *H-World.* https://networks.h-net.org/node/20292/discussions/66052/defining-world-history-vs-global-history

Barnett R. et al. (2018, Apr 11). After the end of history …: Notes from Session 2 of TED2018. *TED Blog.* https://blog.ted.com/after-the-end-of-history-notes-from-session-2-of-ted2018/

Bar-Yam (2002). Complexity rising: From human beings to human civilization, a complexity profile. In Encyclopedia of Life Support Systems (EOLSS), developed under the Auspices of the UNESCO. *EOLSS Publishers, Oxford, UK.* https://necsi.edu/complexity-rising-from-human-beings-to-human-civilization-a-complexity-profile

Basil (2023, Jan 1). Ancient Greece Timeline: 20 Important Events. *Mythology Planet.* https://mythologyplanet.com/ancient-greece-timeline/

Bayoumy T. (2020). Music Bands in the Old Kingdom. Journal of Tourism, *Hotels and Heritage*, 1(1), 40–54. https://doi.org/10.21608/sis.2020.40171.1000

BBC News contributors (2021, Feb 23). Australia: Oldest rock art is 17,300-year-old kangaroo. *BBC News*. https://www.bbc.com/news/world-australia-56164484

BD Editors (2017, Apr 28). Taxonomy. *Biology Dictionary*. https://biologydictionary.net/taxonomy

Becky Dell Music Academy contributors (2023). Western Classical Music. *Becky Dell Music Academy*. Retrieved Aug 1, 2023. https://www.beckydellmusicacademy.co.uk/western-classical-music/

Bengtsson T. et al. (2019). Introduction. In: Bengtsson, T., Keilman, N. (eds) Old and New Perspectives on Mortality Forecasting. Demographic Research Monographs. *Springer, Cham*. https://doi.org/10.1007/978-3-030-05075-7_1

Bentley J.H. (Sep, 2012). The Task of World History, in The Oxford Handbook of World History, ed. by Jerry H. Bentley. *Oxford: Oxford University Press*.

Binkley R. (1998). Biography of Enheduanna, Priestess of Inanna. *Center for Digital Discourse and Culture. Virginia Tech University*

Berdyaev Nikolai (1923). Бердяев Николай. Смысл истории : Опыт философии человеческой судьбы. *Берлин, Обелиск, 1923*. [Nikolai Berdyaev (Author), George Reavey (Translator), Boris Jakim (Foreword) (2009). The Meaning of History. *Semantron Press; 2nd Enl edition, June 26, 2009*]

Bilkadi Z. (1995). The Oil Weapons. *Saudi Aramco World*. 46(1): 20–27.https://archive.aramcoworld.com/issue/199501/the.oil.weapons.htm

Biologyonline.com contributors (2023). Genus. *Biologyonline.com*. Retrieved Oct 10, 2023. https://www.biologyonline.com/dictionary/genus#

Bisher (2021, July 22). Musical staff (Hurrian Hymn no.6). *National Museum Of Damascus*. https://virtual-museum-syria.org/damascus/56-tablet-musical-staff/

Blaug M. (2023). Economics. *Encyclopædia Britannica*. Retrieved July 31, 2023. https://www.britannica.com/topic/economics

Blitz M. (2015, June 16). A New Recreation Shows How Ancient Romans Lifted Wild Animals Into the Colosseum. *Smithsonian Magazine*. Retrieved July 31, 2023. https://www.smithsonianmag.com/travel/how-ancient-romans-got-wild-animals-colosseum-180955580/

Bloomenthal A. (2023). What Is Electronic Money or eMoney? *Investopedia*. Retrieved July 31, 2023. https://www.investopedia.com/terms/e/electronic-money.asp

Blumberg R. B. (2023). Experiments in Plant Hybridization (1865) by Gregor Mendel. *MendelWeb*. Retrieved on September 2, 2023. http://www.mendelweb.org/Mendel.html

Blumberg J. (2022, Oct 24). A Brief History of the Salem Witch Trials. *Smithsonian*. Retrieved July 31, 2023. https://www.smithsonianmag.com/history/a-brief-history-of-the-salem-witch-trials-175162489/

Bollongino R. et al. (2012). Modern Taurine Cattle Descended from Small

Number of Near-Eastern Founders. *Molecular Biology and Evolution*, 29(9): 2101–2104. https://doi.org/10.1093/molbev/mss092

Boogaard K. (2022, June 2). What Is the Cycle Time Formula? *Wrike.* https://www.wrike.com/blog/what-is-cycle-time-formula/

Borowiec S. (2016, Mar 15). AlphaGo seals 4-1 victory over Go grandmaster Lee Sedol. *The Guardian.* https://www.theguardian.com/technology/2016/mar/15/googles-alphago-seals-4-1-victory-over-grandmaster-lee-sedol

Bouchrika Imed (2023, June 28). What Is the Oldest University in the World? *Research.com.* https://research.com/universities-colleges/oldest-university-in-the-world

Bowden B. (2022). History as Philosophy: The Search for Meaning. *Histories*, 2(2): 80–90. https://doi.org/10.3390/histories2020008

Bradsher G. (2020, July 7). The Royal Archives of Ebla: Reference and Processing Archivists 4,000 Years Ago. *National Archives.* https://text-message.blogs.archives.gov/2020/07/07/the-royal-archives-of-ebla-reference-and-processing-archivists-4000-years-ago/#

Braha Sijeta (2016, January). Early Modern English. *ResearchGate.* https://www.researchgate.net/publication/339416540_Early_Modern_English

Brichieri-Colombi S. (2019). The Ramp at Hatnub Quarry: No Solution for Pyramids. *Palarch's Journal of Archaeology of Egypt/Egyptology*, 16(1): 1-21. Retrieved July 31, 2023. http://www.leatherandshoes.nl/wp-content/uploads/2020/12/Brichieri_Colombi_2019_16_1.pdf

Briant P. (2006). From Cyrus to Alexander; a History of the Persian Empire. *Eisenbrauns*

Brockett O. & Franklin H. (1974). History of the Theatre. *Allyn and Bacon*

Brogan D. W. (1949). The Meaning of Human History. *Nature*, 163(4150): 744–744. https://doi.org/10.1038/163744a0

Brown A. (2010). The Alligator Tug Historical Plaque. *ontarioplaques.com.* Retrieved July 31, 2023. https://www.ontarioplaques.com/Plaques/Plaque_Norfolk14.html

Bruening G. & Lyons J. (2000). The case of the FLAVR SAVR tomato. *California Agriculture*, 54(4), 6–7. https://calag.ucanr.edu/Archive/?article=ca.v054n04p6

Bryce T. (2023). The 'Eternal Treaty' from Hittite perspective. *The British Museum.* Retrieved Sep 3, 2023. https://espace.library.uq.edu.au/data/UQ_263207/UQ263207_OA.pdf

Bullock Museum contributors (2023). Texas Instruments integrated circuit. The chip that Jack built. *Bullock Museum.* Retrieved Sep 5, 2023. https://www.thestoryoftexas.com/discover/artifacts/integratedcircuit_spotlight_121214

Bunn M. (2023, July 6). The largest danger at the Zaporizhzhia nuclear power plant: intentional sabotage. *Bulletin of the Atomic Scientists.* https://thebulletin.org/2023/07/the-largest-danger-at-the-zaporizhzhia-nuclear-power-plant-intentional-sabotage/

Butzer K. W. (1976). Early Hydraulic Civilization in Egypt. *University of Chicago Press*

Caicedo A. (2020). Research team traces evolution of the domesticated tomato. *University of Massachusetts Amherst*. Retrieved August 1, 2023. https://www.umass.edu/news/article/research-team-traces-evolution

Cambridge English Dictionary contributors (2023a). System. Cambridge English Dictionary. Retrieved July 30, 2023. https://dictionary.cambridge.org/us/dictionary/english/system

Cambridge English Dictionary contributors (2023b). Proxy war. Cambridge English Dictionary. Retrieved July 30, 2023. https://dictionary.cambridge.org/us/dictionary/english/proxy-war

Cambridge English Dictionary contributors (2023c). Control. Cambridge English Dictionary. Retrieved Sep 5, 2023. https://dictionary.cambridge.org/us/dictionary/english/control?q=control

Capua R. (2015, March). Papyrus-Making in Egypt. *Metmuseum.org*. https://www.metmuseum.org/toah/hd/pyma/hd_pyma.htm

Carrasco D. & Sessions S. (2008). Daily Life of the Aztecs: People of the Sun and Earth (The Daily Life Through History Series). *Hackett Publishing Company, Inc.*

Cartwright M. (2018, Dec 4). Serf. *World History Encyclopedia*. https://www.worldhistory.org/Serf/

Cauchi E. (2015, Apr 3). Ancient Tiryns. *Eternal Greece Ltd*. https://eternalgreece.com/tiryns-2/

Ceccarelli M. et al. (2019). Ball Bearings from Roman Imperial Ships of Nemilake. *Advances in Historical Studies*, *08*(03), 115–130. https://doi.org/10.4236/ahs.2019.83009

Cengage contributors (2023). The Invention Of The Fax Machine. *Encyclopedia.com*. Retrieved Sep 4, 2023. https://www.encyclopedia.com/science/encyclopedias-almanacs-transcripts-and-maps/invention-fax-machine

Chaum D. (1983). Blind Signatures for Untraceable Payments. In: Chaum, D., Rivest, R.L., Sherman, A.T. (eds) Advances in Cryptology. *Springer, Boston, MA*

Childs M. (2011, Nov 1). John McCarthy: Computer scientist known as the father of AI. *Independent*. https://www.independent.co.uk/news/obituaries/john-mccarthy-computer-scientist-known-as-the-father-of-ai-6255307.html

Choi C. Q. (2019, Dec 11). Humanity's Oldest Cave Art Shows Shape-Shifting Supernatural Hunters. *Live Science*. https://www.livescience.com/oldest-rock-art-supernatural-beings.html

Chopra Deepak (2005). The Book of Secrets: Unlocking the Hidden Dimensions of Your Life. *Harmony; Reprint edition (September 27, 2005)*

Christian D. (2009). Contingency, Pattern and the S-curve in Human History.

World History Connected, 6(3).
https://worldhistoryconnected.press.uillinois.edu/6.3/christian.html

Christian D. (Dec 31, 2017). What is Big History? *Journal of Big History. 1*(1): 4-19. https://doi.org/10.22339/jbh.v1i1.2241

Clerk D. (1916). The internal-combustion engine. *Journal of the Royal Society of Arts, 65*(3341): 42–54. https://www.jstor.org/stable/41347131

Cochran T. B., & Norris R. S. (2018). Nuclear weapon. *Encyclopædia Britannica.* https://www.britannica.com/technology/nuclear-weapon

Cohen S. N. et al. (1973). Construction of Biologically Functional Bacterial Plasmids In Vitro. *Proceedings of the National Academy of Sciences, 70*(11), 3240–3244. https://doi.org/10.1073/pnas.70.11.3240

Coleman-Norton P. R. & Bourne F. C. (Authors), Johnson A. C. & Pharr C. (Eds) (2003). Ancient Roman Statutes: A Translation With Introduction, Commentary, Glossary, and Index. *Lawbook Exchange Ltd; Reprint of sole edition (October 3, 2003)*

Computer History Museum contributors (2023a). Timeline of Computer History. The Atanasoff-Berry Computer (ABC) is completed. *Computer History Museum.* Retrieved Sep 5, 2023. https://www.computerhistory.org/timeline/1942/#

Computer History Museum contributors (2023b). 1970: Semiconductors compete with magnetic cores. *Computer History Museum.* Retrieved July 30, 2023. https://www.computerhistory.org/storageengine/semiconductors-compete-with-magnetic-cores/

Computer Timeline contributors (2023). James Russell (compact disk). *Computer Timeline.* Retrieved July 30, 2023. http://www.computer-timeline.com/timeline/james-russel-compact-disk/

Computing History contributors (2023). Welcome to LEO, the first business computer. *Computinghistory.org.uk.* Retrieved Sep 4, 2023. https://www.computinghistory.org.uk/pages/50348/Welcome-to-LEO-the-first-business-computer/

Cook J. (2017, Oct 10). The Lion Man: an Ice Age masterpiece. *The British Museum.* https://www.britishmuseum.org/blog/lion-man-ice-age-masterpiece

Coppa A. et al. (2006). Early Neolithic tradition of dentistry. *Nature, 440*(7085), 755–756. https://doi.org/10.1038/440755a

Cornille A. et al. (2014). The domestication and evolutionary ecology of apples. *Trends in Genetics, 30*(2): 57–65. https://doi.org/10.1016/j.tig.2013.10.002

Costa Goncalo (2021, Nov 28). The Portuguese Colonial Empire. *Portugal.com.* https://www.portugal.com/history-and-culture/the-portuguese-colonial-empire/

Cowgill W. et al. (1998 - 2024). Syntax [in Indo-European languages]. Britannica. Retrieved Sep 10, 2024. https://www.britannica.com/topic/Indo-European-languages/Syntax

Crab S. (2017). 'Clavecin Électrique' or 'Clavessin Électrique'. Jean-Baptiste

Delaborde, France. 1759. *120 Years of Electronic Music*. Retrieved Aug 1, 2023. https://120years.net/wordpress/clavecin-electrique-1759/

Cragg G. M. & Newman D. J. (2013). Natural products: A continuing source of novel drug leads. *Biochimica et Biophysica Acta. 1830*(6), 3670–3695. https://doi.org/10.1016/j.bbagen.2013.02.008

Cramer F. H. (1949). The Hanseatic League. *Current History, 17*(96): 84–89. http://www.jstor.org/stable/45309337

Cripps E. L. (2014). Money and Prices in the Ur III Economy of Umma [Review of Monetary Role of Silver and its Administration in Mesopotamia during the Ur III Period (c. 2112-2004 BCE). A Case Study of the Umma Province, by X. Ouyang]. *Wiener Zeitschrift Für Die Kunde Des Morgenlandes, 104*, 205–232. http://www.jstor.org/stable/24754725

Crites G. D. (1993). Domesticated Sunflower in Fifth Millennium B.P. Temporal Context: New Evidence from Middle Tennessee. *American Antiquity, 58*(1), 146–148. https://doi.org/10.2307/281459

Cross A. (2022, Aug 19). This band has recorded the oldest known folk song in the world. *A Journal of Musical Things*. https://www.ajournalofmusicalthings.com/this-band-has-recorded-the-oldest-known-folk-song-in-the-world/

CRS contributors (2023, May 15). Defense Primer: U.S. Policy on Lethal Autonomous Weapon Systems. *Congressional Research Service (CRS)*. https://crsreports.congress.gov/product/pdf/IF/IF11150#

CTBTO contributors (2023). Infrasound monitoring. *CTBTO*. Retrieved Sep 4, 2023. https://www.ctbto.org/our-work/monitoring-technologies/infrasound-monitoring#

Cue Math contributors (2022). Coordinate Plane. *Cue Math*. https://www.cuemath.com/geometry/coordinate-plane/

Cyril B. & Elliot S. (1974). Ancient Egyptian medicine: the Papyrus Ebers. *Ares*

D'Amico D. (2019, Apr 3). Is humanity progressing? Pinker, Krugman debate the question. *Brown University*. https://www.brown.edu/news/2019-04-02/pinker-krugman

Daniel E. et al. (1998). Magnetic recording: the first 100 years. *Wiley-IEEE Press; 1st edition*

Davis J. (1996). Microvenus. *Art Journal, 55*(1): 70-74. https://doi.org/10.2307/777811

Declercq G. (2000). Anno Domini. The Origins of the Christian Era (Brepols Essays in European Culture). *Brepols Publishers*

Dennell R. (2019). Dating of hominin discoveries at Denisova. *Nature, 565*(7741): 571–572. https://doi.org/10.1038/d41586-019-00264-0

de Kraker A. (2016). Ice and water. The removal of ice on waterways in the Low Countries, 1330–1800. *Water History, 9*(2): 109–128. https://doi.org/10.1007/s12685-016-0152-3

de Ste. Croix G. E. M. (1982). The Class Struggle in the Ancient Greek World:

From the Archaic Age to the Arab Conquests. *Cornell University Press; 1st edition (January 31, 1982)*

de Zurara Gomes Eannes (Author), Beazley C. R. & Prestage E. (Translators) (2010). The Chronicle of the Discovery and Conquest of Guinea Vol. I, *Cambridge University Press (July 1, 2010)*

Department of Ancient Near Eastern Art (2004, October). The Akkadian Period (ca. 2350–2150 B.C.). In Heilbrunn Timeline of Art History. *The Metropolitan Museum of Art.* http://www.metmuseum.org/toah/hd/akka/hd_akka.htm

Deshmukh A. (2022, Feb 11). Mapped: The World's Major Religions. *Visual Capitalist.* https://www.visualcapitalist.com/mapped-major-religions-of-the-world/

Deshpande M. S. (2010). History of the Indian Caste System and its Impact on India Today. *California Polytechnic State University.* https://digitalcommons.calpoly.edu/socssp/44/

Deulofeu J. (2014). La matemàtica de la història: Alexandre Deulofeu o el pensador global, Lapislàtzuli Editorial. [The mathematics of history: Alexandre Deulofeu or the global thinker] *Pròleg de Patrícia Gabancho edition*

Diamond J. (2017). Guns, Germs, and Steel: The Fates of Human Societies. *W. W. Norton & Company; 20th Anniversary edition*

Dictionary.com contributors (2023a). History. Dictionary.com. Retrieved Oct 10, 2023. https://www.dictionary.com/browse/histories

Dictionary.com contributors (2023b). Prehistory. *Dictionary.com.* Retrieved Sep 6, 2023. https://www.dictionary.com/browse/prehistory

Dieter A. (1991). Building in Egypt: Pharaonic Stone Masonry. *Oxford University Press; First Edition, 1st Printing (February 7, 1991)*

Dietrich O. (2011). Radiocarbon Dating the First Temples of Mankind: Comments on 14C-dates from Göbekli Tepe. *Zeitschrift Für Orient-Archäologie.* 4, 12-25. https://www.researchgate.net/publication/258182967_Radiocarbon_dating_th e_first_temples_of_mankind_Comments_on_14C-Dates_from_Gobekli_Tepe

Dimock E. C. et al. (2023, Aug 23). Hinduism. *Britannica.* https://www.britannica.com/topic/Hinduism

Dionysius of Halicarnassus (Author), Stephen Usher (Translator) (1974). Dionysius of Halicarnassus: Critical Essays, Volume I. Ancient Orators. Lysias. Isocrates. Isaeus. Demosthenes. Thucydides (Loeb Classical Library No. 465). *Harvard University Press (January 1, 1974)*

Dioscorides P. & Laguna A. (1555). "De Materia Medica" by Dioscorides. *Library of Congress.* Retrieved August 1, 2023. https://www.loc.gov/item/2021666851/

Dobbs R. et al., (2012). Urban world: Cities and the rise of the consuming class. *McKinsey & Company.* https://www.mckinsey.com/featured-insights/urbanization/urban-world-cities-and-the-rise-of-the-consuming-class

Dolinsky A. (2023). Inventory Management History Part Three Venetian Arsenal - ahead of their time. *Almyta Systems.* Retrieved Sep 4, 2023. http://www.almyta.com/Inventory_Management_History_3.asp

Drezner D. W. (2021, Nov 23). Thinking about the role of time in grand strategy. *The Washington Post.* https://www.washingtonpost.com/outlook/2021/11/23/thinking-about-role-time-grand-strategy/

Du D. (2018). The Evolutionary Road: The Common Goal of Human as a Species. *Open Journal of Philosophy, 8*(5): 481–494. https://doi.org/10.4236/ojpp.2018.85033

Duarte D. (2019, Jan 19). The 7 Mass Media and the 4th Screen. *Treeshake.com.* https://dave-duarte.squarespace.com/blog/2009/1/19/the-7-mass-media-and-the-4th-screen.html

Dunn P. M. (2003). Galen (AD 129-200) of Pergamun: anatomist and experimental physiologist. *Archives of Disease in Childhood - Fetal and Neonatal Edition, 88*(5), F441–F443. https://fn.bmj.com/content/fetalneonatal/88/5/F441.full.pdf

Dwayne H. Mulder (2024). Objectivity. *Internet Encyclopedia of Phylosophy (IEP).* Retrieved Feb 4, 2024. https://iep.utm.edu/objectiv/

Ebert R. J. & Piehl D. (1973). Time Horizon: A Concept for Management. *California Management Review, 15*(4): 35-41. https://doi.org/10.2307/41164456

eCUIP contributors (2023). Astrophysics Fusing Astronomy & Physics. *eCUIP.* Retrieved Sep 3, 2023. https://ecuip.lib.uchicago.edu/multiwavelength-astronomy/astrophysics/06.html

Eden A.H., Moor J.H., Soraker J.H., Steinhart E. (Editors). (2013, April 13). Singularity Hypotheses: A Scientific and Philosophical Assessment (The Frontiers Collection). *Springer. 2012th edition*

Edison Tech Center contributors (2023). The Electric Motor. *Edison Tech Center.* Retrieved Sep 3, 2023. https://edisontechcenter.org/electricmotors.html

Egli L. et al. (2020, Apr 21). Taxonomic error rates affect interpretations of a national-scale ground beetle monitoring program at National Ecological Observatory Network. *Ecosphere, 11*(4): e03035. https://esajournals.onlinelibrary.wiley.com/doi/full/10.1002/ecs2.3035

Ellstrand NC. (2014). Is gene flow the most important evolutionary force in plants? Am J Bot., *101*(5):737-753. https://bsapubs.onlinelibrary.wiley.com/doi/10.3732/ajb.1400024

El-Saady H. (1998). Considerations on Bribery in Ancient Egypt. *Studien Zur Altägyptischen Kultur, 25*: 295–304. http://www.jstor.org/stable/25152765

El-Sharkaw M. (2004). Cassava biology and physiology. *Plant Molecular Biology, 56*, 481–501, 2004. Retrieved August 1, 2023. https://www.academia.edu/en/9606189/CASSAVA_BIOLOGY_AND_PHYSIOLOGY

English T. (2019, Aug 31). The History of Interchangeable Parts in the Industrial Revolution. *Interesting Engineering.* https://interestingengineering.com/innovation/the-history-of-interchangeable-parts-in-the-industrial-revolution

Encyclopedia.com contributors (2018, June 08). Dimension. *Encyclopedia.com.*

https://www.encyclopedia.com/science-and-technology/mathematics/mathematics/dimension

Encyclopedia of Molecular Pharmacology contributors (2008). Electrochemical driving force. 457–457. In: Offermanns, S., Rosenthal, W. (eds) Encyclopedia of Molecular Pharmacology. *Springer, Berlin, Heidelberg.* https://doi.org/10.1007/978-3-540-38918-7_5614

Erickson M. (2011, May 26). Is History Cyclical? Big *Think.* https://bigthink.com/guest-thinkers/is-history-cyclical

Espacenet contributors (1992). EP0554492A1 Method and device for optical input of commands or data. *Espacenet Patent search.* Retrieved Aug 1, 2023. https://worldwide.espacenet.com/patent/search/class_of_resources/008209311/publication/EP0554492A1?q=pn%3DEP0554492

Everts S. (2015, May 12). A Brief History of Chemical War. *Science History Institute.* Retrieved August 1, 2023. https://sciencehistory.org/stories/magazine/a-brief-history-of-chemical-war/#

Fagan B. M. & Beck C. (1996). The Oxford Companion to Archaeology. (Oxford Companions). *Oxford University Press. 1st edition*

Farley C. (2004, July 6). Elvis Rocks. But He's Not the First. *Time.* Retrieved Aug 1, 2023. http://content.time.com/time/arts/article/0,8599,661084,00.html

Finch D. et al. (2021). Ages for Australia's oldest rock paintings. *Nature Human Behaviour.* 5, 310–318. https://doi.org/10.1038/s41562-020-01041-0

Finkelstein J. J. (1968). The Laws of Ur-Nammu. *Journal of Cuneiform Studies,* 22(3/4): 66–82. https://doi.org/10.2307/1359121

Flatow Ira (April 4, 2008). 1860 'Phonautograph' Is Earliest Known Recording. Talk of the Nation. *NPR.* https://www.npr.org/2008/04/04/89380697/1860-phonautograph-is-earliest-known-recording

Fortinet contributors (2023). Top 5 Most Notorious Attacks in the History of Cyber Warfare. *Fortinet.* Retrieved August 1, 2023.https://www.fortinet.com/resources/cyberglossary/most-notorious-attacks-in-the-history-of-cyber-warfare#

Frankenfield J (2020, Mar 13). Artificial Intelligence (AI). *Investopedia.* https://www.investopedia.com/terms/a/artificial-intelligence-ai.asp

Freeth T. & Jones A. (2012, Feb 1). The Cosmos in the Antikythera Mechanism. *NYU Library's Ancient World Digital Library. ISAW Papers 4.* https://dlib.nyu.edu/awdl/isaw/isaw-papers/4/#

Frenzel L. (2019, Oct. 11). Who Really Did Invent the Transistor? *ElectronicDesign.* https://www.electronicdesign.com/technologies/analog/article/21808701/who-really-did-invent-the-transistor

Fritz W. B. (1996). The Women of ENIAC. *IEEE Annals of the History of Computing,* 18(3): 13-28. https://courses.cs.washington.edu/courses/csep590a/06au/readings/00511940-frist.pdf

Fuentes A. (2017). The Creative Spark: How Imagination Made Humans

Exceptional. *Dutton*

Fukuyama F. (1989). The End of History? *The National Interest, 16:* 3–18. http://www.jstor.org/stable/24027184

Gabriel R. (2002). The Great Armies of Antiquity. *Holtzbrinck; Illustrated edition*

Galor O. & Moav O. (2005, Nov 17). Natural Selection and the Evolution of Life Expectancy. *London School of Economics and Political Science.* https://sticerd.lse.ac.uk/seminarpapers/dg09102006.pdf

Galpin F. W. (1929). The Sumerian Harp of Ur, c. 3500 B. C. *Music & Letters. 10*(2), 108–123. http://www.jstor.org/stable/726035

Gardiner A. H. (1923). The Eloquent Peasant. *The Journal of Egyptian Archaeology, 9*(1/2): 5–25, 1923, https://doi.org/10.2307/3853490

Gardiner P. (2023). Philosophy of history - History as a process of dialectical change: Hegel and Marx. *Encyclopædia Britannica.* Retrieved August 1, 2023. https://www.britannica.com/topic/philosophy-of-history/History-as-a-process-of-dialectical-change-Hegel-and-Marx

Garfinkel Y. (2010). Dance in Prehistoric Europe. *Documenta Praehistorica, 37,* 205–214. https://www.researchgate.net/publication/316978385_2010_Dance_in_Prehistoric_Europe_Documenta_Praehistorica_37_205-214

Garlinghouse T. (2022, Aug 16). The Aztec civilization: Mexico's last great Indigenous empire. *Live Science.* https://www.livescience.com/aztec-empire-mexico#:~:text=The%20Aztec%20Empire%20flourished%20in,in%20the%20early%2016th%20century

Gaunitz C. et al. (2018). Ancient genomes revisit the ancestry of domestic and Przewalski's horses. *Science, 360*(6384): 111–114. https://doi.org/10.1126/science.aao3297

Ghosh S. (2015). Human cadaveric dissection: a historical account from ancient Greece to the modern era. *Anatomy & Cell Biology, 48*(3), 153. https://doi.org/10.5115/acb.2015.48.3.153

Gin R. H. & Green B. N. (1997). George Goodheart, Jr., D.C., and a history of applied kinesiology. *Journal of Manipulative and Physiological Therapeutics, 20*(5), 331–337. https://pubmed.ncbi.nlm.nih.gov/9200049/

Glogovčan (2020). World's oldest wheel found in Slovenia. *Slovenia.si.* Retrieved July 31, 2023. https://slovenia.si/art-and-cultural-heritage/worlds-oldest-wheel-found-in-slovenia

Gold S. & Wyat M. (1978, Summer). The Rape System: Old Roles and New Times. *Catholic University Law Review, 27*(4). https://scholarship.law.edu/cgi/viewcontent.cgi?referer=&httpsredir=1&article=2391&context=lawreview

Goldstein J. (1999, March). Emergence as a Construct: History and Issues. *Emergence: Complexity & Organization, 1*(1): 49-72. https://www.tandfonline.com/doi/abs/10.1207/s15327000em0101_4. https://www.researchgate.net/publication/243786253_Emergence_as_a_Const

ruct History and Issues

Goldstone J. A. (2015, May 11). The Great and Little Divergence: Where Lies the True Onset of Modern Economic Growth? *SSRN Electronic Journal*. https://doi.org/10.2139/ssrn.2599287

Gosling F.G. (2010). Manhattan Project National Security History Series. *U.S. Department of Energy*. Retrieved Aug 1, 2023. https://www.energy.gov/sites/prod/files/Manhattan_Project_2010.pdf

Graetz J.M. (1981, August). The origin of space war. *Creative Computing Magazine*. Volume 07 Number 08. *Archive.org*. https://archive.org/details/creativecomputing-1981-08/page/n59/mode/2up

Granerød G. (2013). "By the Favour of Ahuramazda I Am King": On the Promulgation of a Persian Propaganda Text among Babylonians and Judaeans. *Journal for the Study of Judaism*, 44(4-5), 455–480. https://doi.org/10.1163/15700631-12340387

Greely HT (2019, Aug 13). CRISPR'd babies: human germline genome editing in the 'He Jiankui affair'. *J Law Biosci*. 6(1):111-183. https://www.ncbi.nlm.nih.gov/pmc/articles/PMC6813942/

Gregersen E. (2023). History of Technology Timeline. *Britannica*. Retrieved Sep 5, 2023. https://www.britannica.com/story/history-of-technology-timeline#

Griffin E. (2010, Dec 15). A Short History of the British Industrial Revolution. *Palgrave Macmillan; 2010 edition*

Grigoraki Argyro (2022, July). A magical rattle, unlike the others! *National Archaeological Museum*. Retrieved August 2, 2023. https://www.namuseum.gr/en/monthly_artefact/a-magical-rattle-unlike-the-others

Grinin L., Korotayev A. (2015). Great Divergence and Great Convergence: A Global Perspective. *Springer; 2015*

Grinin L., Grinin A., Korotayev A. (2020). Dynamics of Technological Growth Rate and the Forthcoming Singularity. In Andrey V. Korotayev (Ed), David J. LePoire (Ed)The 21st Century Singularity and Global Futures: A Big History Perspective (World-Systems Evolution and Global Futures). *Springer; 1st ed. 2020 edition*. pp.287-344. https://www.researchgate.net/publication/338352919_Dynamics_of_Technological_Growth_Rate_and_the_Forthcoming_Singularity

Groenen M. A. M. (2016). A decade of pig genome sequencing: a window on pig domestication and evolution. *Genetics Selection Evolution*, 48(1). https://doi.org/10.1186/s12711-016-0204-2

Grover C.E. et al. (2022, Dec 13). Dual Domestication, Diversity, and Differential Introgression in Old World Cotton Diploids. *Genome Biology and Evolution*, 14(12): 1-17. https://doi.org/10.1093/gbe/evac170

Guan H. et al. (2022, September). The Rise and Fall of Paper Money in Yuan China, 1260-1368. *The University of Manchester*. http://hummedia.manchester.ac.uk/schools/soss/economics/discussionpapers/

EDP-2207.pdf

Gurevich A. (2021, March 1). World Mythology: Myth, Metaphor, and Mystery. *MHCC Library Press Open Educational Resources.* https://mhcc.pressbooks.pub/worldmythology/

Hansen B. (2012, August). History of Earth's Climate. 7. Holocene. *Dalum Hjallese Debatklub.* Retrieved August 2, 2023. http://www.dandebat.dk/eng-klima7.htm

Harari Y. N. (2015, June 16). Why humans run the world. *Ideas.ted.com.* https://ideas.ted.com/why-humans-run-the-world

Harari Y. N. (2018). Sapiens: A Brief History of Humankind. *Harper Perennial. Reprint edition*

Harrison B. (1962). Meaning and Mental Images. *Proceedings of the Aristotelian Society. JSTOR. 63,* 237–250. https://www.jstor.org/stable/i408488

Harry Ransom Center contributors (2022). The Niépce Heliograph. *Harry Ransom Center.* https://www.hrc.utexas.edu/niepce-heliograph/

Hartmann G. W. (1949). Review of The driving forces of human nature and their adjustment: An introduction to the psychology and psychopathology of emotional behavior and volitional control [Review of the book *The driving forces of human nature and their adjustment: An introduction to the psychology and psychopathology of emotional behavior and volitional control, by T. V. Moore*]. *Psychological Bulletin, 46*(1), 83–85. https://doi.org/10.1037/h0051819

Hasse J. (2017, Feb 24). The First Jazz Recording Was Made by a Group of White Guys? *Smithsonian.* https://www.smithsonianmag.com/smithsonian-institution/was-first-jazz-recording-made-group-white-guys-180962246/

Hawkesworth A. S. (1910). The Temple Library of Nippur. *The Open Court, 1910*(12), Article 12. https://opensiuc.lib.siu.edu/ocj/vol1910/iss12/12

Head M.J. (2018, July 20). IUGS ratifies Holocene subdivision, *Subcomission on Quarternary Stratigraphy.* http://quaternary.stratigraphy.org/iugs-ratifies-holocene-subdivision/

Heathers Admin (2018, Aug 30). Taxonomy Hierarchical Relationship Issues. *Hedden Information Management.* https://www.hedden-information.com/taxonomy-hierarchical-relationship-issues/

Hegel G. W. F. (2018). Lectures On the Philosophy of History, Tr. by J. Sibree. *Franklin Classics*

Helden A. V. et al. (2010). The Origins of the Telescope. *Amsterdam University Press*

Heller A. (1896). Anianus Jedlik. *Nature, 53*(1379), 516–517. https://doi.org/10.1038/053516a0

Hemour S. & Wu K. (2014). Radio-Frequency Rectifier for Electromagnetic Energy Harvesting: Development Path and Future Outlook. *Proceedings of the IEEE, 102*(11): 1667-1691. https://ieeexplore.ieee.org/document/6922611

Henrich J. (2023, June). How Culture Made Us Uniquely Human. *Zygon, 58*(2), 405-424.

https://henrich.fas.harvard.edu/sites/scholar.harvard.edu/files/henrich/files/zygon_-_2023_-_henrich_-_how_culture_made_us_uniquely_human.pdf

Hepburn B. & and Andersen H. (2021). Scientific Method. *The Stanford Encyclopedia of Philosophy.*
https://plato.stanford.edu/archives/sum2021/entries/scientific-method/

Higham T. et al. (2012). Testing models for the beginnings of the Aurignacian and the advent of figurative art and music: The radiocarbon chronology of Geißenklösterle. *Journal of Human Evolution.* 62(6), 664–676.
https://doi.org/10.1016/j.jhevol.2012.03.003

Higham T. et al. (2014). The timing and spatiotemporal patterning of Neanderthal disappearance. *Nature, 512*(7514), 306–309.
https://doi.org/10.1038/nature13621

Hintikka J. et al. (2020, Dec 17). History of logic. *Encyclopedia Britannica.* Retrieved Aug 2, 2023. https://www.britannica.com/topic/history-of-logic

History of England contributors (2023). Early Modern English (c. 1500 - c. 1800). *History of England.* Retrieved Sep 10, 2023.
https://www.thehistoryofenglish.com/early-modern-english

History of Information contributors (2023). John Wilkinson Invents the First Machine Tool: a Boring Machine for Cylinders and Cannons. *History of Information.com.* Retrieved Sep 4, 2023.
https://historyofinformation.com/detail.php?id=4755

Hodder I. (2018). Where Are We Heading?: The Evolution of Humans and Things (Foundational Questions in Science). *Yale University Press; Illustrated edition*

Hodder I. & Meskell L. (2011). A Curious and Sometimes a Trifle Macabre Artistry. *Current Anthropology, 52*(2), 235–263. https://doi.org/10.1086/659250

Homeland Security contributors (2023). Weapons of Mass Destruction. *Homeland Security.* Retrieved Aug 1, 2023. https://www.dhs.gov/topics/weapons-mass-destruction#

Homer (Author), Butler S. (Translator) (2021). The Iliad: Homer's Greek Epic with Selected Writings. *Wine Dark Pres*

Hornblower S. (2023, Mar 10). Ancient Greek civilization. *Britannica.*
https://www.britannica.com/place/ancient-Greece

Hounshell D. A. (1985). From the American System to Mass Production, 1800–1932: The Development of Manufacturing Technology in the United States. *Johns Hopkins University Press (September 1, 1985)*

Howell Trevor H. (1987). Avicenna and his regimen of old age. *Age and Ageing, 16*(1), 58–59. https://doi.org/10.1093/ageing/16.1.58

HP contributors (2023). Computer History: All About the ENIAC. *HP.* Retrieved Sep 5, 2023. https://www.hp.com/ca-en/shop/offer.aspx?p=computer-history-all-about-the-eniac

Huang B. et al. (2020, June 25). Causal Discovery from Heterogeneous/Nonstationary Data with Independent Changes. *ArXiv.org.* Retrieved Aug 1, 2023. https://doi.org/10.48550/arXiv.1903.01672

Humphries J. (2011). Childhood and Child Labour in the British Industrial Revolution. *Cambridge University Press; Reprint edition (October 31, 2011)*

Hutchinson P. (2016, May 23). A window on infinity: rediscovering the short films of the Lumière brothers. *The Guardian*. Retrieved Aug 1, 2023. https://www.theguardian.com/film/2016/may/23/rediscovering-lumiere-brothers-early-cinema-pioneers

The Hummel Class of resources contributors (2023). Who Has The Oldest Class of resources Tree? *The Hummel Class of resources*. Retrieved Aug 1, 2023. Thehummelclass of resources.com. https://thehummelclass of resources.com/who-has-the-oldest-class of resources-tree

Hymowitz T. (2004). Speciation and cytogenetics. In Boerma H. R. (Author, Editor), Specht J. E. (Editor) (2004). Soybeans: Improvement, Production, And Uses (Agronomy). *American Society of Agronomy-Crop Science Society of America-Soil Science Society of America; 3rd edition (January 1, 2004)*

IBM contributors (2023). 701 Translator IBM Press release, January 8, 1954. *IBM Archives. Exhibits. IBM*. Retrieved Aug 2, 2023. https://www.ibm.com/ibm/history/exhibits/701/701_translator.html

Iddamalgoda H. (2022, November). The History Of E-Commerce. *ResearchGate*. https://www.researchgate.net/publication/365202093_The_History_Of_E-Commerce

Indo-European.Info contributors (2023). English = Indo-European. *Indo-European.Info*. Retrieved Sep 10, 2023. https://indo-european.info/dictionary-translator/

Internet World Stats contributors (2023). Internet growth statistics. *Internet World Stats*. Retrieved Sep 5, 2023 https://www.internetworldstats.com/emarketing.htm

Institutoideal contributors (2008, Jan 25). Hungarian Inventors and their Inventions. *Instituto IDEAL*. https://web.archive.org/web/20120322223457/http://www.institutoideal.org/conteudo_eng.php?&sys=biblioteca_eng&arquivo=1&artigo=94&ano=2008

International Circus Hall of Fame contributors (2023). History of the Circus. *International Circus Hall of Fame*. Retrieved Aug 2. 2023. https://circushalloffame.com/history-of-the-circus

International Peace Bureau contributors (2023). Conventional Weapons. *International Peace Bureau*. Retrieved Aug 2. 2023. https://www.ipb.org/conventional-weapons/

International Printing Museum contributors (2023). Gutenberg press. *International Printing Museum*. Retrieved Sep 4, 2023. https://www.printmuseum.org/gutenberg-press

International Telegraph Union contributors (2023). History. *ITU*. Retrieved Sep 3, 2023. https://www.itu.int/en/about/Pages/history.aspx

IPCC (2023), Summary for Policymakers. In: Climate Change 2023: Synthesis Report.Contribution of Working Groups I, II and III to the Sixth Assessment

Report of the Intergovernmental Panel on Climate Change [Core Writing Team, H. Lee and J. Romero (eds.)]. IPCC, Geneva, Switzerland, pp. 1-34, https://www.ipcc.ch/report/ar6/syr/

Issawi C. (2019). Ibn Khaldūn | Muslim Historian. *Encyclopædia Britannica.* Retrieved Aug 2. 2023. https://www.britannica.com/biography/Ibn-Khaldun

Jaenisch R. & Mintz B. (1974). Simian Virus 40 DNA Sequences in DNA of Healthy Adult Mice Derived from Preimplantation Blastocysts Injected with Viral DNA. *Proceedings of the National Academy of Sciences, 71*(4), 1250–1254. https://doi.org/10.1073/pnas.71.4.1250

Javelosa J. (2016, June 10). Bug In Video Game Makes AI Go Rogue, Starts Totally Destroying Players. *Futurism.* https://futurism.com/this-video-games-artificial-intelligence-turned-on-players-using-super-weapons

Javelosa J. (2016, Dec 25). Could We Hack Our Brains to Gain New Senses? Technology is making it possible to experience the world in new ways. *Futurism.* https://futurism.com/could-we-hack-our-brains-to-gain-new-senses

John (2013, Oct 25). Capacitors – Invention History and the Story of Leyden Jar. *Circuits Today.* Retrieved Aug 2. 2023. https://www.circuitstoday.com/capacitors-invention-history-and-the-story-of-leyden-jar

Jones E. (2003). The European Miracle: Environments, Economies and Geopolitics in the History of Europe and Asia. *Cambridge University Press; 3rd edition*

Jones G. (2017, July 18). Business History, the Great Divergence and the Great Convergence. *Harvard Business School General Management Unit Working Paper No. 18-004. SSRN Electronic Journal.* https://doi.org/10.2139/ssrn.3004580

Jordan D. K. (2022, Nov 14). The Eloquent Peasant, 2022-11-24, *David K. Jordan at UC San Diego.* https://pages.ucsd.edu/~dkjordan/arch/egypt/Petrie/EgyEloquent.html

JoUgo B. et al. (2018). Toward a General Theory of Societal Collapse. A Biophysical Examination of Tainter s Model of the Diminishing Returns of Complexity. Arxiv.org. https://arxiv.org/abs/1810.07056

Kahane Guy (2021). Importance, Value, and Causal Impact. *Journal of Moral Philosophy, 19*(6): 577-601. https://doi.org/10.1163/17455243-20213581

Kallenborn Z. (2021, Oct 5). Applying arms-control frameworks to autonomous weapons. *Brookings.* https://www.brookings.edu/articles/applying-arms-control-frameworks-to-autonomous-weapons/#

Kane G. C. et al. (2015, July 14). Strategy, not technology, drives digital transformation. MIT Sloan Management Review. *Deloitte University Press.* https://sloanreview.mit.edu/projects/strategy-drives-digital-transformation/

Kaplan R. M. (2012, March). Johann Christian Reil and the naming of our specialty. *Australasian Psychiatry, 20*(2):157-8. https://pubmed.ncbi.nlm.nih.gov/22457334/

Kappel Krystyna (2016). Ancient Egyptian Harp. Its origins and status within the Ancient Egyptian society. *Academia.edu.*

https://www.academia.edu/31747764/Ancient_Egyptian_Harp_Its_origins_an d_status_within_the_Ancient_Egyptian_society

Kayser J. et al. (2018). Emergence of evolutionary driving forces in pattern-forming microbial populations. *Phyl. Trans. R. Soc. B* 373: 2017.0106. 2017.0106. https://doi.org/10.1098/rstb.2017.0106

Kempe F. (2023, Oct 21). Biden's inflection point and history's sobering lessons. *Atlantic Council.* https://www.atlanticcouncil.org/content-series/inflection-points/bidens-inflection-point-and-historys-sobering-lessons/

Kendler K. S. et al. (2022, May). The Emergence of Psychiatry: 1650–1850. *The American Journal of Psychiatry*, 179(5): 329-335 https://ajp.psychiatryonline.org/doi/abs/10.1176/appi.ajp.21060614

Kentnor H. (2015). Distance Education and the Evolution of Online Learning in the United States. *University of Denver. Digital Commons.* https://digitalcommons.du.edu/cgi/viewcontent.cgi?article=1026&context=la w_facpub

Kerr R. & Wood N. (2004). Science and Civilisation in China Volume 5: Chemistry and Chemical Technology, Part 12, Ceramic Technology. *Cambridge University Press; 1st edition (November 15, 2004)*

Khotsey A. S. (2005). Хоцей А. С. (2005). Проблема смысла истории с точки зрения логики. *Философия и общество.* 3(40):26-71. https://www.socionauki.ru/journal/articles/126642/ [Khotsey A. S. (2005). The problem of the meaning of history from the point of view of logic. *Philosophy and society.* 3(40):26-71. https://www.socionauki.ru/journal/articles/126642/]

Kiernan B. (2004, August). The First Genocide: Carthage, 146 BC. *SAGE Journals, International Council for Philosophy and Human Sciences, 51(3).* https://journals.sagepub.com/doi/10.1177/0392192104043648

Kilmer A. D. (1971). The Discovery of an Ancient Mesopotamian Theory of Music. *Proceedings of the American Philosophical Society.* 115(2), 131–49. http://www.jstor.org/stable/985853

King L. W. (2008). The Avalon Project: Code of Hammurabi. *Yale.edu; Lillian Goldman Law Library.* https://avalon.law.yale.edu/ancient/hamframe.asp

Kingsford P. W. (2023, Aug 21). James Watt. *Britannica.* https://www.britannica.com/biography/James-Watt

Kirchner H.O. K. & Lazar M. (2008, Feb 6). The thermodynamic driving force for bone growth and remodelling: a hypothesis. *J R Soc Interface.* 5(19): 183-93. https://royalsocietypublishing.org/doi/10.1098/rsif.2007.1096

Kisak P F. (Edited by) (2015). Ancient Legal Codes: "The Historicity of Morals & Values". *CreateSpace Independent Publishing Platform. First Edition (October 14, 2015)*

Klein R. (1995). Anatomy, Behavior, and Modern Human Origins. *Journal of World Prehistory*, 9, 167-198. http://dx.doi.org/10.1007/BF02221838

Knerl L. (2019, Dec 7). When was the Fax Machine Invented? *HP.com.* https://www.hp.com/us-en/shop/tech-takes/when-was-fax-invented#

Kodak Digitizing Blog contributors (2023). Who Made the First Video Camera? *Kodak Digitizing*. Retrieved Aug 1, 2023. https://kodakdigitizing.com/blogs/news/who-made-the-first-video-camera

Krentz P. (2020, Sep 24). Battle of Salamis: 480 BC. *Oxford Bibliographies*. https://www.oxfordbibliographies.com/display/document/obo-9780199791279/obo-9780199791279-0196.xml#

Koetsier T. & Blauwendraat H. (2017, June). The Archimedian screw-pump: A note on its invention and the development of the theory. *Pumppower*. http://www.pumppower.com.au/wp-content/uploads/2017/06/Archimedian-Screw-Pump-a-note-on-its-invention.pdf

Koh NK (2008). Proto-porcelain of Shang/Western Han. *Koh Antique*. 22 Mar 2008. http://www.koh-antique.com/celadon/proto.html

Koht H. (Author), Haugen E. (Translator) (1964). Driving Forces in History. *Belknap Press; 1st U.S. ed. edition (January 1, 1964)*

Korotayev A. et al. (2006). Introduction to Social Macrodynamics: Compact Macromodels of the World System Growth. *Moscow: KomKniga, 2006*

Korotayev A. (2018). The 21st Century Singularity and its Big History Implications: A re-analysis. *Journal of Big History*, 2(3): 71 - 118. http://dx.doi.org/10.22339/jbh.v2i3.2320

Kott A. & Perconti P. (2018). Long-Term Forecasts of Military Technologies for a 20–30 Year Horizon: An Empirical Assessment of Accuracy. *Arxiv.org*. https://arxiv.org/ftp/arxiv/papers/1807/1807.08339.pdf

Kovács É. (2011). Polysemy in Traditional vs. Cognitive Linguistic. *Eger Journal of English Studies*, XI: 3-19. https://core.ac.uk/download/pdf/159786966.pdf

Kozbelt A. et al. (2010). Theories of Creativity. In: Kaufman, J.C. and Sternberg, R.J., Eds., *Cambridge Handbook of Creativity, Cambridge University Press, New York*. http://dx.doi.org/10.1017/cbo9780511763205.004

Kraut Richard (2022, Dec 2). Socrates Greek philosopher. *Encyclopaedia Britannica*. https://www.britannica.com/biography/Socrates

Krebs R. R. & Rapport A. (2012). International Relations and the Psychology of Time Horizons. *International Studies Quarterly*, 56(3), 530–543. http://www.jstor.org/stable/23256803

Kuhn Thomas S. (1962). The Structure of Scientific Revolutions. *University of Chicago Press*

Kumar K. (2021, Mar 21). Colony and Empire, Colonialism and Imperialism: A Meaningful Distinction? *Comparative Studies in Society and History, 63: 280 -* 309. https://www.cambridge.org/core/journals/comparative-studies-in-society-and-history/article/abs/colony-and-empire-colonialism-and-imperialism-a-meaningful-distinction/4FB6341AD7B7C63468503BEE873F1995

Kvavadze E. et al. (2009). 30,000-Year-Old Wild Flax Fibers. *Science*. 325(5946): 1359. https://www.science.org/doi/10.1126/science.1175404

Lange M. M. (2011, February). Progress. *Stanford Encyclopedia of Philosophy*. https://plato.stanford.edu/entries/progress/

Langgut D. (2017, June). The Citrus Route Revealed: From Southeast Asia into the Mediterranean. HortScience, 52(6): 814-822. https://doi.org/10.21273/HORTSCI11023-16

Laskaris N. et al. (2011, September). Late Pleistocene/Early Holocene seafaring in the Aegean: new obsidian hydration dates with the SIMS-SS method. *Journal of Archaeological Science, 38*(9): 2475-2479. https://www.sciencedirect.com/science/article/abs/pii/S0305440311001798

Lawergren Bo (2006). Neolithic drums in China. In: Hickmann E, Both AA, and Eichmann R (eds). Studien zur Musik Archäologie V. Orient-Archäologie 20. *Deutsches Archäologisches Institut.* [Lawergren Bo (2006). Neolithic drums in China. In: Hickmann E, Both AA, and Eichmann R (eds). Studies in Music Archeology V. Orient Archeology 20. *German Archaeological Institute*]. https://www.hunter.cuny.edu/physics/faculty/lawergren/repository/files/artic les/neolithic-drums-in-china-lawergren.pdf/view

Laws D. (2013, Nov 06). Who invented the diode? *CHM.* https://computerhistory.org/blog/who-invented-the-diode/

Lean Factories contributors (2023). Venetian Arsenal - Venice Ship Building Using Mass Production. *Lean Factories.* Retrieved Sep 4, 2023. https://leanfactories.com/venetian-arsenal-venice-ship-building-using-mass-production/

Lennox James (2021, July 16). Aristotle's Biology. *The Stanford Encyclopedia of Philosophy.* https://plato.stanford.edu/entries/aristotle-biology/

Lewis M J T (2001). Railways in the Greek and Roman world. *ResearchGate.* https://www.researchgate.net/publication/242240630_RAILWAYS_IN_THE_G REEK_AND_ROMAN_WORLD

Leip B. (2022, Oct 13). Who invented the typewriter? A Brief History. *Typewriters.com.* Retrieved July 31, 2023. https://typewriters.com/blogs/who-invented-the-typewriter-a-brief-history/

Leeuwarder Courant Contributors (2001, Apr 12). Oudste bootje ter wereld kon wekelijk varen. [Oldest boat in the world could really sail]. *Leeuwarder Courant.* https://www.archeoforum.nl/Pesse10.html

Lemelson-MIT contributors (2023). Blaise Pascal Pascaline Calculator. *Lemelson-MIT.* Retrieved Sep 4, 2023. https://lemelson.mit.edu/resources/blaise-pascal

Lentz D. L. et al. (2008, Apr 29). Sunflower (Helianthus annuus L.) as a pre-Columbian domesticate in Mexico. *PNAS, 105*(17): 6232-6237. https://www.pnas.org/doi/10.1073/pnas.0711760105#table/41001172

Li LF et al. (2013, Nov 18). Origins and domestication of cultivated banana inferred from chloroplast and nuclear genes. *PLoS One, 8*(11): e80502. https://journals.plos.org/plosone/article?id=10.1371/journal.pone.0080502

Li Y. et al. (2015, Nov 4). The Earliest Chinese Proto-Porcelain Excavated from Kiln Sites: An Elemental Analysis. *PLoS One. 10*(11):e0139970. https://journals.plos.org/plosone/article?id=10.1371/journal.pone.0139970

Librado P. et al. (2021). The origins and spread of domestic horses from the

Western Eurasian steppes. Nature 598: 634–640.
https://doi.org/10.1038/s41586-021-04018-9

Library of Congress contributors (2022). The Daguerreotype Medium. *Library of Congress*. https://www.loc.gov/collections/daguerreotypes/articles-and-essays/the-daguerreotype-medium

Library of Congress contributors (2023a). Timeline (1914 - 1921). *Library of Congress*. Retrieved 07/25/2023. https://www.loc.gov/collections/stars-and-stripes/articles-and-essays/a-world-at-war/timeline-1914-1921/#

Library of Congress contributors (2023b). Principia. Philosophiæ naturalis principia mathematica. *Library of Congress*. Retrieved Sep 4, 2023. https://www.loc.gov/item/2021667054#

Lisha Pace (2022, Dec 6). South-Pointing Chariot Explained – Everything You Need To Know. *History Computer*. https://history-computer.com/south-pointing-chariot/

Lister T. (2023, Nov 3). Exhausted and disappointed with allies, Ukraine's president and military chief warn of long attritional war. *CNN*. https://www.cnn.com/2023/11/03/world/ukraine-president-warns-long-attritional-war/index.html

Little D. (2020). Philosophy of History. *Stanford Encyclopedia of Philosophy*. https://plato.stanford.edu/entries/history/

Liu L. et al. (2018, October). Fermented beverage and food storage in 13,000 y-old stone mortars at Raqefet Cave, Israel: Investigating Natufian ritual feasting. *Journal of Archaeological Science: Reports*. 21: 783-793. https://www.sciencedirect.com/science/article/pii/S2352409X18303468?via%3Dihub

Lobell J. A. (2012, March/April). New Life for the Lion Man. *Archaeology Archive*. 65(2). https://archive.archaeology.org/1203/features/stadelhole_hohlenstein_paleolithic_lowenmensch.html

Loff S. (2022, Jan 5). Apollo 11 Mission Overview. *National Aeronautics and Space Administration*. https://www.nasa.gov/mission_pages/apollo/missions/apollo11.html

Logan D. C. (2009, March). Known knowns, known unknowns, unknown unknowns and the propagation of scientific enquiry. *Journal of Experimental Botany*, 60(3): 712–714, https://academic.oup.com/jxb/article/60/3/712/453685

Loutre N.F. (2003). Clue from MIS 11 to Predict the Future Climate–A Modelling Point of View. *Earth and Planetary Science Letters*. 212:213-214. https://www.sciencedirect.com/science/article/abs/pii/S0012821X03002358?via%3Dihub.

Lovejoy-inc (2015, Mar 9). Evolution of Gear Couplings. *CouplingAnswers.com*. http://www.couplinganswers.com/2015/03/the-evolution-of-gear-couplings.html

Lucas A. (1936). The wood of the Third Dynasty plywood coffin from Saqqara.

Annales du Service des Antiquités de l'Égypte. 36:141–64

Lynn Abbott & Seroff Doug (1996). 'They Cert'ly Sound Good to Me': Sheet Music, Southern Vaudeville, and the Commercial Ascendancy of the Blues. *American Music*. 14(4), 402–54. https://doi.org/10.2307/3052302

Ma A. (2018, May 16). Thousands of Swedish people are swapping ID cards for microchips. *World economic forum*. https://www.weforum.org/agenda/2018/05/thousands-of-people-in-sweden-are-embedding-microchips-under-their-skin-to-replace-id-cards

Mackey R.R. (2014, Mar 27). Information Warfare. *Oxford Biographies*. https://www.oxfordbibliographies.com/display/document/obo-9780199791279/obo-9780199791279-0024.xml

Macmillan Dictionary contributors (2022). *Macmillan Dictionary*. https://www.macmillandictionary.com/us/dictionary/american/direction

Macrotrends contributors (2023). World Life Expectancy 1950-2023. *Macrotrends*. https://www.macrotrends.net/countries/WLD/world/life-expectancy#

Maggioni L. et al. (2010). Origin and Domestication of Cole Crops (Brassica Oleracea L.): Linguistic and Literary Considerations. *Economic Botany*, 64(2): 109–23. http://www.jstor.org/stable/41001172

Maier J.F. et al. (2017, Jan 17). Model granularity in engineering design – concepts and framework. *Design Science*, 3(e1). https://doi.org/10.1017/dsj.2016.16

Mallory, J. P. (1976). Time perspective and proto-Indo-European culture. World Archaeol 8. Vol 8, pp. 44-56. https://www.jstor.org/stable/124298

Mallory J. P. & Adams D. Q. (2006). The Oxford Introduction to Proto-Indo-European and the Proto-Indo-European World. *Oxford University Press; Illustrated edition (November 9, 2006)*

Maloney T.R. et al. (2022). Surgical amputation of a limb 31,000 years ago in Borneo. *Nature*, 609: 547–551 (2022). https://doi.org/10.1038/s41586-022-05160-8

Malwarebytes contributors (2023). What is Stuxnet? *Malwarebytes*. Retrieved 07/25/2023. https://www.malwarebytes.com/stuxnet

Manning M. J. & Romerstein H. (2004, Nov 30). Historical Dictionary of American Propaganda Annotated Edition. *Greenwood; Annotated edition*

Mansfeld Jaap (1985). Aristotle and Others on Thales, or the Beginnings of Natural Philosophy (With Some Remarks on Xenophanes). Mnemosyne, 38(1/2): 109–29. http://www.jstor.org/stable/4431379

Mark Joshua J. (2019, Oct 9). Sumerians. *World History Encyclopedia*. https://www.worldhistory.org/Sumerians/

Mark Joshua J. (2021, Oct 26). Code of Ur-Nammu. *World History Encyclopedia*. https://www.worldhistory.org/Code_of_Ur-Nammu/

Marks S. & Freeman C. W. (2022). Diplomacy. *Encyclopaedia Britannica*. https://www.britannica.com/topic/diplomacy

Marx Karl & Engels Friedrich (2008). The Communist Manifesto. *Pathfinder Press*. *3rd edition*

Mathematics dictionary contributors (2022). Coordinates. *Mathematics dictionary.*
   http://www.mathematicsdictionary.com/english/vmd/full/c/coordinates.htm

Matson John (2010, Oct 5). Graphene Researchers Geim and Novoselov Win
   Nobel Prize in Physics [Updated]. *Scientific American.*
   https://www.scientificamerican.com/article/geim-novoselov-physics-novel/

May R. (1991, May 1). The Cry for Myth. *W. W. Norton & Company*

Mcbrearty S. & Brooks AS. (2000, November). The revolution that wasn't: a new
   interpretation of the origin of modern human behavior. *J Hum Evol.* 39(5):453-
   563. https://doi.org/10.1006/jhev.2000.0435

McCarthy M. (2007). Report on the wreck of the Sub Marine Explorer (1865) at
   Isla San Telmo, Archipielago de las Perlas, Panama, and the 2006 fieldwork
   season. *Maritime Archaeology.* https://museum.wa.gov.au/maritime-
   archaeology-db/sites/default/files/no._221_submarine_explorer_1.pdf

McGillem C. D. (2023. May 17). Telegraph. *Britannica.*
   https://www.britannica.com/technology/telegraph

McGovern P. E. et al. (2004, Dec 4). Fermented beverages of pre- and proto-
   historic China. *PNAS.* *101*(51) 17593-17598.
   https://www.pnas.org/doi/10.1073/pnas.0407921102

Mcleod Saul (2023, July 31). Thomas Kuhn: Paradigm Shift. *SimplyPsychology.*
   https://www.simplypsychology.org/kuhn-paradigm.html#

Mehta I. (2017, September). Origin and History of Onions. *IOSR Journal Of
   Humanities And Social Science (IOSR-JHSS),* 22(9): 07-10.
   https://www.iosrjournals.org/iosr-jhss/papers/Vol.%2022%20Issue9/Version-
   13/B2209130710.pdf

Meinwald C. C. (2023). Plato. *Encyclopaedia Britannica.* Retrieved 01/20/2023.
   https://www.britannica.com/biography/Plato

Mellars P. (2006, June). Why did modern human populations disperse from
   Africa ca. 60,000 years ago? A new model. *Proceedings of the National Academy
   of Sciences,* 103(25): 9381-9386. https://doi.org/10.1073/pnas.0510792103

Merriam-Webster Dictionary contributors (2023a). World War. *Merriam-Webster
   Dictionary.* Retrieved 07/25/2023. https://www.merriam-
   webster.com/dictionary/world%20war

Mgrdichian Laura (2006, Oct 13). Ancient Hair-Dyeing – A Nanoscience?.
   PhysOrg. https://phys.org/news/2006-10-ancient-hair-dyeing-
   nanoscience.html

Michel J-P. et al. (2011, Jan 14). Quantitative Analysis of Culture Using Millions of
   Digitized Books. *Science,* 331(6014): 76-182.
   https://www.ncbi.nlm.nih.gov/pmc/articles/PMC3279742/pdf/nihms-
   329575.pdf

Miller G. A. (2003, March). The cognitive revolution: a historical perspective.
   Trends in Cognitive Sciences Volume, 7(3): 141-144.
   https://doi.org/10.1016/S1364-6613(03)00029-9

Modis T. (2002). Forecasting the growth of complexity and change. *Technol*

Forecast Soc Chang, 69(4):377–404. https://doi.org/10.1016/S0040-1625(01)00172-X

Modis T. (2006). The Singularity Myth. In Technological Forecasting & Social Change, 73(2): 104-112. https://www.researchgate.net/publication/267207324_The_Singularity_Myth

Modis T. (2012). Why the Singularity Cannot Happen. In Eden, A., Moor, J., Søraker, J., Steinhart, E. (eds) Singularity Hypotheses. *Springer; 2012th edition (April 13, 2013)*

Mondal Sekh Rahim (2020, Mar 31). Ibn-Khaldun's Contribution to Sociology. *Social Trends*, 7: 143-150. https://ir.nbu.ac.in/bitstream/123456789/3575/1/Vol.%207%20March%202020_11.pdf

Money Staff (2023, Feb 13). What Is Fiat Money? *Money*. https://money.com/what-is-fiat-money/

Morgan H. (2011). Early Childhood Education: History, Theory, and Practice. *Rowman & Littlefield Publishers; Second edition*

Morris Ian (2011). Why the West Rules—for Now: The Patterns of History, and What They Reveal About the Future. *Picador. First edition (October 25, 2011)*

Morris R. (1961). The Meaning of Human History (The Paul Carus lectures). *Open Court, 2nd edition*

Morris R. J. T. & Truskowski B. J. (2003, April). The evolution of storage systems. *IBM Systems Journal*, 42(2): 205–217. https://doi.org/10.1147/sj.422.0205

Mossman Sue (2013, Dec 29). Alexander Parkes – Materials man and polymath. *Science Museum*. https://blog.sciencemuseum.org.uk/alexander-parkes-materials-man-and-polymath/

Münzel S. C. et al. (2004). Eine Mammutelfenbeinflöte aus dem Aurignacien des Geißenklösterle. Neue belege für eine musikalische Tradition aus dem Jungpaläolithikum auf der Schwäbischen Alb. [A mammoth ivory flute from the Aurignacian of Geißenklösterle. New evidence for a musical tradition from the Upper Palaeolithic on the Swabian Jura]. *ARCHÄOLOGISCHES KORRESPONDENZBLATT*. 34(4), 447-462. Retrieved August 1, 2023, from https://www.academia.edu/4030578/Eine_Mammutelfenbeinfl%C3%B6te_aus_dem_Aurignacien_des_Gei%C3%9Fenkl%C3%B6sterle_Neue_belege_f%C3%BCr_eine_musikalische_Tradition_aus_dem_Jungpal%C3%A4olithikum_auf_der_Schw%C3%A4bischen_Alb

Murphy D. B. & Davidson M. W. (2011). Fundamentals of light microscopy and electronic imaging. *Oxford: Wiley-Blackwell*

Museum of Fine Arts Boston contributors (1987). Mummy mask. *Museum of Fine Arts Boston*. https://collections.mfa.org/objects/164600/mummy-mask

Music With Ease contributors (2021). Opera Before Gluck. *Music With Ease*. https://www.musicwithease.com/opera-before-gluck.html

Myhrvold N. (2022, Nov 02). Coffee. *Encyclopaedia Britannica*. https://www.britannica.com/topic/coffee

Myles S. et al. (2011, Jan 18). Genetic structure and domestication history of the grape. *PNAS, 108*(9): 3530-3535.
https://www.pnas.org/doi/10.1073/pnas.1009363108

Nargund G. (2009). Declining birth rate in Developed Countries: A radical policy re-think is required. *Facts Views Vis Obgyn, 1*(3): 191-193.
https://www.ncbi.nlm.nih.gov/pmc/articles/PMC4255510/

NASA Content Administrator (2019). Apollo 10. *National Aeronautics and Space Administration.*
https://www.nasa.gov/mission_pages/apollo/missions/apollo10.html

National Library of Medicine contributors (2012, Feb 7). Greek Medicine - Dioscorides. *National Library of Medicine.*
https://www.nlm.nih.gov/hmd/greek/greek_dioscorides.html

National Research Council (US). (1994). Sharing Laboratory resources: Genetically Altered Mice: Summary of a Workshop Held at the National Academy of Sciences, March 23-24, 1993. Washington (DC): *National Academies Press (US).* https://www.ncbi.nlm.nih.gov/books/NBK231336/

Needham J. & Tsuen-Hsuin T. (1985). Science and Civilisation in China: Volume 5, Chemistry and Chemical Technology; Part 1, Paper and Printing. *Cambridge University Press*

Nees Georg (1965, Feb 5). Computergrafik. *Compart.* http://dada.compart-bremen.de/item/exhibition/164

Nekoei A. & Sinn F. (2021, Jan 29). HERSTORY The Rise of Self-Made Women. CEPR Discussion Paper No. DP15736. *CEPR.*
https://repec.cepr.org/repec/cpr/ceprdp/DP15736.pdf

Neuendorf Henri (2016, Feb 5). 100 Years Ago Today, Dada Was Born at Cabaret Voltaire in Zurich. *Art World.* https://news.artnet.com/art-world/dada-100-year-anniversary-420473

Newton Isaac (1848). Newton's Principia. The mathematical principles of natural philosophy, by Sir Isaac Newton. *New-York, D. Adee, 1848, First American Edition.* https://www.loc.gov/item/04014428/

New World Encyclopedia contributors (2022). Orchestra. *New World Encyclopedia.*
https://www.newworldencyclopedia.org/entry/orchestra

New World Encyclopedia contributors (2023). Total war. *New World Encyclopedia.* Retrieved 07/25/2023.
https://www.newworldencyclopedia.org/entry/Total_war

Nichols S. (2022, Sep 14). 400. What Governs History?. *Ligonier.*
https://www.ligonier.org/podcasts/5-minutes-in-church-history-with-stephen-nichols/400-what-governs-history

Nicholson Judith A. (2005, Dec 11). Flash! Mobs in the Age of Mobile Connectivity. *The Fibreculture Journal.* https://fibreculturejournal.org/fcj-030-flash-mobs-in-the-age-of-mobile-connectivity/

Nicholson P. T. & Shaw I. (Eds) (2009). Ancient Egyptian Materials and Technology. *Cambridge University Press. Illustrated edition*

Nielsen M. (2012, Jan 23). If correlation doesn't imply causation, then what does? *Data-driven Intelligence blog.* https://michaelnielsen.org/ddi/if-correlation-doesnt-imply-causation-then-what-does/

NIHF contributors (2022). Alonzo G. Decker: Portable Hand-Held Electric Drill. *National Inventors Hall of Fame.* https://www.invent.org/inductees/alonzo-decker

NIHF contributors (2023a). Otis Boykin. *National Inventors Hall of Fame.* https://www.invent.org/inductees/otis-boykin

NIHF contributors. (2023b). The Invention of the Industrial Robot. *National Inventors Hall of Fame.* https://www.invent.org/blog/inventors/George-Devol-Industrial-Robot

NMU contributors (2023). Historiography. *NMU Writing Center.* https://nmu.edu/writingcenter/historiography

NobelPrize.org contributors (2020, June 20). The Nobel Prize in Physics 1954. *The Nobel Prize.org. Nobel Media AB 2020.* https://www.nobelprize.org/prizes/physics/1954/summary/

Noll A. M. (2014, Nov 12). First-Hand:Howard Wise Gallery Show of Digital Art and Patterns (1965): A 50th Anniversary Memoir. *ETHW.* https://ethw.org/First-Hand:Howard_Wise_Gallery_Show_of_Digital_Art_and_Patterns_(1965):_A_50th_Anniversary_Memoir

Noll A. M. (2016). The Howard Wise Gallery Show Computer-Generated Pictures (1965) A 50th-Anniversary Memoir. *Leonardo 49*(3), 232–39. http://www.jstor.org/stable/43834354

Nomade S. et al. (2016). A 36,000-Year-Old Volcanic Eruption Depicted in the Chauvet-Pont d'Arc Cave (Ardèche, France)? *PLoS ONE. 11*(1): e0146621. https://doi.org/10.1371/journal.pone.0146621

North Dakota Information Technology contributors (2023). Definition of Information Technology. *North Dakota Information Technology.* Retrieved Sep 4, 2023. https://www.ndit.nd.gov/standards/definition-information-technology#

NZ History contributors (2023, Apr 27). Women and the vote. *NZ History.* https://nzhistory.govt.nz/politics/womens-suffrage

O'Brien P. (2008). Global history. *Making History.* https://archives.history.ac.uk/makinghistory/resources/articles/global_history.html

OHIO History Connection contributors (2021, July 6). How History is More Than "The Facts". *OHIO History Connection.* Accessed on 10/19/2023. https://www.ohiohistory.org/how-history-is-more-than-the-facts/

Olmstead A. L. & Rhode P. W. (2001). Reshaping the Landscape: The Impact and Diffusion of the Tractor in American Agriculture, 1910-1960. *The Journal of Economic History, 61*(3): 663–698. http://www.jstor.org/stable/2698132

Olstein Diego (2014). Thinking History Globally. *Palgrave Macmillan; 2015th edition (November 4, 2014)*

Open Culture contributors (2018, Oct 23). How an 18th-Century Monk Invented the First Electronic Instrument. *Open Culture.* https://www.openculture.com/2018/10/18th-century-monk-invented-first-electronic-instrument.html

Oppenheim Adela (2019, February). Egypt in the Middle Kingdom (ca. 2030–1650 B.C.). *The Metropolitan Museum of Art.* https://www.metmuseum.org/toah/hd/mking/hd_mking.htm

O'Toole Kit (2021, Dec 15). 'Rocket 88': One of The Pioneering Songs of Rock. *Culture Sonar.* https://www.culturesonar.com/rocket-88-one-of-the-pioneering-songs-of-rock/

Our World in Data contributors (2023a). Global fossil fuel consumption. *Our World in Data.* Retrieved Sep 4, 2023. https://ourworldindata.org/grapher/global-fossil-fuel-consumption

Our World in Data contributors (2023b). Life expectancy 1770 to 2021. *Our World in Data.* Retrieved Sep 4, 2023. https://ourworldindata.org/grapher/life-expectancy

Our World in Data contributors (2023c). Gender ratio for average years of schooling. *Our World in Data.* Retrieved Sep 4, 2023. https://ourworldindata.org/grapher/gender-ratios-for-mean-years-of-schooling

Oxford Languages contributors (2023). English Dictionary. *Oxford Languages.* Retrieved Sep 10, 2023. https://languages.oup.com/research/oxford-english-dictionary/#

Oxford Learner's Dictionaries contributors (2023a). Anthropology. *Oxford Learner's Dictionaries.* Retrieved on September 2, 2023. https://www.oxfordlearnersdictionaries.com/us/definition/american_english/anthropology#

Oxford Learner's Dictionaries contributors (2023b). Taxonomy. *Oxford Learner's Dictionaries.* Retrieved Sep 6, 2023. https://www.oxfordlearnersdictionaries.com/us/definition/english/taxonomy

Oxford Learner's Dictionaries contributors (2023c). Domain. Retrieved Sep 6, 2023. *Oxford Learner's Dictionaries.* https://www.oxfordlearnersdictionaries.com/us/definition/english/domain?

Oxford Learner's Dictionaries contributors (2023d). History. *Oxford Learner's Dictionaries.* Retrieved Dec 8, 2023. https://www.oxfordlearnersdictionaries.com/us/definition/english/history

Panov AD (2005). Scaling law of the biological evolution and the hypothesis of the self-consistent galaxy origin of life. *Adv Space Res, 36*(2): 220–225. https://doi.org/10.1016/j.asr.2005.03.001

Paris HS. (2015, August). Origin and emergence of the sweet dessert watermelon, Citrullus lanatus. *Ann Bo,. 116*(2):133-48. https://pubmed.ncbi.nlm.nih.gov/26141130/

Parry R. & Harald T. (2021). Ancient Ethical Theory. *The Stanford Encyclopedia of*

Philosophy (Fall 2021 Edition), Edward N. Zalta (ed.).
https://plato.stanford.edu/entries/ethics-ancient/
Partington J.R. (1998). A History of Greek Fire and Gunpowder. The *Johns Hopkins University Press (November 27, 1998*
Pearsall DM (2008). Plant domestication and the shift to agriculture in the Andes. In The Handbook of South American Archaeology (eds H Silverman, WH Isbell). *Springer; 1st ed. 2008. Corr. 2nd printing 2008 edition*
Penn Museum contributors (2023). The Games. *Penn Museum.* https://www.penn.museum/sites/olympics/olympicorigins.shtml
Per J. & Sui T. (2017). How Water Influences Our Lives. *Springer; 1st ed*
Pepelasis A. A. et al. (2023). Tariff. *Encyclopedia Britannica.* Accessed on 07/28/2023. https://www.britannica.com/money/topic/tariff
Petram L. (Author), Richards L. (Translator) (2014). The World's First Stock Exchange. *Columbia Business School Publishing; Illustrated edition (May 27, 2014)*
Pharaoh.se contributors (2023). The Nineteenth Dynasty of Ancient Egypt Dates: 1292-1190 BC. *Pharaoh.se.* Retrieved Sep 4, 2023. https://pharaoh.se/dynasty-XIX
Pinkard Terry (2017). Does History Make Sense?: Hegel on the Historical Shapes of Justice. *Harvard University Press (February 27, 2017)*
Piperno D. R. et al. (2009, Mar 31). Starch grain and phytolith evidence for early ninth millennium B.P. maize from the Central Balsas River Valley, Mexico. *PNAS, 106* (13): 5019-5024. https://www.pnas.org/doi/10.1073/pnas.0812525106
Plato (2013). LAWS By Plato -Project Gutenberg. Translated By Benjamin Jowett. *The Project Gutenberg EBook of Laws.* 2013. https://www.gutenberg.org/files/1750/1750-h/1750-h.htm
Pöhlmann E. & West M. L. (2001). Documents of Ancient Greek Music. *Oxford University Press*
Pomeranz Kenneth (2001). The Great Divergence: China, Europe, and the Making of the Modern World Economy. *Princeton University Press*
Popper Karl (1935). Logik der Forschung. *Verlag von Julius Springer, Vienna, Austria* [English edition - Karl Popper (2002). The Logic of Scientific Discovery (Routledge Classics). *Routledge; 2nd edition*]
Popper Karl R. (2020). The Open Society and Its Enemies. *Princeton University Press (September 15, 2020)*
Powell E. A. (2023). Telling Tales in Proto-Indo-European. *Archaeology.* Retrieved Sep 10, 2023. https://www.archaeology.org/exclusives/articles/1302-proto-indo-european-schleichers-fable#
Prakash Tara (2019, February). Egypt in the Old Kingdom (ca. 2649–2130 B.C.). *The Metropolitan Museum of Art.* https://www.metmuseum.org/toah/hd/oking/hd_oking.htm
Press G. (2013, May 9). A Very Short History Of Big Data. *Forbes.* https://www.forbes.com/sites/gilpress/2013/05/09/a-very-short-history-of-big-

data/?sh=64cca50f65a1

Price M. (2022, Sep 7). World's oldest amputation: Foot removed 31,000 years ago—without modern antibiotics or painkillers. *Science.* https://www.science.org/content/article/world-s-oldest-amputation-foot-removed-31-000-years-ago-without-modern-antibiotics-or

Pyrgies Joanna (2021, July 3). War and peace in the Standard of Ur. *Archaeotravel.eu.* https://archaeotravel.eu/war-and-peace-in-the-standard-of-ur/

Quirke S. (2004). Egyptian Literature: 1800 BC, Questions and Readings. *Golden House Publications, 2004*

Radivojević M. & Kuzmanović-Cvetković J. (2014, January). Copper minerals and archaeometallurgical materials from the Vinča culture sites of Belovode and Pločnik: overview of the evidence and new data. *Starinar. 2014(64):7-30.* https://www.researchgate.net/publication/273312957_Copper_minerals_and_archaeometallurgical_materials_from_the_Vinca_culture_sites_of_Belovode_and_Plocnik_Overview_of_the_evidence_and_new_data

Radivojević M. & Roberts B. W. (2021). Chapter 52 Balkan metallurgy in a Eurasian context in Miljana Radivojević et al. (eds) The Rise of Metallurgy in Eurasia: Evolution, Organisation and Consumption of Early Metal in the Balkans. *Archaeopress*

Rahmstorf L. (2006). In Search of the Earliest Balance Weights, Scales and Weighing Systems from the East Mediterranean, the Near and Middle East. in 'Weights in context. Bronze Age weighing systems of Eastern Mediterranean: chronology, typology, material and archaeological contexts. Proceedings of the International Colloquium, Rome 22–24 November 2004, eds. M. E. Alberti, E. Ascalone & L. Peyronel, Studi e Materiali 13, *Rome: Istituto Italiano di Numismatica,* 2006, 9-45

Railton D. (2018, May 31). Are humans still evolving? *Medical News Today.* https://www.medicalnewstoday.com/articles/321942

RAND Corporation contributors (2023). Cyber Warfare. *RAND Corporation.* Retrieved 07/25/2023. https://www.rand.org/topics/cyber-Warfare.html

Raspe Rudolph Erich (2015). The surprising adventures of Baron Munchausen. *CreateSpace Independent Publishing Platform (February 25, 2015), New Edition*

Ratliff E. (2020, June 16). We Can Protect the Economy From Pandemics. Why Didn't We? Wired. https://www.wired.com/story/nathan-wolfe-global-economic-fallout-pandemic-insurance

Razifard H. et al. (2020, April). Genomic Evidence for Complex Domestication History of the Cultivated Tomato in Latin America. *Molecular Biology and Evolution,* 37(4): 1118–1132. https://doi.org/10.1093/molbev/msz297

Rebecca (2022, Nov 30). Electromechanical Relay – History of The Electromechanical Relay. *History Computer.* https://history-computer.com/electromechanical-relay-history-of-the-electromechanical-relay/

Reedy C. (2017, Oct 16). Kurzweil Claims That the Singularity Will Happen by 2045. *Futurism*. https://futurism.com/kurzweil-claims-that-the-singularity-will-happen-by-2045

Rehm J. & Biggs B. (2021, Dec 23). The four fundamental forces of nature. *Space.com*. https://www.space.com/four-fundamental-forces.html

Renger J. M. (2023, Aug 25). Hammurabi. *Encyclopædia Britannica*. https://www.britannica.com/biography/Hammurabi

REN (2014, September). Faith Forum: Is humanity going in the right direction?. *Reno Gazette Journal*. https://www.rgj.com/story/life/2014/09/20/humanity-going-right-direction/15946917

Rens Bod (2016). A New History of the Humanities: The Search for Principles and Patterns from Antiquity to the Present Reprint Edition. *Oxford University Press; Reprint edition*

Rhodes M. (1961). An Analysis of Creativity. *The Phi Delta Kappan*. 42 (7):.305–310, https://www.jstor.org/stable/20342603

Richardson K. et al. (2023). Earth beyond six of nine planetary boundaries. *Science Advances*. 9(37). https://www.science.org/doi/10.1126/sciadv.adh2458.

Ritchie H. (2022, Nov 30). How many species are there? *Our World in Data*. https://ourworldindata.org/how-many-species-are-there

Ritchie H. & Roser M. (2022). Energy mix. *Our World in Data*. https://ourworldindata.org/energy-mix

Ritchie H. et al. (2022). Fossil Fuels. *Our World in Data*. https://ourworldindata.org/fossil-fuels

Ritchie H. et al. (2023). Population Growth. *Our World in Data*. https://ourworldindata.org/population-growth

Robinson D. K. (2020, Mar 31). Gustav Theodor Fechner: Psychophysics and Natural Science. *Oxford Research Encyclopedias. Psychology*. https://doi.org/10.1093/acrefore/9780190236557.013.487

Robinson K. (1998). All our futures: Creativity, culture, education (PDF). *National Advisory Committee on Creative and Cultural Education*. http://sirkenrobinson.com/pdf/allourfutures.pdf

Rolt L. T. C. (2022, Apr 18). Richard Trevithick. *Encyclopaedia Britannica*. https://www.britannica.com/biography/Richard-Trevithick

Roser M. et al. (2023). Life Expectancy. *Our World in Data*. Retrieved Sep 4, 2023. https://ourworldindata.org/life-expectancy

Roser M. et al. (2019). World Population Growth, revision in May 2019. *Our World in Data*, https://ourworldindata.org/world-population-growth

Roskin M. G. (2023). Political Science. *Encyclopaedia Britannica*. https://www.britannica.com/topic/political-science/Enduring-debates-in-political-science

Rotenstreich N. (1971). The Idea of Historical Progress and Its Assumptions. *JSTOR. History and Theory*, 10(2): 197–221. https://doi.org/10.2307/2504292

Royal Institution contributors (2023). Michael Faraday's generator. *The Royal*

Institution. https://www.rigb.org/explore-science/explore/collection/michael-faradays-generator

Rubinson Karen S. (1990). The textiles from Pazyryk. *Penn Museum. 32*(1). https://www.penn.museum/sites/expedition/the-textiles-from-pazyryk/

Russo E. (2003, January). Special Report: The birth of biotechnology. *Nature. 421* (6921): 456–457. https://www.nature.com/articles/nj6921-456a

Rutherford Adam (2019). The Book of Humans: A Brief History of Culture, Sex, War and the Evolution of Us. *W&N (May 16, 2019)*

Ryan Tim (2023). A Brief History Of Western Union Money Transfer Services. Street Directory. Accessed on 07/28/2023. https://www.streetdirectory.com/travel_guide/161051/money_management/a_brief_history_of_western_union_money_transfer_services.html#

Saaty R.W. (1987). The analytic hierarchy process—what it is and how it is used. *Mathematical Modelling. 9(3-5):* 161-176. https://doi.org/10.1016/0270-0255(87)90473-8

Sack H. (2014, May 11). The very first Printed Book – The Diamond Sutra. *SciHi Blog.* http://scihi.org/diamond-sutra/

Sagan Carl (1986). The Dragons of Eden: Speculations on the Evolution of Human Intelligence. *Ballantine Books; Reprint edition (December 12, 1986)*

Said-Metwaly Sameh et al. (2017). Approaches to Measuring Creativity: A Systematic Literature Review. *Creativity. Theories – Research - Applications, 4*(2): 238-275. https://doi.org/10.1515/ctra-2017-0013

Samuel A. (2017, Feb 21). Meet Alan Emtage, the Black Technologist Who Invented ARCHIE, the First Internet Search Engine. *JSTOR Daily.* https://daily.jstor.org/alan-emtage-first-internet-search-engine/

Sand P. H. (2018, July 27). Mesopotamia 2550 B.C.: The Earliest Boundary Water Treaty. *Global Journal of Archaeology and Anthropology.* 5(4):555669. https://www.researchgate.net/publication/328256971_Mesopotamia_2550_BC_The_Earliest_Boundary_Water_Treaty

Sandberg A. & Bostrom N. (2008). Global Catastrophic Risks Survey, Technical Report #2008-1. *Future of Humanity Institute, Oxford University: pp. 1-5.* https://www.fhi.ox.ac.uk/reports/2008-1.pdf

Sander van der Leeuw (2016, July 8). Complex Systems Theory, Sustainability, and Innovation. *Global Institute of Sustainability, Arizona State University's Julie Ann Wrigley Global.* https://sustainability.asu.edu/media/wrigley-lecture-series/complex-systems-theory/

San Diego House of Hungary contributors (2023). Foregoers Miksa Déri, Ottó Bláthy, Károly Zipernowsky. *San Diego House of Hungary.* https://sdmagyar.org/foregoers/miksa-deri-otto-blathy-karoly-zipernowsky/

Sansone D. (1985). The Date of Herodotus' Publication. *Illinois Classical Studies, 10*(1): 1–9. http://www.jstor.org/stable/23062529

Satapathy C. (1999). Did India Give the World Its First Customs Tariff? *Economic and Political Weekly, 34*(8), 449–451. http://www.jstor.org/stable/4407669

Schafer E. D. (2023). Digital technology. *Encyclopedia.com*. Retrieved Sep 5, 2023. https://www.encyclopedia.com/history/dictionaries-thesauruses-pictures-and-press-releases/digital-technology#

Schatzkin Paul (1977). Who invented what -- and when?? *The Farnsworth Chronicle*. http://www.farnovision.com/chronicles/tfc-who_invented_what.html

Schick T. (1986). Perishable Remains from the Nahal Hemar Cave. *Mitekufat Haeven: Journal of the Israel Prehistoric Society / מתקופת האבן י"ט* (1986): 95-97. http://www.jstor.org/stable/23373152

Schier A. (2023, Feb 13). Amazon's Driverless Zoox Taxi Hits The Streets Of Foster City. *Patch*. https://patch.com/california/sanmateo/amazons-driverless-zoox-taxi-hits-streets-foster-city

Schinkel, A. (2006, June). The Object of History. *Essays in Philosophy*, 7(2). https://research.vu.nl/ws/portalfiles/portal/2230641/197407.pdf

Schliemann Heinrich et al. (1885). Tiryns: The prehistoric palace of the kings of Tiryns, the results of the latest excavations. *Scribner's Sons*

Schneider B. R. (2023a). Biological weapons in history. *Encyclopaedia Britannica*. Retrieved 07/25/2023. https://www.britannica.com/technology/biological-weapon/Biological-weapons-in-history

Schneider B. R. (2023b). Chemical weapon. *Encyclopaedia Britannica*. Retrieved 07/25/2023. https://www.britannica.com/technology/chemical-weapon

Schnurmann C. (2003, September).' Wherever profit leads us, to every sea and shore...': the VOC, the WIC, and Dutch methods of globalization in the seventeenth century. Renaissance Studies. 17(3): 474-493. https://www.jstor.org/stable/24413463

Scholten A. (2016). International Law Aspects of Forced Deportations and Expulsions. *Congress on Urban Issues, Malaga*. https://www.aacademica.org/andrew.scholten/9.pdf

Schoppert S. (2017, Jan 8). Six of the Deadliest Proxy Wars of the Cold War. *History Collection*. https://historycollection.com/six-deadliest-proxy-wars-cold-war/3/

ScienceDaily contributors (2004, Apr 9). Oldest Known Evidence Of Cat Taming Found In Cyprus. *ScienceDaily*. https://www.sciencedaily.com/releases/2004/04/040409092827.htm

Science Museum contributors (2018, Nov 9). Meet LEO, the world's first business computer. *Science Museum*. https://www.sciencemuseum.org.uk/objects-and-stories/meet-leo-worlds-first-business-computer#

SciNews (2019, Dec 11). Earliest hunting scene in prehistoric art. *YouTube*. https://www.youtube.com/watch?v=UphEiocyvN0

Science Reference Section, Library of Congress (2022, Feb 22). Who is credited with inventing the telephone? *Library of Congress*. https://www.loc.gov/everyday-mysteries/technology/item/who-is-credited-with-inventing-the-telephone

Sebastian P. et al. (2010, July 23). Cucumber (Cucumis sativus) and melon (C. melo) have numerous wild relatives in Asia and Australia, and the sister species of melon is from Australia. *PNAS, 107*(32): 14269-14273. https://doi.org/10.1073/pnas.1005338107

Sempa F. P. (2022, January). Spengler, Toynbee, Burnham, and the Decline of the West. *Kirk Center.* .https://kirkcenter.org/essays/spengler-toynbee-burnham-and-the-decline-of-the-west/

Senft T. M. (2023, July 18). Videoconferencing communications. *Britannica.* https://www.britannica.com/technology/videoconferencing

Sexton E. (2023). Asymmetrical Warfare. *Encyclopaedia Britannica.* Retrieved 07/25/2023. https://www.britannica.com/topic/asymmetrical-Warfare

Shambaugh G. (2023). Economic Warfare. *Encyclopaedia Britannica.* Retrieved 07/25/2023. https://www.britannica.com/topic/economic-Warfare

Shannon C. E. (1948, July). A Mathematical Theory of Communication. *Bell System Technical Journal, 27*(3): 379-423. https://doi.org/10.1002/j.1538-7305.1948.tb01338.x

Sharp Tim (2022, Feb 28). The world's first commercial airline. *Space.* https://www.space.com/16657-worlds-first-commercial-airline-the-greatest-moments-in-flight.html

Shaw I. (Editor) (2004). The Oxford History of Ancient Egypt. *Oxford University Press; New Ed edition (February 19, 2004)*

Shchelin Pavel (2022). Павел Щелин. Теория Войны: Почему Путин ведет два самых разрушительных типа войны против Украины. *ХВИЛЯ.* 22.03.2022. https://hvylya.net/analytics/249398-teoriya-voyny-pochemu-putin-vedet-dva-samyh-razrushitelnyh-tipa-voyny-protiv-ukrainy [Shchelin Pavel. War Theory: Why Putin is waging two of the most devastating types of war against Ukraine. *HVILYA.* 22.03.2022. https://hvylya.net/analytics/249398-teoriya-voyny-pochemu-putin-vedet-dva-samyh-razrushitelnyh-tipa-voyny-protiv-ukrainy - in Russian]

Schleck J. & Sen A. (2017). Introduction: Alternative Histories of the East India Company. *Journal for Early Modern Cultural Studies, 17*(3): 1–9. https://www.jstor.org/stable/90020547

Shepherd D. G. (1990). Historical development of the windmill. *OSTI.gov.* https://www.osti.gov/servlets/purl/6342767

Shryock A., Smail D.L. (2011). Deep History: The Architecture of Past and Present. *University of California Press, First Edition*

Sightseeing Tours Italy contributors (2022). Circus Maximus – Rome's Original Stadium. *Sightseeing Tours Italy.* https://www.sightseeingtoursitaly.com/tips-articles/circus-maximus-romes-original-stadium/

Silver D. et al. (2017, Oct 19). Mastering the game of Go without human knowledge. *Nature. 550*(7676): 354–359. https://www.nature.com/articles/nature24270

Silverberg R. (1964). Great Adventures in Archaeology. *Dial Press*

Simmons J. & Wolfgram R. Zack "Doughnut" (2014, Mar 6). Natural resources during the Industrial Revolution. *Prezi*. https://prezi.com/nuou4gww7bfx/natural-resources-during-the-industrial-revolution/

Sinn F. & Nekoei A. (2021, May 27). The origin of the gender gap. *CERP*. https://cepr.org/voxeu/columns/origin-gender-gap

Slobodskoy Fr. Seraphim (2023). Apostolic Council in Jerusalem. *Orthodox Church of the Mother of God*. Retrieved Sep 3, 2023. https://churchmotherofgod.org/salvation-history/new-life-church-history/2448-apostolic-council-in-jerusalem.html

Small A.H. (Jan 2015 - Jan 2016). "Hear My Voice". National Museum of American History. Retrieved Sep 4, 2023. https://americanhistory.si.edu/documentsgallery/exhibitions/hear-my-voice/4.html

Smith G. (2008). Newton's Philosophiae Naturalis Principia Mathematica. *The Stanford Encyclopedia of Philosophy*. https://plato.stanford.edu/entries/newton-philosophy/

Smith M. R. (1973). John H. Hall, Simeon North, and the Milling Machine: The Nature of Innovation among Antebellum Arms Makers. *Technology and Culture*, 14(4): 573–591. https://doi.org/10.2307/3102444

Smithsonian Institution (2022, July 7). Climate Effects on Human Evolution. *Smithsonian National Museum of Natural History*. https://humanorigins.si.edu/research/climate-and-human-evolution/climate-effects-human-evolution

Smoot S.O. (2018, Winter). Notes on the Satire of the Trades. Middle Egyptian texts, (NMC1202). Winter 2018 Semester, *Academia. pp. 1-14*

Snooks G.D. (2019). Is Singularity a Scientific Concept, or the Construct of Metaphysical Historicism? Implications for Big History. *IGDS. Working Papers, No. 17 (February)*: 1–37. https://www.researchgate.net/publication/331113459_Is_Singularity_a_Scientific_Concept_or_the_Construct_of_Metaphysical_Historicism_Implications_for_Big_History_REVISED_EDITION

Solmsen F. (1936). The Background of Plato's Theology. *Transactions and Proceedings of the American Philological Association, 67*: 208. https://doi.org/10.2307/283196

Songfacts contributors (2022a). I got the blues by Antonio Maggio. *Songfacts*. https://www.songfacts.com/facts/antonio-maggio/i-got-the-blues

Songfacts contributors (2022b). You Belong To Me by Jo Stafford. *Songfacts*. https://www.songfacts.com/facts/jo-stafford/you-belong-to-me

Sorokin Pitirim A. (1927, September). A Survey of the Cyclical Conceptions of Social and Historical Process. *Social Forces, 6*(1): 28-40. https://academic.oup.com/sf/article-abstract/6/1/28/2231400

South Tyrol Museum of Archaeology contributors (2016a). Ötzi the Iceman. *South*

Tyrol Museum of Archaeology. https://www.iceman.it/en/the-iceman/

South Tyrol Museum of Archaeology contributors (2016b). The Iceman the oldest glasier mummy. *South Tyrol Museum of Archaeology.* http://www.iceman.it/wp-content/uploads/2016/09/TheIceman-MP-engl.pdf

Spar I. (2009, April). Gilgamesh. *The Metropolitan Museum of Art.* https://www.metmuseum.org/toah/hd/gilg/hd_gilg.htm

Sparavigna A. C. (2011). Ancient concrete works. *Arxiv.org.* https://arxiv.org/ftp/arxiv/papers/1110/1110.5230.pdf

Spector R. H., The Editors of Encyclopaedia Britannica (2023). French rule ended, Vietnam divided. *Encyclopaedia Britannica.* Retrieved 07/25/2023. https://www.britannica.com/event/Vietnam-War/French-rule-ended-Vietnam-divided

Spencer J. (2023). History Of The Cell Phone (1973 to 2023). *Practically Networked.* Retrieved Sep 4, 2023. https://www.practicallynetworked.com/history-of-the-cell-phone/

Spengler Oswald (2020). The Decline of the West. Two Volumes in One Paperback, *Cosimo Classics (December 9, 2020)*

Sperling D. & Gordon D. (2009). Two billion cars: driving toward sustainability. *Oxford University Press, New York*

Spier F. (2008). Big history: the emergence of a novel interdisciplinary approach. *Interdisciplinary Science Reviews. 33*(2): 141-152. https://www.tandfonline.com/doi/abs/10.1179/030801808X259754

Spitzer J. & Zaslaw N. (2005, Sep 1). The Birth of the Orchestra: History of an Institution, 1650-1815. *Oxford University Press*

Staal J.F. (1965, April). Euclid and Pāṇini. *Philosophy East and West, 15* (2): 99–116. https://www.jstor.org/stable/i260801

Stacker contributors (2022). History of hip-hop. *Stacker.* https://stacker.com/stories/5482/history-hip-hop

Stada Media contributors (2022). Video Production vs Film Production: What Is The Difference? *Stada Media.* https://stadamedia.co.uk/blog/video-production-vs-film-production-what-is-the-difference

Stalker P. J. (2005). Gaming In Art: A Case Study Of Two Examples Of The Artistic Appropriation Of Computer Games And The Mapping Of Historical Trajectories Of 'Art Games' Versus Mainstream Computer Games. *University of the Witwatersrand. Johannesburg.* http://ljudmila.org/~selectparks/dl/PippaStalker_GamingInArt.pdf

Statista contributors (2023a). Number of mobile phone users worldwide from 2015 to 2020. *Statista.* Retrieved Sep 5, 2023. https://www.statista.com/statistics/274774/forecast-of-mobile-phone-users-worldwide/

Statista contributors (2023b). Total number of US states, at the end of each year, since the Declaration of Independence in 1776. *Statista.* Retrieved Sep 5, 2023. https://www.statista.com/statistics/1043617/number-us-states-by-year/

Stephens Mitchell (1991). History of Television. *From Grolier Encyclopedia of Knowledge* (Volumes 1-20 - Complete Set.
https://stephens.hosting.nyu.edu/History%20of%20Television%20page.html

Stern E. M. & Schlick-Nolte B. (1994). Early Glass of the Ancient World 1600 B.C A.D. 50. *Hatje Cantz Publishers.* https://www.hatjecantz.de/early-glass-of-the-ancient-world-671-1.html

Stevi Jackson (2016, Mar 1). Women's studies, gender studies and feminism. *Discover Society.* Articles, Issue 30.
https://archive.discoversociety.org/2016/03/01/womens-studies-gender-studies-and-feminism/

Stiner M. C. et al. (2022, Jan 18). An endemic pathway to sheep and goat domestication at Aşıklı Höyük (Central Anatolia, Turkey). *PNAS, 119*(4). https://www.pnas.org/doi/10.1073/pnas.2110930119

Stix Gary (2014, Sep 1). What Makes Humans Different Than Any Other Species. *Scientific American.* https://www.scientificamerican.com/article/what-makes-humans-different-than-any-other-species

Stribling J. et al. (2008, December). Data quality, performance, and uncertainty in taxonomic identification for biological assessments. *Journal of the North American Benthological Society, 27*(4):906-919.
https://www.researchgate.net/publication/216200337_Data_quality_performance_and_uncertainty_in_taxonomic_identification_for_biological_assessments

StudySmarter contributors (2023). Digital Technology. *StudySmarter.* Retrieved Sep 5, 2023. https://www.studysmarter.co.uk/explanations/business-studies/business-development/digital-technology/

Sturgeon W. et al. (1824). No. III. Improved electro-magnetic apparatus. *Transactions of the Society, instituted at London, for the Encouragement of Arts, Manufactures, and Commerce, 43*: 37–52. http://www.jstor.org/stable/41325678

Swamy K.R.M. (2023, Feb 25). Origin, distribution, taxonomy, botanical description, genetics, genetic diversity and breeding of cucumber (Cucumis sativus L.). *International Journal of Development Research, 13*(02): 61542-61559. https://doi.org/10.37118/ijdr.26219.02.2023

Swatman R. (2015, Aug 19). 1971: First Ever Email. *Guiness World Records.* https://www.guinnessworldrecords.com/news/60at60/2015/8/1971-first-ever-email-392973

Synnott J. et al. (2015). A review of the polygraph: history, methodology and current status. *Crime Psychology Review,* 1(1): 59-83. https://www.tandfonline.com/doi/full/10.1080/23744006.2015.1060080

Szabadvary F. (1985, Aug 5). The history of chemical laboratory equipment. Invited lecture delivered at the XVIIth International Congress of History of Science, Berkeley, USA. *Periodica Polytechnica (Budapest University of Technology and Economics).* https://core.ac.uk/reader/236622340

Tainter J. A. (1990). The Collapse of Complex Societies (New Studies in

Archaeology). *Cambridge University Press; Reprint edition (March 30, 1990)*

Tanenbaum M. et al. (2023, Jan 19). Mass production. *Britannica.* https://www.britannica.com/technology/mass-production

Tankard J. W. (1972). Public Opinion Polling by Newspapers in the Presidential Election Campaign of 1824. *Journalism Quarterly, 49* (2): 361–365. https://journals.sagepub.com/doi/abs/10.1177/107769907204900219

Taplin O. & Podlecki A. J. (2022, Dec 06). Aeschylus Greek dramatist. *Encyclopaedia Britannica.* https://www.britannica.com/biography/Aeschylus-Greek-dramatist

Teilhard P. (2008). The phenomenon of man. *Harper Perennial Modern Classics, 1st edition*

Thalmann O. et al. (2013, Nov 15). Complete mitochondrial genomes of ancient canids suggest a European origin of domestic dogs. *Science, 342*(6160):871-4. https://pubmed.ncbi.nlm.nih.gov/24233726/

The Ancient Egypt Site contributors (2014, Jan 26). 1st Intermediate Period (2150-2040). *The Ancient Egypt Site.* http://www.ancient-egypt.org/history/1st-intermediate-period/index.html

The Ancient Egypt Site contributors (2014, Sep 25). 3rd Dynasty (2650-2575). *The Ancient Egypt Site.* http://www.ancient-egypt.org/history/early-dynastic-period/3rd-dynasty/index.html

The Ancient Egypt site contributors (2014, Aug 19). 12th Dynasty (1991-1783). *The Ancient Egypt site.* http://www.ancient-egypt.org/history/middle-kingdom/12th-dynasty/index.html

The Aerospace Corporation contributors (2023). Brief History of GPS. *The Aerospace Corporation. Aerospace. org.* Retrieved Sep 3, 2023. https://aerospace.org/article/brief-history-gps

The Archeologist contributors (2021, Dec 17). Ptolematic Egypt: Ancient Egypt under Greek Rule. *The Archaeologist.* https://www.thearchaeologist.org/blog/ptolemaic-egypt-ancient-egypt-under-greek-control#:~:text=The%20Ptolemaic%20Kingdom%20was%20an,Cleopatra%20VII%20in%2030%20BC

The Art Story contributors (2010). Performance Art Movement Overview. *The Art Story.* https://www.theartstory.org/movement/performance-art/

The Britannica Dictionary contributors (2023). Development. The Britannica Dictionary. Accessed 20 Oct. 2023. https://www.britannica.com/dictionary/development

The British Museum contributors (2022). Object: The Standard of Ur. *The British Museum.* https://www.britishmuseum.org/collection/object/W_1928-1010-3

The British Library contributors (2023a). Rigveda. *The British Library.* Retrieved Sep 3. 2023. https://www.bl.uk/collection-items/rig-veda#

The British Library contributors (2023b). Collection items: Gutenberg Bible. *British Library.* Retrieved Sep 4, 2023. https://www.bl.uk/collection-

items/gutenberg-
bible#:~:text=The%20Gutenberg%20Bible%20was%20printed,vellum%20and
%2036%20on%20paper

The British Library contributors (2023c). Old English. *British Library*. Retrieved Sep 10, 2023. https://www.bl.uk/medieval-literature/articles/old-english#

The British Library contributors (2023d). Middle English. *British Library*. Retrieved Sep 10, 2023. https://www.bl.uk/medieval-literature/articles/middle-english#

The British Museum contributors (2023a). Papyrus; hieratic literary text: Teaching of Khety (the so-called "Satire on Trades"). *The British Museum*. Retrieved Sep 4, 2023. https://www.britishmuseum.org/collection/object/Y_EA10182-4

The editors of Archaeology (2016, May/June). The World's Oldest Writing. *Archaeology*. https://www.archaeology.org/issues/213-1605/features/4326-cuneiform-the-world-s-oldest-writing

The Editors of Encyclopaedia Britannica (1999). Automaton. *Encyclopedia Britannica*. Retrieved 06/10/2024. https://www.britannica.com/technology/automaton

The Editors of Encyclopaedia Britannica (2019). Ebers papyrus. *Encyclopedia Britannica*, 7 Aug. 2019. Retrieved 07/25/2022. https://www.britannica.com/topic/Ebers-papyrus

The Editors of Encyclopaedia Britannica (2020). Council of Jerusalem. *Encyclopaedia Britannica*. https://www.britannica.com/event/Council-of-Jerusalem

The Editors of Encyclopaedia Britannica (2022a). Tarquin king of Rome [616-578 BC]. *Encyclopaedia Britannica*. Retrieved 11/28/2022. https://www.britannica.com/biography/Tarquin-king-of-Rome-616-578-BC

The Editors of Encyclopaedia Britannica (2022b). Cai Lun. *Encyclopaedia Britannica*. Retrieved 11/28/2022. https://www.britannica.com/biography/Cai-Lun

The Editors of Encyclopaedia Britannica (2022c). Mule mammal. *Encyclopaedia Britannica*. Retrieved 11/28/2022. https://www.britannica.com/animal/mule-mammal

The Editors of Encyclopaedia Britannica (2022d). John Wesley Hyatt American inventor. *Encyclopaedia Britannica*. Retrieved 11/28/2022. https://www.britannica.com/biography/John-Wesley-Hyatt

The Editors of Encyclopaedia Britannica (2022e). Joseph Swan English physicist and chemist. *Encyclopaedia Britannica*. Retrieved 11/28/2022. https://www.britannica.com/biography/Joseph-Wilson-Swan

The Editors of Encyclopaedia Britannica (2022f). Kinesiology. *Encyclopedia Britannica*. Retrieved 11/28/2022. https://www.britannica.com/science/kinesiology

The Editors of Encyclopaedia Britannica (2023a). Imhotep. *Encyclopedia Britannica*. Retrieved 01/20/2023 https://www.britannica.com/biography/Imhotep

The Editors of Encyclopaedia Britannica (2023b). Thales of Miletus. *Encyclopaedia Britannica*. Retrieved 01/25/2023. https://www.britannica.com/biography/Thales-of-Miletus

The Editors of Encyclopaedia Britannica (2023c). Blood Libel. *Encyclopaedia Britannica*. Retrieved 01/20/2023. https://www.britannica.com/topic/blood-libel

The Editors of Encyclopaedia Britannica (2023d). Colosseum. *Encyclopaedia Britannica*. Retrieved 01/20/2023. https://www.britannica.com/topic/Colosseum

The Editors of Encyclopaedia Britannica (2023e). Thomas Savery. *Encyclopaedia Britannica*. Retrieved 01/20/2023. https://www.britannica.com/biography/Thomas-Savery

The Editors of Encyclopaedia Britannica (2023f). Alessandro Volta. *Encyclopaedia Britannica*. Retrieved 02/14/2023. https://www.britannica.com/biography/Alessandro-Volta

The Editors of Encyclopaedia Britannica (2023g). Ems telegram, *Encyclopaedia Britannica*. Retrieved 07/25/2023. https://www.britannica.com/event/Ems-telegram

The Editors of Encyclopaedia Britannica (2023h). Herodotus Greek historian. *Encyclopaedia Britannica*. https://www.britannica.com/biography/Herodotus-Greek-historian

The Editors of Encyclopædia Britannica (2023i). Corruption. *Encyclopædia Britannica*. https://www.britannica.com/topic/corruption-law

The Editors of Encyclopædia Britannica (2023j). Serfdom. *Encyclopædia Britannica*. https://www.britannica.com/money/topic/serfdom

The Editors of Encyclopaedia Britannica and Chmielewski K. (2023). The First Atomic Bombs Tested and Used During World War II. *Encyclopaedia Britannica*. Retrieved 07/25/2023. https://www.britannica.com/story/discover-more-about-the-first-atomic-bombs-tested-and-used-during-world-war-ii#

The Encyclopedia of World Problems contributors (2023). Radiological Warfare. *The Encyclopedia of World Problems*. Retrieved 07/25/2023. http://encyclopedia.uia.org/en/problem/radiological-Warfare

The Hard News Cafe contributors (2004, June 11). What's the gripe between 'hard' and 'soft' sciences? The debate rages on. *Utah State University*. https://www.usu.edu/today/story/whats-the-gripe-between-hard-and-soft-sciences-the-debate-rages-on#

The Kennedy Center contributors (2022). Hip Hop: A Culture of Vision and Voice. *The Kennedy Center*. https://www.kennedy-center.org/education/resources-for-educators/classroom-resources/media-and-interactives/media/hip-hop/hip-hop-a-culture-of-vision-and-voice./

The Metropolitan Opera contributors (2022). Obsessions with Orpheus. The Metropolitan Opera.

https://www.metopera.org/discover/education/educator-guides/eurydice/obsessions-with-orpheus/

TheMusicHistory contributors (2022). Pop Music History Facts and Timeline. *TheMusicHistory.com*. https://themusichistory.com/pop-music-history-facts-and-timeline.html

The National WWII Museum contributors (2020, Aug 6). The Most Fearsome Sight: The Atomic Bombing of Hiroshima. *The National WWII Museum*. https://www.nationalww2museum.org/war/articles/atomic-bomb-hiroshima

The Ohio State University contributors (2023). Real-World Relativity: The GPS Navigation System. *The Ohio State University*. Retrieved Sep 3, 2023. https://www.astronomy.ohio-state.edu/pogge.1/Ast162/Unit5/gps.html#

The World Bank contributors (2023a). Labor Force, female (% of total labor force). *The World Bank*. Retrieved Sep 4, 2023. https://data.worldbank.org/indicator/SL.TLF.TOTL.FE.ZS

The World Bank contributors (2023b). The State of Women's Legal Rights. Women, business and the law 2023. *The World Bank*. Retrieved Sep 4, 2023. https://wbl.worldbank.org/content/dam/sites/wbl/documents/2023/Chapter%201%20The%20State%20of%20Women%E2%80%99s%20Legal%20Rights.pdf

The World Bank contributors (2023c). Population, total - United States. *The World Bank*. Retrieved Sep 5, 2023. https://data.worldbank.org/indicator/SP.POP.TOTL?locations=US

The World Bank contributors (2023, Feb 28). Pace of Reform Toward Equal Rights for Women Falls to 20-Year Low. PRESS RELEASE NO: 2023/050/DEC. *The World Bank*. https://www.worldbank.org/en/news/press-release/2023/03/02/pace-of-reform-toward-equal-rights-for-women-falls-to-20-year-low#

The Siberian Times reporter (2016, Aug 23). World's oldest needle found in Siberian cave that stitches together human history. *The Siberian Times*. https://siberiantimes.com/science/casestudy/news/n0711-worlds-oldest-needle-found-in-siberian-cave-that-stitches-together-human-history/

Tromp J. (2016, Jan 20). Number of legal Go positions. *Git Hub*. https://tromp.github.io/go/legal.html

Troward T. (2007). The Creative Process In The Individual. *The Book Tree. January 1, 2007*

Thompson H. A. (1992). The Stoa of Attalos II in Athens. *Athens/Princeton: American School of Classical Studies at Athens*

TomiAhonen Consulting (2018, Dec 1). Excerpt from Report: 7th Mass Media in 2008. TomiAhonen Consulting. https://londoncalling.co/wp-content/uploads/TomiAhonenConsulting-7thMassMedia2008-ReportExcerpt.pdf

Torvich Victor (2021). Subsurface History of Humanity: Direction of History. *Independently published*

Torvich V.V. (2020a, January-March). Humankind as a system. Part 1. Slozhnyye

systemy [The complex systems], 1 (7): 61-72.
https://web.archive.org/web/20200925004940/https://thecomplexsystems.com/
wp-content/uploads/2020/07/Torvich-V.V..pdf

Torvich V.V. (2020b, April-June). Humankind as a system. Part 2. Slozhnyye
systemy [The complex systems], 2 (8): 42-59.
https://web.archive.org/web/20220401053646/https://thecomplexsystems.com/
wp-content/uploads/2020/10/ss-2-8-2020.pdf, p.42-59

Torvich V.V. (2020c, July-September). Торвич В.В. Человечество как система.
Часть 3. Сложные системы, 3 (36): 74-93. [Humankind as a system. Part 3.
Slozhnyye systemy [The complex systems], 3 (36): 74-93 - In Russian].
https://web.archive.org/web/20230211175809/https://thecomplexsystems.ru/w
p-content/uploads/2020/12/TorvichVV.pdf

Torvich V.V. (2021a, July-September). Торвич В.В. Модели системы
человечества. Сложные системы, 2 (39): 12-31. [Models of humankind
system. Slozhnyye systemy [The complex systems], 2 (39): 12-31 - In Russian].
https://web.archive.org/web/20230211175918/https://thecomplexsystems.ru/w
p-content/uploads/2021/06/Torvich-V.V..pdf

Torvich V.V. (2021b, October-December). Торвич В.В. Региональные модели
системы человечества. Часть 1. Сложные системы, 4 (41): 4-11. [Regional
models of humankind system. Part 1. Slozhnyye systemy [The complex
systems], 4 (41): 4-11 - In Russian].
https://web.archive.org/web/20220630140919/https://thecomplexsystems.ru/w
p-content/uploads/2022/01/Torvich-V.V..pdf

Totaro R. (2022, Mar 22). How elevators changed architecture. *Domus*.
https://www.domusweb.it/en/architecture/2022/03/08/how-elevators-
changed-architecture.html

Tupy M. L. (2013, October). Human Progress: Not Inevitable, Uneven, and
Indisputable. *CATO Institute.* https://www.cato.org/commentary/human-
progress-not-inevitable-uneven-indisputable

Tweney D. (2010, Aug 12). 1888: Road Trip! Berta Takes the Benz. *Wired.com*,
https://www.wired.com/2010/08/0812berta-benz-first-road-trip/

UNESCO World Heritage Centre contributors (2023). Bisotun. *UNESCO World
Heritage Centre.* https://whc.unesco.org/en/list/1222/#

United Nations contributors (2016). Identifying social inclusion and exclusion -
the United Nations Chapter 1. *United Nations.*
https://www.un.org/esa/socdev/rwss/2016/chapter1.pdf

United Nations contributors (2023a). Human Trafficking. *United Nations Office on
Drugs and Crime.* Retrieved Sep 3, 2023.
https://www.unodc.org/unodc/en/human-trafficking/human-trafficking.html

United Nations contributors (2023b). World Day Against Child Labour 12 June.
United Nations. Retrieved Sep 3, 2023.
https://www.un.org/en/observances/world-day-against-child-
labour/background#

United Nations contributors (2023c). Universal Declaration of Human Rights - the United Nations. *United Nations.* https://www.un.org/en/about-us/universal-declaration-of-human-rights#

University of Edinburgh contributors (2022). The Life of Dolly. *The University of Edinburgh.* https://dolly.roslin.ed.ac.uk/facts/the-life-of-dolly/index.html

University of Georgia contributors (2023). A Brief History of the Internet. *University System of Georgia.* Retrieved Sep2, 2023. https://www.usg.edu/galileo/skills/unit07/internet07_02.phtml#

University of Southampton contributors (2016, Feb 18). Eternal 5D data storage could record the history of humankind. *University of Southampton.* https://www.southampton.ac.uk/news/2016/02/5d-data-storage-update.page

UN News contributors (2022, Sep 18). Closing gender pay gaps is more important than ever. *UN News.* https://news.un.org/en/story/2022/09/1126901

Urquhart J. (2006, Jan 14). How Islam changed medicine: Ibn Sina (Avicenna) saw medicine and surgery as one. *BMJ. 332*(7533): 120. https://pubmed.ncbi.nlm.nih.gov/16410600/

US Census Bureau contributors (1999). Historical Estimates of World Population. *United States Census Bureau.* https://www.census.gov/data/tables/time-series/demo/international-programs/historical-est-worldpop.html

US Census Bureau contributors (2012). Total World Population - Census Bureau, Table 1331. Population and Population Change by Development Status:1950 to 2050. *US Census Bureau, Statistical Abstract of the United States.* ftp://ftp.census.gov/library/publications/2011/compendia/statab/131ed/tables/12s1329.pdf

US Department of Defense contributors (2002, Feb 12). News Transcript: Presenter Donald H. Rumsfeld, DoD News Briefing - Secretary Rumsfeld and Gen. Myers. *U.S. Department of Defense.* https://irp.fas.org/news/2002/02/dod021202.html

US Department of State contributors (2023a). The Bretton Woods Conference, 1944. *U.S. Department of State. Archive.* https://2001-2009.state.gov/r/pa/ho/time/wwii/98681.htm

US Department of State contributors (2023b). The League of Nations, 1920. *Office of the Department of State United States of America.* Retrieved Sep 2, 2023. https://history.state.gov/milestones/1914-1920/league

Valk J. (2020, November). Crime and Punishment: Deportation in the Levant in the Age of Assyrian Hegemony. *Bulletin of the American Schools of Oriental Research*, 384. https://doi.org/10.1086/710485

Vann R.T. (Nov 28, 2023). World history. *Britannica.* https://www.britannica.com/topic/world-history

Vasilev M. I. (2015, Feb 5). The Policy of Darius and Xerxes Towards Thrace and Macedonia (Mnemosyne, Supplements / History and Archaeology of Classical Antiquity, 379). *Brill Academic Pub (February 5, 2015)*

Veldink A. (2023). The origin and meaning of Digital Transformation. *Linkedin.*

Retrieved Sep 5, 2023. https://www.linkedin.com/pulse/origin-meaning-digital-transformation-anneke-veldink/

Vergiani V. (2020). Bhartrhari on Language, Perception, and Consciousness. In Jonardon Ganeri (Editor) The Oxford Handbook of Indian Philosophy (Oxford Handbooks). *Oxford University Press; 1st edition*

Vermeij G. J. (2011). A Historical Conspiracy: Competition, Opportunity, and the Emergence of Direction in History. *Cliodynamics*, 2(1): 187-207. https://escholarship.org/uc/item/6gh17580

Vernadsky V. I. (1977). Вернадский В.И. Размышления натуралиста: Научная мысль как планетное явление, Книга вторая. *Издательство Наука*, 1977 [V.I.Vernadsky, Notes by a Naturalist: Scientific Thought as a Planetary Phenomenon, Book Two, *Nauka Publishing House, 1977*]

Victoria and Albert Museum contributors (2006, Oct 31). Sock. *Victoria and Albert Museum.* https://collections.vam.ac.uk/item/O128882/sock-unknown/

Vidale Massimo & Zahir Muhammad (2017). Early Evidence of Bead- Making at Mehrgarh, Pakistan: A Tribute to the Scientific Curiosity of Catherine and Jean- François Jarrige. In Alok Kumar kanungo (ed.) Stone Beads of South and Southeast Asia. Archaeology, Ethnography and Global Connections. *Indian Institute of Technology.* pp.233-254. https://www.academia.edu/38492223/Early_Evidence_of_Bead_Making_at_M ehrgarh_Pakistan_A_Tribute_to_the_Scientific_Curiosity_of_Catherine_and_J ean_Fran%C3%A7ois_Jarrige

Vigne Jean-Denis. et al. (2004). Early Taming of the Cat in Cyprus. *Science*, 304(5668):259. https://pubmed.ncbi.nlm.nih.gov/15073370/

Villa P. & Roebroeks W. (2014, Apr 30). Neandertal Demise: An Archaeological Analysis of the Modern Human Superiority Complex. *PLoS ONE, 9*(4): e96424. https://doi.org/10.1371/journal.pone.0096424

Vincent-Lancrin S. (2008). Chapter 10. The Reversal of Gender Inequalities in Higher Education: An On-going Trend. *OECD. Higher education to 2030 - Volume 1: Demography. p.265 - 298.* https://www.oecd.org/education/ceri/41939699.pdf

Vizmuller-Zocco J. (1985). Linguistic Creativity and Word Formation. *Italica, JSTOR.* 62(4): 305–310. https://www.jstor.org/stable/i220769

Vocabulary.com contributors (2023). Humankind. Vocabulary.com Dictionary, Vocabulary.com. Accessed on 10/19/2023. https://www.vocabulary.com/dictionary/humankind#

Vodafone contributors (2017, Dec 4). 25 years since the world's first text message. *Vodafone.* https://www.vodafone.com/news/technology/25-anniversary-text-message

Vyshedskiy A. (2019, July 29). Language evolution to revolution: the leap from rich-vocabulary non-recursive communication system to recursive language 70,000 years ago was associated with acquisition of a novel component of imagination, called Prefrontal Synthesis, enabled by a mutation that slowed down the prefrontal cortex maturation simultaneously in two or more children – the Romulus and Remus hypothesis. *RIO Journal.* https://riojournal.com/article/38546/

Waal F. de. (2014, Sep 1). Why Humans and Other Primates Cooperate. *Scientific American.* https://www.scientificamerican.com/article/why-humans-and-other-primates-cooperate

Wachsmann S. (1995). Paddled and Oared Ships Before the Iron Age. In John Morrison (ed) The Age of the Galley: Mediterranean Oared Vessels Since Pre-classical Times. *Chrysalis Books; First Edition (January 1, 1995)*

Wade M. (2019). Voskhod 1. *Encyclopedia Astronautica.* http://www.astronautix.com/v/voskhod1.html

Walker Amélie A. (1997, September/October). Neolithic Surgery. *Archaeology. NewsBriefs.* 50(5). https://archive.archaeology.org/9709/newsbriefs/trepanation.html

Walter P. et al. (2006). Early Use of PbS Nanotechnology for an Ancient Hair Dyeing Formula. *Nano Lett.* 6: 2215–2219. https://pubs.acs.org/doi/10.1021/nl061493u

Wambulwa M. C. et al. (2021, Aug 06). From the Wild to the Cup: Tracking Footprints of the Tea Species in Time and Space. *Front. Nutr., Sec. Nutrition and Sustainable Diets,* 8. https://doi.org/10.3389/fnut.2021.706770

Wang JX et al. (2008, December). Ancient Chinese literature reveals pathways of eggplant domestication. *Ann Bot.* 102(6): 891-897. https://academic.oup.com/aob/article/102/6/891/104734

Wang P. et al. (2020). The genome evolution and domestication of tropical fruit mango. *Genome Biol,* 21(60). https://doi.org/10.1186/s13059-020-01959-8

WebMD Editorial Contributors (2021, Oct 25). What Is Mob Mentality? *WebMD.* https://www.webmd.com/mental-health/what-is-a-mob-mentality

Weiss E. & Zohary D. (2011, October). The Neolithic Southwest Asian Founder Crops Their Biology and Archaeobotany. *Current Anthropology,* 52(S4). https://www.journals.uchicago.edu/doi/full/10.1086/658367

Weldon S.P. (2015, Jan 12). Big History, Deep History, and the Problem of Scale. *Inhabiting the Anthropocene.* https://inhabitingtheanthropocene.com/2015/01/12/bigdeephistory

West John B. (2014, May 30). Galen and the beginnings of Western physiology. *Am J Physiol Lung Cell Mol Physiol.* 307: L121–L128. https://doi.org/10.1152/ajplung.00123.2014

White J. L. (1999). First of a Series: Pioneering Polymer Industry Developments: Bayer and the First Synthetic RubberFirst of a Series. *International Polymer Processing.* 14(2): 114-114. https://doi.org/10.3139/217.9902

Wicks F. (1999, July 1). The Blacksmith's Motor. *ASME. Mechanical Engineering.* 121(07): 66–69. https://doi.org/10.1115/1.1999-JUL-8

Wikipedia contributors (2016). List of most valuable crops and livestock products. *Wikipedia.* 2016. Data for 2016 from

https://www.fao.org/faostat/en/#data/QV.

https://en.wikipedia.org/wiki/List_of_most_valuable_crops_and_livestock_products

Wikipedia contributors (2023a). Timeline of prehistory. *Wikipedia*. Retrieved Sep 6, 2023. https://en.wikipedia.org/wiki/Timeline_of_human_prehistory

Wikipedia contributors (2023b). Timeline of ancient history. *Wikipedia*. Retrieved Sep 6, 2023. https://en.wikipedia.org/wiki/Timeline_of_ancient_history

Wikipedia contributors (2023c). Timeline of post-classical history. *Wikipedia*. Retrieved Sep 6, 2023. https://en.wikipedia.org/wiki/Timeline_of_post-classical_history

Wikipedia contributors (2023d). Timelines of modern history. *Wikipedia*. Retrieved Sep 6, 2023. https://en.wikipedia.org/wiki/Timelines_of_modern_history

Williams L. P. (2022, Feb 07). Science and the Industrial Revolution. *Britannica*. https://www.britannica.com/science/history-of-science/The-founding-of-modern-biology

Wilkins Alasdair (2011, May 25). The story behind the world's oldest museum, built by a Babylonian princess 2,500 years ago. *Cizmodo*. https://io9.gizmodo.com/the-story-behind-the-worlds-oldest-museum-built-by-a-b-5805358

Wilmut I. et al. (1997). Viable offspring derived from fetal and adult mammalian cells. *Nature*. *385*, 810–813. https://doi.org/10.1038/385810a0

Winchester A.M. (2022, Dec 23). Genetics. *Encyclopaedia Britannica*. https://www.britannica.com/science/genetics

Wood J. (2023). History of the Radio. *Tech Wholesale*. Retrieved Sep 4, 2023. https://techwholesale.com/history-of-the-radio.html

Woodward K., Woodward S. (2015). Gender studies and interdisciplinarity. *Palgrave Commun* 1, 15018. https://doi.org/10.1057/palcomms.2015.18

Woolfe J. A. (1992). Sweet potato: An Untapped Food Resource. *Cambridge University Press; 1st edition (March 27, 1992)*

Worldometer contributors (2023). World Population by Year. *Worldometer*. Retrieved Sep 5, 2023. https://www.worldometers.info/world-population/world-population-by-year/

World Nuclear Association contributors (2020, November). Outline History of Nuclear Energy. *World Nuclear Association*. https://world-nuclear.org/information-library/current-and-future-generation/outline-history-of-nuclear-energy.aspx

World Population Review contributors (2023). Countries Where Women Cannot Vote 2023. *World Population Review*. https://worldpopulationreview.com/country-rankings/countries-where-women-cant-vote

Wu X. etc. (2012, June 29). Early pottery at 20,000 years ago in Xianrendong Cave, China. *Science*. *336*(6089):1696-700.

https://www.science.org/doi/10.1126/science.1218643

Wulf Andrea (2016, June 7). The Unsung Hero of Western Science. *The Atlantic*.
https://www.theatlantic.com/science/archive/2016/06/the-man-who-invented-botany/485780/

Xiang H. et al. (2014, Dec 9). Early Holocene chicken domestication in northern
China. *Proc Natl Acad Sci U S A*, *111*(49):17564-9.
https://pubmed.ncbi.nlm.nih.gov/25422439/

Yale University Office of President contributors (2023). Biography of Grace
Murray Hopper. *Yale University Office of President*. Retrieved Sep 4, 2023.
https://president.yale.edu/biography-grace-murray-hopper#

Yin-Poole W. (2016, June 3). Elite: Dangerous Latest Expansion Caused AI
Spaceships to Unintentionally Create Super Weapons. *Eurogamer*.
https://www.eurogamer.net/articles/2016-06-03-elite-dangerous-latest-expansion-caused-ai-spaceships-to-unintentionally-create-super-weapons

Your Genome contributors (2021, July). Are humans still evolving. *Your Genome*.
https://www.yourgenome.org/stories/are-humans-still-evolving

Zabelin I.M. (1970). Забелин И. М. (1970). Человечество - для чего оно ? In
Человек и человечество. Человек и природа. "Этюды оптимизма".
Советский писатель, Moskva, 1970. [I.M. Zabelin. Humankind - what is it for?
In Man and humanity. Man and nature. "Studies of Optimism". *Soviet Writer,
Moscow, 1970*]

Zarrillo et al. (2018). The use and domestication of Theobroma cacao during the
mid-Holocene in the upper Amazon. *Nat Ecol Evol*, *2*: 1879–1888.
https://pubmed.ncbi.nlm.nih.gov/30374172/

Zhang F. (2024). Inventions of the Industrial Revolution. *Timetoast*. Retrieved
April 22, 2024. https://www.timetoast.com/timelines/unification-of-germany-10525b6a-4d6b-4bfb-94fd-df6c95d74cdb

Zhen Liu et al. (2018, Jan 24). Cloning of Macaque Monkeys by Somatic Cell
Nuclear Transfer. *Cell*. *172*(4): 881–887.e7.
https://www.cell.com/fulltext/S0092-8674(18)30057-6

Zurita N.F.S. & Tumer I.Y. (2017, Aug 6-9). A Survey: Towards understanding
emergent behavior in complex engineered systems. *Proceedings of the ASME
2017 International Design Engineering Technical Conferences & Computers and
Information in Engineering Conference IDETC/CIE. Cleveland, Ohio, USA.*
https://www.researchgate.net/profile/Nicolas-Soria-Zurita/publication/320335580_A_Survey_Towards_Understanding_Emergent_Behavior_in_Complex_Engineered_Systems/links/59de68aea6fdcca0d320463e/A-Survey-Towards-Understanding-Emergent-Behavior-in-Complex-Engineered-Systems.pdf

Image Credits

Image Credit 1 - © This file is licensed under the Creative Commons Attribution-Share Alike 3.0 Unported license. - https://commons.wikimedia.org/wiki/File:Ice_Age_Temperature.png. This figure was prepared by Robert A. Rohd from publicly available data and is incorporated into the Global Warming Art project; "Ice Age Temperature"
Image Credit 2 - © This file is licensed under the Creative Commons Attribution-Share Alike 3.0 Unported license. - https://commons.wikimedia.org/wiki/File:Holocene_Temperature_Variations.png. This figure was prepared by Robert A. Rohd from publicly available data and is incorporated into the Global Warming Art project; "Holocene Temperature Variations"

Index

10000 BC – 1 BC, 191
10500 BC - 2023 AD, 194
10500 BC - 6500 BC, 260
11000 BC - 2023 AD, 280
12000 BC - 2023 AD, 196
1316 - 1650, 253
1590 - 1853, 254
1600 BC - 597 BC, 249
173 - 1455, 252
17500 BC - 6500 BC, 245
1767 - 2023, 255
1800 BC - 1700 AD, 304
1924 – 2023, 285
2000 BC – 1316 AD, 263
2000 BC - 2023 AD, 298
2100 BC - 1241 BC, 248
2300 BC – 534 BC, 283
2500 BC - 1698 AD, 272
2500 BC - 2023 AD, 296
2700 BC - 2000 BC, 262
3300 BC – 1000 BC, 282
334 BC - 895 AD, 251
3750 BC - 2000 BC, 247
42000 BC - 10500 BC, 192
42000 BC - 2023 AD, 185

500 BC - 1700 AD, 305
534 BC - 1698 AD, 279
550 BC - 1759 AD, 290
597 BC - 334 BC, 268
6500 BC - 2700 BC, 261
776 BC - 168 BC, 250
8000 BC – 3000 BC, 281
8400 BC - 2700 BC, 246
937 BC - 128 BC, 270
Abū Bakr al-Rāzī, 94
Adam Rutherford, 20
Aeschylus, 103
Agustín Fuentes, 20
Alan Emtage, 130
Alessandro Volta, 123
Alexander Bain, 154
Alexander Graham Bell, 154
Alexander Parkes, 96
Alexander the Great, 268
Alliances, 139
Alonzo Decker, 121
Amelia Carolina Sparavigna, 91
Anne Kilmer, 85
Antonio Maggio, 85
Antonio Meucci, 154

Ányos Jedlik, 118
Apostle Peter, 141
Archduke Francis Ferdinand, 134
Archimedes, 120
Archytas of Tarentum, 121
Aristotle, 99
Armstrong, 127
Art and music, 78
Artificial Intelligence (AI), 179
Asakura, 116
Auguste and Louis Lumière, 87
Avicenna, 100
back time horizon, 258
Beatrice Mintz, 95
Behavioral Modernity, 33
Bela Julesz, 88
Bertha Benz, 71
Big history, 21
Boykin, 123
Bunsen and Kirchhoff, 164
Cai Lun, 90
Carl Linnaeus, 51
Carl Sagan, 239
Carlos Glidden, 130
Carriers of subject of trade, 114
Categories of electrical machines, 117
Categories of Means of Warfare, 133
Categories of storage devices, 128
Charles Wheatstone, 154
Charlie Bachman, 129
Christopher Latham Sholes, 130
Classes of resources, 335
Claude Shannon, 177
Claudius Galenus, 100
Clifford Berry, 176
Complex System Models of Humankind, 199
Complex Systems, 40
complexity, 21
Components of electronic machines (devices), 117
Components of international trade, 114
Conventional history of humankind, 333
Conventional history of humankind timeframe, 333
Creativity Index of Humankind, 337
Creativity Index of Humankind for resources (CI-H), 337
Criteria for a Search of the Driving Force, 212
Criteria in a Search for New Classes of Resources, 337
Cyrus, 153
Dafna Langgut, 111
Damien Finch, 80
Daniel Little, 16
Darius I of Persia, 135
David Chaum, 116
David Christian, 17
deep history, 47
deep-level history, 9
Digital technology, 176
Dionysius of Halicarnassus, 144
Dioscorides, 100
Direction of movement, 124
Distant education, 150
Domains of resources, 335
Domesticated Animals, 107
Domesticated Plants (Fruits), 107
Domesticated Plants (Seeds and Grains), 107
Domesticated Plants (Vegetables), 107
Dominance of Statistical Errors, 238
Driving Force Hypothesis, 215
Duncan Black, 121
Durability Criterion for Classes of Resources, 337
Durability Criterion for Resources, 336, 337
Edouard-Leon Scott de Martinville, 161

Education Levels, 150
electronic communication channels, 153
Elements of mechanical machines, 117
Emergent Behavior, 69
Empires, 139
End of Holocene, 323
Energy storage devices, 117
Enheduanna, 102
Ennigaldi, 104
Erasistratus of Ceos, 99
Ewald Georg von Kleist, 122
Expand-ability Criterion for Classes of Resources, 337
External information storage and processing, 128
Families of resources, 335
Feng Jisheng, 136
Ferdinand Braun, 123
First 1400 times increase in fossil fuel consumption, 169
First 400 times increase in fossil fuel consumption, 169
First 50 times increase in fossil fuel consumption, 169
First 800 times increase in fossil fuel consumption, 169
First A Single-Atom-Thick Material, 93
First Acknowledgment of AI creativity by people globally, 179
First Aerophone (Flute), 81
First Airplane, 125
First Alcohol, 94
First Amphibious vehicle, 125
First Amputation, 98
First Anatomy, 99
First Animation, 81
First Anthropology, 104
First Apples, 110
First Archeology, 104
First Architecture, 80

First Artificial Intelligence (AI), 179
First Asymmetric Warfare, 135
First Authored Literature, 102
First Automata, 120
First Bananas, 109
First Barley, 111
First Bearings, 120
First Beer, 94
First Big data processing, 166
First Biological storage device, 131
First Biological Warfare, 136
First Biology, 99
First Blues Music, 85
First Cabbage, 112
First Cacao (Chocolate), 111
First Capacitor, 122
First Cassava (Yuka), 112
First Cats, 108
First Cell (mobile) phone, 155
First Chemical Warfare, 136
First Chicken, 108
First Child Labor, 146
First Choral Music, 83
First Chordophone (Harp), 82
First Circus, 83
First Cloned Mammal, 95
First Cloned Primate, 96
First Coffee, 111
First Cognitive Science, 104
First College (University), 150
First Colonial Empire, 140
First Commodity money, 115
First Communication via hologram, 156
First Compiler, 166
First Composite Materials (Cartonnage), 92
First Composite Materials (Concrete), 91
First Composite Materials (Plywood), 92
First Computer in business, 166
First Computer/Digital Art, 88

First Computing machine, 121
First consumption of gas and oil
    together overcome coal, 169
First consumption of oil became top
    one, 169
First Conventional war, 133
First Corn (Maize), 109
First Corruption, 143
First Cost-effective digital storage,
    177
First Cotton, 113
First Country where women right
    to vote accepted legally, 174
First Couplings, 120
First Cows, 108
First Cucumber, 110
First Cyber Warfare, 137
First Dance, 80
First Data storage with a projected
    lifespan of 13.8 billion years, 131
First Database, 129
First Debt bondage / bonded labor,
    145
First Decisive usage of Internet, 178
First Decisive usage of mobile
    phones, 177
First Dentistry, 99
First Diffusion of scientific
    knowledge, 167
First Digital computer, 176
First Digital transformation
    definition, 178
First Diode, 123
First Diplomacy, 101
First Disinformation, 106
First Division and specialization of
    human labor, 158
First Dogs, 107
First Domestic violence, 144
First Driver-less ground cargo
    vehicle with an engine, 127
First Economic Warfare, 135
First Economics, 102

First Eggplant, 110
First Electrical battery, 123
First Electrical generator, 122
First Electrical motor, 122
First Electrical transformer, 122
First Electricity-powered machine,
    118
First Electronic logic gate, 176
First Electronic machine (devices),
    121
First Electronic money, 115
First Electronic Music Instrument,
    87
First Electronic transfer, 116
First Elevator, 126
First E-mail, 155
First Empire, 140
First Enriched Uranium 235, 93
First Equipment to observe objects,
    163
First Ethics, 103
First Export, 116
First Faience, 91
First False News, 105
First Falsifiability as a criterion, 167
First Fax, 154
First Felt, 90
First Fiat money, 115
First Film, 87
First Flash Mob, 84
First Framework for international
    monetary policy, commerce, and
    finance, 140
First Fuel-powered machine, 118
First Gears, 120
First Gender Studies, 100
First Genealogy and Family Tree,
    103
First General international
    organization, 142
First Genetically Modified (GM)
    Food (Tomato), 90
First Genetically Modified (GM)

organism, 95
First Genetically Modified Human, 96
First Genetics, 104
First Genocide, 145
First Gerontology, 100
First Glass, 92
First Global network (Internet), 142
First Grape, 109
First Graphic Art (Drawing), 80
First Ground transportation with the use of animals, 125
First Ground vehicle with an engine, 127
First Hip-Hop Music, 86
First History, 104
First Horses, 108
First Human trafficking, 146
First Human-powered machine, 117
First Hybrid (Mule), 95
First Icebreaker, 125
First Idiophone (Rattles), 82
First Inclined plane, 119
First Increase in life expectancy in developed counties (English and Wales) is primarily driven by declining old-age (60-year-old) mortality, 172
First Information Warfare, 136
First Integrated circuit (microchip), 177
First Intergovernmental organization, 142
First Jazz Music, 86
First Judiciary, 101
First Kinesiology, 100
First Knitted Materials, 90
First Leather, 89
First Less than 20% gap with men in years of schooling, 175
First Less than 21% gap with men in earnings, 175
First Lethal autonomous weapon systems, 137
First Lever (balance weights), 119
First Library, 129
First Lie Detector, 106
First Life expectancy at birth over 28 years, 171
First Linguistics, 103
First Liquid Fuel (Kerosene), 94
First Liquid preparations (Medicine), 94
First Logic, 101
First Machine Translation, 130
First Magnetic storage device, 130
First mandatory education, 151
First Mango, 110
First Marketplace, 114
First Marketplace for securities trade, 115
First Massive forced displacement / deportation, 145
First Mathematical theory of communication, 177
First Matter identification technique, 164
First Mechanical calculator (Pascaline), 166
First Medicine (Physician), 99
First Membranophone (Drum), 82
First Metal (Copper), 92
First Mob Mentality, 105
First Modern production factory, 159
First Multi-city economic and defensive alliance, 141
First Multinational corporation, 142
First Multi-times increase in coal mining, 169
First Museum, 104
First Music ensemble (band), 82
First Musical Composition & Notation, 84
First Mythology, 102
First Near-Earth orbit spaceship,

126

First Non-kinetic weapons Warfare, 135

First Nuclear Warfare, 137

First Nuclear-energy-powered machine, 118

First Olympic Games, 101

First Onion, 112

First Online learning, 152

First Online trade, 115

First Opera, 84

First Opinion Poll, 105

First Optical storage device, 131

First Orange, 110

First Orchestra, 83

First Over 10% share of "self-made" women at the top of the social hierarchy, 174

First Over 3% of women of working age have legal equality to men, 175

First Over 39% percentage of employed women, 174

First Over 50% share of women in higher education in OECD countries, 174

First Painting, 78

First Paper, 90

First Papyrus Paper, 90

First Performance Art, 84

First Pharmacology, 99

First Philosophy, 101

First Photography, 87

First Physiology, 100

First Pigs, 108

First Pills (Medicine), 93

First Plastic (Parkesine), 96

First Playwright, 103

First Political Science, 101

First Pop Music, 86

First Porcelain, 93

First Post, 153

First Potato, 112

First Pottery, 91

First Power tools, 121

First Precision interchangeable parts, 158

First Prefabrication, 157

First Preschool education, 151

First Printing (Printing Medium), 129

First Production factory, 159

First Propaganda, 105

First Proxy war, 134

First Psychiatry, 106

First Psychology, 106

First Pulley, 119

First Radio, 154

First Resistor, 123

First Rice, 109

First Robot, 121

First Rock Music, 86

First Rutway for cargo and ships, 126

First School, 150

First Scientific paradigm, 167

First Screw, 119

First Sculpture, 79

First Search Engine, 130

First Semiconductor Material, 93

First Semiconductor storage device, 131

First Serfdom, 145

First Sexual violence (including rape), 144

First Sheep and Goats, 108

First sizable increase in renewable energy sources consumption, 170

First Slavery, 144

First Social exclusion, 144

First Sociology, 102

First Song/Folk Song Music, 85

First Sonic or ultrasonic or infrasonic device, 164

First Soybeans, 112

First Spike in fossil fuel mining, 168
First Standardized parts, 157
First Steam-powered machine, 118
First Storytelling, 79
First Submarine, 125
First Sugar cane, 109
First Sunflower, 111
First Surgery, 99
First Sweet potato, 112
First Synthesized Nanoparticles, 92
First Synthetic Fiber, 96
First Synthetic Polymer, 96
First Synthetic Rubber, 97
First Tea, 112
First Telegraph, 154
First Telephone, 154
First Television, 88, 155
First Ten times increase in an
    average annual growth rate of
    life expectancy at birth, 172
First Text (First Writing, First
    Writing Medium), 128
First Text message, 155
First Textile, 89
First Theatre, 83
First Theology, 102
First Threat of Radiological Warfare
    use, 137
First Tomato, 110
First Total war, 133
First Trade barrier, 116
First Trade network, 114
First Train with engine, 126
First Transgenic Mouse, 95
First Transistor, 123
First Transport from Earth to the
    Moon, 126
First Transport from Moon orbit to
    the Moon, 127
First Transportation with a use of
    watercraft, 124
First Treaty between city-states, 139
First Treaty between nations, 139

First Typing, 130
First Use of electromagnetism, 148
First Use of energy to run machines,
    158
First Use of general relativity, 149
First Use of gravity, 147
First Use of machine tools, 158
First Use of quantum physics, 149
First Use of scientific method, 167
First Use of specialized machinery,
    158
First Use of strong nuclear force,
    148
First Use of weak nuclear force, 148
First Video Art, 87
First Video conferencing, 155
First Video Game, 88
First Virtual Keyboard Typing, 130
First War over the sacred (not
    material) thing, 134
First Warfare with the use of
    gunpowder, 136
First Watermelon, 110
First Water-powered machine, 118
First Wedge (ax), 119
First Western Classical Music, 85
First Wheat, 109
First Wheel and axle, 119
First Wind-powered machine, 118
First World monotheistic religion,
    141
First World religion, 141
First World war, 134
Forces of Nature, 147
Francis Fukuyama, 18
Frank Haven Hall, 130
Frans de Waal, 20
Fritz Hofmann, 97
Gard Granerød, 105
Geim, 93
General models of humankind, 334
George J. Goodheart, Jr., 100
Gerald Schatten, 96

Gerhard Bosinski, 80
Gisela Fischer, 80
Giulio Caccini, 84
Global history, 22
Global International Organizations, 139
Global Networks, 139
Gomes Eannes de Zurara, 146
Grace Hopper, 166
Granularity, 65
Granularity Levels, 189
Guglielmo Marconi, 155
Gustav Theodor Fechner, 106
Hans E. Korth, 130
Hans Lippershey, 164
Hans Martens, 163
Hard materials, 89
Harm to a group of people, 143
Harm to a person, 143
Hattusili III, 139
He Jiankui, 96
Hegel, 14
Henry Ford, 159
Henry IV, 84
Herbert Boyer, 95
Herbert Hoover, 155
Herodotus, 104
Herophilus of Chalcedon, 99
hierarchical classification system, 51
High-level model of humankind, 334
Homer, 95
How Fast Humankind Is Moving?, 308
I. S. Unshlikht, 106
Ian Hodder, 19
Ian Morris, 18
Ibn Khaldūn, 102
Ike Turner, 86
Imhotep, 99
Importance Criterion for Classes of Resources, 337
Importance Criterion for Resources, 336

Independent communication channels, 153
Individual Dates Imprecision, 235
Inedible Domesticated Plants, 107
Infant Don Henry, 146
Information technology, 165
International Organizations, 139
International Treaties, 139
Involvement of women in humankind activities, 173
Irnerius, 150
Is Humankind Development a Controllable Process?, 310
Isaac Newton, 167
J. Lyons, 166
Jack Kilby, 177
Jacopo Peri, 84
James Peachey, 125
James Russell, 131
James Watt, 158
Jerome Carden, 120
Joe Ceburn West, 125
Johann Christian Reil, 106
Johann F. Oberlin, 151
Johannes Gutenberg, 160
John A. Larson, 106
John Atanasoff, 176
John Bardeen, 123
John Gray, 18
John McCarthy, 179
John Wesly Hyatt, 96
John Wilkinson, 158
Joseph Henry, 121, 122
Joseph Nicéphore Niépce, 87
Joseph Swan, 96
Juli Gutiérrez Deulofeu, 13
Julius H. Kroehl, 125
Kalinkos, 135
Karl Benz, 71
Karl Marx, 11
Karl Popper, 167
Karoly Zipernowsky, 122

Khety, 150
King Darius I, 105
King Hammurabi, 144
Klaus Schmidt, 80
Known Unknowns Factors, 338
Kool Herc, 86
Leonard Woolley, 82
Levels of Taxonomy of Resources, 335
Life expectancy growth, 171
Limiting and Liberating Effects, 66
Louis-Jacques-Mandé Daguerre, 87
Low-level model of humankind, 334
Ma Jun of Cao Wei, 120
Mabrouk A. El-Sharkaw, 112
Machine types, 117
Main physics theories, 147
Man-Made Existential Disasters, 322
Man-Made Materials, Substances, Organisms, 89
Mansur Sajjadi, 81
manufacturing engineering, 157
Marc Brunel, 158
Margaret Meek Lange, 17
Maria de Medici, 84
Marian L. Tupy, 17
Martin Cooper, 155
Martin Graetz, 88
Mass education, 150
Mass production, 157
Mass production techniques, 157
Mass transportation, 124
Mass Use Criterion for Classes of Resources, 337
Mass Use Criterion for Resources, 336
Means of Warfare, 133
Measuring the Creativity of Humankind, 275
Mebaragesi, 133
Media of the Mass transportation, 124
Medium of exchange, 114
Megan Erickson, 18
Michael Faraday, 122
Michael Noll, 88
Middle-level model of humankind, 334
Miguel Alonso, 20
Miksa Deri, 122
Misclassification Errors, 238
Morris Raphael Cohen, 16
Multi-Layer Schema of, 334
Musical notation, 78
Myth, 102
Nabonidus, 104
Napoleon, 123
Nathan Rotenstreich, 16
Neil Papworth, 155
Nikolai Berdyaev, 15
Nikolai Tesla, 154
Non-electronic communication channels, 153
Novoselov, 93
Objectivity, 234
Organisms, 89
Oswald Spengler, 13
Ottavio Rinuccini, 84
Otto Titusz Blathy, 122
Otto von Bismarck, 136
Ötzi, also called the Iceman, 119
Panini, 103
Pascal, 166
Patrick Lancaster Gardiner, 17
People and societies as objects of study, 98
Pericles, 135
Philippe Walter, 92
Philo Taylor Farnsworth, 88
Pieter Van Musschenbroek, 122
Plato, 101
Polybius, 145
Pythaides, 83
Ramesses II, 139

Ray Kurzweil, 322
Ray Tomlinson, 155
Razifard, 110
Regional models of humankind, 334
related to history, 98
related to mental health, 98
Related to physical health, 98
related to place in society, 98
related to society and world, 98
Relation to society, 150
Resource Creation Time (RCT), 337
Resources, 335
Richard Trevithick, 126
Right to education, 151
Robert Street, 118
Romulus, King of Rome, 144
Rudolph Jaenisch, 95
Samuel F.B. Morse, 154
Samuel W. Soule, 130
Sapiens, 31
Savery, 118
Scientific method, 165
Scipio Aemilianus, 145
Self-operation machines, 117
Simple machines, 117
Socrates, 104
Soft materials, 89
Soft-hard materials, 89
Sources of power, 117
Spitzer John, 83
Stanley Cohen, 95
Stephen Nichols, 20
Steve Russell, 88
subjectivity, 234
Substances and liquid materials, 89
Subsurface history of humankind, 333
Super-high-level model of humankind, 334
Taxonomic Errors, 54
Taxonomy, 51
Technology beyond the limitations of human senses, 163

Terry Pinkard, 16
Thales, 101
The First layer is the events layer, 334
The Fourth layer is the driving force layer, 334
The Second layer is the motivation layer, 334
The Third layer is the opportunities layer, 334
Theophrastus, 99
Thespis, 83
Thillaie Delaborde, 87
Thomas Davenport, 122
Thomas Kuhn, 167
Time horizon, 258
Tool types, 117
tools for generic social impact, 98
Tools, devices, and machines from man-made materials, 117
Trade with the use of an intermediary, 114
Transnational entities, 139
Transport Driving force, 124
Types of art with the use of many people, 78
Types of goods delivery infrastructure, 114
Types of inventories of recorded information, 128
Types of music, 78
Types of musical instruments, 78
Types of non-musical art, 78
Types of recording, transforming, and retrieving information, 128
Types of technology-based art, 78
Types of war, 133
Ur-Nammu, 101
Usage of Domesticated Plants and Animals, 107
Usage of natural resources on a massive scale, 168
Usage of people as a resource on a

massive scale, 143
Usage of the Scientific method and
information technology, 165
Use of forces of Nature, Relativity,
and Quantum physics, 147
Václav Prokop Diviš, 87
Valdemar Poulsen, 130
Variables and Invariables, 70
Vitruvius, 126
Walter Brattain, 123
Walter Gifford, 155
Walther Bothe, 176
Which Force Is Driving Humankind
Development?, 310
Why Humans Rule the Earth?, 308
Willard Libby, 148

William Fothergill Cooke, 154
William Sturgeon, 148
world history, 6
World history, 21
World Religions (each over 6% of
the world religious population),
139
Would We Still Be Sapiens?, 321
Yaneer Bar-Yam, 21
Yang Xingmi, 136
Yosef Garfinkel, 80
Zabelin, 17
Zacharias Janssen, 163
Zaslaw Neal, 83
Zhuangzi, 118
Zigong, 118